# FLASH

## OF

# GENIUS

# FLASH

## OF

# GENIUS

And Other True Stories of Invention

# JOHN SEABROOK

 ST. MARTIN'S GRIFFIN  NEW YORK

www.stmartins.com

Design by Susan Walsh

These essays, some in slightly different form, were first published
by The New Yorker magazine.

ISBN-13: 978-0-312-53572-8
ISBN-10: 0-312-53572-4

First Edition: September 2008

10 9 8 7 6 5 4 3 2 1

*This book is for Harry*

# CONTENTS

# ACKNOWLEDGMENTS

I have been richly blessed with three great editors over my years at *The New Yorker*. The first, Nancy Franklin, edited the title story—in fact, I think she came up with the title. The second, Deborah Garrison, edited "The Spinach King" and helped me through the gut-wrenching process of writing about my family. The third, longest-lasting, not to say long-suffering, and still-standing editor, the amazing Cressida Leyshon, edited most of the pieces in this book, and there is no way to overstate how much she has contributed to it.

I have also benefitted enormously from the support and guidance of Robert Gottlieb, Tina Brown, David Remnick, Dorothy Wickenden, and Daniel Zalewski, as well as from the unsung labors of all the fact-checkers, copy editors, proofreaders, and editorial assistants who have worked on one or another of these pieces over the years.

Thanks to my agent, Joy Harris, who has stuck by me through my entire career as a writer, and to my editor at St. Martin's, Elizabeth Beier.

Thanks also to my old pal Eric Schlosser, who has guided me when I didn't know where I was going, and who has always been in my corner.

For the gift of seeing my work on the big screen—and, gee!, they make your name so much bigger in the movies than in print—I am grateful to Michael Lieber, who was the first to see a movie in this material, and who had his own struggles with Bob Kearns. In making the film, *Flash of Genius,* Marc Abraham took his time and waited until he had just the right script, and the right actors, and made a movie with a big heart. And (pointing up at the sky) here's to you Philip Railsback for writing a truer adaptation of my work than I could have hoped to write myself. You should have seen it.

I remember saying to Bob Kearns back in 1990, when I was trying to persuade him to let me write about him, "One day this story is going to be a movie, and everyone will see that badge you're wearing that says 'inventor' on it." Bob didn't stay alive long enough to see the movie—in which he is uncannily well rendered by Greg Kinnear—but I am pleased that Phyllis Kearns, and the six Kearns kids, can enjoy this.

Thanks to my dad and his brothers for kindling my vicarious interest in engineers, builders, and doers. I have always tried to design my pieces according to their sound engineering principles.

I'd also like to thank all the people I interviewed and chased around the country and the world. From the gold prospectors I met in the Owl Café, in Battle Mountain, Nevada, way back in 1988—my very first piece for *The New Yorker*—to the Chinese scrap-metal kings, who are part of the most recent piece here, and all the people in between who shared their stories and dreams with me: I couldn't have written these stories without you.

*E come sempre, tante grazie, Lisa bella, amore mio. Per tutto.*

# INTRODUCTION

Robert Kearns, the subject of this book's title story, was an archetype of the industrial world: a lone inventor with a good idea. He was a little guy in every sense of the word (in stature, he was Leprechaun-like) who believed that one of the biggest corporations in Detroit, an institution he worshipped—the Ford Motor Company—had infringed his patents. He took Ford to court, and serving as his own attorney for part of the trial, he won. Now that his story is being told, more or less as it happened, on the screen, in Marc Abraham's film *Flash of Genius,* Bob Kearns might inspire future lone inventors to pursue similarly single-minded quests against big corporations, in the hope of winning millions, like him. But before anyone emulates Kearns, one should ask, What did Bob Kearns intend, in devoting his life to defending his patents, and what is his legacy?

I came across Kearns for the first time in the spring of 1990, in a *New York Times* story written by Edmund Andrews. Kearns was then in the final phase of his epic legal battle against Ford. He claimed to have invented the intermittent windshield wiper, and a jury in Detroit had found his patents valid but had been unable to agree on how much to award him. Ford, hoping to avoid an even larger jury-mandated fee—Kearns could have won up to $325 million—had offered Kearns thirty million dollars, a sum that

Kearns refused on principle, saying "this case has never been about money." Since patent cases are usually *all* about money, Kearns's refusal confounded not only his horrified lawyers, but the entire patent bar. When the jury was unable to agree on how much Kearns should get, the judge in the case, Avern Cohn, of the U.S. District Court for the Eastern District of Michigan, declared a mistrial. Cohn, a silver-haired Detroit native with a patrician bearing, had already shown limited tolerance for Kearns's shortcomings as an attorney, and made no secret of the fact that he thought Kearns should have settled for thirty million. He promised the case would be retried soon. Something about the fact that all this fuss was over a quotidian object like the intermittent windshield wiper—a useful improvement, to be sure, but hardly a world-changing one—intrigued me. I mentioned the case to Robert Gottlieb, then the editor of *The New Yorker*, and he suggested I go out to Detroit and see if there was a story there.

I remember the day I walked into Judge Cohn's chambers and asked his chief of staff, Judy Cassady, if I could see the Kearns file. She gave a cigarette laugh and led me down to the courthouse basement, where the papers for the case were stored. At that point the Kearns case was twelve years old—it was one of the longest-running cases in Michigan's history. Dozens of filing boxes, each crammed with legal documents, filled a wall of shelves. Judy showed me a desk where I could sit, said, "See you in a month," and left. I settled in, took the lid off the first box, and began to read.

I had thought that the Kearns story was about an invention and a theft—a pretty straightforward bit of business. But as I slowly made my way through the accumulated papers of what were not one but three lawsuits—against Ford, Chrysler, and General Motors too, with the possibility of dozens more against other automakers—I realized that Kearns *v.* the auto industry was about the nature of invention itself, and about the federal government's attempts to regulate and legislate "invention," a concept that Judge Learned Hand had called "as fugitive, impalpable, wayward, and vague a phantom as exists in the whole paraphernalia of legal concepts."

There was no question that Kearns had invented an intermittent windshield wiper; the marvelous details of the invention story I read in the depositions, the same details the film makes so vivid—such as the aquarium filled with water and sawdust in which Kearns tested his wipers in the family basement—were absolutely credible. His invention sounded like Learned Hands's "inventive act": the story of how it came to be involved his damaged eye, his wedding night, and a champagne cork. There was also no question that the Ford wiper design closely resembled Kearns's. The question was whether Kearns deserved a limited monopoly for his idea, or whether, as Ford argued, the wiper circuit was obvious—transistor, capacitor, resistor—and the intermittent windshield wiper, as is so often the case with invention, was simply in the air, part of the technological zeitgeist. After reading the entire Kearns file, I no longer thought this was a simple story of invention and theft. It was an epic story of technological evolution, neatly packed inside a dispute over windshield wipers.

The stories in this collection are about inventors, innovators, engineers, and entrepreneurs, some of whom are trying to get something built (or, in the case of the Antikythera Mechanism, rebuilt) and some of whom are coping with the consequences of their inventions. Not all of them are underdogs, like Kearns; some, like Dan Dienst, are overlords trying to outmaneuver the little guys. But whether the subject is Bryan Sykes, the creator of the MatriLine DNA testing kit; or Leslie Robertson, who designed the structure of the World Trade towers; or Leonardo, the MIT robot that is a collaboration of Cynthia Breazeal and Stan Winston; or the Weather Channel, created by John Coleman, a former weatherman, and Frank Batten, a media business executive; or Roger Salquist and his ill-fated Flavr Savr tomato, I have always been interested in the circumstances, unforeseen obstacles, and unimagined outcomes of "inventive acts." Chuck Hoberman thought he was making sculpture when he invented a timeless toy, the Hoberman Sphere. Will Wright, on the other hand, started out to make a dollhouse for his young daughter, and ended up inventing the Sims, one of the most successful computer game franchises ever. The Arctic seed vault is a political invention that took twenty years of international wrangling to create, and required one obsessive individual, Cary Fowler, to make it happen. The modern-day gold rush I reported on from Battle Mountain, Nevada, was also a kind of invention, created by the combination of a cheap method of refining—heap leaching—and the high price of gold. Some of the people here are self-invented—like David Karp, the former junkie who became the Fruit Detective.

Whole industries exist because of some inventor's flash of genius. That notion has always thrilled me. Inventors are the artists of the industrial world. Like artists, they give form to blankness—and their inventions feed, clothe, house, succor, amuse, and cure millions. (Whose creations touched more people's lives—Andrew Wyeth, the painter, or his brother Nat Wyeth, who invented the recyclable PET plastic bottle for DuPont?)

Where does this flash of genius come from? What's the story behind it? A great idea is often conditioned by chance, born of mundane circumstances, but becomes spectacular and transcendent—worthy of Archimedes' bathtub shout of "Eureka!" (I found it!)—once it enters the world. A great idea can be protected by patent laws, but it often leaks out of the legal containers that society has fabricated for it and becomes part of the common heritage of humanity.

My grandfather, C. F. Seabrook, whom I write about in "The Spinach King," was an inventor—not of a device but of a system, a way of mechanizing agriculture. He automated as many steps in the production of food, specifically frozen vegetables, as he could from the planting to the harvest to the packaging. His three sons went to work for him, and in the course of creating something that had never been done before they all were faced with engineering challenges every day. I grew up listening to them talk about how they solved those problems. I came to admire problem solvers, doers, builders, and inventors, in spite of the fact (or because of it?) that I have no talent for doing myself. When I was a child, the invention that impressed me most was my uncle Courtney's: according to family lore, he came up with the idea to package frozen vegetables in boil-in-the-bag pouches. As far as I can tell, Seabrook Farms was the first to use this method. The company never applied for a patent; my father says they didn't know much about patents, and they were too busy to file for them. Nonetheless, I regard Uncle Courtney as the inventor of the boil-in-the-bag method of cooking frozen vegetables—and as such he is one of the progenitors of this book.

The material at the heart of most of these stories didn't yield itself willingly to the trembling embrace of literary nonfiction. Technical facts about gear ratios, the chemical components of DNA, the hybridization of corn, and the processing of scrap metal resist the music and rhythm of language. But this was my material—it had chosen me long before I knew I was a writer—and if I could wish this book into anyone's hands, I would send it to the writer who, like me, is struggling to describe the booming and buzzing industrial world he or she perceives all around, but which seems never to get assigned in freshman Lit class. My starting faith in doing this work was that language and narrative could make unpromising material— metal alloys, structural engineering, algorithms, heap leaching, traffic, windshield wipers, and patent law—come alive.

When I was in Detroit on my first Kearns reporting trip, in May 1990, I went to see Dennis Kearns. Dennis, as the oldest son, had claimed the position of spokesman for the family, and although I wasn't sure all of his five siblings accepted him as that, I got the message that if I wanted to meet his father, I'd have to meet Dennis first. We met for dinner in a barbecue place. Dennis was working as a private investigator then and had a certain tough-guy swagger about him. But we hit it off pretty well, and he gave me the green light to go meet his dad, who was then living in Houston. Arnold, White & Durkee, Kearns's law firm at that time (he would soon fire them and take over the case himself) were based in Houston, and Kearns had taken an apartment there in order to be close to them.

I spent three days in Houston, and it rained hard the whole time—a hot, tropical rain that steamed as it hit the asphalt. The weather, and the cramped confines of Kearns's apartment, which was literally papered with legal documents, helped contribute to the sense of claustrophobia I felt in his presence. I am drawn to eccentric, difficult characters who are engaged in obsessive, single-minded pursuits; almost every one of the stories in this book is about someone like that. Michael Wright, one of the researchers on Antikythera Mechanism, has some Bob Kearns in him, and David Karp, the Fruit Detective, has a splash too, while Cary Fowler, the world's seed banker, has a few things in common with Kearns as well. But for pure, unwavering devotion to his goal, not one of them could touch Kearns.

By the time I met him, Kearns had gone through three different law firms—Harness, Dickey & Pierce of Detroit; Lane, Aitken & McCann of Washington, D.C.; and McDougall, Hersh & Scott of Chicago, and was now on his fourth. His first lawyers, in their memorandum to the court asking to be removed from the case, spoke of "constant verbal reprimands by Dr. Kearns to his attorneys whenever [they] attempted to cooperate in the slightest with defense council." His second attorney, Dick Aitken, who also asked to be removed from the case, said in a hearing that Kearns had become so suspicious of him that "I suspect that my phone conversations are being recorded. Free communication is no longer possible . . . under the circumstances, I think it is clear that Dr. Kearns would be better served by a new attorney." His third set of lawyers also petitioned the court to remove them from case. "The undisputed facts are replete with instances of disharmony and outright confrontation between Dr. Kearns . . . and counsel," wrote the judge who heard their plea, and "the court has no choice but to grant counsel's motion to withdraw."

For three days, in a high-pitched nasal voice that cut through the drumming of the rain, Kearns lectured me on all the different ways that the U.S. District Court for the Eastern District of Michigan was failing to uphold his rights as an American citizen and an inventor. He argued his entire case, pausing frequently to find some passage in a deposition or in a legal text. I had the sense that although I happened to be in the room, he wasn't talking to me. Kearns was easy to admire, harder to like.

I figured to follow the story through the penalty phase of the Ford trial, which ended with the jury awarding Kearns ten million dollars. But when the Chrysler trial came around a year later, I was still reporting. By the time the piece was published in *The New Yorker*, in January 1993, almost three years had passed. Michael Lieber, who had been the moving force in turning Joseph Mitchell's well-known *New Yorker* piece "Joe Gould's Secret" into a film of the same name starring Stanley Tucci, saw cinematic potential in the

Kearns story and brought it to Marc Abraham, a well-known Hollywood producer, who optioned it, and decided he wanted to direct the material himself. Marc is a big Frank Capra fan, and the little guy in Kearns inspired him. The producers then got into their own negotiation with Kearns, and the family, over the rights to the story, and from time to time I'd hear from Lieber that Kearns was driving them crazy and wondering whether there was anything I could do. I could only sympathize.

In the fifteen years since "The Flash of Genius" appeared, the U.S. patent system has deteriorated. There's been a large increase in the number of patents filed, without a proportionate increase in the number of patent examiners to process them. Costs have continued to rise—it now costs a minimum of thirty thousand dollars to obtain a patent. And there's been a big spike in patent litigation. Last year, approximately six thousand defendants were sued nationwide in about twenty-eight hundred patent cases. At the same time, the notion of what is patentable has become more confused, with the tremendous increase in software patents, many of which are for business methods that should never be patentable in the real world, and so are of dubious merit. No one can patent a car auction, for example, but it is possible to get a patent for a method of auctioning cars online. Many of these patents are eventually reexamined by the Patent Office and ruled invalid, but not before years of litigation. A well-known example is Amazon's patent on the One Click method of purchasing, which the company's founder, Jeff Bezos, obtained himself. Amazon's competitors, like Barnes & Noble, argued that patenting One Click was like patenting the express checkout line in a supermarket. The Patent Office eventually did reexamine and limit Bezos's patent, but not before Amazon had enjoyed a monopoly on One Click buying for nearly ten years.

The U.S. patent system exists to treat an evil with a lesser evil, which means that it occupies a peculiar state of moral relativism. The evil is that the people who do come up with useful improvements often do not receive proper credit for them. Sometimes their ideas are stolen outright, but most times they flow almost as if by gravity into the larger stream of material progress. The only sure way an inventor can keep an invention to himself is never to disclose it to the world. But what would be the point of that?

In order to promote technical progress, the patent system proposes a compromise: if the inventor agrees to reveal his invention, he can have an eighteen-year head start on the competition—a limited monopoly. Although monopoly is widely believed to be harmful to entrepreneurship and innovation—the granting of monopolies by the British crown was one of the colonists' most bitter complaints—a limited monopoly was and still is seen as the best way to ensure technical progress, as well as to protect the inventors' rights. However, the founders invested this last aspect of patent law—protecting inventors—with much less importance than inventors like Bob Kearns have given it. Indeed, Jefferson and Franklin both seem to have found the concept of inventors' rights disagreeable (and they were inventors themselves), perhaps because they foresaw the monstrous legal battles that it would ensue, as litigants hacked away at the vexed question of who gets credit for what.

When I was reporting "The Flash of Genius," the phrase "patent troll" was not yet in general use. A patent troll, as defined by Peter Detkin, a former general counsel of Intel, who popularized the term, is a person or company that uses a "paper patent"—a patent on a design for an invention that the holder has no intention of developing into an actual invention and uses it to sue a large company for infringement. In the early 1990s, there was a good deal of talk about "submarine patents," and of a Chicago-based inventor named Jerome Lemelson, who was the master submariner. Lemelson's technique, which he perfected with his lawyer, Gerald Hosier, was to identify fecund patches of technological progress, such as machine vision, and file for patents on tools and techniques the still developing field would probably need. Then, by regularly amending the patent applications, they would keep the patent "pending"—which means that the patent has been filed but not granted yet, so that the clock on the limited monopoly has not yet begun to tick—until other inventors and entrepreneurs had created and developed the market. Then Lemelson and Hosier would complete their patents, and their submarine would emerge in the midst of the surprised, unwitting infringers, who would either settle or get their pants sued off. By the early 1990s, when I interviewed him for my piece on Kearns, Lemelson held more than 350 patents and was worth hundreds of millions. I thought I had been fair to Jerry Lemelson—there are some who consider him one of the greatest frauds of the twentieth century—but he wasn't happy with my sketch of him, and after the article was published, he wrote me a vaguely threatening letter. But he obviously had bigger fish to fry. When he died, in 1997, he set aside more than $130 million to create the Lemelson Foundation, an organization devoted to encouraging genuine inventors and entrepreneurs.

Hosier's younger partner and protégé, Ray Niro, extended Lemelson's technique, by pursuing alleged infringers more aggressively, with broader patent claims and more harassing lawsuits. Starting from the position that the Patent Act makes no distinction between patents that resulted in manufactured goods and mere paper patents, which exist solely as legal rights, Niro and his fellow trolls seek to buy patents from inventors who are not attempting to enforce them, or from bankrupt technology businesses. The broader the patent the better, and if the inventor happens to be an independent individual, better still. (For example, Niro represents the owner of a patent that covers the posting of a JPEG file on a Web site—virtually every site on the Internet with pictures on it infringes this patent.) Having secured the patent, the troll then accuses a large firm of infringing it. Since the cost of defending such a suit is at least a million dollars, often much more, the firm may decide the more prudent course of action is to settle. So, even though the troll has done nothing to advance the technology in question, he is able to profit handsomely from the patent system.

In defense of their deplorable practices, Niro and his fellow patent trolls point to the fact that no one who buys real estate without intending to live on it is called a "land troll," so why should the case be any different for intellectual property? Nonetheless, the naked greed and unsupportable (if legal) tactics of the trolls—the general sense that easy money is available to those who are unscrupulous enough to demand it—besmirches the whole system, and provokes respectable companies that should know better to play by the same rules. Every week seems to bring a new outrage. In March 2008, Gibson, the guitar

maker, claimed that Activision, the company behind the wildly successful video game Guitar Hero, was infringing Gibson's patent on a
virtual guitar! Activision, in turn, brought a lawsuit to clarify its rights.
Not many of the millions of kids now discovering the guitar through
Guitar Hero are likely to buy a Gibson product, if Gibson comes between
them and their fun. The case makes it clear that the record industry isn't
the only branch of the music business to enjoy a patent on stupidity.

When you consider these abuses, you have to wonder whether
the patent system makes sense anymore. Lawmakers, hoping to rescue the system, are pushing a Patent Reform Act through Congress,
and it seems likely to become law. It proposes changes in the methods available to challenge a patent's validity, and also the ways in
which damages are calculated, in the hope of bringing the modern
system more in line with the founders' intentions. I hope the lawmakers succeed, because without the patent system, individual inventors and small companies would have no chance against big
companies, who could easily dominate their respective industries
with market share alone. And dominant companies are not always
the most innovative players in the field, because often innovation
threatens their business model. That's why the telegraph companies
didn't invent the telephone, and the music industry didn't create
iTunes, and Microsoft didn't start Google.

By demonstrating the individual inventor's power in court, and
by showing how high royalty rates could be, Kearns ironically helped
create the patent trolls that plague the system today. But Kearns
was the farthest thing from an extortionist. Kearns was a moral absolutist, who found himself in a morally relative world. Had he been
in it for the money, he could have made a lot more of it. But as suc-
cessive waves of his lawyers discovered, to their horror, Kearns was
in it for the principle. It will be doubly ironic if reform of the patent
laws—reforms the Kearns case indirectly helped inspire—end up
making it harder for real inventors like Kearns to get to court.

Kearns had planned, after wrapping up the Chrysler case, to
move on and prosecute the other twenty-six automakers around
the world, all of whom had also infringed his patent. Having estab-

lished a royalty rate of eleven cents per wiper in the Ford case, Kearns stood to earn many hundreds of millions in damages. (As the attorney for a Japanese manufacturer said, "There aren't enough zeroes to pay Kearns what he's owed.") But Judge Cohn quickly put an end to that scenario. He held Kearns, who planned to continue to represent himself, to account for failing to reduce the number of claims within the court-ordered deadline, and used this technicality to dismiss all future cases. Kearns got one big zero. "He goose-egged us," as Dennis told me recently.

Toward the end of his life, Kearns did enjoy the recognition of inventors around the world. He received hundreds of letters from other independents, many telling their own infringement horror stories, and thanking him for winning one for the little guy. But the ten million he received from Ford, and the thirty million he won from Chrysler, didn't change Kearns's behavior much, nor did it mellow his sense of injustice and indignation. In fact, he didn't cash the Chrysler check for nearly eight years. Kearns was angry that Judge Cohn had awarded ten million of the money to the lawyers that had represented Kearns in the first phase of the Ford trial—Arnold, White & Durkee of Houston. Kearns, with typical obstinacy, said that if Cohn was going to give his money away, he didn't want any of it. (Arnold, White, for its part, couldn't figure out how to distribute the ten million, and in the subsequent arguing over the windfall, the venerable firm imploded.) The money sat in the court's account and then in Kearns's safe deposit box. Kearns continued to drive a 1965 Chrysler New Yorker (1965 happens to be the last model before Chrysler introduced the intermittent wiper as an option). Finally, around 2000, Tim Kearns persuaded his dad to go to the bank with the check, and he did. It was still good.

For the last five years of his life, Kearns suffered from Alzheimer's. "He'd get in the car and forget where he was going, and then he'd forget how to get back from where he was," Dennis told me. He refused to stop driving, and the family was forced to petition the state to have his license taken away. After that he didn't go far from the house. His money finally came in handy: the family could afford round-the-clock nursing care. He died, at the age of seventy-seven, in February 2005.

Did Kearns actually invent the intermittent windshield wiper? Had Kearns never lived, intermittent windshield wipers would still exist; someone else would have invented them. Had Edison never lived, we would still have electric lights and phonographs and movie cameras. (Indeed, it now appears that a French inventor, Parisian Édouard-Léon Scott de Martinville, recorded sound seventeen years before Edison did.) Had my uncle Courtney never lived, we'd still have boil-in-the-bag frozen vegetables. But while it is true that the zeitgeist seems to be mainly responsible for invention, still it is important to believe that individual inventors matter. It is a founding myth of industrial culture, and even if the individual inventor is often an illusion, it is an important and necessary one, and the myth is true often enough to make the fantasy believable.

In the end, Kearns had his story to tell, and the combined legal and corporate power of Ford and Chrysler were no match for the power of that story. That was what drew me to Kearns—it was not just his story I found compelling, but the way that story came to matter in a clash over technological innovation. The power that the invention story carried in patent disputes inspired me to hope that I could use stories to illuminate material that was full of bewildering technical details. Stories themselves are like inventions—little literary mousetraps that writers hope to spring on a reader's attention. I hope these will capture yours.

# FLASH

## OF

# GENIUS

# THE FLASH OF GENIUS

In November 1962 Bob Kearns was driving his Ford Galaxie through the streets of Detroit when it started to rain lightly. Kearns turned the wipers on low. In those days, even the most advanced wipers had just two settings, one for steady rain and one for heavy rain; in a mizzling rain, they screeched back and forth across the glass, mesmerizing the driver and occasionally causing accidents. Kearns, whose vision was already impaired as a result of an accident nine years earlier—on his wedding night, he was hit in the left eye by a flying champagne cork—was straining to see through the windshield, half thinking about his lousy wipers and half thinking about his bad eye, when he had what *The Wall Street Journal* later called "the kind of inspiration that separates inventors from ordinary people." Kearns thought, Why can't a wiper work more like an eyelid? Why can't it blink? The idea for the "Kearns blinking eye wiper" entered his mind.

A little more than three decades after his good idea came to him, Kearns went to trial against General Motors. Kearns, who was sixty-five years old, had already defeated Ford and Chrysler in court, and he stood to collect more than twenty million dollars from them for infringing his patents on the intermittent windshield wiper. After the GM trial, Kearns planned to start on foreign automakers, beginning with Ferrari and working his way through virtually the entire automobile industry worldwide. He was a hero to thousands of inventors with their own patent-infringement horror stories to tell. And he was a barnacle that had fastened itself to the underside of our patent system so tenaciously that the most powerful corporations in the world could not pry it off.

Kearns was a small man, a few inches taller than elfin. His voice was high, nasal, and toneless, and his shoulders were stooped, perhaps from years of peering down at patent texts. His skin was pinkish, and his hair was startlingly white. According to Dennis, his oldest son, it turned white all at once, in 1976, when Kearns took apart an intermittent-windshield-wiper apparatus made by Mercedes and discovered that the great German carmaker had apparently infringed his wiper patents, too.

Kearns represented himself against Chrysler, and planned to do so again against GM. His offices, Kearns Associates, were directly across the street from the Detroit federal courthouse, where his cases were tried. He could usually be found at his desk, half hidden behind heaps of motions and countermotions and books on trial procedure. The Associates were mainly Kearns's family. He had six children, and the lawsuit had become the dominant event in their lives—and now their children were growing up with the case. The family was close, and the lawsuit had brought them closer. Four of his children were working full time for their father. The case is what they did. None of them had any legal training. They had learned on the job to write briefs, service documents, and deal with maneuvers pulled on them by the hundreds of lawyers working for the Big Three. "For the kids, the lawsuit is all we've ever known," Kearns's daughter Kathy, told me. "I mean, for us this is normal."

There was widespread feeling in patent departments of corporations around the country that Kearns's case represented a frightening precedent. An inventor named Gilbert Hyatt, who was recently granted a basic patent on the microprocessor, was the latest example of the trend. In theory, Hyatt had billions coming to him from the dozens of corporations that used microprocessors. "This kind of stuff makes people who work for corporations very nervous," Marty Adelman, a law professor and patent expert at Wayne State University, told me. "The story today is not the big company screwing the little guy but the little guy screwing the big company. It's getting easier and easier for the little guy to do it."

The United States patent system was designed for the independent inventor—for the person whom Nikola Tesla described as "the lone worker who follows the fleeting inspiration of a moment and finally does something that has not been done before." Two hundred years ago, when Thomas Jefferson created our patent system, all inventors were independent. Now most inventors work in huge corporate research centers. Individuals surrender their ideas to the corporation, and for doing so they receive regular salaries. But the patent system, together with the law that has accrued around it, still rests on the eighteenth-century idea of the inventor, and in court a lone inventor with a patent is a formidable opponent for any corporation to face. "I read all the patent cases, and rarely has there been a case in the last five years where the corporation has beaten an independent inventor," Adelman said. "I tell all the corporate people who call me to testify against individuals, 'Jesus, guys, you're up against it.'"

The most frightening thing about Kearns, from the automobile companies' point of view, was that he didn't seem particularly interested in money. He wanted justice. "They think they can pay me thirty million dollars and put me on a park bench," he told me. "Well, Bob Kearns is not somebody's lackey." He said he simply wanted to make windshield wipers. That was all he had ever wanted. He would go on suing until automobile companies around the world were stopped from manufacturing his wiper, and he could make it himself.

The United States Patent and Trademark Office is in Crystal City, a government development in Arlington, Virginia. The buildings are glass and steel, and sleek, in the modern federal style, and the place has a sort of splendid isolation about it that goes nicely with being the city of invention. On the ground floor of the Patent Office is the Search Room, a vast space filled with patents. The Patent Office has the largest collection of patents in the world. Here or upstairs, in the library, are Balinese patents and Manchurian patents, and English patents dating back to 1623. There are German dyestuff patents that were confiscated by the United States during the First World War and became part of the foundation of the American chemical industry. More than six million United States patents have been issued since 1790, when the first one went to Samuel Hopkins, of Pittsford, Vermont, for a new way of making potash, and they are all stored here, in paper form, stacked faceup in an immense lattice of metal cubbyholes—about a hundred bright ideas to each cubby, and thousands of inspirations to each long, dark row. Feathery dust lies on some of the older patents. Patent searchers can be found in the aisles, scouring their fingertips lightly together to remove the dust, and plucking flakes of rotting patents from their jackets and sweaters.

A graph of the fall and rise in the popularity of patents over the last hundred years would look like this: U. Having weathered a long siege of antimonopoly sentiment in the middle of this century, patents are now almost as popular as they were in the 1890s. In 1992, the Patent Office received 185,446 patent applications, more than in any previous year, and 109,728 patents were granted, almost twice as many as a decade earlier. The Patent Office cites these numbers as evidence that the spirit of Edison and Bell is alive, that America is as innovative as ever. This may be true. It is certainly true that patents are more valuable than they used to be.

One reason is the influence of the United States Court of Appeals for the Federal Circuit, which was created in 1982 in part to hear all patent appeals. Before that, patent appeals went to circuit courts of appeal. Most judges despise patent cases. A patent case can tie up a judge's calendar for months, sometimes for years, and often involves technical issues that the judge doesn't understand. Also, patent law is maddeningly subjective and imprecise, and apt to plunge all but the stoutest minds into dizzying swirls of logic. In a patent case a judge is asked to dissect the indivisible stream that is technical progress, to say where one man's inspiration ends and another's begins. For these reasons, circuit judges tended to dismiss patents as invalid simply to get rid of the cases. Between 1950 and 1975, three out of every four patents in the circuit courts were ruled invalid or not infringed. Certain circuits were notorious for their hostility toward patents: in the Eighth Circuit, almost no patents were held valid. The federal circuit court was created to bring fairness and logic to the system, and most people agree that it has. It has also dramatically increased the value of patents. The court has found three out of every four patents valid or infringed. Many of the judges who sit on the court are former patent attorneys, so they are inclined to be more sympathetic to patents than most people are. In the federal circuit, patents are held to be valid until proved otherwise, and not the other way around.

The boundaries of what is patentable have expanded. In 1972 a molecular engineer named Ananda Chakrabarty applied for a patent on a microbe he had engineered that would help break down crude oil. The Patent Office rejected his application, citing a clause in the patent code which says that life-forms are not patentable. Chakrabarty appealed, and in 1980 the Supreme Court ruled in his favor, 5 to 4, creating a brand-new sector of intellectual property: life. The National Institutes of Health subsequently applied for thousands of patents on human genes. The prospect that the U.S. government might soon own the gene that causes, say, green eyes naturally creates a certain amount of controversy, with some people predicting a kind of land grab at the cellular level—the Japanese patenting brown eyes, Swedes patenting blond hair, Italians patenting Roman noses.

Independent inventors are pleased by the renewed popularity of patents because stronger patents give them greater leverage with the manufacturers and licensing companies they sell their inventions to. Automobile and computer manufacturers—businesses that assemble many pieces of technology into a product, as opposed to businesses whose product is a single technology—are not so pleased. They now have to pay royalties for parts that used to be free; or, if they decide to infringe a patent, they can no longer be reasonably confident of getting away with it.

The boom in intellectual property has been good for the Patent Office; patents are its principal source of income, which pays the salaries of its patent examiners. They work on six floors above the

Search Room, their desks and floors awash in patent applications. The Commissioner of Patents, Harry F. Manbeck, has a spacious office on the top floor of the building.

A trim, forceful, no-nonsense sort of fellow, he was naturally pleased with the robust good health that the patent system currently enjoys. "I think there is an increasing awareness of the importance of technology in America, and of the need to protect our technology from incursions by others," he said. "Having said that, I think it is remarkable, isn't it, that the system that was used for granting the first patent"—he waved toward a framed copy of that document, hanging on a wall behind a secretary—"is essentially the same as the system used in granting Patent No. 5,000,000, for . . ." He shot a glance, over his spectacles, toward an aide.

"Ethanol Production by Escherichia Coli Strains Co-Expressing Zymomonas PDC and ADH Genes," said the aide, reading from a clipboard.

"Right," Manbeck said. He leaned back, laced his hands behind his head, and directed his gaze out the window. Across an expanse of the Potomac floodplain, airplanes were landing at National Airport.

Bob Kearns grew up in River Rouge, a working-class neighborhood on the west side of Detroit. Two things about the place captured Kearns's imagination. One was Our Lady of Lourdes Cathedral, a big redbrick Catholic church, which, he remembers, imported water from the real Lourdes. The other thing was the Ford Motor Company's Rouge plant, the largest industrial complex in the world. Kearns's father, who was a roll turner for the Great Lakes Steel Corporation, had once taken his son to visit the Rouge, and Kearns recalls that he had been "just so impressed by the magnitude of what Ford's was doing." Lumber from Ford forests; ore and coal and coke from Ford mines; silica sand from Ford quarries, for making windshields; rubber from Ford plantations in Fordlandia, in Brazil, for making tires—all flowed into the Rouge aboard Ford trains and Ford ships, to be refined and machined and assembled into Fords. At the Rouge, a car could be made from raw materials in four days.

As a teenager, Kearns worked in some of the job shops that used to fill the streets and alleys of Detroit. One place made the molding around the opera windows on Cadillacs. That was its entire business. Another place made the dies for the tools that were used to install one part of the landing gear of C-5 transport planes. The father of one of Kearns's friends had designed a better car-door handle—the familiar bar of curved steel with the push button under it—which helped prevent the door from opening if the car rolled. The man made a fortune supplying GM. "The automotives, the automotives," Kearns once said to me. "That's all there was. If you were an inventor, and you really wanted to reach people, you invented for the automotives. I remember when Charley Wilson"—the president of GM in the forties and fifties—"said, 'What's good for GM is good for America.' I really believed that was true."

Kearns's first invention was a comb that dispensed its own hair tonic. It did not get beyond the model stage. He experimented with an amplifier for people who had undergone laryngectomies and with a new kind of weather balloon. In 1957 he invented a navigational system that he hoped the military would use in its Sidewinder missiles. His ex-wife, Phyllis, remembers him dancing her around the kitchen and saying he was going to buy her two Cadillacs, one for each foot. "It was so exciting," Phyllis recalls. "It was always so exciting, living with Robert—such an adrenaline high." The navigational system didn't pan out either. Kearns tried again.

When the idea for the intermittent wiper came to him, Kearns and his wife and their four young children were living in a brick house on Rutherford Street, on the north side of Detroit. Kearns, who had a master's in mechanical engineering from Wayne State University, was commuting to Case Western Reserve, in Cleveland, where he was working toward his Ph.D. He believes that his great idea grew in some mysterious way out of the eye injury he had received on his wedding night, in a country inn in Ontario. "Phyllis was in the bathroom, you know, changing, and I was sitting on the bed opening the champagne. And I'd never opened champagne before. And—pow! The cork goes off, hits me directly in the left eye, I fall back on the bed bleeding all over the sheets, Phyllis comes out of the bathroom screaming. I mean, it was a mess."

Kearns worked on the wiper on weekends during the first half of 1963. He constructed a glassed-in office for himself on one side of the basement, where he could work without interference from the kids. The other half was Phyllis's laundry room. "I'd be over here, doing laundry, up to my ears in kids, and he'd be over there behind the glass with his feet up," Phyllis recalled. "Well, he said he did his best work with his feet up."

By the summer, Kearns had built a working model of his invention. He could vary the time the wipers dwelled at the base of the windshield; he could vary the speed with which they swept it; he had even figured out a way of making the wipers automatically adjust their interval to the amount of water on the glass. He put his wiper control in a red metal box that on the outside had the words "For Engineering Tests Only. Do Not Open. Proprietary Design Property of Kearns Engineers," and two friends installed the box in the Galaxie.

Phyllis: "If it rained, we would stop whatever we were doing, run out to the car, turn the wipers on, and drive around. Doing life tests, Robert called it."

Bob: "I had figured out that the elasticity of rainwater was different from the elasticity of hose water, and I wanted to set the thing just right."

Phyllis: "Oh, I felt so proud, driving that car in the rain. I'd get both my hands right up at the top of the steering wheel, where people passing could see them, so they knew I wasn't just switching the wipers on and off."

In October, Kearns decided that the time had come to demonstrate his invention to a car manufacturer. He chose Ford because it had supplied him with some wiper motors to experiment on and because "to me Ford was always the greatest." Through his brother Marty, who worked in body engineering at Ford, he made contact with a man named John Ciupak, who he believed "had a substantial position in windshield wipers," and Ciupak said he should come over to the engineering complex in Dearborn, Ford's headquarters. Kearns drove the Galaxie over. He met Ciupak inside and brought him out to the parking lot. He demonstrated variable speed, variable dwell, and moisture responsiveness. He let Ciupak try. They spent about forty-five minutes at it altogether, and Ciupak seemed impressed. However, he explained to Kearns that his field was wiper linkages and blades—that Joe Neill, the executive engineer, was the man Kearns needed to speak to.

Three days later, Kearns, once again driving the Galaxie, reappeared for his appointment with Neill. He was surprised to find about ten Ford engineers waiting for him in the parking lot. They took turns running the wipers; they poked around under the hood; they crawled under the dash. One at a time, several engineers took Kearns aside and asked him how his wiper worked. "I didn't want to tell them how I'd done it, but I didn't want to be impolite either," Kearns recalled. Eventually, Neill appeared. He had a Mercury brought out of the lab, and, keeping Kearns at a distance, demonstrated to him that, as chance would have it, Ford was working on an intermittent wiper, too. Nonetheless, Neill said, Ford would like to look at Kearns's invention, if Kearns would like to show it to Ford.

Neill then said he would like to know how much Kearns's wipers cost to build. He also arranged for Kearns to get instructions on Ford's specification tests: the wipers had to run three million cycles, and they had to be able to operate at 270 degrees, the maximum temperature under the hood. Kearns left in a state of euphoria. Many years later, recalling that day in a court document, he wrote, "I was in heaven!"

Ted Daykin was one of the Ford engineers who came out into the parking lot to inspect Kearns's Galaxie in 1963. Daykin spent thirty-eight years, his entire career, working as an engineer at Ford, and took early retirement two years ago. He was almost exactly the same age as Kearns, received a similar education, and also devoted many years to windshield-wiper experiments, but the two men were nothing alike. Daykin looked about ten years younger than Kearns, and he appeared to be one of the steadiest of men. He and his wife, Prill, lived in a spacious ranch-style house in Dearborn, within a mile of the Ford engineering laboratories where Ted did his life's work. Around the living room were framed photographs of the Daykin family: their daughter, Elizabeth, who was also an engineer at Ford;

Elizabeth's husband, Gregory, who worked in product planning for General Motors; and the Daykins' son, Robert, who worked on the Pontiac account for a local advertising agency.

Daykin began experimenting with windshield wipers in 1957, when his supervisor asked him to design an electric wiper motor. Electricity was the new auto technology then. Electric windows, electric locks, electric trunk catches were the latest gadgets. But wipers were one of the quiet backwaters of automotive technology. The standard wiper was driven by intake from the engine manifold, which was connected by a series of hoses to the wiper motor. The wipers wiped from the center of the windshield out, leaving a big unwiped V in the middle.

Ford had asked Daykin and his colleagues to invent a wiper system in which the blades moved parallel to each other. "See, Chrysler had come out with parallel blades in 1955, and people liked them," Daykin said. "So Ford wanted parallel blades. But the problem with parallel blades is that your surface area is too large for the mechanism to drive the wipers effectively." Daykin's electric motor, linked to parallel blades, appeared as a standard feature on 1959 Mercurys and as an option on 1959 Lincolns, and it was immediately popular. At that time, the beauty of the option business was just beginning to dawn on the auto industry. By keeping the base price of the car low—even selling the car at a loss—Ford could bring customers into the dealerships, then sell them a bunch of options that were extremely profitable for Ford.

Windshield wipers were a potentially rich source of options. "The success of those parallel blades got management thinking, Well, what other wiper options can we come up with?" Daykin said. "So I was told to organize a windshield-wiper group, and to play around and see what else we could invent. You know, a lot of people don't really spend a lot of time thinking about their wipers. They turn them on, they turn them off, and that's about it. But the fact is that there are dozens of inventions that go into the way your wipers work. What causes wipers to complete their wipe cycle when they're turned off midwipe? How, when they have returned to the base of the windshield, do they park themselves out of the driver's sight? In the industry, we call that feature 'depressed park.' How are wipers synchronized with the wash mechanism—what makes the wiper go on automatically when you push the washer, and give you two or three wipes? How about the rear-window wiper? Well, when you talk about that stuff you're talking about the inventions of windshield-wiper engineers." In the early sixties, Daykin and his colleagues busied themselves with inventing features like those. "Of course, one of the things we worked on was the intermittent wiper. How do you design a circuit where the wiper comes to a stop at the base of the windshield and then goes into its cycle again? The intermittent wiper was—well, I won't say it was the Holy Grail for wiper engineers. But it was the obvious next step for wipers to take."

The basic problem to solve in inventing an intermittent windshield wiper was the timing device—the thing that sends current to the wiper motor at regular intervals. What should the timing device be? One of the engineers working with Daykin had designed a circuit that relied on a bimetallic timer. The timer worked like a thermostat, on the principle that two different kinds of metal will expand and contract at different rates when their temperature changes. The problem with this invention was that it took some time to heat up. On very cold days, it might not work at all. Also, getting the wiper to dwell for short periods was difficult because of the time it took for the switch to heat and cool.

In late 1961 Ford's principal supplier of windshield-wiper components, a Buffalo-based company called Trico Products, brought a new intermittent device to Ford. It was a small vacuum chamber, about the size and shape of a bathtub stopper, that contained a plunger and spring and had two small air hoses attached to it. The outlet hose ran to the engine manifold, and the inlet hose ran to the dashboard, where it was attached to a small dial. The engine, as it cooled itself, sucked in air through the outlet hose, producing suction in the vacuum chamber, and so drawing the plunger down and compressing the spring. The driver used the dial mounted on the dash to control the flow of air into the vacuum chamber. The spring moved a switch in the wiper circuit to the "off" position, and the wipers dwelled. The spring eventually caused the plunger to rise and moved the switch to the "on" position. The wipers wiped.

As a piece of engineering, the Trico system was not especially distinguished. It was something of a Rube Goldberg contraption. It had twenty-nine moving parts, which meant a lot of potential for breaking down. When the driver accelerated, the vacuum was insufficient to run the intermittent mode, and the wipers would default to high speed. Trico, in trying to sell the wiper to Ford, advertised this as a specially designed passing feature—useful, say, in overtaking a truck on a rainy day. "The engineers saw it for what it was, which was a design flaw," Daykin said. "But the planners thought that the passing feature was really neat." Management decided to offer Trico's intermittent wiper as an option on 1965 Mercurys, and the wiper division went to work developing it. This was the intermittent wiper that Kearns saw when he paid his first visit to the engineering building.

Kearns's intermittent wiper was an elegant piece of engineering. It had four parts, and only one of them moved. It was a leap forward, beyond electricity and into electronics. Though Kearns did not realize it, he was on the threshold of the next revolution in automotive technology. He had worked for the Bendix Corporation in the midfifties, and had some experience with electronic control systems, which were then used only in high technology, like computers. A transistor, a capacitor, and a variable resistor were the three basic components of Kearns's circuit. The resistor and the capacitor together were the timer, and the transistor worked as the switch. The resistor, which the driver could adjust with a knob, controlled the rate of current flowing into the capacitor. When the voltage in the capacitor reached a certain level, it triggered the transistor; the transistor turned on, and the wipers wiped once. The running of the wiper motor drained voltage out of the capacitor; it sank below the threshold level of the transistor, and the transistor turned off. The wipers dwelled until the capacitor recharged.

"There's no question that Dr. Kearns's wiper circuit was interesting," Daykin said. "He had a three-brush motor, with dynamic brake and intermittent on one speed only—his system was a concatenation of a lot of different ideas. But we figured there was just no way in the world it was patentable. An electronic timing device was an obvious thing to try next. How can you patent something that is in the natural evolution of technology?" Daykin shook his head. He said he had spent much of his last year at Ford helping to prepare for the Kearns case, and the experience had caused him to think a lot about the patent system. "I think about all those Ford engineers I worked with developing wiper systems. Dozens of inventors—maybe a hundred—contributed to your intermittent windshield wiper. There were men from Trico, Magnetti Marelli, Rover, Prestolite, Delco, General Motors, Chrysler, and Ford. I don't know who some of them were—nobody does. They were the real inventors of the intermittent windshield wiper, not Kearns."

Prill could be heard in the dining room, setting the table for a family lunch. "Patents were meant to encourage innovation, after all, not static ownership," Daykin said. "Can you imagine where we would be if each one of those engineers had gone after a patent? We'd all still be driving around with two-speed wipers."

Having received the go-ahead from Ford, Kearns began testing his intermittent wiper. He figured that putting it through three million cycles would take six months. He bought an aquarium, installed the wipers in it, filled the tank with a mixture of oil and sawdust to simulate a load on the wiper, and set it over on Phyllis's side of the basement. It was Phyllis's job, when her husband was away, to keep an eye on the tank; occasionally, she would stir its contents with a cooking spoon. When Kearns came home from Case Western Reserve on weekends, he devoted himself to wiper experiments. On Friday night, sometimes all night, Phyllis would watch the oscilloscope, an EKG-like monitor for measuring electrical impulses, while Bob tried components in different configurations. On Saturday, he would be out in the driveway all day, bent over the Galaxie, making adjustments. He would fill the neighbors in on his progress. A salesman from Motorola or Delco might stop by, with a quote on resistors. On Saturday evening, the whole family gathered in the living room and inked in circuit diagrams, for making printed circuit boards. On Sunday, after church, Bob drove Phyllis and the kids around Detroit, scouting out sites for the Kearns wiper factory. "Dad had picked out jobs for each of us," his son Tim recalled. "My brother Dennis was going to be the company lawyer, I was going to be the chief engineer, and my brother Robert would be the head mechanic." By the late fall of 1963, Phyllis was pregnant again. "How about a girl?" she remembered Bob saying. "We need a computer programmer."

The wipers completed their three-million-four-hundred-thousandth wipe on November 16, 1964. (Kearns had let the wipers run another four hundred thousand cycles for good measure.) He called Ford with the good news, but Ford didn't seem overexcited. His financial situation was becoming dire. His family was large; his income as a doctoral fellow was not, and he was spending a considerable portion of it on wiper components. Also, he needed money to get his patents. Phyllis was supportive—"I thought the sun was never going to set on Robert," she says—but Phyllis's mother had begun to wonder why her son-in-law didn't get a regular job in the auto industry, like so many of his classmates. "Oh, but giving up the rights to his patents would have killed Robert," Phyllis said. "He would have died."

Kearns finally took action: "I waited for a rainy day, then I drove over to see Dave Tann." Tann was one of six brothers who had expanded the business started by their father, a small tool-and-die shop, into the Tann Corporation, a midsize manufacturing company that supplied carmakers with various parts and tools—fenders, dashboards, hood ornaments, dies for stamping out hoods. He was the sort of man Kearns imagined himself becoming. Kearns brought Tann out to the car and showed him the intermittent wiper. "Dave got in the car, drove around awhile, and came back all excited," Kearns recalls. "'This is great! This is great!' he kept saying. He wouldn't give me my car back. He said, 'Here, we'll swap. Take my Cadillac.' So I drove that home, and he took mine." They agreed that Kearns would assign his rights to the intermittent wiper to Tann, and Tann would take over the cost of getting the patents. In addition, Tann would pay Kearns a thousand dollars a month to continue his wiper R & D, plus royalties when the wiper went into production. Kearns went home that afternoon with his first year's payment, twelve thousand dollars in cash. "Robert came home, got me and the kids into the kitchen, and covered the whole kitchen counter with money," Phyllis said. "That was a great day."

Dick Aitken, Tann's patent attorney, filed the first patent application for Kearns's intermittent wiper in December of 1964. When it comes to writing patent applications, patent attorneys talk about "staking out the four corners of the invention," and Aitken did an excellent job of staking them as far apart as he could. The first patent was granted in November 1967. Meanwhile, Tann had made contact with Ford, and he and Kearns had given a formal presentation to a group of Ford engineers and executives. "Dave bought a new car to make the demonstration with," Kearns said. "And that car was Henry Ford's favorite color—black. It had black everything. Black tires, black wheels, and black leather seats. Dave said, 'Black is what Ford likes? Well, we'll give 'em what they like.' That was how Dave Tann did things." The demonstration was a hit, and it led to a series of demonstrations to other parts of the Ford organization.

Finally, Roger Shipman, a Ford supervisor, announced to Kearns that he had "won the wiper competition." He told Kearns that his wiper would be used on the 1969 Mercury line. Kearns was given the prototype of a windshield-wiper motor to commemorate the occasion. The other engineers welcomed him aboard Ford's wiper team. Then, according to Kearns, Shipman asked him to show his wiper control to the rest of the team. Wipers were a safety item, Shipman explained, and the law required disclosure of all the engineering before Ford could give Kearns a contract. This sounded reasonable to Kearns, so he explained to the Ford engineers exactly how his intermittent wiper worked.

About five months later, Kearns was dismissed. He was told that Ford did not want his wiper system after all—that the other engineers had designed their own. Kearns remembered that one of the engineers taunted him as he was leaving. Then, about six months after the dismissal, Shipman called Kearns, told him his wiper still had a chance for the 1969 model year, and asked him to come in again. "And, just like a lover, I went back again," Kearns said. "Because what else could I do? Ford was my market. Plus I did not really believe at that time that Ford would infringe my patent. I mean, I believed in Ford. I'm a believer."

Thomas Jefferson was the first superintendent of our patent system, and our first patent examiner. Among the public men of the late eighteenth century, he was by far the best qualified for the job. He was an inventor himself: he invented a moldboard for plows, a swivel chair, a pedometer, a camp stool, and a copying device, among other things. He was interested in inventors, and seems to have understood them.

Another quality that made Jefferson the right person to run the patent system was that he distrusted patents. Patents, being monopolies, were dangerous in a republic conceived in part as an anti-monopoly haven. Starting a patent system was like providing the young economy with enough rope to hang itself. Jefferson was familiar with the havoc that patents had caused in the British economy. In England, in the late sixteenth century, Elizabeth I had discovered that when Parliament refused to give her money she could raise it herself by selling monopoly rights to noblemen. In 1623, to put a stop to that practice, Parliament passed the Statute of Monopolies, which declared monopolies illegal. However, the statute contained an exception for patents: to encourage innovation, Parliament allowed genuine inventors the right to hold limited monopolies on their inventions.

The trouble was that Parliament did not figure out how to determine who was a genuine inventor and what a genuine invention was. It was easy for Elizabeth's successor, James I, and for his son, Charles I, to go on selling monopolies to bogus inventors who could afford to buy them. This was one reason that, in 1649, Parliament chopped off Charles's head.

Jefferson thought he could fix the basic flaw in the British system. His solution was the principle of examination. The principle is that certain innovations have a quality that elevates them to the status of inventions, and thus makes them eligible to be held as private property, while innovations that lack this quality are the common property of humanity. Learned people can, by study and power of reason, determine which inventions deserve a patent and which do not. Examination is the greatest American contribution to the institution of patents, and it has been copied by virtually every industrial nation in the world. Like a lot of ideas associated with the Enlightenment, it sounds a lot better than it works.

Jefferson and his fellow-examiners struggled to come up with a definition for *invention*. Jefferson declared that in order to be patentable an invention had to be new and useful, but he found that some new and useful inventions were too frivolous to be worth "the embarrassment of an exclusive patent," as he put it. He did make sure the law stated that a patent could go only to "the true and sole inventor." Of course, when Jefferson used the word *inventor* he had in mind a farmer or a small manufacturer who in the course of harvesting a crop or making a doorknob would discover a shortcut or devise a new tool that would make the job easier or the product better. The idea of an industrial-research laboratory, a place staffed by thousands of inventors working for a single organization, could hardly have occurred to Jefferson.

In 1906 a patent lawyer named Edwin Prindle published a series of articles in the magazine *Engineering* in which he explained to businesses how they could use patents to restrain trade. "Patents are the best and most effective means of controlling competition," he wrote. "They occasionally give absolute command of the market, enabling their owner to name the price without regard to cost of production. . . . Patents are the only legal form of absolute monopoly." Patent lawyers recommended the use of what are called improvement patents, by which the life of a patent—in the United States, its life is seventeen years—could be extended almost indefinitely. First, one had to get control of a basic patent on a new technology, and the best way of doing that was to organize a trust and buy the patent from the inventor. If no basic patent existed, the trust could simply buy up all the minor patents in the field. Then, every year or two, inventors working for the company could come up with a slightly improved version of the technology and patent it, and the seventeen-year clock would start over. The lawyers suggested hiring large numbers of inventors, to build a fortress of improvement patents around the basic patent and keep competitors far from the company's technology. These inventors would, of course, have to sign contracts surrendering the right to their ideas. While this was not in the spirit of the patent system designed by Jefferson, it was technically legal: the law could not prevent the inventor from assigning his idea, once it had become his private property, to someone else.

The first corporations were essentially large blocks of patents. Western Union grew from Samuel Morse's patents on the telegraph, International Harvester from Cyrus McCormick's patents on the reaper, General Electric from Edison's patents on the lightbulb, and AT & T from Bell's patents on the telephone. Independent inventors began to find it difficult to compete with inventors hired by the corporations. A lot of them took jobs in corporate research laboratories—they were willing to exchange the chance of getting rich for the certainty of a regular salary. The ones that remained independent turned to inventing gadgets and toys to survive. Opining on whether or not this is a good thing is one of the set pieces of technology histories. Some people see the rise of hired inventors as a natural part of the evolution of technology; others see it as a wrong turn.

James B. Conant: "As theory developed in physics and chemistry and penetrated into practice, as the degree of empiricism was reduced in one area after another, the inventor was bound to disappear."

John Kenneth Galbraith: "Technical development has long since become the preserve of the scientist and the engineer. Most of the cheap and simple inventions have, to put it bluntly, been made."

Philo Farnsworth: "We must not lose track of the fact that inventions as such, important inventions, are made by individuals and almost invariably by individuals with very limited means."

Nikola Tesla: "Invention is predominantly individualistic. Everything of prime moment comes from some individual unconnected with any commercial organization."


In 1969 Ford came out with a new, electronic intermittent windshield wiper, the first in the industry. It used a transistor, a resistor, and a capacitor in the same configuration that Kearns had designed. It cost Ford about ten dollars to make, and it sold for thirty-seven dollars. At first, Ford offered the intermittent wiper as a stand-alone option, and it sold slowly. Then Ford packaged it with another gadget—the remote-control side mirror, which was one of Ford's most popular options—and wiper sales took off. In 1974 General Motors began putting the intermittent wiper on its cars, and in 1977 it appeared on Chrysler's. Saab, Honda, Volvo, Rolls-Royce, and Mercedes, among others, soon followed. By 1989, Ford alone had sold 20.6 million cars with the intermittent wiper and made a profit that has been calculated at $557 million. Altogether, about thirty million intermittent wipers are sold around the world each year.

Kearns tried to get an explanation from Ford, but he soon discovered that "there's a diode in the line when you talk to Ford—the information only goes one way." His lawyers wrote letters to Ford's legal department, informing it that Ford was infringing Kearns's patents. Eventually, they received a letter back saying that Ford was not infringing Kearns's patents and that, in any case, Kearns's patents were invalid. "I just felt very diminished," Kearns said. "It's like you're a nothing, you're a gnat. You don't count. You just don't count."

Kearns wanted Tann to sue Ford. "As a practical matter, we couldn't sue Ford for patent infringement, because they were one of the family's main sources of business," Tann said later, of his company. "We needed Ford's goodwill to keep our business alive."

Several years passed. Kearns got his patent rights back from Tann. He moved his family to Gaithersburg, Maryland, to take a job with the Bureau of Standards, testing the skid resistance of various kinds of road surfaces. Kearns was in his midforties now. On July 8, 1976, Dennis Kearns stopped in at a Mercedes service center, bought a wiper control, and brought it home to his father. Kearns went down to the basement and took it apart. "And I saw capacitor, resistor, transistor—it was all there," he recalled. "Even the great Mercedes had infringed my patents." He wandered distractedly out of his home, hitchhiked to Washington, and got on a Greyhound headed south. Somehow he had become convinced that Richard Nixon wanted him to go to Australia, to build an electric car. "Then

I realized I'd never spent any time with my kids. I'd been so consumed with my work on the wiper that I'd never even shown them how to fly a kite. So I went and bought these two kites. When the police picked me up a few days later, I was in Tennessee, in a park, holding these two kites."

In 1978 Kearns filed suit against Ford for patent infringement. Eventually he added other car companies to the suit, but Ford was the principal focus of his hatred. "I just had an overwhelming feeling that what Ford had done was wrong," Kearns said. "It was unjust, and it was illegal." In his suit he asked for $350 million in lost profits, multiplied by three—the maximum penalty for willful infringement—plus interest and costs, for a total of $1.6 billion.

Henry Ford loathed patents. One of Ford's lawyers once boasted, "There is no power on earth, outside of the Supreme Court, which can make Henry Ford sign a license agreement or pay a royalty." Ford thought that the patent system should be abolished, because, he said, it "produces parasites, men who are willing to lay back on their oars and do nothing," and because patents afford "opportunities for little minds, directed by others more cunning, to usurp the gains of genuine inventors—for pettifoggers to gain a strategic advantage over honest men, and, under a smug protest of righteousness, work up a hold-up game in the most approved fashion."

Ford's opinion of the patent system was galvanized by the Selden Patent. In 1879 George B. Selden, a resident of Rochester, had filed a patent application in which he claimed to have invented the automobile. In his application Selden described a machine with a gasoline-driven, combustion-type engine that sat in front of the driver; a clutch; a foot brake; a drive shaft; and front-wheel drive. Selden had never built such an automobile. He wasn't an especially skilled mechanic. He was a patent lawyer, in fact. Selden believed that in the not-too-distant future people were going to be riding around in motorized cars of the type he envisioned, and he wanted to have a monopoly on them.

For the next sixteen years, Selden kept his application pending in the Patent Office, using his professional skills to draw the process out, amending the application now and then, waiting for the men who were actually building automobiles to produce one that was marketable. In 1895 he decided that the moment had come, and he caused himself to receive Patent No. 549,160. An East Coast auto manufacturer named Albert Pope, who was backed by a syndicate of investors, made a royalty agreement with Selden and acquired the rights to his patent. In keeping with business practices of the day, Pope and his backers formed a trust, and called it the Association of Licensed Automobile Manufacturers. The ALAM declared that any car manufacturer that did not get a license from the trust and pay a royalty of 1.25 percent of the sales price of each car it sold would be infringing the Selden Patent and would be sued. By 1905, 85 percent of the auto industry was under license to the ALAM. Selden was promoted as the inventor of the automobile.

In 1903 Henry Ford, then an unknown engineer from Detroit, had formed the Ford Motor Company. He applied for a license from the ALAM but was judged to be merely a fly-by-night assembler of parts, not a bona fide automobile manufacturer, and was turned down. Ford decided to make and sell his cars anyway. He announced that he had no intention of paying his tithe to the Selden Patent, that the patent was unjust, and that the machine Selden described could never have worked in the first place. The ALAM wasted no time in suing Ford for patent infringement. The drama of Ford, a barely educated, plainspoken Midwesterner, defying the entire automobile industry, as well as some of the most powerful interests on Wall Street, was irresistible to the public, and it made Ford famous.

Ford did not shrink from the attention. He expanded his position into a general attack on the patent system. "I believe absolutely in free competition, and in abolishing patents, which kill competition," he said. In *Monopoly on Wheels,* a 1961 book about the Selden case, William Greenleaf writes, "By endowing his own struggle for a place in the sun with a luminous appeal to fundamental principles, [Ford] translated a wearisome patent suit into one man's struggle for the right to enjoy unhampered opportunity. This was a potent theme in a day when the politics of Progressivism was sweeping the land and the movement for social democracy was still nourished by the hopes and ambitions of the small businessman." In 1911 Ford won the Selden case on appeal, breaking the patent, destroying the ALAM, propelling himself into the dominant position in the auto industry, and ensuring that future generations of Americans would regard Henry Ford, not George Selden, as the inventor of the automobile.

For the rest of his life, Ford virtually ignored the patent system. "As a rule Ford adamantly refused to adopt parts and components patented by others," Greenleaf writes. "Instead, he ordered his engineers to evolve their own designs." Other carmakers designed their own parts too. This gave the young automobile industry the unique advantage of having free access to technology as soon as it was invented. Ford was a kind of Promethean figure, taking a revolutionary new technology out of the hands of the elite and giving it directly to the people. This was not necessarily the best thing for those who invented the technology—the designers of carburetors, sparkplugs, radiators, rubber tires, power steering, overdrive, the convertible top, rack-and-pinion steering, the rear-window defroster, cruise control, air bags, and intermittent windshield wipers. However, Ford, in defense of his position on patents, often pointed out that his own invention—a light, cheap, durable car that could be mass-produced, like matches or pins, at a time when the industry was committed to the automobile as a luxury product—would have been impossible if he had been forced to pay for the inventions of other men. "I invented nothing new," he once declared. "I simply assembled into a car the discoveries of other men behind whom were centuries of work, and the discoveries of still other men who preceded them. Had I worked fifty or even ten or even five years before I would have failed. So it is with every new thing. Progress happens when all the factors that make for it are ready, and then it is inevitable. To teach that a comparatively few men are responsible for the great forward steps of mankind is the worst sort of nonsense."

When Kearns filed suit against the Ford Motor Company in 1978, Ford did what corporations usually do in patent cases: it began stalling, in the hope that Kearns would lose heart or run out of money. Patent cases are richly endowed with opportunities for stalling. The heart of Ford's defense was that Kearns's patents were invalid because, according to the Doctrine of Nonobviousness, his intermittent wiper was not an invention at all.

The Doctrine of Nonobviousness is the current solution to the problem that confounded Jefferson: how to define invention. Over the last two centuries, many people have tried to define it. The 1929 edition of *Walker on Patents,* the standard patent textbook, stated, "What constitutes invention is a very perplexing question." In 1937 this was revised to read, "An invention is the result of an inventive act." An inventive act was generally considered to be a flash of insight that comes when the inventor is not striving for it, as in the case of Nikola Tesla, who was strolling through a park in Budapest and reciting some lines from Goethe when the concept of alternating current suddenly came into his mind and he diagrammed it in the dust with a stick; or of Edwin Land, who was taking photographs of his three-year-old daughter one morning in Sante Fe and, when she asked him why the pictures couldn't be seen immediately, conceived the Polaroid process. The invention story was an important part of the invention itself.

Most judges are not scientists. The average judge's view of invention tends to have more to do with Coleridge's theories about the imagination than with the judge's experience inside an engineering lab. As the twentieth century got older, and the gap between the liberal arts and the applied sciences got larger, the problem got worse. The last straw came in 1941, when the Supreme Court issued its "flash of creative genius" decision, in *Cuno Engineering Corporation v. Automatic Devices Corporation.* The invention in question was the first cordless automobile cigarette lighter. The Court decided that it was not patentable because it lacked the characteristics of an invention. Justice William O. Douglas, writing for the majority, stated that "the new device, however useful it may be, must reveal the flash of creative genius, not merely the skill of the calling."

Patent professionals began to feel that the legal view of invention was inconsistent with the way things actually got made, and that a more scientific, less romantic definition of invention was needed. A panel of patent experts produced the Doctrine of Nonobviousness, which became law in the Patent Act of 1952. The doctrine states that a patentable invention must be nonobvious to a person of ordinary skill in the art at the time the invention is made. While this definition is generally believed to be an improvement over the flash of genius, it isn't perfect: there is a how-many-angels-can-dance-on-the-head-of-a-pin aspect to nonobviousness that makes it possible to argue cases almost indefinitely, and often the side with more legal resources wins.

The lawsuit against Ford became Kearns's life. He put every penny he had into it. He was driven by an uncynical, almost spiritual belief in justice and an equally pure hatred of the automobile industry. At a hearing in 1980, Kearns said, "I want you to understand that I am wearing a little badge here, and that badge says that I am an inventor, and it says I am a net contributor to society. And it is like maybe you can't see the badge, and these other gentlemen can't see the badge, and I don't think anybody is going to be able to see the badge until my trial is finished in this courtroom and I will find out whether I am wearing the badge or not." After his breakdown over the Mercedes wiper, he was unable to work. He collected disability from his employer, the Bureau of Standards, and he and his son Tim assembled and sold digital-difference-to-analog converters out of the basement of their home in Gaithersburg. Tim said, "I guess you could say the lawsuit has ruined my father's life, but I don't choose to look at it that way. It is his life. If there's a tragic aspect to it, it is that my father has never invented anything else. It would be interesting to know how many people's lives have been saved by the intermittent wiper, and how many more lives could have been saved by his next invention. We'll never know, because he couldn't let this one thing go. But he just couldn't."

Phyllis Kearns stuck it out as long as she could. "We'd gear ourselves up for a hearing in ninety days," she said. "And then, on the eighty-ninth day, the phone would ring, and I would hear Bob screaming and yelling, and it would turn out that Ford had dumped a bunch of new documents on us, and the hearing would be postponed. Now, I had never heard shouting in the house before. My parents had never shouted. It got to the point where I just couldn't take it." Phyllis left her husband in 1980. "Robert expected me to have the same focus he did, and I just didn't have it."

From time to time, when I felt the concept of what a patent was slipping away, I would get in touch with Jerry Lemelson. Lemelson had received over five hundred patents—more than any other independent inventor alive. He inherited the title in 1991, upon the death of Edwin Land, who had 533. If Lemelson continued to average twenty patents a year—a pace he had sustained for three decades—he would catch Edison, the Henry Aaron of patents, with 1,093, by the time he was ninety-seven. Lemelson was sixty-nine then. He was a compact fellow, with a bald head and a comical New York squawk. He spoke quickly. Behind each of his inventions was a story about how it came to him, and Lemelson told it in the manner of a standup comedian, except that instead of a punch line at the end there was an invention. Lemelson thought in patents, and sometimes he dreamt in patents. It's hard to think of a technology Lemelson hadn't patented. Once, when I was talking to him on a cordless telephone, we had one of those electronic drifts which such phones are subject to. "Darn," Lemelson said. "I invented this thing too."

When Lemelson invents, he first selects a particular field—say, microsurgery, which he was currently looking into. (He had a patent on an electronically controlled tourniquet.) He might hire a patent searcher to obtain copies of all the patents in that art or he might go down to the Patent Office and read the patents himself. He tried to imagine the path along which the art will develop, and to construct a patent application that sat squarely in the middle of it, so that even if the invention was never manufactured—and only one in every seven of Lemelson's inventions was actually made—his patent would be like a tollgate on a highway, at which all travelers must stop. Lemelson's great advantage over other inventors is that he writes all his patent applications himself. Though in theory a patent application is merely a rendering of the invention in language, in reality it is a kind of invention itself. "It takes great skill to craft a patent application," he said. "You have to stake the four corners of your invention broadly enough so that they give you maximum protection. You tend to avoid adjectives. You don't say 'transistor' when you can use 'controllable electronic valve'—that sort of thing. Of course, if you write too broadly you may invalidate your claim because it will tread on the prior art. But if you write too narrowly you may miss the thing about the technology that turns out to be truly valuable."

In 1992, thanks to deals with Sony, Sanyo, Siemens, and others, Lemelson reportedly earned two hundred million dollars. He had filed suit against Motorola, Kodak, and Apple. Several years earlier, he moved his residence from New Jersey to Nevada. "I don't mind saying that the reason for it is that it's a lot easier to litigate from out there," he said. "When I litigate in New Jersey or New York, it takes five to ten years to get to trial. Out in Nevada, it only takes a year."

Lemelson was a corporation's worst nightmare. To his critics he was merely an inventor of paper patents, exploiting the power that the patent system gave the independent inventor. As Lemelson saw it, though, litigation was the only way an independent inventor could protect his rights. "Occasionally, it is possible to earn money selling licenses—it's a lot easier these days than it used to be," he said. "But the simple fact is that most manufacturers would rather infringe a patent than pay a license. Have you heard of NIH—the Not Invented Here syndrome? Well, it's a disease that American industry in general suffers from. The attitude is 'If we didn't invent it, we're not interested.' Or 'If it's such a good invention, how come we didn't think of it?' Or 'Hey, we have all these thousands of engineers on our payroll—why should we have to pay someone else for an idea?' It is virtually impossible for an independent inventor to invent for an American U.S. corporation. They're just not interested in inventions that they don't make."

Clifford Sadler was an executive in the patent department of Ford. Sadler, known to his colleagues as Kip, was a lean, likable fellow with silver hair and a droll sense of humor. He listened to my questions with his head to one side, his fingers making a lawyerly tent in his lap. "Electronics was simply the way the world was going," he said. "I would say it's to Dr. Kearns's credit that he perceived this. But for Dr. Kearns to say he invented the electronic intermittent windshield wiper is, we feel, sadly unrealistic. Even in 1963, the resistor-capacitor timing device was a standard piece of engineering—it was sophomore-in-college stuff."

Sadler stretched his long legs out in front of him, rocked back in his chair, and sighed. "I think Dr. Kearns honestly believed he was part of the Ford design team," he said. "But Ford never saw it that way. As far as the engineers were concerned, Kearns was a sort of pest. He was always stopping by the lab and saying, 'Hey, what's going on? Need any help?'—that sort of thing." Sadler said that under no circumstances had Ford copied Kearns's design. "As for infringement, we had our lawyers examine Kearns's patents, and in their view the patents were invalid." He added that Kearns's great ambition—to be a supplier of windshield wipers to Ford—was misguided. "Ford has more than two thousand suppliers," he said. "In no case that I can think of has an independent inventor who has no manufacturing track record ever become a supplier to the auto industry. It just doesn't happen."

The Ford case came to trial in January 1990—twelve years after it was filed. Most of Kearns's patents had expired by then. The waters of progress had closed over his head. Judge Avern Cohn divided the trial into two parts: one to determine whether Kearns's patents were valid and infringed and, if they were, one to determine how much Ford should pay for infringing them.

Marty Adelman, the Wayne State law professor, was an expert witness in the Ford case. He told me that once Kearns got into the courtroom the odds of his winning shifted dramatically in his favor. "The inventor has a piece of paper with a big blue ribbon on it that issues from the Patent Office and that he can wave around in front of the jury, and the jury tends to say, 'Oh, he has a patent, he must be right,'" Adelman said. "The corporation is placed in the very formidable position of trying to convince the jury that the Patent Office is wrong.

"The inventor has a story to tell. The cardinal rule for any patent attorney representing an independent inventor is to tell the invention story. You know—how he got the idea. It comes to him in a dream, or when he's in the shower or mowing the lawn. In Kearns's case, the guy gets hit in the eye with a champagne cork on his wedding night, he starts thinking about how the eye works, and ends up inventing a wiper that works like an eyelid. A classic invention story. That's not how things get invented in the lab. It's the heroic theory of invention versus the social theory of invention, and in front of a jury the former is going to win every time. The judge can lecture the jury till he's blue in the face about the Doctrine of Nonobviousness, but the flash of genius is what people want to hear."

Adelman thought for a moment and added, "Of course, in the Kearns case the really scary thing is that Kearns is probably crazy. I mean, any rational holdup artist would have taken the money."

The first trial lasted three weeks, and the jury deliberated for another week. It found that Kearns's patents were valid and that Ford had infringed them. Ford, concerned about the size of the award that a jury in Wayne County might give Kearns, offered to settle the case for thirty million dollars. Kearns, against everyone's advice, turned the money down. "To accept money from Ford would have been like admitting it was okay for them to do what they did," he said.

So there was a second trial, and the second trial awarded Kearns $5.2 million, or about thirty cents a wiper plus interest. Kearns wasn't there for the verdict, having left the proceedings in protest two weeks earlier. Without even telling his family, Kearns had returned to Gaithersburg ("INVENTOR IN WIPER LAWSUIT DISAPPEARS" was the headline in the *Detroit Free Press*), got his camping equipment, pitched a tent in Little Bennett Regional Park in West Virginia, and was living off pork and beans. Meanwhile, Judge Cohn, his patience wearing thin, suggested that if Kearns did not reappear and accept the money he might begin proceedings to determine whether or not Kearns was mentally competent. Finally, Kearns and Ford settled for $10.2 million.

On June 10, 1992, the night before the Chrysler verdict was announced, Kearns went out on the town with his family: Dennis; Tim; Tim's girlfriend, Francine; Maureen; Maureen's fiancé, Paul; and Kathy. Wherever they went in downtown Detroit, bartenders and waiters came up and wished them good luck. Kearns's spirits were high. He was confident that he had persuaded the jury to award him a sum of money large enough to hurt Chrysler seriously—he believed that the sum would be around forty million—and to send a message to corporations everywhere that patent infringement does not pay. "I believe I laid it on 'em pretty straight," he said.

The Kearnses ate dinner at the Pontchartrain Hotel. The possibility that the family might become extraordinarily wealthy the following morning wasn't discussed. The money was like a guest at the table to whom no one had been introduced. People talked about it obliquely. Everyone chose a number and put twenty dollars in a pool. After dinner was over and Kearns had left, Kathy said, "The main thing is that Dad seems happy." She said no one was under the illusion that the next day would be the end of anything. "I remember during the Ford case my father's girlfriend Jean used to say, 'Well, soon it will all be over, and he'll be mine.' Finally, I had to say, 'Jean, are you crazy? Don't you get it? This is never going to end.'"

The next morning, the courtroom began filling up at eight-thirty. Lou Mihaly, Kearns's college roommate, came, with his wife, Pinkie. The attendant from the Fort Washington Garage, where Kearns parked his car, came. Phyllis was there. She had driven up from Maryland the night before, with their son Robert. That night, Kathy had said to me, "It's obvious that Mom still cares for Dad. I mean, you can see it in the way she is just thrilled when he comes up behind her and puts his hands on her shoulders. But she just can't live with the lawsuit. It's too crazy." Now Phyllis said she was trying not to be nervous by focusing on the fact that the jury had already made its decision and nothing she felt or did could change it. She clenched her hands into fists and said, "Oh, I want willful infringement so badly."

Shortly after nine, the jury came in. Judge Cohn asked his clerk, Judy Cassady, if she would read the verdict. Ms. Cassady read, "Did you find that Dr. Kearns proved by clear and convincing evidence that Chrysler acted willfully when it infringed any of Dr. Kearns's patents? Answer: no." Phyllis gasped softly. Ms. Cassady went on, "What amount do you find is a reasonable royalty on a per-unit basis for the total of twelve million five hundred and sixty-four thousand one hundred and seven units? Answer: ninety cents per unit."

In the silence that followed, one could almost hear people multiplying 12.5 million by .9. It came to about eleven and a half million dollars. With the years of interest, the total would be around eighteen million.

Judge Cohn thanked the jurors for their efforts and dismissed them. Then he said good-bye to the lawyers. "I'm sure I will see you here again," he said in the direction of Kearns.

The Kearns family moved out into the corridor. The garage attendant reached for Kearns's hand, and Kearns accepted his congratulations somewhat awkwardly. Reporters encircled him. Kearns looked grim. "I would have to say I'm disappointed," he said. The family, standing around, seemed unsure of what to do. It wasn't clear whether anyone felt like whooping it up over eleven and a half million dollars; it was perfectly clear that it would be considered bad form if anyone did. They talked about who had won the pool. Eventually Kearns said he had to get over to the office, and he moved toward the elevators, with a crowd of family and reporters trailing him. Down in the lobby, a woman pointed at the entourage and said, "Who's that?"

One of the guards said, "That's the man who invented the intermittent windshield wiper."

The family walked down West Lafayette Street. In the elevator, on the way up to Kearns's office on the fourteenth floor, no one spoke. Kearns stared at the ceiling. "I just don't understand it," he said finally, to no one in particular. "I just don't understand why they didn't hold for willfulness."

The family spilled out onto the fourteenth floor. The former tenants had recently left, taking even the wall-to-wall carpeting with them, so they walked over slabs of epoxy-encrusted concrete. The view from the windows was of downtown Detroit—empty hotels and department stores, abandoned machine shops. In an unused room sat a disembodied windshield-and-dashboard assembly from a 1965 Dodge Dart, with a windshield-wiper system rigged up to it, which Kearns had used in the trial.

The family went into the Kearns offices. It was only ten-thirty—too early to go out to lunch. Phyllis suggested that she make some coffee. Her ex-husband seemed to be slipping away into one of his hopeless moods. "The moral is that unlawful conduct does pay," he said. "I don't see how any of us could go home to our children and say it does not." He sat at his desk. He looked like a man outdoors in very cold weather who was concentrating hard on staying warm.

—1993

# THE FRUIT
# DETECTIVE

One hot summer day not long ago, just as the specialty food stores around town were putting up First of the Season signs to advertise their peaches, a rare and extraordinary shipment of apricots appeared in Manhattan. They were white apricots, which you can almost never find in the United States. Unlike the familiar tawny-colored varieties, these had pale, almost translucent skin, with a yellow blush. And unlike the cottony supermarket fruit, the white apricots tasted great: a rush of sugar, with a complex, slightly acidic aftertaste. The flesh almost melted in your mouth, and the juice was so plentiful that you had to bend over while eating one, to avoid staining your shirt.

The apricots were available at Citarella and only at Citarella—a fact that pleased the store's produce manager, Gregg Mufson, a great deal. Like his competitors at the other high-end specialty stores around town, such as Eli's, Dean & DeLuca, and Grace's, Mufson tried to titillate his customers by giving them uncommon fruits— curiosities that they might have encountered in a restaurant, on their travels, or on the Food Network. "Anything new, anything different, and if I can get it directly from the grower it's even better, because there's no middleman," said Mufson, who was in his midthirties and wore a neatly trimmed goatee. "I want them to go 'Wow!' I want to blow their minds with something. They'll eat these apricots, and they won't forget that taste, and then they'll come back and buy some more of my fruit." Mufson paid attention to the food press, so that he could be sure to have the trendy fruits and vegetables in stock. "When the *Times* did an article on rambutans"—bright-red, golf-ball-size, tendril-covered fruits from Southeast Asia, with translucent, sweet-tart flesh—"we sold ten cases of them in a couple of days." Appearance, he added, is the most important quality in attracting people to new fruit—the more colorful the better—followed by sugar. "Basically, if it's sweet, people like it," he said.

At first, not many customers paid much attention to the new apricots. "That's a white apricot," one of the produce workers in the store said when a customer asked about the fruit. "First one I ever seen," he added. But the customer went for the Apriums—yellow-skinned, pink-fleshed plum-apricot hybrids, which have become popular in the past few years.

Soon, however, word about the white apricots got out. The pastry chef at Citarella thought they were one of the best fruits he'd ever tasted. The chef Daniel Boulud bought two cases of white apricots and was "crazy for them," Mufson said; Boulud used them to make apricot galettes. The owner of Citarella, Joe Gurrera, gave a white apricot to Martha Stewart when she came into the East Hampton branch of the store, and "she was blown away by it," Mufson reported. "Blown a-way." The store sold out of its supply in a couple of days; the next shipment disappeared even more rapidly. Mufson was delighted. "My boss gave me a compliment! My boss never gives me compliments. He said, 'This is the best fruit ever. We got to get more of this stuff.' All I can say is David really scored this time."

David is David Karp, a sometime "provisioner" for specialty stores like Citarella, and a noted fruit writer. He is the Fruit Detective, a persona he invented around the time he worked as a provisioner for Dean & DeLuca. His job is to range around the country and the world and find exotic fruits, or uncommon varieties of common fruits. In recent years, he has traveled to Madagascar to investigate vanilla, to Sicily to hunt for blood oranges, and to the Australian outback to research bush fruits. But most of his work is performed in California. The Fruit Detective is a familiar figure at the Santa Monica Farmers' Market—he's the one in the pith helmet with the leather chin strap, his fruit knife in a holster on his belt, looking like a slightly demented forest ranger as he interrogates farmers with rapid-fire questions and eats their fruit. Readers of Karp's articles, which appear regularly in the *Los Angeles Times* and *Gourmet,* follow him on his quest for pomelos, Asian pears, mulberries, and persimmons. Most people experience a truly great piece of fruit very rarely—that perfect peach you ate one summer day long ago, a taste you hope for in every subsequent peach you eat but never quite recapture. Karp's goal is to have that experience again and again.

I first heard about the Fruit Detective from a friend, an organic farmer in southern New Jersey named Torrey Reade.

"Anything new on the farm?" I asked her one day.

"Well, we had a visit from the Fruit Detective."

"What's a fruit detective?"

Torrey wasn't sure, exactly, except that the fellow was passionate, almost manic, about fruit. "He left his business card—wait, I think I may have it in my wallet."

The card said "David Karp, Fruit Detective." It had raised lettering that looked slightly crooked, and it gave a residence in Venice, California. The name reminded me that I once knew a David Karp, whose passage from brilliant Upper East Side private-school kid to heroin addict was a sad but familiar story of money, drugs, and wasted talent. I stood there rubbing my finger over the lettering, wondering what had become of that David Karp, while Torrey described her encounter.

"We were trying to grow Charentais melons," she explained, "which is a French exotic, and he had heard about us from a health-food store in Princeton. Somehow he found us and came down to see about getting some for Dean & DeLuca. He was wearing this funny hat and shorts—no one in South Jersey wears shorts in the summertime, because of the bugs. We showed him our melons, which he liked but didn't love, and then he started asking, 'What else do you have?' So we told him about the pear tree that was growing near the old privy. He demanded to see it immediately. It produces these tiny, inedible pears, but he thought it might be an heirloom variety and got very excited—he was actually hopping around in the weeds."

The more she described the Fruit Detective, the more he sounded like my David Karp. I kept the card and, over the winter, sent the Fruit Detective an e-mail. After he confirmed that he was the person I was thinking of, we talked on the phone and made plans to have lunch the next time he came to New York on "fruit work."

I hadn't known David Karp well, but I had heard a lot about him from some friends who had grown up with him in Manhattan and told memorable Karp stories. Karp's father, Harvey Karp, was an extraordinarily successful businessman, whose house in East Hampton was reputed to be a palace. David was brilliant. He was fluent in Latin and, it was said, read only the poets of late antiquity. He published a translation of the sixth-century writer Venantius Fortunatus when he was twenty. Not only did he get 800s on the SATs but he got 800s on a friend's SATs too—and he did it while coming down from LSD. He also knew more about punk rock than any of his friends, and he was well versed in drugs.

After graduating from Wesleyan, in 1979 (word of the SAT caper had got back to the authorities, and he and his friend were suspended for a year, but he finished in three years), Karp worked on Wall Street in risk arbitrage and option trading, where he was soon making more than a hundred thousand dollars a year. He collected rare books and rare wines. He produced a Lydia Lunch album, 13.13, in 1982, and cultivated friends in the downtown rock world. But his dabbling in heroin had turned into an every-weekend habit, and in 1984, after drugs were found in his desk at work, Karp got fired. At this point, a less apocalyptic spirit might have stepped back from the dark side; Karp moved into the Hôtel Plaza Athénée in Paris with his fashion-model girlfriend and a supply of heroin, and indulged in a life of total hedonism—sleeping all day, living off pastries from Lenôtre, getting high and staying up all night reading Saint Augustine (in Latin), and, when his drugs ran out, taking the Concorde back to New York to buy some more. Eventually he ran through most of his money and returned to New York, where he was soon supporting his habit by selling off his book collection and by dealing heroin to friends and friends of friends.

Karp has been completely sober—no drugs, alcohol, or cigarettes—for almost twelve years. In 1990, after waking up on a floor strewn with broken glass and Cap'n Crunch cereal ("Junkies love sweet stuff"), he had allowed his parents to put him in detox at Gracie Square Hospital, and he then spent seven months in rehab in Southern California, doing the twelve-step program. On returning to the world, he called up a college friend, Eric Asimov, who wrote the "$25 and Under" column for the *Times,* and proposed a free-lance piece about apricots. Fruit was connected in Karp's mind to the great love of his life, a woman he had met in college, with whom he had shared an interest in collecting fruit-crate art and the elaborately decorated wrappers around blood oranges. "I thought it would intrigue her if I became a fruit expert," he explained. He'd try to find great fruit, and woo her with it. He got the fruit, but not the woman. "This is very pathetic," he told me. "The story of unrequited love. But what can I say? She was the love of my life." In the course of pursuing her, he began amassing "dossiers" on different fruits, which contained the names of thousands of fruit growers, breeders, marketers, wholesalers, and retailers. Ten years later, he was a unique source of information on the fruit industry—a vital link between the "knowers" who love obscure fruit and the "growers" who cultivate it.

Karp moved to California in 1999, because that's where so much of the nation's fruit comes from, and he lived in a small cottage in Venice with his cat, Sahara, who, he was convinced, once saved him from dying of an overdose by licking his face until he woke up. When he wasn't searching for fruit, he collected books about fruit, compiled songs about fruit, and corresponded with fruit lovers all over the world—chefs, specialty stores, and amateur fruit enthusiasts who simply wanted to know the difference between a Pluot, an Aprium, and a plumcot. Did he have time for other interests? Aardvarks, Karp said. "I love them, because most people think they're unattractive, but I think they're incredibly soulful." Once, when he was visiting the Philadelphia Zoo, he climbed into the anteater pen, hoping to commune with the animals, but instead experienced "a nasty confrontation with the business end of an anteater."

We met in April. In the intervening years, Karp had lost the hair on the top of his head. "I've grown glabrous," he said, using the term of art for a fuzzless nectarine. He looked very fit, not at all like a former junkie—more like a guy who eats a lot of fruit.

Over lunch, he told me that he had recently wrapped up a research project on bitter almonds ("I'm not, generally speaking, a nut enthusiast") and was hot on the trail of European greengage plums, which are common abroad but extremely rare in the United States. "Have you had one? Oh, my God, you'll die when you taste one—it's an atom bomb of flavor. I'm convinced there's a small planting somewhere in California, and I won't stop until I find it." He didn't eat much of his pasta, and what he did eat he liberally coated with dried chili peppers, a shaker of which he carries in his black canvas bag. He scolded me for drinking a Coke: "That stuff is bad for you. Have you ever seen what it will do to a penny?"

After he had finished his lunch, he said, "Okay, ready to eat some mind-blowing fruit?" It is Karp's custom, whenever he meets people for a meal, to bring along remarkable fruit. Eric Asimov recalls an occasion when the Fruit Detective turned up with a bright-red fruit from West Africa called a miracle fruit (*Synsepalum dulcificum*), which, Karp said, had a startling effect on the taste buds: for an hour after you've eaten it, even the sourest foods taste sweet. "I tried one, and then I ate a sour lemon," Asimov said. "I was stunned at how sweet it became."

Karp took from his bag a large, heart-shaped, scaly, greenish fruit that I had never seen before—a cherimoya, a fruit native to South America. Taking out his grapefruit knife, he concentrated his full attention on slicing into the white, custardy flesh and peeling several sections for me. The focus he brought to this task, the specialized equipment he used, and the obvious tactile pleasure he felt in the procedure, combined with the prospect of an imminent mind-blowing experience, were all powerfully reminiscent of the David Karp of twenty years ago. And, as promised, the fruit was amazing.

One day in 1962, a Mormon missionary walked into a Safeway in Los Angeles and asked for a Chinese gooseberry. The produce manager didn't know what that was, so he asked the main produce buyer for Safeway, who, in turn, called Frieda Caplan, the founder of Frieda's Finest, a local wholesaler of specialty produce items. She didn't know either. A few months later, a broker representing New Zealand farmers was walking around the L.A. wholesale produce market, trying to sell Chinese gooseberries. The other produce buyers weren't interested, but Caplan, remembering the Safeway buyer's query, said, "I'll take all you've got," and that turned out to be 2,400 pounds. "No one is ever going to buy something called a Chinese gooseberry," a shipping official told Caplan. The rind of the gooseberries was kind of furry and reminded him of New Zealand's national bird, so he suggested naming the fruit after it—the kiwi.

People who grow and market unusual fruits tell that story a lot, usually as a way of illustrating the potential that exists in the American marketplace for something new. Although the United States is the most ethnically diverse country on earth, that diversity is not reflected in the fruit stocked by the average supermarket. The mango, which is one of the most popular fruits worldwide, is not among the top-ten American fruits (which are, in descending order, bananas, apples, watermelons, oranges, cantaloupes, grapes, grapefruit, strawberries, peaches, and pears). Our vegetables are considerably more diverse than our fruits. Portobello mushrooms, arugula, fennel, radicchio, mesclun, Swiss chard, and jicama—all specialty items ten years ago—are now in American supermarkets across the country, but sapotes, lychees, and loquats are not. American travelers in Asia and Latin America find many delicious fruits—jackfruit, longan, and breadfruit—that are never available fresh at home. This is because the United States Department of Agriculture has outlawed the importing of certain foreign-grown tropical fruits to prevent the spread of tropical pests. But in 2000 the USDA began allowing papayas and rambutans grown in Hawaii to be imported to the mainland after they had been treated with electron beams—the same

THE FRUIT DETECTIVE     39

process that neutralizes anthrax spores in the mail (though anthrax requires a much higher dose). The new technology, many in the exotic-fruit world believe, has expanded Americans' awareness of the fruit that the rest of the world eats, and brought a cornucopia of new items to the produce department.

Part of being a fruit detective means figuring out what will be the next kiwi. That's not Karp's only interest; he spends at least as much time tracking down the classic varieties of familiar fruits as he does sleuthing exotics. But the intrigue and potential payoff implicit in the next big fruit are irresistible. When I saw Karp in April, he was enthusiastic about the prospects of the pitahaya, which is grown in Central America and in Asia, where it's known as dragon fruit. He talked up dragon fruit during his meeting with Gregg Mufson, of Citarella, a few days after our lunch. "Giant, flaming-pink, spineless member of the cactus-pear family, the most spectacular-looking fruit I've ever seen," Karp told Mufson, practically spitting with excitement. He said that, while some varieties aren't so tasty—"they taste like a snow cone, like they were made of gelatinized mousse with sugar"—others are much more interesting: the magenta-colored flesh has the texture and flavor of watermelon, sometimes with a hint of strawberry.

Mufson was initially skeptical about dragon fruit, but after listening to Karp he got more curious.

"Know where we can get some?" he asked.

"I have a connection," Karp said, with a manic gleam in his eye.

Karp told Mufson that although no foreign-grown pitahayas were currently allowed into the country, he knew of a "top secret" planting, which was about three hours south of Los Angeles, outside the desert town of Borrego Springs. The planting was a partnership among a specialty-produce grower, Kevin Coniff, who had propagated a variety of pitahaya for Southern California; a farmer, Thomas Antel, who owns the land where the pitahaya plants were growing; and a large wholesaler of fresh produce, D'Arrigo Brothers, which was putting up the money. The reason the pitahaya planting was secret was that the partnership, or "consortium," as Karp delighted in calling it, was trying to develop an exclusive American market for dragon fruit, and they didn't want their plans publicized before they were ready. "It's like opening a movie in L.A. or New York. They'll want to get it into fancy markets and affluent areas, with a lot of foodies and food press, and the word spreads from there."

Mufson said that D'Arrigo Brothers had done something similar with broccoli rabe. Over the past ten years, the company created hardier varieties of broccoli rabe, so that what was once a specialty item has become available year-round, with D'Arrigo Brothers controlling most of the distribution. "Nearly all the broccoli rabe that comes into New York, the D'Arrigos handle it," Mufson said.

Karp slapped his fist into his palm. "They're up to the same thing with dragon fruit!" he exclaimed. "Boy, this sounds like a case for the Fruit Detective, if ever there was one."

Mufson stared at him. He had never met anyone like the Fruit Detective before.


In mid-June, I flew out to Los Angeles and joined Karp for five days of fruit work. Before this trip, I imagined David Karp as a man who had been redeemed by fruit—someone who had found in fruit a way of escaping his demons. What I came to realize over the course of our five days together—five very long days—was that Karp had not really banished his demons at all. He'd just found a way of channeling his particular needs and talents (the desire for esoteric knowledge, the pursuit of extreme pleasure, a sympathy for shady characters, and experience in dope dealing) into a career as a purveyor of amazing fruit—a career, it turns out, that serves those needs and talents very nicely.

Much of our time together was spent in the cramped cab of Bessie, as Karp calls his white Ford Ranger pickup truck, which became ever more cramped as it filled with fruit during our travels. Days began early and ended late, but Karp was never tired. "All I need is my morning fruit fix," he'd say cheerfully, offering me a slice of "exquisite" Snow Queen white nectarine from Reedley, California, as I blearily slid into the cab.

We stopped at farmers' markets and roadside stands along the way. Karp has been known to conduct stakeouts of certified farmers' markets that he suspects of being "cheaters" (farmers who buy fruit from wholesalers, remove the stickers, and sell it as their own); if he finds proof, he may publish the cheaters' names in the L.A. *Times*. We didn't catch any on our trip, but when Karp found people selling fruit that was inaccurately labeled he would instruct them on its true heritage. In one market, he found farmers from Vera Ranch, near Vallejo, selling plums called mirabelles, which, he explained to the woman behind the counter, weren't mirabelles but myrobalans. "These are much too large, totally out of season, and there is a tartness in the skin of mirabelles these don't have, and mirabelles generally have a clingstone"—a pit that is attached to the flesh.

"Wow," said the woman. "You know your stuff."

In the truck, we talked of fruit constantly. Karp is especially passionate about stone fruit—apricots, peaches, nectarines, plums, and cherries—and, because it was cherry and apricot season, we spent a lot of time on those fruits. We discussed the genealogy of different varieties, and the way the great varieties were described in the works of fruit literature that Karp most admires—chiefly, Robert Hogg's *The Fruit Manual: A Guide to the Fruits and Fruit Trees of Great Britain* (fifth edition, 1884) and Edward A. Bunyard's *The Anatomy of Dessert* (1929). Karp quoted, from memory, passages about the "melting" quality Bunyard prized; after a while, it was hard to tell when he was quoting and when he wasn't. "At its ripest, it is drunk rather than eaten," he'd say, referring to Coe's Golden Drop plum. Discussing the transparent gage, he pronounced, "A slight flush of red and then one looks into the depths of transparent amber as one looks into an opal, uncertain how far the eye can penetrate." If I got something wrong or forgot a point about fruit made in an earlier conversation, Karp was quick to correct me. By the end of five days of fruit talk in the fruitmobile, I was counting the minutes to the time I could say good-bye and not have to talk about fruit anymore.

I also watched Karp eat a lot of fruit. I saw him grazing in a cherry orchard with the farmer, who, after sampling cherries for half an hour, had to run for the bathroom. Craig Ledbetter, an apricot breeder with the Department of Agriculture, whom we met near Fresno, said, "David eats fruit that I wouldn't touch, and I eat a lot of fruit. Soft, half-rotten stuff on the ground—he has no problem putting that into his mouth."

On our first day, we drove down to Borrego Springs, in the hope of seeing the pitahaya planting. But Thomas Antel, the landowner, would let us view the plants only from across the road. Karp, clad in his pith helmet, attempted to extract information from Antel about the consortium's intentions. (When I asked later if the pith helmet was really necessary, Karp said that he was always getting clobbered by falling fruit, and that last year in Hawaii he had been struck on the head from the height of twenty feet by a durian—a delicious but terrible-smelling fruit familiar in Asia. "Without my helmet, that durian would have killed me," he said.)

"So how are the plants doing?" Karp asked, taking out his notebook.

"It's a learning experience, David, a learning experience," Antel said, looking nervously at the notes Karp was taking. "What can I tell you? I wish I could show you the plants, but there's too much money involved to screw this up." He rubbed his face hard with both hands, and his mood seemed to darken. "People feel a sense of entitlement, like they can just come down here and see what we're doing."

Karp was undaunted. "Where did the breeder get his breeding stock from?" he demanded. "Because they say there are some varieties that taste better than others."

"They may be right, David, they may be right. Look, I can't talk about this. There's some very big players involved in this thing, and they don't care who gets hurt—that's just the way it is."

The agricultural landscape in which the Fruit Detective operates is made up mostly of small organic fruit-growing operations—farms of mainly a hundred acres or less, many of which produce the older varieties of plums, apricots, peaches, and apples that were loved by generations of Americans before the coming of the hardier but flavorless supermarket varieties. These farmers survive by looking for niches. A niche could be a classic variety of fruit that the big commercial growers don't produce, such as the Blenheim apricot, which is, in the Fruit Detective's opinion, one of the best-tasting fruits in the world. Or a niche could be a brief window of time in the growing season of a particular item when the commercial producers don't have any fruit and the small farmer can name his price. But since the passage of the North American Free Trade Agreement in 1994, many of the larger growers of commodity fruits, such as tomatoes and mangoes, are finding that they can't compete with the cheaper labor and production costs in Mexico, and so they are also looking for niches in order to survive.

"The marketing window keeps getting smaller and smaller," said Andy Mariani, who farms eighty acres, most of which are devoted to cherries—Black Republican and Rainier, among other varieties—in the Santa Clara Valley. "We used to have a window here between cherries from Stockton and cherries from Washington. First, it was a couple of weeks, then a couple of days. Now it's almost nothing. The Stockton growers use sprays to retard the ripening process, so they can sell when the price is highest." Mariani's cherry harvest was in full swing on the day we visited, and, as a result of an abrupt downturn in cherry prices caused by the Stockton farmers, he had lost his "candy bar"—an expression sometimes used in the fruit world to describe a lucrative crop. "We just lost seventy-five thousand dollars in one day," Mariani said. "I would have been better off in the stock market."

Karp worships farmers like Mariani and, as a writer, takes every opportunity to promote their efforts. Eric Asimov said, "David is more like a wine writer than like a food writer. He brings that level of connoisseurship and obsessive attention to detail—the importance of the soil, the cultivation methods, and the growing region. Wine writers talk about the importance of *terroir,* or place; David is the first writer to bring that concept to fruit." He added, "Grape growers make the cover of wine magazines, but you never read about the great peach or cherry growers, except in David's pieces."

Most food writing is about cooking—it's less about the ingredients than about the rendering of those ingredients, and the consuming of them in communal settings. Karp is interested in the primal act of tasting—eating fruit right from the tree, vine, or bush. ("I'm not a foodie," he says. "I'm a fruitie.") His goal is sensual pleasure, but he has a rarefied idea of what fruit should taste like. The particular kind of taste he's after is one that the nineteenth-century writers on fruit described as "high flavor"—a fecund, almost gamy taste that, according to Karp, has been all but lost as fruits have been bred for mass production and long-distance shipping. "High flavor is the flavor of a pheasant, hung until high," he said. "You bite into the fruit, you taste the sugar, the texture, the acidity, and there's an almost overpowering aroma. That's what fruit should taste like. But Americans don't know that, because most of the fruit we eat is trash fruit."

We found the white apricots on a small farm in Brentwood, about an hour east of San Francisco. The farmer was Ross Sanborn, who is eighty-two years old. He wore faded denim overalls and had a full head of white hair and a face deeply browned from years in the sun. ("Hey, looks like you're going on a safari!" he said when he saw Karp.) Sitting in the shade of his porch, Sanborn told us that he had been trying to breed white apricots for almost thirty years, working with plant material he obtained from Morocco and Iran in the nineteen-seventies. Finally, he said, he believed he had come up with what he'd hoped was "the perfect 'cot." He called it an Angelcot.

After we had finished talking, we followed Sanborn out to the part of the orchard where the white apricots were growing. Karp went up to a tree, picked an Angelcot from it, and held it in the tips of his long fingers, caressing the velvety "pubescence," which is the fruitie term for the fuzz. "There's something so sensuous about apricots—of all the fruits, they are the most like a woman's breast," he said, denying himself the pleasure of tasting the fruit as long as he could. He unsheathed his fruit knife, neatly halved the 'cot, and examined the pit. Then he bent at the waist and brought the pitless half up to his mouth, inhaled, and bit. The fruit melted. The juice ran down his chin. A bite, then another bite, and all that remained of the apricot were the bits of flesh sticking to the Fruit Detective's face.

—2002

# GAME MASTER

In 1972 an engineer and former carnival barker named Nolan Bushnell started a video-game company, in Santa Clara, California. As an engineering student at the University of Utah in the 1960s, Bushnell had become obsessed with an early computer game called Spacewar. The game's developers, a group of graduate students who were part of the Tech Model Railroad Club at MIT, an early proving ground of computer hackers, had never considered selling the game; their idea was to demonstrate the appeal of interactivity, and to take a first small step toward simulating intelligent life on a computer. Bushnell's ambition was more worldly. He wanted to manufacture coin-operated game-playing machines and license them to amusement arcades. He foresaw a new kind of midway hustle, in which the hustler would be inside the machine. "The things I had learned about getting you to spend a quarter on me in one of my midway games," he later said, "I put those sales pitches in my automated box." From this unlikely marriage—the computer lab and the carnival—the video-game industry was born.

The first product of Bushnell's company, Atari, was Pong, a simple, elegant game in which two players manipulated electronic paddles and sent a blip back and forth across a black-and-white screen. The game had two basic components. It was a simulation of table tennis, managing to render most of the game's rules, structure, and logic onto the screen. And it was an animation—a moving picture designed to complete the feedback loop between the eyes, the brain, and the fingers on the game controls. The game was designed by a former All-State football player named Al Alcorn, who was Atari's second employee. As Heather Chaplin and Aaron Ruby tell the story in *Smartbomb,* their history of the industry, Bushnell took the handmade Pong game to Andy Capp's Tavern in nearby Sunnyvale, and within weeks people were lining up outside the bar in the morning, before opening time, to play it. By 1974, Pong had made it to a pizza parlor in Hanover, New Hampshire, where I played it, and for the rest of that summer my dearest desire was to go back and play it again.

The games that followed Pong—Space Invaders, Asteroids, Missile Command, and Pac-Man, among others—were even more captivating, but the simulations remained the stuff of arcades and midways: sports, space aliens, zombies, shoot-'em-ups. In the 1980s, as the speed and storage capacity of computers and game-playing consoles grew, designers continued to improve the graphics. The simulation side of the games, however, never came close to realizing the Tech Model Railroad Club's old ambition of reproducing real-life dynamics on the screen. The bestselling video game in 2006 is Madden NFL, in which you get to play pro football from the perspective of star players. Madden NFL is a far more sophisticated simulation than Pong was, but the content of the game is no closer to real life.

In the late 1980s, a new type of video game quietly emerged—the God game. Computer animation is a brute-force project of converting graphic art into three-dimensional polygons, the building blocks of digital pictures. But to create a truly absorbing simulation, one that offers some insight into the nature of real life, is a much more difficult proposition. The designer must play God, or at least the notion of God in Boethius's *Consolation of Philosophy*—a god that can anticipate the outcome of the player's actions and yet allows the player the feeling of free will.

Among the pioneers of the God game was Peter Molyneux of Great Britain, who created Populous in 1989. The game gives the player omniscient power over a variety of simulated societies. (You can help them or torture them as you wish, although your actions have consequences in the game.) Another important God-game designer, Sid Meier, has based his Civilization series, which began to appear in 1991, on historical processes, such as scientific discovery, war, and diplomacy. But the master of the genre—the god of God games—is Will Wright. Beginning in 1989, with SimCity, in which the object is to design and manage a modern city, and continuing with The Sims in 2000, in which you care for a family in an ordinary suburban environment, Wright created situations that redefined the boundaries of what a game can be. "It occurred to me that most books and movies tend to be about realistic situations," he has said. "Why shouldn't games be?" To game designers, Wright is the Zola of the form: the man who moved the subject matter of games away from myth, fantasy, and violence and toward ordinary social life.

For six years, Wright had been working on a new game, which would be released in September 2008. It was anticipated with something like the interest with which writers in Paris in the early twenties awaited Joyce's *Ulysses*. At first, Wright called the project Sim Everything, but a few years later he settled on the name Spore. Drawing on the theory of natural selection the game sought to replicate algorithmically the conditions by which evolution works. Conceptually, Spore was radical: at a time when most game makers were offering ever more dazzling graphics and scenarios and stories, Wright and his backer, Electronic Arts, were betting that players wanted to create the environments and stories themselves—that what players really like about games is exploring what Wright calls "possibility space." "Will has a reality-distortion field around him," his former business partner, Jeff Braun, told me. "He comes up with the craziest idea you've ever heard, and when he's finished explaining it to you the world looks crazy—he's the only sane person in it."

Wright's office was in a corner of a six-story building a few blocks from San Francisco Bay, in Emeryville, California. It had a balcony where he could smoke. The walls were covered with drawings in colored markers, which bore cryptic messages like "Star

Map Issues." Wright, then forty-six, was tall and skinny, with a long, narrow face and slender fingers. He dressed in the same clothes everyday—black New Balance sneakers, faded black jeans, a button-down shirt, a leather jacket, and thick aviator-style glasses. His skin was shiny and reddish-brown, in that way that a smoker's skin can look—half tanned and half cured. He sometimes had a wispy mustache and goatee. You don't really have a conversation with him; you mention an idea, and that triggers five or ten associations in Wright's mind, which he delivers in quick bursts of data that are strung together with "um"s.

When I walked into his office, Wright jumped up and, after shaking my hand, said, "Here, try this, um, it's this really cool toy I found recently," and handed me a wireless controller for a small robotic tank that was sitting on the floor. It was facing another tank, which Wright was controlling. He started moving his tank around and shooting mine, watching me curiously, waiting to see how long it would take me to understand what was going on. I felt an odd tingling sensation in my hands, but I didn't pay any attention to it at first. Eventually I realized that I was getting shocked: every time Wright's tank shot mine, an electric charge passed from the controller into my hands.

Wright had been working on a PowerPoint presentation of a talk he had been asked to give about Spore. "It's supposed to be about how I came up with the game, but what I really want to talk about is the history of astrobiology, so I'm doing both," he said. He moved over to the two computers in his office and clicked through some images, while describing the basic structure of Spore. At first, I was baffled. Up to this point in his career, Wright had been including more and more social realism in his games. But Spore was a surprise—at a glance, it looked like a "cartoony bug game," as one contributor to a gaming Web site put it. The buildings didn't have the crisp urban lines of SimCity; they looked more like the architecture in Dr. Seuss books. Wright had also introduced weapons and conquest. The violence wasn't gratuitous—in some cases, you had to kill to survive—but it wasn't sugar-coated either. Not only did you kill other creatures in Spore, but you had to eat them.

At the first level of the game, you are a single-celled organism in a drop of water, which is represented on the screen as a two-dimensional environment, like a slide under a microscope. By successfully avoiding predators, which are represented as different-colored cells, you get to reproduce, and that earns you DNA points (a double helix appears over your character). DNA is the currency in the early levels of Spore, and as you evolve you can acquire better parts—larger flippers for faster swimming, say, or sharper claws for defeating predators. Eventually you emerge from the water onto the second level—dry land—and your creature must compete with other creatures and mate with those of your own kind, which the computer generates, until you form a tribe. You can play a violent game of conquest over other tribes or you can play a social game of conciliation. If you make clever choices, according to the logic of the simulation, you will survive and continue to evolve. Along the way, you get to acquire ever more powerful tools and weapons, and to create dwellings, towns, cities. When your city has conquered the other cities in your world, you can build a spaceship and launch into space. By the final level, you have evolved into an intergalactic god who can travel throughout the universe conducting interplanetary diplomacy and warfare.

The images that Wright called up on the computer were supposed to illustrate the game, but they gave little sense of what it would look like. There was a slide that showed the equation for gravity, a slide about panspermia theory (the idea that life on earth began with organic matter brought from space by comets and other "dirty snowballs"), and a picture of the cast of the early-eighties TV show *The Dukes of Hazzard*. Wright paused to say that, according to his calculations, based on the speed of radio waves, a hundred and fifty stars have received *The Dukes of Hazzard* by now.

Spore isn't a multiplayer game, like the immensely popular World of Warcraft, which runs on "massively parallel" computers (a distributed system employing many networked machines); it's what Wright jokingly calls a massively parallel single-player game. If you enable an Internet feature, Spore servers will "pollinate" your copy of the game with content created by other players. In order to create the best content for your style of play—"the right kind of ecosystem for your creature," as Wright puts it—Spore builds a model of how you play the game, and searches for other players' content that fits that model. If you create a hyperaggressive Darwinian monster, for example, the game might download equally cutthroat opponents to test you. In other words, while you are playing the game, the game is playing you.

Wright asked if I would like to try the Spore "creature editor," which is the first major design tool in the game. On the screen was a kidney-shaped blob that looked like Mr. Potato Head before you add the features. Wright showed me the menus for creating my creature's skeleton, body, eyes, and skin. I used the mouse to stretch the blob into a torso, changing the shape and length of the spine as I did so. I chose the parts from the left side of the screen—flippers, beaks, three-jointed legs—all of which would cost DNA points at this stage of the game. Wright explained, "You can choose different mouths—carnivore, herbivore, omnivore—which will determine not only how you will eat in the world but what type of voice the creature has." On the right side of the screen were graphics that showed the evolutionary advantages and consequences of each choice—speed, power, stealth, etc. Switching to the paint menu, I applied a base coat of purple, then some orange stripes; the computer automatically shaded the colors, so that my creature's skin looked professionally textured.

"Okay, now go to test mode," Wright said.

I clicked a button and my creature sprang to life and started lumbering around the screen. It was a goofy-looking thing—a hammer-fisted apatosaurus with a potbelly, a long neck, and floppy dog ears. But it was a fully animated character, something that Pixar might have created, and I had made it in about three minutes. I felt as if I were playing with digital clay.

Electronic Arts was the largest producer of video games in the world, with more than seven thousand employees, and studios in North America, Europe, and Asia. It made or licensed software for many game-playing platforms, including computer games for PCs and Macs; console games for Nintendo, Sony, and Microsoft game boxes; handheld games for the Nintendo Game Boy (and the

Nintendo DS) and for the Sony PSP; and online games for playing on the Web. EA had begun to make "mobile games," for playing on cell phones, a new and rapidly growing market.

EA was founded in 1982 by Trip Hawkins, a former marketing manager at Apple Computer, as "the new Hollywood," and it was at first supposed to be a haven for video-game auteurs. Hawkins proposed to treat designers, who had hitherto been regarded as mere engineers, as artists, and to design sexy packaging that would evoke album covers, with the names of the creators emblazoned on the front. "Can a video game make you cry?" was one of the company's early challenges. Over the years, EA shifted its strategy toward games based on "proven content"—licensed stories and characters from film, sports, and TV, rendered in game form. EA has also developed sports-simulation games, based on professional sports leagues, featuring the players themselves. As Steven L. Kent recounts in *The Ultimate History of Video Games*, it began in 1984, with Dr. J and Larry Bird Go One-on-One, a basketball game for which EA paid Erving and Bird to use their names and images. But now, EA has created a sports-gaming empire. The 2006 version of Madden NFL, which was originally published in 1990, sold two million copies in its first week of release. In recent years, the company has acquired a Microsoft-like reputation for hard-nosed business practices—buying smaller development studios that can no longer afford the rising costs of game production, and shutting out potential competitors with exclusive licensing deals.

The EA campus was in Redwood Shores, California, at the northern edge of Silicon Valley. Employees dressed in shorts; there was a gym; the games in the company store were less than half price; and several meeting rooms were designed to look like sports bars. But according to two class-action suits for "unpaid overtime," one filed by EA game artists and another by programmers, working for EA hasn't always been as much fun as it appeared to be. Although both suits have been settled and EA had revised its overtime policy, during crunch times eighty-hour weeks continued to be the norm.

While I was at EA, I was given a demonstration of The Godfather, one of the company's new games. You begin as a low-level criminal and attempt to become, through the clever use of violence and extortion, the head of the crime family. One of the game's innovations is that, in addition to killing opponents, you can also wound them by shooting them in the kneecaps or shoulders—and if you only wound them you can still extort money from them, and thereby advance in the game. I also saw the most recent installment of the Tiger Woods golf franchise. The golfer allowed EA to attach motion sensors to his body and face, and the data were rendered in computer graphics. The result is, among other things, a remarkable computer-animated version of Woods's famous smile—the way the upper lip slides up over the teeth is perfect. After hitting a good drive, you get to hear Woods whisper, "On the screws, Tiger."

After the demos, I met Larry Probst, then the chief executive of EA, who started in the company's sales department in 1984. Probst explained that EA allowed Wright to put together a development team by choosing some of the most talented artists and programmers from EA's vast network of game makers. The company also constructed a separate headquarters for the seventy-five-member team in Emeryville, about fifty miles north of the corporate campus near Orinda, where Wright was living. It was counting on Spore to help shore up its bottom line. The company's stock price had dropped almost 30 percent since April, and its 2006 sales figures were 20 percent lower than the previous year's. Probst blamed the company's problems on one of the cyclical downturns that hits the game industry every four or five years when a new generation of gaming machines become available; in the fall, both the PlayStation 3, from Sony, and Nintendo's Wii system would go on sale. Traditionally, gamers stop buying the current generation of games in anticipation of those that will be developed for the new machines.

But there were reasons to believe that EA's problems were more systemic—indeed, that the entire game industry was on the verge of a fundamental restructuring. Not since the early 1980s, when video games began moving from amusement arcades into homes, had the future seemed so uncertain. While each generation of hardware offers the capacity for increasingly realistic graphics—like Tiger's smile—it also requires producers to devote more programming hours to filling that capacity. Twenty years ago it was possible for one man to create an entire video game; today development teams of a hundred or more are the norm. Moreover, EA's basic product, which is a boxed game costing around fifty dollars, isn't as appealing as it once was. Many adult players prefer "casual games," which can be played on cell phones and in shorter sessions online. Instead of buying games at a store and bringing them home, customers want games they can get on the Web. Just as some in the film industry have begun to wonder about the economic feasibility of films that cost upward of fifty million dollars to produce, so people in the game industry wonder whether big-budget games can survive in a climate that favors downloadable games that are cheap, short-lived, and disposable.

During our conversation, Probst seemed most enthusiastic about the market for casual games, especially games for cell phones, which earned EA more than a hundred million dollars in 2005. "Think about what happens when three billion Chinese people have cell phones," he said at one point. But how do you convince a casual gamer, who is just looking for distraction, to play a game that is about evolution, city building, conquest, and interstellar travel? I asked Probst about this, and he said, "You tell people it's a Will Wright game."

Wright belongs to the last generation of game designers (and indeed, human beings) who grew up before personal computers and game consoles existed. He built models of things as a kid: "ships, cars, planes—I loved to do that," he told me. When Will was ten, he built a balsa-wood replica of the flight deck on the *Enterprise,* which won an award at a Star Trek convention. He was also fond of the board games made by Avalon Hill, such as PanzerBlitz, a strategy game loosely based on tank warfare on the Eastern Front.

Wright's father, Will, Sr., and grandfather were graduates of Georgia Tech's engineering school, and Wright keeps their graduation pictures hanging on a wall in his house, alongside a picture of himself. His forebears are crewcut men in sober suits, about to embark on successful careers in making useful things. Then, there's Will, Jr., who never graduated from college, and who didn't fit into the family tradition—a gangly man-boy with a sweet, slightly stoned-looking grin. "Something went wrong with this one," Wright said, peering at the picture.

In the 1960s, Wright's father developed a new way of making plastic packing materials and started a successful company, which allowed the Wrights to live comfortably in Atlanta. Will's dad was also an excellent golfer. His mother, Beverlye Wright Edwards, was an amateur magician and actress. Wright flourished in the local Montessori school, with its emphasis on creativity, problem solving, and self-motivation. "Montessori taught me the joy of discovery," Wright told me. "It showed you can become interested in pretty complex theories, like Pythagorean theory, say, by playing with blocks. It's all about learning on your terms, rather than a teacher explaining stuff to you. SimCity comes right out of Montessori—if you give people this model for building cities, they will abstract from it principles of urban design."

In the evening, Will and his father would sit on the porch and talk about the stars, NASA's Apollo program, and the possibility of life on other planets. Wright was planning to be an astronaut, and his goal was to create colonies in space that would help relieve the pressure of overpopulation. His father thought this was a wonderful idea.

When Will was nine, his father died of leukemia, and his mother took him and his younger sister, Whitney, back to Baton Rouge, her hometown. Will went to Episcopal, a conventional prep school. He didn't like it as much as the Montessori school, although he enjoyed discussions about God with the faculty. "That's where I became an atheist," he said. He started at Louisiana State University when he was sixteen; two years later, he transferred to Louisiana Tech. He excelled only in subjects that he was interested in: architecture, economics, mechanical engineering, military history. He had impractical goals—in addition to starting colonies in space, he wanted to build robots. He dropped out again after two years, drove a bulldozer for a summer, and then, in the fall of 1980, went to the New School, in Manhattan, where he studied robotics. He lived in an apartment over Balducci's in Greenwich Village and spent a lot of time on Canal Street scrounging parts from the surplus electronics stores that used to line the street and using them to build a robotic arm.

In the summer of 1980, Wright answered an ad in a car magazine: Richard Doherty, a rally enthusiast, was looking for participants to compete in a point-to-point race between Farmingdale, Long Island, and Redondo Beach, California. Wright had a Mazda RX-7, which he and Doherty modified with a larger fuel tank and a roll cage. They wore night-vision goggles so that they could drive fast in the dark without headlights and avoid the cops. "Will said we should take the southern route, even though it was longer, because if we got stopped he'd be able to talk to the cops," Doherty told me. "We did get stopped in Georgia. We were doing a hundred and twenty, with no headlights, but it didn't take Will more than a couple of minutes to make the officer see why he had to let us go without a ticket." They won the race, establishing a new record of thirty-four hours and nine minutes.

After a year at the New School, Wright went back to Baton Rouge to live with his best friend. His family expected Will to take over the plastics company, but Will wasn't interested. (Eventually they sold the business.) Souping up cars for rally racing was his main passion that summer, until his roommate's sister, Joell Jones, came to Baton Rouge for a visit. Jones was eleven years older than Wright; their families had been friends and he had known her when he was a teenager. Now she lived in Oakland, where she was a painter and a social activist. She was back in Baton Rouge to recuperate after severing a nerve in her wrist. To extend the range of motion in her hand, Wright built a device out of metal and rubber bands. "Will would talk to me passionately about the need to colonize space, and I would say that it was more important to feed people on earth," Jones told me. "Somehow we fell in love." When Jones went back to Oakland, Wright asked if he could come and live with her; she agreed, on the condition that he didn't interfere with her painting. They married in 1984.

In the early 1980s, coin-operated machines began to decline in popularity and home-video games began to take hold. Atari, which had popularized home-gaming consoles, was superseded by Nintendo, a venerable Japanese playing-card company, with its Nintendo

Entertainment System. As hardware, the NES was an improvement over the Atari machines (Atari's joystick controller was replaced with the directional "+" pad, which the player operated with his thumbs), but it was software, in the form of a Nintendo game cartridge called Super Mario Bros., that made Nintendo the industry leader. Shigeru Miyamoto, who had designed Nintendo's Donkey Kong for arcades, redesigned the game, changing the carpenter in the game, whose name was Jumpman, to a plumber, whom he called Mario, and adding a brother named Luigi and a far greater array of aids (golden coins, magic mushrooms), obstacles (fire-spitting enemies), and underground passageways, many of them drawn from Miyamoto's boyhood memories of exploring caves in the mountains near his home in Sonobe.

By the time Super Mario appeared, the syntax for game play was firmly established; it remains the standard grammar. The player progresses through the game by defeating antagonists, restoring his energy with "power-ups" he finds along the way, accumulating bonus points to rise to progressively harder levels, many of which feature a "boss" who must be defeated in order to earn a "save game" and not have to repeat the level. Although Super Mario, which debuted in the United States in 1985, had a goal (to rescue Princess Peach from a giant reptile named Bowser), it also encouraged exploration for its own sake; in this regard, it was less like a competitive game than a "software toy"—a concept that influenced Will Wright's notion of possibility space. "The breadth and the scope of the game really blew me away," Wright told me. "It was made out of these simple elements, and it worked according to simple rules, but it added up to this very complex design."

In the late nineties, Sony's PlayStation console replaced the NES as the dominant home game-playing system, and Microsoft's Xbox, introduced in 2001, became the second-bestselling machine. But neither Sony nor Microsoft has had Nintendo's influence on basic game design.

In 1991 yet another phase in the game business began when a young programmer named John Carmack, who was, together with John Romero, a partner in a Dallas-based company called id Software, figured out how to program 3-D graphics for a PC, enabling the designers to give more depth to interior spaces and to create more realistic movements. According to *Masters of Doom,* David Kushner's 2003 book, when Romero first saw Carmack's 3-D program, he exclaimed, "This is it. We're gone!" Romero designed the graphics and game play for an ultraviolent game that called on his own love of 1950s horror comics published by EC comics, combined with a heavy-metal sensibility. The result was Doom, the defining first-person shooter, in which you play a "space marine," and the object is to kill the zombies that come at you as you advance deeper into Hell. Everything about the game was designed to inflame a teenage boy's fantasies of power while causing grave distress to his parents. In 1999 the elders' worst fears about the antisocial effects of first-person shooters seemed to be realized when Dylan Klebold and Eric Harris, the teenagers who massacred twelve of their classmates and one teacher at Columbine High School in Colorado, were revealed to be obsessive players of Doom. Congressional hearings on violence in video games followed. More recently, the San Andreas version of the Grand Theft Auto series, in which the object is to pimp and steal your way to the top (you can get power-ups from mugging prostitutes), caused Hillary Clinton to cosponsor the Family Entertainment Protection Act, which would ban the sale of violent games to minors. Clinton also accused the makers of violent and sexually explicit games of "stealing the innocence of our children and making the difficult job of being a parent even harder."

One day in his office, Wright showed me an e-mail he had received from Lara M. Brown, a professor of political science at California State University, Channel Islands, in response to an essay he had written for *Wired* about the educational value of video games. Brown, who uses technology in her own teaching, wrote, "Most of us are in agreement that this younger generation—raised on video games—has learned to be reactive, instead of active, and worse, they have lost their imaginative abilities and creativity because the games provide all of the images, sounds, and possible outcomes for them. Our students tend to not know how to initiate questions, formulate hypotheses, or lead off a debate because they like to wait to see what 'comes at them.' They also have difficulty imagining worlds (places and/or historical times) unless you (as a professor) can provide them with a picture and a sound to go along with the words. . . . In essence, they seem to have lost the ability to visualize with their minds."

Wright, though, believes that video games teach you how to learn; what needs to change is the way children are taught. "The problem with our education system is we've taken this kind of narrow, reductionist, Aristotelian approach to what learning is," he told me. "It's not designed for experimenting with complex systems and navigating your way through them in an intuitive way, which is what games teach. It's not really designed for failure, which is also something games teach. I mean, I think that failure is a better teacher than success. Trial and error, reverse-engineering stuff in your mind—all the ways that kids interact with games—that's the kind of thinking schools should be teaching. And I would argue that as the world becomes more complex, and as outcomes become less about success or failure, games are better at preparing you. The education system is going to realize this sooner or later. It's starting. Teachers are entering the system who grew up playing games. They're going to want to engage with the kids using games."

Shortly after moving in with Jones, Wright began making a helicopter simulator on his personal computer (a Commodore 64). Eventually the simulator evolved into a shoot-'em-up in which the player flies the helicopter over various cities and islands, trying to bomb buildings and blow up bridges. Wright showed the game to Gary and Doug Carlston, the founders of Broderbund, one of the earliest PC-gaming software companies. In 1984 Broderbund brought it out as a PC game called Raid on Bungling Bay, and it appeared as a Nintendo cartridge the following year. It was only a moderate success for the PC, but it sold a million cartridges, mainly in Japan, and because of Nintendo's generous royalty agreement with Broderbund, Wright says, "I made enough money to live on for several years."

In designing Raid on Bungling Bay, Wright noticed that he "was more interested in creating the buildings on the islands than in blowing them up." He started thinking of a game in which the point would be to design buildings or, maybe, to build a city. A neighbor suggested that Wright take a look at a 1969 book called *Urban Dynamics,* by Jay Wright Forrester, an MIT professor, which argued that urban planning could be carried out more rationally by a computer simulation than by humans, because the computer wouldn't be blinded by intuitive biases. In a later book, *World Dynamics,* Forrester laid out his proposal for a simulation that could manage the entire planet.

Computer simulations had been around since the 1950s, when military planners, climatologists, and economic forecasters began programming models of particular scenarios and dynamics and using them to predict outcomes. One early and well-known biological simulation was the Game of Life, created by a mathematician named John Horton Conway in 1970. The game, which simulated the growth and death of a living creature, was based on the principle of "cellular automata," in which the programmer assigns simple rules to discrete units, or cells. It can be played on a plain two-dimensional grid, in which black squares represent live cells and white squares represent dead ones. Each cell reacts to the state of the cells around it. The rules are: (1) any live cell with fewer than two live neighbors dies of loneliness; (2) any live cell with more than three neighbors dies of overcrowding; (3) any live cell with two or three neighbors lives; (4) any dead cell with three neighbors returns to life. Conway's purpose was to show how a simple structure of cells could be organized algorithmically to simulate complex, lifelike systems in which unpredictable or "emergent" outcomes occur.

Wright figured out how to combine Forrester's and Conway's ideas to imitate the dynamics of a city. The player would be responsible for adjusting around a hundred variables in a way that allows the city to thrive. You establish transportation networks, power grids, hospitals, and schools. Each decision affects many other variables: a rising crime rate leads to a declining population, which erodes the tax base, which requires the cutting of some essential services—less funding for the hospital, for example.

Wright built a prototype of the game and worked on it for Broderbund, but the company could not see the commercial potential for a game you couldn't win. Eventually Broderbund gave back the game's rights to Wright, and he set out to find a backer.

One night, at a pizza party in Alameda, Wright met Jeff Braun, a young businessman who was looking to get into video games. As Braun explained, "Will showed me the game and he said, 'No one likes it, because you can't win.' But I thought it was great. I foresaw an audience of megalomaniacs who want to control the world." Together, they founded Maxis, and brought out SimCity in 1989. (Broderbund eventually joined the venture as a distributor; by then Wright had added a feature that allowed players to destroy their cities with various disasters—a volcano, an earthquake, an alien attack, a meteorite shower.)

SimCity was slow to catch on, but seventeen years later the game had earned the company $230 million. A sizable number of players who first became interested in urban design as a result of the game have gone on to become architects and designers, making SimCity arguably the single most influential work of urban-design theory ever created.

In 1986 Wright and Jones had a daughter, Cassidy, and Jones made Wright promise to share the parenting equally so that she could continue painting. "He really did stick to that," she told me. "He spent a lot of time with Cassidy." While he was at home with his daughter, Wright began to turn over the idea for a new game, a kind of interactive dollhouse that adults would like as much as children. "I went around my house looking at all my objects, asking myself, What's the least number of motives or needs that would justify all this crap in my house? There should be some reason for everything in my house. What's the reason?"

One morning in 1991, as Wright awoke in his house in the Oakland Hills, he thought he smelled smoke and called 911. Over the next half hour, the smoke got worse. "I thought, Uh-oh, this isn't trending well." He and his wife decided it was time to evacuate (Cassidy was away at a friend's house). They grabbed some family photos, jumped into Jones's car, and drove away. When they returned, three days later, the Oakland Hills firestorm had destroyed everything. Nothing was left except for some lumps of melted metal, the remains of their other car. In the months that followed, as

Wright went about replacing his belongings, he started thinking about all the things people needed. "I hate to shop," he said, "and I was forced to buy all these things, from toothpaste, utensils, and socks up to furniture."

Three works helped Wright understand how he could turn these life experiences into a game. One was the book *A Pattern Language*, by Christopher Alexander and his colleagues at the Center for Environmental Structure in Berkeley. The book identifies 253 timeless ways of building, which are classified as patterns—"Stair Seats," "Children's Realm," etc.—and it shows how these patterns can create satisfying living spaces. The idea is that the value of architecture can be measured by the happiness of the people who live in it. The second was the psychologist Abraham Maslow's 1943 paper "A Theory of Human Motivation," in which Maslow described a pyramid-shaped hierarchy of human needs, with "Physiological" at the bottom, and above it "Safety," "Love," "Esteem," and, at the top, "Self-actualization." The third inspiration was Charles Hampden-Turner's *Maps of the Mind,* which compares more than fifty theories about how the mind works. Putting these works together, Wright formulated a model with which to "score" the happiness of the people in his dollhouse by their status, popularity, and success and by the quality of the environment the player designs for them—the more comfortable the house, the happier the people. Wright told me, "I don't believe any one theory of human psychology is correct. The Sims just ended up being a mishmash of stuff that worked in the game."

From a technical perspective, Wright's singular achievement in The Sims was to design a new kind of "object-oriented" operating system that modeled the complexity of social dynamics. As Chris Hecker, one of the developers on the Spore team, explained to me, "In Will's games, the objects themselves are encoded to interact with the environment around them. So if you introduce an espresso machine you buy from the online Sims mall, the Sims will be able to make espresso without having to reprogram the game. All you have to do is drop the object into the environment and it will make other stuff happen. The objects create 'verbs,' as we say."

The original Sims had eight motives or needs—hunger, hygiene, bladder, comfort, energy, social, fun, and room—all of which are affected by objects in the world around them. Life for a Sim is the pursuit of happiness, but happiness depends on social interaction and consumption, and consumption requires money. For example, the cheapest bed in The Sims 2, which costs 300 "simoleons," brings your Sim 1 point of comfort and 2 points of energy; a 3,000-simoleon bed carries 7 points of comfort and 6 of energy. Wright has said that he intended the game as a parody of consumerism, because "if you sit there and build a big mansion that's all full of stuff, without cheating, you realize that all these objects end up sucking up all your time, when they had been promising to save you time."

Almost no dedicated Sims player, Wright included, actually follows the rules of the game, which force you to spend many hours working in menial jobs in order to be able to afford nicer stuff. Most players use the "cheats" that are widely available on the Internet and have been built into the game by the programmers. Cheats are short pieces of code you can type into the game that let you get around the rules. Typing "motherlode" into The Sims 2, for example, endows your Sims with 50,000 simoleons. But using cheats doesn't really feel like cheating, because playing The Sims doesn't really feel like a game. It seems more like gardening, or fixing up your house. One of the game's small triumphs is to make work seem like fun. As my fourteen-year-old niece exclaimed recently, when I asked her what she liked about playing The Sims, "You've got one Sim who you've got to get to school, and another who needs to get to his job, and their kid has been up all night and is in a bad mood, and the house is dirty—I mean, there's a ton of things to do!"

When Wright took his idea to the Maxis board of directors, Jeff Braun says, "The board looked at The Sims and said, 'What is this? He wants to do an interactive dollhouse? The guy is out of his mind.'" Dollhouses were for girls, and girls didn't play video games. Maxis gave little support or financing for the game. Electronic Arts, which bought Maxis in 1997, was more enthusiastic. (Wright received seventeen million dollars in EA stock for his share of the company.) Wright's games are so different from EA's other releases that it was hard to imagine the two being united in the same enterprise. But the success of SimCity had already established Sim as a strong brand, and EA, which by then, fifteen years after its founding, was becoming a Procter & Gamble–style brand-management company, foresaw the possibility of building a Sim franchise. Released in 2000, The Sims was an immediate hit; it went on to become the bestselling PC game of all time. EA has since licensed it to many other playing platforms, and issues regular Sims "expansion packs," featuring new content, like Livin' Large, House Party, and Hot Date. (Wright has had nothing to do with the expansion packs.) The Sims franchise had earned EA more than a billion dollars so far. EA's only misstep was The Sims Online, the multiplayer version released in 2002, which failed to attract the masses of players drawn to other multiplayer games, such as World of Warcraft and Runescape.

The Sims brought a huge new population to gaming—girls. That did not come as a complete surprise to Wright, since women made up 40 percent of his Sims development team, and his daughter Cassidy, then fourteen years old, had helped him tinker with the prototypes. When he was a kid, Wright told me, "I never played with dolls, which is more of a social thing than playing with trains—it's about the people in the house. Cassidy helped me see that. She and her friends got into the purely creative side of the game, rather than the goal-oriented side, which really influenced me a lot." Cassidy was traumatized to discover that the Sims could burn down their house, and die in the fire, if they weren't careful around the stove. Wright left that feature in the game.

An unintended result of The Sims' success is that Wright transformed the tactile experience of playing with dolls, which has been a part of children's development for thousands of years, into a virtual experience. The enormous success of The Sims means that children today can grow up without having the hands-on model-making experiences that Wright enjoyed as a child and that inspired him to make games in the first place.

One evening I went with Wright to the house he and Jones moved into after the Oakland Hills fire. He drove a black two-door BMW with a fancy radar detector. The car was a mess, inside and out; Wright never washes it because he wants it to look like one of the banged-up starships in *Star Wars*. Parking it in the garage, he led me into the house through a short hallway that was full of oddly shaped pieces of machined steel. Wright explained that these were left over from the days when he competed in gladiatorial robot contests called BattleBots, in which engineers attempt to build the most destructive remote-controlled robot vehicles possible. These ferocious machines fight in large Plexiglas boxes, ramming into each other at high speeds, trying to disable their opponents by flipping them over; the tournaments are like geek cockfights. One of Wright's robots, which he designed with the help of Cassidy, was called Kitty Puff Puff. It fought its opponents (which had names like the Eviscerator and Death Machine) by sticking a piece of gauze to its opponent's armature and then driving in circles around it until the opposing robot was so cocooned in gauze that it couldn't move. Eventually the organizers banned cocooning.

The house, a split-level, was on a hilltop in Orinda, and it had a lovely view of Mount Diablo in the distance. Jones's paintings—colorful, biomorphic abstractions—were hung on the walls, and in the yard were her sculptures: architectural-looking objects made of found metal. But Wright's stuff took up most of the space. Just inside the front door was the control console of a Soyuz 23 spacecraft from the 1970s, which Wright bought from a former State Department official. Upstairs was his collection of unusual insects. Cassidy was away at college, but her prints—whimsical collages that feature drawings of rabbits and electric sockets—were also on display, and I saw a comic book she made, *The Adventures of Not Asian Girl*. On a porch off the living room were large blocks of alabaster that Wright was in the process of sculpting with hand tools into smooth, Brancusi-like shapes, a hobby that Jones had suggested to her husband as a way of expressing his artistic side. The rock dust and overflowing ashtrays on the porch suggested that he had been devoting a considerable amount of time to grinding stone lately.

The house was also filled with books. Some are what Wright calls "landmarks"—foundations for the design of one or another of his games. "Most of the games I've done were inspired by books," he told me. SimEarth, a simulation of the earth's ecology, was based on the Gaia hypothesis of James Lovelock, and SimAnt, an ant-colony simulation, was based on E. O. Wilson's *The Ants*. The key landmarks for Spore, however, were not books. They were Drake's equation and *The Powers of Ten*. The former, which he'd shown me on the computer screen in his office, is a formula devised in 1961 by Frank Drake, a radio astronomer, to estimate the number of possible worlds in our galaxy that might be populated with beings that could communicate with us. (About ten thousand, according to Drake's calculations.) The latter is a short film by Charles and Ray Eames, made in 1977, which begins with a man lying on the grass in a Chicago park, and then shows a series of images of the same shot, each taken from a position ten times farther away than the last one, until the viewer reaches the limits of the universe at $10^{24}$ meters (ten to the twenty-fourth power). Then it returns to the opening image and goes the other way, zooming into the man's skin, until at $10^{-16}$ you reach the limits of the inner world—the space inside a proton.

"I love *The Powers of Ten*," Wright said, "and I've always been a big fan of the Eameses. At the same time, I am really interested in the terms of Drake's equation, and when I began working on Spore I was using it to map some of the game play. At some point I realized that the terms of Drake's equation mapped neatly to the scale of *The Powers of Ten*. So I rolled the two up into Spore."

Wright seems to be more interested in making games than he is in integrating his ideas into a coherent philosophy. After you have played The Sims long enough, for example, you begin to recognize all the ways in which the simulation is not like real life. (The Sims 2, which came out in 2004, added more refinements to the basic design; in addition to the motives and needs, there are four different aspirations.) The Sims is only as realistic as the social theories it's based on, and these theories have been combined not according to scientific principles but for the purposes of entertainment. The Sims doesn't really model human dynamics; it merely gives you a model for exploring your own idea about how families work (just as playing with dolls does). Wright is not a visionary, in the sense that he is not the author of a worldview; he tailors his ideas according to the technical parameters of the simulation and the logic of games.

Whether the game involves fighting intergalactic battles or modeling climate change, the simulation works according to a logic of its own. Wright may be the game industry's greatest auteur, but to a large extent he has abdicated authorship of his own creation.

Jones came home with some Mexican takeout, and we ate from the containers, in the living room. Jones is soft-spoken, but she had a quiet authority around the house. She seemed a bit subdued. I asked her if she played her husband's games. "No, I don't. I'm not really interested in games," she said pleasantly. Later, she added, "Our daughter Cass used to say, 'We lived through the process of making the games, so we don't need to play them.' I think it frustrates Will that I don't play his games. Clearly, his games matter, on a deep level, to many people—take these online diaries people keep about their Sims. Wow. I don't know if they're avoiding their lives or learning about them. Me, I don't want to play a game to learn about myself." Several months later, when I heard that Wright and Jones were thinking about separating, and Wright had moved out, I recalled Jones's words.

I asked Wright if he was working on a new game. He said that, for the first time in his career, he was not. He was researching the Soviet space program, and hoping to produce a documentary film about it. He said he was seriously considering a return to rally racing this November by competing in the Baja 1000—a race across the desert. (He later changed his mind.) He had a Hollywood agent and a TV development deal with ABC for a reality show exploring our relationship with technology in the home. But tonight, at least, he did not seem particularly engaged by any of these plans. With the prospect of Spore's launch ahead of him, he seemed a little lost.

In May of 2006, I joined some twenty thousand members of the game industry—developers, marketers, distributors, buyers, press—in downtown Los Angeles for the industry's big trade show, Electronic Entertainment Expo, or E3. Electronic Arts, which had hoped in vain that Wright would have the game ready for the convention, was instead offering conventioneers the opportunity to see Wright demonstrate the game, inside a special Spore Hut that was set up next to EA's enormous pavilion.

By Wednesday morning at ten o'clock, when the trade floor opened, Wright was installed inside the hut, which could accommodate about thirty people. The line to get into the Spore Hut quickly grew to two hours long, snaking through the trade floor. Wright's mission was to play all the way through the game, which he estimates would require seventy-nine years if one played every aspect of it (Wright is designing cheats), in seventeen to twenty minutes, over and over, for two days.

On the trade floor, screens showed guns, cars, football players, and Lycra-clad virtual babes, featuring "better breast shadowing, better breast physics, and deeper breast customization," as one gaming blog put it. It felt as if we were all inside some gigantic video-game machine—the place Nolan Bushnell had imagined thirty-five years earlier.

In the EA pavilion I joined a clump of gamers watching each other play Battlefield 2142, the latest sequel to EA's popular shooter. I took a turn, but kept breaking out in a sweat and being greeted with the alarming sight of my face reflected on the screen—scrunched up, red, demonic-looking. Staggering out of the EA pavilion and into the cyber midway, I tried some of the nonviolent games, including Guitar Hero, in which the designers have ingeniously turned the controller into a guitar that you play by pushing buttons; it's like karaoke air guitar. I also tried SingStar Rocks!, a PlayStation game that measures your pitch, phrasing, and timing, and scores you as you sing. (Unfortunately, I chose Nirvana's "Come as You Are," which is not an easy song, and then compounded my problems by trying to sing in Kurt Cobain's register. "Awful" was the game's judgment of my performance, and it bothered me all day.) Finally, I got a demo of Left Behind, which is a Christian-themed video game based on the popular series of books by Tim LaHaye and Jerry B. Jenkins. You play a Christian in the streets of postapocalyptic Manhattan, and the object is to convert as many nonbelievers as you can before the Judgment Day. You get power-ups for finding bits of Scripture, and praying raises your spirit level—which is represented by a graphic "slider" at the top of the screen. However, you have to kill hostile nonbelievers, and can acquire some suitable weaponry for the job. Violence drains your spirit level, but if you click on the pray button you can bring it up again.

The influence of Will Wright was not immediately obvious on the trade floor. His sandbox aesthetic is more noticeable in online virtual communities like Second Life, created by Linden Lab and based in San Francisco, which uses a similar operating system to The Sims Online. Second Lifers can buy space in a SimCity-like community and use it for commercial transactions—conducted in virtual currency that can be exchanged for real money out in the real world. Aspiring musicians can perform onstage while their music is streamed over an audio channel. Second Life seems like a logical outcome of Wright's simulation games—and it isn't technically a game at all. When I asked Wright about Second Life, he said, "I think what you're going to see now on Second Life is people who will start to develop games—someone will invite other people to kick a soccer ball around, and it will go from there."

Wright's situation inside the hut was a little like his situation in the game industry—he seemed both enthroned and imprisoned. I half expected to find Bushnell at the door, charging people a quarter to see the geek. I could dimly make out Wright, seated behind a raft of computers on a raised platform behind the chairs, smears of color from the monitors reflecting on his glasses. There was a large screen on one wall, where the game was projected. He had been demonstrating Spore for about five hours straight when I got there, without lunch or cigarette breaks, although the EA handlers had brought him a Mocha Frappuccino, his favorite drink, from Starbucks.

I took my seat. There were little holes in the ceiling, with light behind them, to simulate stars. The walls of the hut were decorated with models of creatures that other players had designed. The lights went down and the game began in the drop of water. "Okay, so we start, and I'm trying to survive here—whoops, the guy wants to eat me." Wright narrated the game in the first person, and he seemed to be having fun. Using the creature editor, he put together a part-reptilian, part-avian creature, with yellow and purple stripes, four spindly legs, and talons at the end of its arms; it looked both cute and fierce. "Okay, now I have to survive and eat—whoops, I'm going to run away from that guy. Whoops, not that way—this is a harsh world right now." His creature ate another creature's egg. "Okay, now that I've eaten I feel like mating," and he located a mate the computer had generated for him. The creatures went at it, discreetly, behind a puff of smoke, to the sound of smooth jazz. "Procedurally generated mating," Wright said, with a smoker's chuckle.

Wright hurtled through the levels, evolution moving at hyperspeed as his creature acquired houses, tools, weapons, vehicles, and cities. While he was narrating his creature's adventures, Wright was also explaining how, in passing through the different levels of the game, the player would be progressing through the history of video games: from the arcade games, like Pac-Man, to Miyamoto's Super Mario, to the first-person shooters. At the tribal level you are playing a Peter Molyneux–style God game, and at the global level you are playing Sid Meier's Civilization. Finally, Wright reached the status of intergalactic god, with the power to visit other worlds. "Now we're going to go over to this place, which you can tell by the sliders has intelligent life on it, and this is actually a moon, a moon of this gas giant here. Okay, this is an alien civilization and there are a lot of different things I can do here diplomatically—I can actually use fireworks. Okay, they seem to like that. Actually, now they're starting to worship me as a god. So I might decide to pick one of these guys up." A tractor beam came down from his spaceship and sucked up one of the creatures. The natives started shooting at him. "Oops. They were upset by that."

At a certain point in the performance, the crazy ambition of Spore became clear: Wright was proposing to simulate the limitless possibility of life itself. The simulation falls between Darwinism and intelligent design, into new conceptual territory. Wright had worked out the algorithm for life, as described by the philosopher Daniel C. Dennett, in *Darwin's Dangerous Idea*. Dennett writes, "Here, then, is Darwin's dangerous idea: the algorithmic level is the level that best accounts for the speed of the antelope, the wing of the eagle, the shape of the orchid, the diversity of species, and all the other occasions for wonder in the world of nature. . . . Can it really be the outcome of nothing but a cascade of algorithmic processes feeding on chance?" The old dream of the MIT hackers who came up with Spacewar—to recreate life on a computer—was coming true forty years later, right here in the Spore Hut, in the form of a spindly, striped creature that looked a little like Will Wright himself.

After Wright's encounter with the other planet, he pulled back to reveal a vast galaxy of other worlds, some computer generated, some created by other players in the game who had reached the status of intergalactic gods—"more worlds than any player could visit in his lifetime," he said. As people in the audience gasped at the vastness of the possibility space, Wright's spaceship zoomed into the interstellar sandbox, looking for an uninhabited planet to colonize, just as young Will had promised his father he would.

—2006

# CHILD'S PLAY

In 1913 an Illinois stonemason named Charles Pajeau created a toy after seeing his children playing with pencils and empty thread spools—he called it Tinkertoy. In 1916 John Lloyd Wright, the son of the architect, invented Lincoln Logs, a toy inspired by watching the earthquake-proof "floating cantilever construction" of his father's Imperial Hotel in Tokyo. During the Second World War, a mechanical engineer named Richard James was working on ships' suspension systems when a torsion spring fell off his desk and flopped over, and the way it wiggled struck him as funny. His wife, Betty, paging through the dictionary, came upon a word for the toy: Slinky. In 1982 a NASA nuclear engineer named Lonnie Johnson was working at home on a high-pressure pump when a jet of water accidentally shot across the bathroom. Since then, more than two hundred million Super Soakers have been sold.

Seventeen years ago, Chuck Hoberman was a kinetic sculptor, with a degree in fine art from Cooper Union and a degree in mechanical engineering from Columbia University. He and his wife, Carolyn, who was also an artist, lived in a seventh-floor walkup just below Canal Street, in a dilapidated building with a sign outside that said, "Gentleman—Please Do Not Urinate on the Door. It Is Unsanitary." Chuck was interested in transformations—mechanical objects that could change their size without changing their shape. "I was obsessed with the idea of making objects disappear," he told me. "Not as a magic trick, but where the object could self-transform—change itself by itself." He tried to imagine a scissors hinge, like those you see in old-fashioned elevator doors, except in three dimensions, so that the structure could expand into a dome or a sphere. What would the geometry of such a structure look like? Early in the morning, before going off to his job at an engineering firm, Chuck would sit in his "study" (created by hanging a sheet between the desk and the bed), folding pieces of paper into triangles, pentagons, and polyhedrons. He worked on the problem for several years, but he made no progress.

The Hobermans are Buddhists, and one day in the spring of 1987 they were visiting their teacher's retreat, at a farm in the Hudson Valley. "I was listening to a great Tibetan lama who was teaching the philosophy of mind, a kind of brick-by-brick construction of the proper view of consciousness," Chuck recalled. "Each point was introduced, examined from the point of view of several different schools of Buddhist thought, then synthesized into a conclusion that led to the next point. I was supposed to be meditating, but I was drifting. It was a beautiful spring day, and the room was warm. Then there was a click, and in an instant I saw the solution to my obsession. I saw a linkage—a hinged loop of pieces moving in space. I could see how two, three, many linkages could be attached to one another to build up an entire transforming volume."

Chuck took out a patent on the idea, which was described in the technical literature as a "Doubly-Curved Truss Structure." He thought of his structure as art, but he wanted to prove that it had a practical, money-making purpose as well; utility is an essential part of Chuck's aesthetic. He had a series of conversations with Martin Mikulas, who was then the head of structural concepts at NASA's Langley Research Center, about developing his invention for space travel. He also spoke to a tent manufacturer about making a tent that wouldn't require poles, a luggage-maker about creating suitcases and trunks that could fold up for easier storage, and a medical-equipment manufacturer about making instruments for noninvasive surgery. Everyone Chuck spoke to was certain that he had invented something valuable, but no one was sure exactly what it was.

The notion that what Chuck Hoberman had invented was a toy came from Anthony Gentile, who, along with his twin brother, John, is a partner in Abrams Gentile Entertainment, a firm that creates toys and brokers ideas to larger manufacturers. Most independent inventors need toy brokers in order to gain access to the industry. Hasbro and Mattel, which between them account for about 35 percent of the industry's twenty billion dollars in annual domestic sales, don't even consider independent solicitations.

The Gentiles had read about Chuck's invention in the Patents column of the *Times,* and asked him to meet them at their offices, situated across from the boarded-up Broadway saloon Legz Diamond's, on West Fifty-fourth Street. "John and Anthony are these intense New York guys, and they both talk really fast," Chuck recalled. "They look exactly the same, and there was one of them on either side of me—it was like listening to them in stereo."

"When we met Chuck, he had his sights set on outer space," Anthony Gentile told me. "You know Chuck; he's a big thinker. He was talking about building space stations and whatnot, and we said to him, 'That sounds great, Chuck, but how about this—a collapsible playhouse that you can fold up small enough to fit into your back pocket!'"

The Gentiles hired Chuck to develop that idea and several other toys, and they had a prototype of the playhouse manufactured, which they showed to Mattel in the hope of working out a licensing deal. "Mattel loved that toy," Anthony said, "except for the price point—which was, like, fifty dollars. And let me tell you, everything in the toy business is about price point." In recent years, as the toy industry has seen its claim on playtime challenged by video games, toymakers have become intensely focused on price; more than 65 percent of American toys sell for twenty dollars or less. "I could make a doll levitate, with no strings—a miracle!" Anthony says. "But if I can't do it for nineteen ninety-five they're not interested."

Chuck worked for the Gentiles for two years, developing ideas for toys, but none of them sold, and when his contract ended he was ready to return to his career as an artist. A curator of design at the Museum of Modern Art asked him to create a piece for a MoMA show, and Chuck made a dome that could open from the center, like an iris. He also built the two-story-high transforming sphere that visitors to the Liberty Science Center in Jersey City encounter just inside the main entrance. These projects didn't earn Chuck much money, but they did bring him artistic credibility, and that was what he really wanted.

Carolyn had a different vision. "I had been going to toy fairs, meeting people, and I found the toy world to be very interesting," she told me. She persuaded Chuck to focus on making a toy sphere. What Chuck came up with was an unlikely toy, a transformer that changes its shape as it expands, from a sea-urchin-like bundle of hinges into a sphere of delicately attenuated struts. Each hinge unfolds while at the same time pivoting, so that its relationship to the other hinges remains the same. The struts inscribe a series of triangles and pentagons that intersect with each other, and the points of intersection form geodesic circles that are similar to the shapes described by Buckminster Fuller, who was an inspiration for Chuck.

Carolyn found a manufacturer in New Jersey that could make the parts for the toy sphere, and together they raised money to pay for the materials and the production costs. Carolyn also designed the packaging for the product, which they called the Hoberman Sphere, and which consisted of more than four hundred acrylic pieces that required assembly at home. The Hobermans took it around to the major toy fairs, including those in New York, San Francisco, and Nuremberg. They didn't get many orders from retailers, but they did get invaluable advice from other toymakers, notably Dennis Binkley, the founder of Geospace International, in Seattle. He convinced the Hobermans that, for financial reasons, their product should be made in China. "He also told me our packaging was terrible," Carolyn says with a laugh.

In May of 1995, Carolyn accompanied Binkley on his next trip to China. "The factory said to us, 'Do you need the toy to snap together?'" she recalled. "And we said, 'No, I guess not.' And they said, 'Could we make it out of polypro?,' and we said, 'Sure.'" Samples of this new Hoberman Sphere—a lightweight, polypropylene thirty-inch toy that now required no assembly at home—came back from China later that year. In 1997 the Hobermans brought out a twelve-inch version, and the Store of Knowledge, a high-end retail chain, bought practically the entire supply.

The Hobermans' big break came on August 16, 1998, when the Reverend Walter Shrophire, Jr., of Foundry United Methodist Church in Washington, D.C., used a Hoberman Sphere as a visual aid in a sermon that he was giving about the big bang. Bill and Hillary Clinton were in the audience; the president was scheduled to give his grand-jury testimony in the Monica Lewinsky matter the following morning. After the sermon, Hillary Clinton asked the minister where he had found that marvelous toy, saying she was looking for something to give Bill for his birthday. The minister offered his sphere, and Hillary passed it along to the president as they stood in the church. Outside, reporters were shouting questions about Monica Lewinsky. People watching the news that evening saw the president, ignoring the press, smiling cryptically as he stared into the Hoberman Sphere, slowly opening and closing it.

"We had no idea what had happened, because our daughter had been born on August eleventh and we were oblivious to everything," Chuck said. "When we finally checked our messages, we heard all these people saying, 'Congratulations! You're famous!'"

By 2003, the Hoberman Sphere could be found everywhere, from science-museum gift shops to Wal-Mart and Toys Я Us. The Hobermans run Hoberman Designs, which was based in a large, high-ceilinged loft in lower Manhattan, employed some twenty-five people, and did ten million dollars' worth of business a year. With nearly five million units sold, the sphere seemed well on its way to becoming a classic toy, a twenty-first-century Slinky, and one of the few toys of recent vintage that are likely to be popular for a long time.

That might have been the end of the story—and it would be a happy ending, more or less, like the story of Richard and Betty James, the inventors of the Slinky. (Richard abandoned the business and his family to join a religious cult in Bolivia, but his wife took over, moved the Slinky factory near the Jameses' hometown of Hollidaysburg, Pennsylvania, where it remains one of the town's largest employers, and made Slinky the world-famous toy that it is today. In 2000, at the age of eighty-six, Betty James was inducted into the toy industry's Hall of Fame.)

But the toy industry has changed since the Second World War, and the difference between the Jameses' and the Hobermans' experience is one way of measuring just how much. Toymakers have always created toys that appealed to parents. The Erector set (1913) and Monopoly (1935) were products that parents could fondly believe were preparing their children to be builders and bankers. In the years after the war, though, toymakers began to make products that appealed exclusively to kids—toys that, in many cases, parents actively disliked, which was the principal source of their appeal. Toys like Rock'em Sock'em Robots, from 1966 (the ad's tagline, "You knocked my block off," taught me how to intimidate my younger brother), were the heirs to toys like Gooey Louie (1995): "Pick his nose until his brain explodes." Dolls such as Shirley Temple (1934) and Ginny (1951)—which, in their infantile appearance, were meant to elicit a maternal response from the children who played with them, and thus to begin preparing girls for motherhood—gave way to Barbie, a doll that was not the child's baby but her role model, the girl she longed to become.

John Brewster, a toy historian, has written of the early-twentieth-century toymakers, "They were marketing a particular social morality—one that stressed industry, probity, and individual endeavor." Play was the work of children, and building blocks and baby dolls were the tools that children used to become adults. But by the mid-1970s, toys had stopped trying to prepare children for anything other than a perpetual childhood. As David Elkind, a professor of child development at Tufts University and the author of the classic book *The Hurried Child*, told me, "Many toys no longer perform a socializing function, as they used to. Toys are no different from any other consumer product—it's all about selling something."

This evolution in the design and marketing of toys marked the first time that children younger than twelve were explicitly targeted as consumers. The toy industry taught the makers of other kinds of consumer products that children were a potentially lucrative market, and that "aspirational age marketing" (selling the charm of feeling older) could be used to sell not only Barbie dolls but clothes, fast food, cosmetics, and electronics. Meanwhile, as fashion and trendiness became the driving concerns of the toy industry, the notion of a classic, a toy made to last, all but disappeared. (Even Binney & Smith, the makers of Crayola crayons since 1903, has seen the need to spruce up its choice of colors with Tickle Me Pink and Macaroni and Cheese crayons.) For the contemporary toymaker, it is less important to invent one classic toy than it is to invent a toy that can be updated regularly with new colors, styles, models, and related products. "What retailers are impressed by is how much real estate you take up on the shelf," Anthony Gentile told me. "You want that whole wall of pink that you see when you get to the Barbie section." By inventing a timeless toy—one that didn't need to be improved—Chuck had limited himself to a tiny piece of retail real estate.

In the years since the introduction of the original sphere, the Hobermans have developed an entire line of spheres, from a twelve-inch, glow-in-the-dark model to a fifty-four-inch megasphere. They have also extended their patented linking concept to other toys, including Flip Outs (a sphere that changes color when you spin it) and Growbots (structures that transform into robotic-looking creatures). So far, none of Chuck's newer concepts have caught on like the original toy, but the Hobermans had high hopes for their new product for the holiday season, the Sonic Sphere.

The Hobermans introduced the toy at the 2003 American International Toy Fair, which was held at the Jacob Javits Convention Center, in New York, in February. I went to the fair to see the toy for myself, joining the crowd of toy inventors, producers, distributors, packagers, retailers, and journalists who were poking around hundreds of exhibitors' booths. As I wandered the aisles of the vast space, I felt a sense of wonder at all the amazing things that toys can do these days (sing, dance, teach, work out), but at the same time I failed to find, among the many thousands of gewgaws, a single item that I wanted to take home to my son. Toys must be two often contradictory things in order to succeed. They have to be fun to play with, but they also have to look, while sitting on the shelf of the toy store, as if they would be fun to play with (the industry refers to this as "playability"), which in many cases results in an emphasis on superficial, attention-grabbing attributes. The only toys I saw at the fair that appealed to me were those I had played with as a child. (The toy industry has accommodated this desire, regularly bringing back toys in twenty-year cycles, like oldies on the radio, so that parents can duplicate their own Toyland experiences through their children. The season's retro toys include Strawberry Shortcake, Teenage Mutant Ninja Turtles, and My Little Pony, all of which were originally popular in the eighties.)

One reason so many sophisticated modern toys are less compelling than their humble forebears is the technology itself. Twenty years ago, the advent of electronics was hailed as "the greatest thing in our industry since the development of plastic," in the words of Arnold Greenberg, the former chairman of Coleco. In 2003, for the first time, more than half of the toys produced by U.S. toymakers had an electronic chip inside. But so far technology had resulted in a striking dearth of good toys. Although this new generation of toys were advertised as "interactive," they're actually less interactive than traditional toys. Mitchel Resnick, a professor of learning research at the MIT Media Lab who studies technology and toys, told me, "The question I ask about tech toys is, Does the technology keep the agency of play with the child, or does it shift the agency to the toy?" High-tech toys are so sophisticated that they're almost capable of playing by themselves—children aren't required.

I found the Hobermans on the mezzanine level of the Javits Center, under a large banner that said "Hoberman Designs." The sound of a steel drum was coming from a nearby exhibitor's booth. The music was supposed to be fun and wacky, but in the cavernous hall it sounded tinny and sad; Chuck said it was driving everybody crazy. "But the drummer has been paid for the whole day, so he's going to play," he added.

Chuck was dressed in a green suit, an orange shirt, and wire-rimmed glasses. He is tall, thin, and pale, and wears his red hair cut short. He was moving around the spacious Hoberman pavilion, meeting people, taking characteristically long strides, and yet his glad-handing seemed forced, not like the natural blarney I've encountered in other toy men. Chuck often looks slightly ill at ease in public, especially when he's on display as "the inventor." Carolyn, who was standing near her husband, appeared to be having more fun. "I like selling," she told me. "Chuck doesn't. He's too shy. But I really enjoy talking to people, hearing what they have to say."

Chuck, forty-seven, ran the design and product-development side of the business, and Carolyn, fifty-one, oversaw sales and intellectual-property protection. For Chuck, the greatest challenge had been finding a way to be successful in the toy business without betraying his artistic standards. He explained, "As an artist, my view was that one's work is the expression of an individual speaking to a viewer who is also an individual. And as an inventor, I'd always loved the fact that the Patent Office only recognizes the inventors on the patent. So my mind-set as we started the business was that marketing was a kind of abuse of statistics. The population is divided into arbitrary categories, but an individual can never be a category." (When time allowed, Chuck continued to seek opportunities to use his designs in artistic and architectural contexts; the mechanical curtain for the stage at the 2002 Winter Olympic Games in Salt Lake City was a Hoberman design.)

Chuck hated the whole notion of focus groups, which are ubiquitous in the toy industry. After all, the Hobermans' company had been founded not on a marketing gambit but on a mystical revelation that occurred while Chuck was meditating. "I didn't *want* to know why people liked the sphere," Chuck told me. "They liked it because I liked it, and that was enough."

The event that changed Chuck's thinking took place in 2002, when the Hobermans introduced their Discover Dome—a demisphere sheathed in origami-style folded paper that had fun facts about planets and dinosaurs printed on it. "We simply said, 'If we build it, they will come,'" Chuck recalled. "In retrospect, I think we all suffered from mass hypnosis." Their fellow toymakers loved the ingenious domes, but kids weren't interested, and the price, $29.99, was too high for most parents. The Discover Dome bombed, and the Hobermans were stuck with thousands of unwanted toys.

As a result of the dome disaster, Chuck had another revelation. "I realized we had to get serious," he said. The company proclaimed 2003 "The Year of the Sphere" in its marketing literature, and Chuck's own image was incorporated into the brand (the packaging bore a photograph of his bespectacled red head). The Hobermans also began conducting focus groups—going to private and public schools around New York City and asking the kids what kind of toy they'd like to have. The kids said they wanted a toy with music and flashing lights—something "interactive"—so Chuck designed the Sonic Sphere.

Like many of the exhibitors at the toy fair, the Hobermans had hired actors to impersonate children playing with the product, in order to demonstrate how much fun it is. (Real children aren't permitted at the fair.) A woman was playing with the Sonic Sphere, rotating it to make different types of vocal and instrumental sounds emerge from the small orange plastic speaker in the center, and expanding and collapsing it to change the pitch and rhythm of the sounds. "So I'm hanging out here in my bedroom, and I can be my own DJ!" the player playing at play said.

The Sonic Sphere was getting good reviews from other toymakers. Brooke Abercrombie, the president of Neurosmith, stopped by. "What a great way to translate motion into sound!" she said. But Chuck couldn't tell whether he had a hit on his hands. "It's not like designing the sphere," he said. "Instead of doing something that pleased me and that, it turned out, kids loved, now we're trying to invent what we think kids will love—which is a very different stance."

In June, the Hobermans went to the Licensing International trade show, which was also held at the Javits Center. Unlike the toy fair, with its Saharan wastes of gimcrackery, at the licensing fair there are no physical objects—the trade is entirely in characters, narra-tives, and brands. Licensed toys—largely movie, music, and TV properties—which were once a tiny part of the toy industry, have steadily grown to encompass more than 30 percent of domestic toy sales. Movie tie-ins are declining, mainly because of the relative failure of the action figures that Hasbro produced for the second *Star Wars* trilogy, but tie-ins to popular TV characters like Sponge-Bob SquarePants are on the rise. (SpongeBob alone generated more than half a billion dollars' worth of licensed products in 2002.)

Toymakers use the word *toyetic* when they're discussing whether an entertainment property has what it takes to be a successful toy. The movie *Men in Black* spawned a lot of licenses, but it wasn't par-ticularly toyetic because the characters are limited to wearing one color. The Harry Potter phenomenon, which also launched a tsu-nami of licensed products, hasn't proved to be particularly toyetic either, perhaps because children would rather read the books than play with the toys.

At the beginning of his toymaking career, Chuck would never have considered taking a license—an arrangement under which the toymaker pays the entertainment company for the right to use its character (and often has to guarantee a minimum payment to the licensor, regardless of how many of the toys are sold). A licensed toy doesn't have to be particularly ingenious, because its appeal has less to do with what the toy does than with what it represents. The Hoberman Sphere is the antithesis of this kind of product: it's a toy that is what it does, and does what it is. The other drawback of li-censed toys is that they deny children the most absorbing aspect of play: creating narratives. An ordinary cardboard packing box can be an enchanting toy if you imagine that it's a secret fort. But a toy that relies on a screen-based character or story doesn't require much imagination. Licensing is the fast-food version of toys—all you have to do is consume.

Nevertheless, like his view of focus groups, Chuck's opinion of licensing was evolving. "I feel this is American culture at its most distinctive," he said of the power of branding that was on display at Licensing International. "There is something very twenty-first cen-tury about the idea that *Lara Croft Tomb Raider* represents a part of the global economy." At the Nickelodeon pavilion, he put on 3-D glasses and watched a SpongeBob episode in the SpongeBob Tiki hut, and then had a talk with some people from Nickelodeon about the possibility of creating a Hoberman product based on the lovable yellow sponge, in time for *SpongeBob* the movie, which was due in theaters in the fall of 2004.

Chuck was still hedging against a licensing deal—"What's the point, really?" he said to me gloomily—but Carolyn was open to the idea. "You know, we need to think big," she said. "Sometimes I imagine a Hoberland, a place where everything transforms. There's a Legoland; why not Hoberland?"

Now the toy-buying season is here again, and, if this season is like others in recent memory, parents will be lining up around the block, in the snow, outside Toys Я Us, to get a toy that, of the thousands of new toys released this year, is the only toy that every child must have. The must-have toy is the apotheosis of the marketing of toys as fashion accessories. Will this year's must-have toy be Kasey the Kinderbot, a learning toy from Fisher-Price, which, in addition to helping kids read and write, also promises to teach them about manners, self-awareness, and emotions—all for $39.88 at Wal-Mart? (Parents will presumably be willing to spend more than twenty dollars for a toy that relieves them of the responsibility of parenting.) Will it be the rare P-Rico Plush doll, from the popular Homies series? Or will it be the Sonic Sphere, from Hoberman Designs?

There was no must-have toy in 2002, or the year before that; the last MHT was Furby, a robotic feline, in 1998. Some industry analysts, like Kurt Barnard, the publisher of *Barnard's Retail Trend Report,* see this as evidence of the toy industry's continuing slippage in its competition with video games—PlayStation 2 and Xbox were the MHTs of the past couple of years. "What the toy industry needs to figure out is how to make toys that are as compelling as video games," Barnard told me. "Until that happens, it's going to have problems." But another industry observer, Christopher Byrne, an independent toy analyst, sometimes known as "the Toy Guy," sees the decline of the must-have toy as a sign that toy buyers are becoming more rational about toys. "Parents have awakened to the fact that the toy they practically killed themselves to get may not have had the appeal that they expected," he told me. "I can't argue with more than forty-four million Furby toys sold, but how many of those did kids play with for a long time?"

The Sonic Sphere was at Wal-Mart and Toys Я Us stores across the country, and the Hobermans were monitoring the weekly numbers. "The volume isn't huge, but the trend is encouraging," Chuck said. "So far, it looks good." Chuck also mentioned, to my surprise, that he'd decided to take a SpongeBob license. "I know, I know, we're selling out," he said with a smile, seeing my raised eyebrows. "But the good thing about SpongeBob is that he can change his shape whenever he wants, which fits nicely into our aesthetic." He went on, "We're knocking around a couple of ideas, one of which is an exploding SpongeBob head, or maybe a head that turns into a pineapple."

Chuck spoke with a confidence that I had not heard from him before. By following his lifelong interest in transformations, I thought, he had himself been transformed—from an artist into a toymaker. But I was wrong about that. Not long after we spoke, Chuck changed his mind and dropped the SpongeBob idea. "A SpongeBob toy might have made us some money, but it just wasn't what we're really about," he explained. "I have to believe that there really is a group of people—regular people shopping at Toys Я Us and Wal-Mart—who share this basic wonder that I have when they touch a plastic linkage that somehow embodies the geometries that underlie natural structures, regardless of whether SpongeBob or Spider-Man's face is on the toy. There's no point in making a throwaway item just because it might sell. There's got to be more to what we do than that."

—2003

# SOWING FOR
# APOCALYPSE

A cold drizzle was falling over Saint Petersburg, and the gray morning light filtered through the grimy windows of the ceremonial rooms of the Vavilov Research Institute of Plant Industry, one of the oldest seed banks—and the most storied—in the world, situated on Saint Isaac's Square. In one of the rooms, a woman in a smock sat at a table with a brown packet, and its contents, pea seeds, spilled out over the table in front of her. She did not look up from sorting through the seeds as two visitors passed, and, with her lips moving silently, she appeared to be lost in thought, or prayer.

Cary Fowler had an appointment to meet the director general of the Vavilov Institute, Nikolai Dzyubenko, in order to discuss the institute's seeds. Fowler, an American, is the world's seed banker. It's a nebulously defined position, yet a critical one. As the executive director of the Global Crop Diversity Trust, which funds the Svalbard Global Seed Vault, in Norway, Fowler was engaged in the Noah-like task of gathering the seeds of about two million varieties of food plants—both the familiar domesticated crops and many of their wild relatives—in order to create the first global seed bank.

We tend to imagine apocalypse coming in the form of a bomb, an asteroid, or a tsunami, but should a catastrophe strike one of the world's major crops, Fowler and his fellow seed bankers may be all that stand between us and widespread starvation. Any of the diseases currently active in the United States—the rust fungus attacking soybeans; the potato late blight (the same one that caused the Irish potato famine), which turns potatoes into a black mass of rot; the Western bean cutworm, which feeds on corn plants—has the potential to turn into a devastating nationwide scourge. Should that happen, the only remedy—genetic resistance—might lie in an obscure variety stored in a seed bank.

The Vavilov Institute is a monument to the extraordinary sacrifices people have made in order to save seeds. During the winter of 1941–42, when Hitler's troops were blockading Leningrad, cutting off food and supplies, the scientists who worked there protected the seeds stored inside the buildings, which amounted to several tons of nutritious food, from the starving Russians outside. At night, thousands of rats would invade the laboratories; the staff guarded the seed collections with metal rods. When some collections of potatoes needed resowing during the winter, institute workers found a plot outside Leningrad, near the front. Eventually much of the collection was smuggled out over frozen Lake Ladoga, to a hiding place in the Ural Mountains. A. G. Stchukin, a specialist in peanuts, died of starvation in the building, as did D. S. Ivanov, a rice specialist, both surrounded by thousands of packets of seeds.

The story of what happened at the Vavilov Institute has a mythic resonance in the mind of every seed banker, and Fowler glanced around almost reverently as he walked through the shadowy halls. One of his personal heroes is Nikolai Vavilov, the Russian biologist and plant breeder for whom the institute is named—and the first man to dream of creating a world seed bank. For Fowler, coming here to arrange for the institute to send seeds to the Svalbard vault in time for its opening, in February 2008, was, in a sense, finishing the job that Vavilov had started. And Vavilov himself was following in a tradition of seed saving that reaches back into prehistory.

Agriculture is thought to have begun around 8000 B.C., in the semiarid mountains of Mesopotamia. Flint sickles and grinding stones discovered in the region suggest that the first farmers collected wild grains, which were developed over time into wheat and barley. Plants were also domesticated by other civilizations in other parts of the world, almost certainly independently. In Southeast Asia, farming began with the domestication of rice, around 6500 B.C.; in Mesoamerica, maize and squash were domesticated between 8000 and 5000 B.C. In each case, a legume was domesticated along with a grain or cereal: lentils with wheat in the Mediterranean; beans with maize in South America; soybeans with rice in Asia. Eating both together provided early humans with the right balance of protein and fat. Of the 250,000 known plant species in the world, only about two hundred are cultivated for food, and the vast majority of the world's food comes from just twenty crops, in eight plant families. It is a measure of the skill of the early farmers that almost all the plants we use in agriculture today were domesticated before historical times.

From the beginning, farmers must have realized that by saving a certain portion of the seeds from the previous year's crop they could ensure themselves of a future harvest. (In Jarmo, Iraq, archeologists have found seed deposits that date from 6750 B.C.) Seed saving was one of the most important acts that a farming community performed. Seeds had to be protected from weather and animals—insects as well as mammals. One early method of preservation was to pack seeds and ash inside baskets and then bury the baskets in the ground. Seeds were also sealed inside adobe structures, and kept in elevated thatched huts. When the community moved, it took its seeds along too.

Biologically, a seed is an embryo of a plant. Around the embryo is usually a layer of endosperm, where the food for the embryo is stored, and around that is the seed coat, which protects the embryo until its moisture and heat sensors say that it is time to germinate. The embryo can survive for many years, under the right conditions, but not forever. In the 1890s, when the tombs of the Egyptian pharaohs were being opened by archeologists, hucksters tried to promote what were said to be ancient Egyptian wheat seeds—the idea being that after such a long rest the seeds would be especially productive. But there's no evidence that any of these seeds germinated.

A seed is also a plant's legs. Wind and water spread seeds, as do birds, bears, foxes, and many other animals, but man has proved to be the longest-distance distributor. When Columbus arrived in the New World in 1493, on his second voyage, he brought the seeds of plants known only in the Old World, among them wheat, onions, citrus, melons, radishes, olives, grapes, and sugarcane, and he took away seeds of plants known only in the New World, including corn, potatoes, tomatoes, peppers, pumpkins, squash, pineapples, and sweet potatoes. During the colonial period, the world's ecological boundaries were redrawn, as domesticated plants were carried far afield and used to establish agricultural economies in other parts of the world. The Royal Botanic Gardens at Kew, outside London, was the headquarters of Great Britain's botanical empire; from there, administrators coordinated the efforts of plant collectors at regional botanical stations from Jamaica to Fiji. As Lucile Brockway explains in her classic book *Science and Colonial Expansion,* published in 1979, cash crops, taken mostly from Latin America, where labor was scarce, were planted in Asia, where labor was abundant. The cinchona tree, from whose bark quinine is made, was transported from the Andes and then planted in India by the British; the anti-malarial treatment then enabled the colonization of Africa. The British also took natural rubber from Brazil, where the plant was first domesticated, and created a rubber industry in Southeast Asia that by the 1920s had greatly diminished Brazil's share of the rubber business. Sugarcane, which probably originated in India, went west and became the main plantation crop of the West Indies. Coffee from Ethiopia was domesticated and introduced to India by the Arabs, and then cultivated by the Dutch in Java. Most of the coffee that grows in Latin America today traces its ancestry to a single coffee plant from Java that was taken to the Amsterdam Botanic Garden in 1706.

Before seeing Dzyubenko, Fowler was shown around some of the old rooms by a member of the institute, a tall, thin man with a long beard. Most of the exhibits concerned the life of Vavilov, who was born in 1887, the son of a prosperous Moscow merchant. Vavilov's education as a plant breeder coincided with the rediscovery, in 1900, of the work of Gregor Mendel, an Austrian monk who had died in 1884, and whose pea-breeding experiments were overlooked during his lifetime. Mendel established the fundamental laws of inheritance, and Vavilov, among others, was prescient enough to grasp their implications. Plant breeding, which had hitherto been an art, would now be a science. By crossing and backcrossing progeny with parents in order to isolate desirable qualities—higher yields, stronger roots, frost resistance—plant breeders could select traits from a broad spectrum of varieties and combine them to create superior seeds. In order to realize the power of these new tools, however, breeders needed easy access to a large pool of genetic diversity. That was the quest to which Vavilov devoted his life. With the aim of creating hardier and higher-yielding Russian crops, Vavilov embarked on a series of expeditions to collect and catalogue ancient domesticated varieties (known as *landraces*) of wheat, barley, peas, lentils, and other crops, as well as their wild relatives, reasoning that because they were well adapted to their natural environments they must contain valuable genes that could be incorporated into Russian crops. Over the next two decades, Vavilov himself collected more than sixty thousand samples, in sixty-four countries; altogether, his teams collected 250,000 samples. The present-day collection is based on those seeds.

Most people understand crop diversity in terms of choice—it's the difference between the sweet, creamy flavor of a Gala apple and the tart, crisp taste of a Granny Smith. But agricultural diversity is much more than that; it is a record of more than ten thousand years of human experience with crops, and of the struggle to produce food in changing ecosystems and climates. Crop diversity may be the most precious natural resource we have, because, as Stephen Smith, a research fellow at Pioneer Hi-Bred, one of the world's largest seed companies, has said, "How humans use diversity in farming determines our food, our health, and our economic well-being, and that in turn determines our political security." Crops such as corn and potatoes have been forced to adapt to vastly different climates in distant places: climate change has been a constant in the lives of crops for millennia. That is why seed banks, which are the primary repositories of crop diversity, are so important: the genes in them may represent our best hope for feeding ourselves in a warming world.

Vavilov observed that crop diversity is scattered unevenly around the world. There are certain places where it is abundant—Asia Minor for wheat and barley, the Andes for potatoes—and other places, such as Russia and the United States and Northern Europe, where there is very little. Vavilov eventually mapped eight centers of diversity, loosely grouped in a belt around the planet's middle. (Scientists speculate that the last Ice Age killed off diversity in much of the Northern Hemisphere, leaving a small center around the Mediterranean, where asparagus was first domesticated, and another in Eastern Europe, where barley and peas grew in abundance.) Building on the earlier work of a Swiss botanist named Alphonse de Candolle, Vavilov developed a theory that since diversity occurs over time, the centers of greatest diversity must also be the centers of origin for those crops. In 1926 he published *The Centers of Origin of Cultivated Plants*. Vavilov's insight (which was subsequently qualified by other researchers) became the basis for national claims of sovereignty over seeds.

But war and politics prevented Vavilov from realizing his dream of a world seed bank. Like so many other Soviet scientists, he fell afoul of Stalin. Vavilov came from a wealthy family, was not a member of the Communist Party, and was friendly with Nikolai Bukharin, a rival of Stalin's. Furthermore, genetics was considered a form of "metaphysics," and geneticists the enemies of Bolshevism. Vavilov was arrested in 1940, charged with treason and espionage, and interrogated, sometimes under torture, for eleven months. His trial was held on July 9, 1941; the tribunal took only five minutes to find him guilty and sentence him to death by firing squad. Later, Vavilov's sentence was commuted to twenty years in a prison at Saratov, on the Volga River. There Vavilov died, of starvation, on January 23, 1943. He was buried in a common grave.

Fowler was familiar with these details of Vavilov's life, but he listened politely as his guide repeated them. Fowler is six feet tall, fifty-seven years old, with curly reddish hair, glasses, and a southern accent and courtliness that derive from his upbringing in Memphis, Tennessee. He had not removed his green parka—the rooms were

chilly—and he carried a briefcase, which contained artists' renderings of what the Svalbard vault will look like. Dressed in a blue
blazer, with a buttoned shirt collar hanging loosely around his neck,
he looked like a schoolboy who had spruced up for a class photograph. His eyes are deep-set, and his prominent forehead sometimes
makes it hard to discern whether they are open or shut. This morning, he looked very pale; he had told me earlier, as we left the hotel,
that he thought he was coming down with the flu. But that wasn't
going to keep him from his appointment with the director.

In addition to discussing the transfer of some of the institute's
seeds, Fowler wanted to broach the delicate subject of what condition the seeds were in. As a seed bank, the Vavilov had been in long
decline. "No one I know would claim to know what is really happening there," Fowler had written to me before the trip. "The most important question being, To what extent are the collections still alive?
Certainly much has died. But how much? Some experts in particular crops claim that a lot still exists. But for other crops we know
that the conditions of conservation/regeneration could only have led
to large losses."

Nikolai Dzyubenko occupied Vavilov's former office, on the south
side of the square. The wooden floors creaked and groaned loudly as
we approached the room. Dzyubenko wore pink-tinted glasses, and
his eyes were expressionless. He sat directly underneath a portrait
of Vavilov, whose face was smiling, eager, and full of energy and
optimism. The room looked both grand and tawdry; all the old ele-
gance had floated up to the ceiling, like smoke, and clung to the
elaborately painted plaster and the chandeliers. Fowler, gritting his
teeth against his worsening flu, took out his papers and began to
describe the Svalbard Global Seed Vault.

"It's seventy-eight degrees north, very remote, and the town has
an excellent infrastructure," he said. "There will be a big ceremony
in February, for the opening, and we'd very much like to work with
you on getting some of the Vavilov seeds sent there in time for that."
A heavyset man, who was wearing a green sweatshirt that said "Australia" in yellow letters on the front, interpreted.

Dzyubenko answered that, technically, moving the seeds to Svalbard would not be difficult, "but since we are not independent, and

since the Vavilov collection is a public treasure, this must be discussed with our superiors at the Academy of Sciences in Moscow—the decision cannot be made at this level. So it will take some time to discuss it." I glanced over at Fowler, to see if this prospect—waiting for the wheels of Russian bureaucracy to turn, before seeds from the institute could get to Svalbard—discouraged him at all. But he merely pressed his lips together, and nodded.

After their talk, Dzyubenko flung open the doors to the next room, to reveal a small feast of pastries, fruits, cold meats, cheeses, juice, and vodka that had been prepared in the American's honor. Fowler felt too queasy to eat any of it, though he did manage to touch the vodka to his lips for a toast. I thought that he would skip the tour of the storage facilities that the director had planned, but he insisted on going through with all of it, including a visit to a new cold-storage room. Another room, full of large stainless-steel liquid-nitrogen storage vats, looked impressive—until Fowler noticed that the digital readouts on all but one of the vats said "Error."

In the Bronze Age, when agriculture had become firmly established as a primary source of food, few calamities would have been as devastating to a community as the loss of its seed stores, or the destruction of its crops. But in our time we almost never hear about these kinds of catastrophes. During the United States–led invasion of Iraq in March 2003, the looting of Iraq's national archeological museum received considerable attention, but almost no one noted that the country's national seed bank was destroyed. The bank, in the town of Abu Ghraib, contained seeds of ancient varieties of wheat, lentils, chickpeas, and other crops that once grew in Mesopotamia. Fortunately, several Iraqi scientists had placed samples of the country's most important crops in a cardboard box and sent them to an international seed bank in Aleppo, Syria. There they sit, on a shelf in a cold room, waiting for a time when Iraq is stable enough to store them again.

Afghanistan's bank, which contained rare varieties of almonds and walnuts and also fruits including grapes, melons, cherries, plums, apricots, peaches, and pears—many of which originated in the region—was destroyed in the 2001 overthrow of the Taliban. Scientists in Kabul had taken the extra precaution of hiding the national seeds in the basements of two houses in the towns of Ghazni and Jalalabad. But when they returned after the fall of the Taliban they discovered that looters had dumped the seeds on the floor. "Apparently, they were after the jars," Fowler told me. Those randomly scattered seeds represented dozens, perhaps hundreds, of unique varieties—Afghanistan's agricultural heritage.

Natural disasters can also destroy seed banks. In the Philippines, a 2006 typhoon flooded a seed bank; there were reports of jars of seed floating in the ocean. In 1998 Hurricane Mitch demolished the national seed bank of Honduras. Nicaragua lost its national seed bank in the 1971 earthquake. Or banks can simply succumb to neglect.

Most of the fourteen hundred public and private seed banks in the world appear to be in a less precarious condition. There are national agriculture banks, which contain the seeds of crops grown in an individual country. There's also a network of international seed banks, funded by some sixty countries and organizations and managed by the Consultative Group on International Agricultural Research, which store specific crops. The bank in Aleppo, where the Iraqi scientists sent their seeds, has one of the world's largest collections of wheat and barley seeds. The main rice seed bank is in Los Baños, the Philippines, and the maize bank is in Mexico City. There are also banks for wildflowers, trees, and wild species of plants. Some are "ex situ"—off-site—and others are "in situ," conserved in fields. The New England Wild Flower Society preserves North American native plants in "sanctuaries" throughout the Northeast. In 2000 the British Royal Botanic Gardens launched the ex-situ Millennium Seed Bank, an ambitious project (and a favorite of Prince Charles) that includes preserving all the native seed-bearing species growing in Great Britain. There is a movement to construct banks for disappearing breeds of domesticated animals; sperm and embryos are cryogenically preserved in liquid nitrogen at a temperature of minus 196 degrees Celsius. However, when it comes to the wild species of the world, animals as well as plants, our current preservation efforts are grossly inadequate. At the G-8 summit in

Germany, in June 2007, scientists predicted that as much as two-thirds of the world's wild species could be nearly extinct by 2100 because of habitat destruction, overfishing, and climate change. The resulting explosion of pests and the loss of pollinators would be only two of the devastating consequences for agriculture.

And even a well-run bank isn't an iron-clad guarantee against extinction. Most seed banks were created as short-term storage facilities in order to develop new seeds—something like genetic libraries. In the past thirty years, they have been modified to include long-term storage facilities, which preserve varieties that are no longer grown in fields—they're more like museums or zoos. Many gene banks aren't adequately equipped or funded for long-term storage. Fowler told me, "We think that fifty percent of the unique collections in developing nations are in danger. Half. That's pretty stunning, when you think about it. As one scientist said to me, 'We call them seed banks, but actually they're more like morgues.'"

From the beginning of the United States' history, its people have been preoccupied with seeds. The early settlers faced a landscape largely devoid of domesticated crops, with the notable exception of maize, which Native Americans had brought from Central America. Among economic crops, only blueberries, cranberries, hops, and a type of sunflower originated in North America; a meal made exclusively of local ingredients would be meager. Therefore it was necessary to import plants and seeds from other countries. Thomas Jefferson, who once wrote, "The greatest service which can be rendered to any country is to add a useful plant to its culture," smuggled rice seeds out of Italy by sewing them into the lining of his coat. Just as immigration brought cultural diversity to the United States, so the immigrants brought botanical diversity, in the seeds they carried with them, which were often concealed in the brims of their hats and the hems of their dresses. In 1862, in the midst of the Civil War, Congress, at the urging of Abraham Lincoln, established the Department of Agriculture, in order to collect "new and valuable seeds and plants . . . and to distribute them among agriculturalists." Great plant explorers like David Fairchild, who was Alexander

Graham Bell's son-in-law, and Frank Meyer, for whom the Meyer
lemon is named, introduced new crops to the United States, where
they thrived.

By 1898, when the USDA established the Office of Foreign Seed
and Plant Introduction, the government was distributing some
twenty million seed packages a year to farmers. A network of state
breeding stations helped develop the most productive varieties for
each region. Beginning in the late 1940s, the government established regional seed banks that focused on individual crops: a center
in Ames, Iowa, was devoted to maize; the apple and grape research
station was in Geneva, New York; the potato center was established
in Sturgeon Bay, Wisconsin. In the 1950s the government constructed a national seed bank—the Fort Knox of seeds—in Fort
Collins, Colorado, the cornerstone of what is known today at the
National Plant Germplasm System. The bank holds nearly five hundred thousand kinds of seeds—its holdings include both varieties
grown domestically and backups for other, international collections.
It is a model for the Svalbard vault. The main storage vault is kept at
eighteen degrees below zero Celsius: the ink in my pen froze as soon
as I entered the room.

Fowler explained the basic principles of storing seeds in banks.
When the seed comes in from the field, it is sorted, labeled, cleaned,
and dried to a humidity level of about 5 percent. Dryness and cold
are the most important factors, to slow down the seed's metabolism
and to ensure that it won't germinate. Breeders' collections are generally stored at room temperature or a little below and are intended
to last for only a few years; base collections are kept at between minus ten and minus twenty degrees Celsius, a temperature at which
some seeds can live for more than a hundred years. (Grains, such as
wheat and barley, tend to live the longest.)

In any well-run bank, samples of the seeds have to be regularly
germinated to ensure that the seeds are still viable. If the germina-
tion rate drops below a certain point, new plants must be grown in
the field from the seed and new seeds collected from those plants.
"It's not too complicated, but there's a lot of labor involved, and it's
expensive," Fowler said. "Plus, there are equipment failures, poor

management, funding cuts, natural disasters, civil strife—you name it."

Fowler's interest in agriculture began on his maternal grandmother's three-hundred-acre farm near Madison, Tennessee, which he visited every summer as a boy. "There was cotton, corn, soybeans, chickens running in the backyard, a couple of milk cows—it was a real old-fashioned farm," he told me. "We'd go to the experimental plots at the local agricultural station for our seeds, and my grandmother would talk to everyone about the different varieties and make selections. She wanted me to take the farm over. She would always ask me, 'Do you want to be a farmer?' We spent a lot of time driving down dusty roads while she gave a running commentary on the quality of crops and soils, pointing things out. But I was more interested in the stuff I was studying in school—Sartre, freedom and determinism, the role of the individual in society, that kind of stuff. And I knew I wanted to be politically active, though I wasn't sure in what area."

During the school year, Fowler lived with his parents in Memphis, where his father was a defense attorney and later a judge. He took an active part in civil-rights demonstrations, and was present in the church on the night that Martin Luther King made his last speech; King was assassinated in Memphis the next day. When he graduated from Simon Fraser University, in Canada, in 1971, he received conscientious-objector status, "which greatly upset my father, who had enlisted the day after Pearl Harbor," Fowler told me. After working in a hospital in North Carolina as a clerk for about a year, he was released from service, and planned to go to Sweden to study for a Ph.D. in sociology at Uppsala University, forty miles north of Stockholm.

That year, however, Fowler discovered an oddly shaped mole on his stomach. By the time it was biopsied, the cancer had spread all over his body.

"'Do you have life insurance?' the doctor asked me," Fowler recalled.

"'No,'" I said. "'Why?'"

"'Because you have six months left to live.'"

The doctors did what they could, removing part of his stomach where the melanoma had appeared, but the prognosis was still grim.

"So I went home and waited to die," Fowler said. "Every time I'd feel the slightest twinge in my body, I'd wonder, Is this the cancer? Is it starting? Am I going to die now?" But he didn't die, and after about a year he decided, This is no way to live, and he went back to pursuing his sociology Ph.D. The doctors were so astounded that they sent Fowler to Memorial Sloan-Kettering in New York for a test of his immune system. Although it seemed to weaken when it was resisting the cancer, it became remarkably effective once the cancer started.

"Ten years later, I was given a diagnosis of testicular cancer," he said. He underwent a painful procedure that involved injecting dye into his feet and then circulating it through his lymphatic system; an X-ray would show how far the cancer had spread. "I lit up like a Christmas tree," Fowler said. "The cancer was everywhere. Though they didn't tell me at the time, they had never had a patient who had survived that kind of cancer." The doctors elected to do extensive radiation treatments; Fowler still has a map of tattoos all over his body that guided the radiation machine. Once again, Fowler told me, "The cancer just disappeared."

I asked how his cancers had influenced his work in saving seeds. Fowler replied, "The first one, I didn't handle it very gracefully. I was scared. Really scared. And the reason I was scared was that I hadn't done anything—I hadn't contributed constructively to society. And that was frightening."

Farmers began to turn away from the ancient practice of saving seeds early in the twentieth century. Plant breeders had discovered that, when two inbred lines are crossed with each other, the next generation explodes in "hybrid vigor," producing more robust plants than those that were allowed to pollinate randomly (known as "open pollination"). If the progeny of two pairs of inbred lines are themselves crossed (a "double cross"), their offspring will be even more vigorous. However, if those crosses and double crosses are then allowed to reproduce naturally, through open pollination, only a fraction of their progeny will show hybrid vigor.

Corn is among the easiest plants to hybridize, because the male parts, which are the tassels that contain the pollen, and the female parts, which are the ear and the silks, are widely separated. It is relatively simple, though labor-intensive, to cross two inbreds by sowing the two lines side by side in nearby rows, and removing male parts of the plants from one line, to ensure that it is fertilized by the other. (This method of emasculating corn plants still provides summer employment to thousands of teenagers throughout the Midwest.) American agriculturalists in general were slow to recognize the potential of hybrid corn, but several American breeders championed the new technique. One of them, Henry A. Wallace, happened to be the son of Warren Harding's Secretary of Agriculture, Henry C. Wallace, and his enthusiasm was heard in high places. In 1924 a Henry A. hybrid, which he dubbed Copper Cross, won a gold medal in the Corn Show at the Iowa Corn Yield Test. In 1926 Wallace founded the Hi-Bred Corn Company, later Pioneer Hi-Bred, to market his seeds.

Pioneer was by no means the first private seed company. A seed trade, catering to farmers who didn't want to take the time to clean and sort their seed, had existed since the early 1800s. But farmers had only to buy the seed once, and then generate more seed themselves. With hybrids, however, farmers had to buy the seed every year if they wanted to enjoy the benefits of hybrid vigor. From a commercial point of view, plant breeders had hit the jackpot—a "biological patent" on seed. Pioneer reaped the benefits of this good fortune, and eventually became the dominant seed company in the world.

In 1933 hybrid corn amounted to about 0.5 percent of the planted corn acreage in the United States. By 1945, thanks in part to promotion by the USDA, that figure had risen to 90 percent. Throughout the Depression, American farmers, who could have grown and saved their own seed by using traditional open-pollinated varieties, instead

bought hybrid seed from corn companies; the increased yields justified the expense.

Beginning in the 1940s, American-made hybrid seeds were sent
around the world as part of a vast agronomic program that came to
be known as the green revolution. Norman Borlaug, an American
plant breeder, used a strain of Japanese semidwarf wheat, known
as Norin 10, which had been bred in Japan and brought to the
United States in 1946, during the Allied occupation, to create a
wheat with a stalk short enough to support a larger, more productive head. First in Mexico, and later in Pakistan and India, Borlaug's wheat allowed local farmers to double, and in some cases
quadruple, their yields. In 1966 the International Rice Research
Institute created a variety of stunted rice called IR8, a cross of an
Indonesian type with a Chinese strain, which was widely planted
in Asia.

The green revolution was a complicated blend of altruistic and
imperial motives, played out through seeds. The notion that humans
now had the power to banish the specter of starvation and famine,
which has haunted our species for millennia, was a potent one. The
green revolution is estimated to have fed roughly a billion people
who might otherwise have starved. In developing countries, production of cereals doubled. By the mideighties, the average person in
these countries consumed 25 percent more calories per day than in
the early sixties. But the development and distribution of the superseeds, which was funded by the World Bank, the United States seed
trade, the Rockefeller Foundation, and the Ford Foundation, was
also a clever way of planting American-style agrarian capitalism in
developing nations that might otherwise be in danger of succumbing
to Communism. In Fowler's 1993 book *Shattering*, written with Pat
Mooney, a Canadian activist, he points out that the new hybrids
"produced not just crops, but replicas of the agricultural systems
that produced them. They came as a package deal and part of the
package was a major change in traditional cultures, values, and
power relationships both within villages and between them and the
outside world." Now, instead of growing crops for local consumption, farmers began growing crops for export. And, like the Ameri-

can farmers before them, Mexican, African, and Asian farmers lost the incentive for saving seed.

In 1973 Fowler started working for a journal called *Southern Exposure*. "It was dedicated to improving the image of the South, and they were working on an issue about the disappearance of family farms," he said. "I got really involved in the subject. I had grown up in these two worlds, with a love of agriculture but with no sense of how that would fit in with what I was really interested in—politics, the law, social justice. Now I began to put things together." Two years later, he became a researcher for Frances Moore Lappé, who was writing a book called *Food First*. Lappé was the author of *Diet for a Small Planet*, which became a bestseller in 1971, promulgating the message that Americans could help solve world hunger by shifting to a predominantly vegetarian diet. But, with *Food First*, Lappé wanted to analyze global food policy. Like many others, she was beginning to see that the aims of the green revolution weren't as simple as they appeared. Hunger was not only the result of a scarcity of food; it could also be caused by a production system that replaced traditional, sustainable agriculture, as practiced by peasant farmers, with a global export system that was driven by foreign agribusinesses. Lappé had rented a house in Hastings-on-Hudson, where Fowler spent a year, working with Lappé and her coauthor, Joseph Collins.

In the course of his research, Fowler read Jack Harlan's articles on the loss of crop diversity, including "The Genetics of Disaster" and "Our Vanishing Crop Genetic Resources." Harlan, a professor of genetics at the University of Illinois, argued forcefully that the adoption of modern hybrid seeds around the world was causing the traditional varieties, grown by farmers for millennia, to become extinct. Landraces were, after all, thoroughly domesticated; if they weren't cultivated, they couldn't survive. In their place, the hybrids created monocultures. And because hybrids are created by crossing purebred lines, these monocultures contained a narrower spectrum of genes. That meant that a single disease could wipe out much of the national crop. In the spring of 1970, a type of corn blight invaded cornfields in the southern United States. By the end of the year, it had killed 15 percent of the American crop; some southern states lost 50 percent of their corn. In 1972 the National Academy of Sciences released a report on the genetic vulnerability of major crops, which found that 70 percent of the United States corn crop consisted of just six varieties.

The very success of plant breeders' efforts was eliminating the raw material that made their work possible. In the United States, the nation's agricultural diversity, which had been rich in 1900, was vanishing from fields. A survey in 1983 found that, since 1903, the number of readily available varieties of cabbage dropped from 544 to 28; carrot varieties dropped from 287 to 21; cauliflower varieties fell from 158 to 9; and varieties of pears fell from 2,683 to 326. In many cases the new commercial hybrids that replaced the traditional varieties no longer tasted as good—they were bred more for production than for flavor.

Farmers, enjoying vastly greater yields with the new hybrids, couldn't be expected to go back to planting the traditional varieties. (The backlash to industrial monocultures did, however, help to inspire widespread interest in "heirloom" seeds, which began with the founding of the Seed Savers Exchange, in 1975, and also led to the creation of local farmers' markets, where at least some of the old varieties can be found.) In the case of many landraces, the only alternative to extinction was preservation in the breeders' ex-situ storage centers—the seed banks. But most of these banks were short- or medium-term storage facilities, and even the long-term centers, like the national seed bank at Fort Collins, were at the time poorly funded and staffed, and hardly qualified to serve as the last line of defense against the mass extinction of landraces.

Fowler's undergraduate thesis had focused on Jean-Paul Sartre's notion of human agency in politics, and he wanted to concentrate on the issue of genetic resource preservation. In 1977 Fowler began working with Pat Mooney, who persuaded him to direct his political activism at the principal international venue within which food-policy matters are decided—the United Nations Food and Agriculture Organization, or FAO, which is based in Rome. Together, they marshaled opposition on the issue of patenting of seeds, which had come to the fore with the passage of the United States Plant Variety Protection Act in 1970. This law, which was strengthened in 1980, and supplemented that year by a Supreme Court decision allowing the patenting of novel forms of bacteria, gave plant breeders a broad legal basis for claiming ownership of genetic resources.

As far back as Luther Burbank, the celebrated American plant breeder who was a contemporary and friend of Thomas Edison, breeders had complained about the injustice of awarding intellectual-property protection to novel mechanical devices and denying it to botanical inventions, even though a new plant might benefit millions. Soybeans, for example, which constitute the fourth-largest crop in the world, are self-pollinated, and can't be crossbred easily. Before the Plant Variety Protection Act, a breeder who wished to develop an improved variety of soybean could not expect much of a return on his investment, because farmers would have to buy the seed only once. But with the protection of the act, which made it illegal to save patented seeds, the seed industry could justify much greater investment in research and development, because farmers would have to buy new seed or pay a license fee every year.

From the perspective of many developing nations, however, the American-led movement to patent seeds was an outrage. The industrialized countries of the North, having helped themselves to genes from the centers of diversity in the South, and having used them to create agricultural industries, were now asking the South to buy those genes back, in the form of patented seeds. According to Jack Kloppenburg, a professor of rural sociology at the University of Wisconsin, crops that originated in the Near East and Latin America make up 66 percent of global food crop production; crops originating in North America and Europe represent less than 5 percent, combined. The North was guilty of "bio-piracy"—a slogan that became popular in the 1980s. Armed with Vavilov's theory that the centers of diversity must be the centers of origin, India, Brazil, and Iran, among other countries, began to press their case in the FAO for sovereignty over these resources. If the North wanted to claim ownership of patented seeds, the South would claim ownership of the genes from which those seeds were made. The Seed War was engaged.

By the mideighties, a "genetic OPEC" had begun to take shape. On coffee plantations in Central America, where a disease called coffee rust was a common threat, breeders wanted to return to Ethiopia, the origin of the coffee plant, and find a variety within the seed bank there that would be rust-resistant. But Ethiopia wouldn't allow breeders access to the coffee genes stored in its seed bank. The Jamaican government refused to allow the genes of allspice to be exported; India did the same with black pepper and turmeric seeds; Ecuador locked up its cacao seeds; Taiwan embargoed sugarcane; and Iran denied the world access to its pistachio collection.

Back in 1979, Fowler and Mooney had begun attending the FAO's annual conferences in Rome. The FAO, which was heavily weighted with Third World representatives, offered a mostly sympathetic forum to the notion of seeds as a genetic commons, part of the shared heritage of humanity, and it was generally hostile to the notion of seeds as commodities. At the 1981 conference, the Mexican delegation, having consulted with Fowler and Mooney, proposed the idea of an international seed bank. It would contain seeds from national and international seed banks, and patented seeds created by private seed companies. The North could have free access to the seeds from the centers of diversity only if the South could have free access to the patented seeds. This proposal was enthusiastically embraced by many developing nations, and at the 1983 conference, the international seed bank became a central part of a nonlegally binding document known as the International Undertaking on Plant Genetic Resources for Food and Agriculture, which was signed by more than a 110 countries around the world.

The bank was denounced by seed companies in the United States and other developed countries. The American Seed Trade Association said that the Undertaking "strikes at the heart of free enterprise and intellectual property rights." Seedsmen argued that patented seeds represented an enormous investment of labor and capital on their part; the unimproved coffee seeds in Ethiopia's seed bank weren't valuable until that investment was made. But Fowler maintained that even primitive landraces represented many generations of selection by farmers who lived around the centers of diversity, going back thousands of years. As he wrote in his book *Unnatural*

*Selection,* which was published in 1994, "Can we really say that the modern plant breeder who turns out a disease-resistant tomato, wheat, or rice variety has done something more grand or worthy of reward than the farming community that first identified and conserved the disease-resistant characteristic in its fields?" He and Mooney began to advocate the concept of "farmers' rights," demanding a monetary system that would recognize the contributions made by farmers in developing nations from which the seeds were taken. As Fowler explained to me, "We were pointing out how unfair it was that after a century and a half of free and unimpeded gene flow from South to North, for the North to come along and say, okay, now you have to pay for the genes—genes we took from you—because now we have a patent on them."

Gene splicing, first performed by Stanley Cohen and Herbert Boyer in 1973, allowed seed companies to offer a limitless range of products. Today's plant breeders can incorporate genes from plants that are not sexually compatible with each other. Indeed, because all living things share the same coded language of DNA, breeders can choose genes from outside the plant kingdom altogether—genes from bacteria, and even from fish, were used to create new kinds of genetically modified organisms, or GMOs. This technology, in turn, led to a new type of seed company, the avatar of which is Monsanto, an agrichemical corporation headquartered in Saint Louis, which is the largest seed company in the world; other leading seed corporations include Bayer, Syngenta, and Dow, all of which have roots in the chemical or the pharmaceutical sector rather than in the seed trade. Whereas Pioneer was a seed company that turned to genetic engineering as a way of improving its product—seeds—Monsanto was a chemical company that saw seeds as a delivery vehicle for its product, which was genes. Instead of creating seeds through hybridization, as Pioneer did, Monsanto would license genetically engineered traits to seed companies. Monsanto's Bt corn, which was introduced in the midnineties, incorporated genes taken from a soil bacterium, *Bacillus thuringiensis,* that provides these Bt crops with resistance to certain pests. In 2006, about 40 percent of the U.S. corn crop was Bt corn. Food made with this and other types of genetically modified organisms is sold in virtually every supermarket in the United States, and does not require labeling. However, in Europe, and in some other parts of the world, GMOs have attracted widespread protest by consumer groups and are subject to much tougher regulations.

The consolidation of the seed industry, which began in the 1970s, has continued in the era of genetic engineering; 55 percent of the seeds used to grow the world's food are sold by just ten global corporations. Large amounts of capital are required to create today's superseeds: biotech companies estimate that the research and regulatory costs of getting a single new genetically engineered trait on the market are as much as a hundred million dollars; a seed that offers two or three "stacked" traits—the state of the art in seed technology—may cost three hundred million dollars. These new seeds could help us cope with climate change and population growth, by producing crops designed to survive on less water, in hotter conditions, with even greater yields. At Pioneer Hi-Bred, which was bought by DuPont in 1999, three quarters of the company's seeds are GMOs; corn plants are being developed for increased ethanol production, drought tolerance, and resistance to rootworm, corn borer, and fungal disease. Many new plant varieties are being designed for industrial uses. Corn, soybeans, sunflowers, and canola can all be used in the production of ethanol and biodiesel. Soybeans are being developed to produce higher yields of oil for ink, with an aim toward replacing traditional petroleum-based inks used in printing. In the United States, corn yields continue to rise; in 2006, American farmers produced nearly 11 billion bushels, with an average yield of 149 bushels an acre. Worldwide, a new green revolution could be in the offing.

The bad news is that the rest of the world isn't as enthusiastic about the new superseeds, perhaps because some countries are still coping with the social consequences of the last green revolution. Other countries worry about the long-term effects of GMOs, which are banned from some markets. Many Europeans feel that genetic engineering is still too new and untested, and too many things could go wrong, from the unwanted pollination of conventional plants by the GMO plants, to unexpected health and dietary effects caused by eating GMO food, to an unforeseen blight that could wipe out a GMO monoculture. Moreover, the old idea of feeding the world's hungry masses, which helped sell the first green revolution, hasn't been embraced as warmly this time. Instead, there is suspicion among developing nations that such talk is all an elaborate "double cross." As Jack Kloppenburg wrote in 2004, in his book *First the Seed*, "The powerful tools of biotechnology are now being wielded largely by a narrow set of corporations which claim to want to use them to eliminate hunger, protect the environment, and cure disease, but which in fact simply want to use them as quickly as they can to make money just as fast as possible."

Plant breeders and seedsmen bitterly criticized Fowler and Mooney for politicizing the debate about genetic resources. By indirectly encouraging developing nations to deny plant breeders access to their seed banks, the activists were placing the responsibility for the conservation of those resources with countries whose unstable or dysfunctional governments couldn't be counted on to take the necessary measures. Many scientists felt that politics had no place in decisions about genetic conservation. Few wanted the governance of agricultural plants to follow the route that was eventually taken to guide the trade in medicinal plants—the Convention on Biological Diversity, which took effect in 1993. With the CBD, nations like Brazil, whose rain forests have long drawn bioprospectors looking for new plant-based drugs and therapies, affirmed sovereignty over the genes within their borders. That system makes some sense when applied to the production of pharmaceuticals, which are distributed to narrowly focused markets, but not to food, which is a worldwide resource. Even the countries within the centers of diversity depend heavily on imported crops to feed their populations. A similar treaty for world agriculture might mean that, in order to develop a variety of wheat using strains from numerous countries, individual agreements would have to be negotiated with every country. That was unthinkable.

At an FAO meeting that Fowler attended in 1981, the octogenarian

Sir Otto Frankel, who was then among the world's most prominent plant scientists, angrily denounced Fowler in a Roman restaurant. Fowler told me, "Here I thought I was trying to do something good, and so to have one of the leading lights in the field just go off on me really made me question what I was doing." Among the people who witnessed the confrontation was Jack Harlan, who had inspired Fowler to take up the cause of genetic resources in the first place. Later, after Frankel left, Fowler went on, "I asked Harlan if he thought we were doing something that was bad, unproductive, destructive, and he said, 'I would never tell you that,' and then he said, 'They're going to fight you and call you names for five years, then there will be a period when things get a little bit better, and then in ten to fifteen years they will adopt all of your ideas but claim the credit for it themselves.' And that's pretty much what happened. At the third International Technical Conference, in 1983, I was viewed as a dangerous radical, and by the fourth conference, in 1996, I was in charge."

In 1993 the FAO hired Fowler to oversee the drafting of a Global Plan of Action for the Conservation and Sustainable Utilization of Plant Genetic Resources—a first step toward a rational, worldwide seed-bank management plan. The International Treaty on Plant Genetic Resources for Food and Agriculture, which was adopted by the UN in 2001 and has been ratified by most of the countries of the world, laid the legal groundwork for a global seed bank. The treaty was both a victory and a defeat for Fowler. It recognized a version of the concept of "farmers' rights," and established a system of compensation for genes used in the creation of patented seeds. However, in return, the developing nations agreed to drop their opposition to the principle of patenting seeds. In effect, Fowler had compromised one of his original principles, common heritage, in order to achieve the other.

Fowler and his colleagues knew where they wanted the vault to be—on the Norwegian archipelago of Svalbard. Although Norway took sovereignty over Svalbard in 1925, the archipelago has a long tradition as an international *terra nullius*—a no-man's-land. In the early 1980s, a backup site for the Nordic Gene Bank was created in a coal mine near the town of Longyearbyen. It contained the seeds from the five Nordic countries—Iceland, Finland, Norway, Sweden, and Denmark. Norway had proposed expanding the facility into a world seed vault, but with the Seed War then raging, the idea was untenable. Now, however, with the treaty in place, and with a rising awareness of the ecological threat posed by climate change, the idea of an ultimate backup to all the other seed banks—a Doomsday vault—seized the imagination of officials in both Norway and Rome. In June 2006, the groundbreaking ceremony at Svalbard was widely covered in the press all over the world.

The vault is not the seed bank that Fowler envisaged back in the eighties—a common bowl from which the world could feed as one. Far from it: each nation will have access to only its own seeds. Nor does the vault much resemble the world bank that Vavilov envisioned—a kind of breeders' utopia, in which the seeds of every kind of food plant in the world are available. In 2006 thirty million new acres of GMOs were planted, bringing the total worldwide acreage to 252 million acres—about 7 percent of the world's crop-land. Altogether, more than ten million farmers from twenty-two countries planted biotech crops in 2006. But few, if any, of these seeds were going into the Svalbard vault. Seed companies had shown little interest in putting them there, and in any case, Norway severely restricts bringing GMOs into the country, even though, as Fowler put it to me, the seeds in the vault would be kept in "multi-ply packages, inside sealed boxes, inside an air-lock chamber, behind multiple locked doors, inside a mountain, frozen to minus twenty, in an Arctic environment in which no seed would survive even if it escaped."

As the use of biotech crops continues to grow, the seeds in the vault will represent an ever-smaller share of the seeds actually growing in fields around the world. An apt symbol of this is what happened in Iraq, the birthplace of agriculture, following the United States–led invasion. Even though Iraq's traditional varieties were preserved in Aleppo, the United States encouraged the use of seeds provided by American companies, many of them GMOs, which were distributed by the United States military as part of Operation Amber

Waves. Order 81, issued in 2004 by Paul Bremer, the head of the Coalition Provisional Authority, prohibited Iraqi farmers from reusing these seeds, forcing them instead to purchase licenses from corporations to receive new seed each year.

I accompanied Fowler to Svalbard to visit the site of the Doomsday vault. We flew from Oslo to Longyearbyen, a settlement of some two thousand inhabitants, and the northernmost destination on earth serviced by regularly scheduled flights; it's about eight hundred miles from the North Pole. From the air, I could see the craggy, snow-covered peaks thrusting some five thousand feet into the air—the mountain range discovered by the Dutch explorer Willem Barents in 1596, when he ran into it while trying to sail over the top of the world. For the next two hundred years, Svalbard was an international center of whaling, but by the end of the eighteenth century the bowhead whale had been hunted to extinction in these waters. In the eighteenth and nineteenth centuries, Svalbard was used by hunters, mainly Russians and Norwegians, whose greatest prize was the thick white coats of the polar bears that roamed the islands and the surrounding ice floes. (The polar bears survived, barely, although now climate change is threatening them with extinction once again.) The huts of some of the most famous hunters and trappers of the era remain, scattered on the snow.

Longyearbyen is on Spitsbergen, the largest of the islands, which means "jagged mountains" in Dutch. Its regular inhabitants live in neat wooden structures that are painted in bright colors. In the early twentieth century, Svalbard became a center of coal mining, and on the crags above the town, the old mining trellises, which were used to bring coal out of the mines, can be seen: stark structures with thick cables strung between them. There is still some mining on Spitsbergen, but these days the Longyearbyen economy is driven mainly by the thousands of tourists who come during the summer months to explore one of the last true wildernesses in Europe, and to watch the Fourteenth of July glacier, at Krossfjord, on the northern side of Spitsbergen, calve into the Barents Sea.

Rune Bergstrom, the chief environmental officer for Svalbard, drove us to the site of the vault, halfway up one of the mountains visible from Longyearbyen. As we left town, he pointed out the graves of miners who died in the influenza epidemic of 1918. Scientists hoping to study the virus had taken tissue samples from the bodies in 1998. We followed a winding road up a steep ridge that was lightly covered with a fine, dry snow—a kind of Arctic sand. Along the road we saw two Svalbard reindeer: odd, goat-size animals, with comically stunted legs and long, awkward-looking antlers.

The vault is tunneled into the sandstone rock face of one of the mountains, near the old mine in which the backup to the Nordic Gene Bank is stored. The design is straightforward: from the entrance, a long tube lined with steel and concrete leads straight back to three large rectangular concrete rooms, which houses the seeds, on shelves. Surrounding the entrance of the shaft is a twenty-seven-foot-tall concrete structure. A series of colored lights are embedded in the top—an artist's installation. In November, as the four-month-long polar night settles over Svalbard, the lights begin to pulse, producing a curtain of light that changes according to the lighting conditions of the Arctic. It is visible far across the Barents Sea, out on the ice floes that the polar bears roam. When the sun returns, in late February, the lights go out and the reflective surface glows with the light of the never-setting sun.

To get a better sense of what it felt like to be deep inside the mountain, we visited the Nordic bank. It was a relatively warm day—about twenty degrees Fahrenheit. In a mining shed, we donned blue overalls, helmets, headlamps, and gas masks, and followed a miner down the abandoned mine, stepping carefully over railway trestles on the tunnel floor. From time to time, we could see black seams of unmined coal in the walls. About two hundred yards in, we came to a large wooden door, which was frozen shut. The miner pounded on it with a sledgehammer until finally it swung open to reveal a smaller door, which was also frozen. Behind that was a large black steel cage, filled with crates. Frost covered the bars, and the ice crystals glistened in the beam of our headlamps. Fowler climbed inside the cage and opened one of the wooden lids. Inside, packed in foam peanuts, were sealed glass ampules, with acquisition numbers etched in the frosty glass. The ampules contained seeds, about five hundred of each variety, of 237 species.

Back outside, I wondered what would happen if the sea levels rise as much as some scientists predict they will. "We are a hundred and thirty meters above sea level," Fowler replied, his breath frosting. "The max sea-level rise under the worst-case climate-change scenario is eighty meters, so whatever happens the seeds should be safe." But who can predict what will happen if the ice melts? A northern sea lane could open year-round between Europe and Asia (the passage that Willem Barents was looking for in 1596, when his vessel became trapped in the ice), and Svalbard could take on the strategic importance that Malta held for centuries, when it was a midpoint between the Christian and Islamic worlds. Will the seeds themselves be viable in a world that warm? Even if they can grow, they won't have evolved the defenses necessary to ward off all the new pests and diseases that will appear. On the other hand, perhaps a few of the seeds inside the vault will hold the answers for the farmers of the future. "When you think about it, the plants have already been there," Fowler said. "When Columbus brought maize to Europe—that was a climate change. When maize then went to Africa, that was a climate change. We need to figure out how the plants were able to adapt to these changes, and repackage those traits."

Far away in the distance, I could see one of the old hunters' shacks, and I thought of the bowhead whale, hunted to extinction by eighteenth-century whalers, and of the polar bears, struggling for survival on the ice floes. Species extinction seems to be the baseline in humanity's relationship with the natural world; the notion of sanctuary is a relatively new and tenuous idea. But Fowler's craggy face, seen against the mountains, showed no trace of doubt.

—2007

# THE TREE OF ME

Why is it that in the United States, the first country in the world to overthrow the accident of birth, people are so fascinated with their ancestors? According to a Maritz poll, 120 million Americans are interested in family history. The National Genealogical Society estimates that family history is now the second most popular hobby in the United States, after gardening. Genealogy is also the second most searched-for subject on the Web. (Porn, of course, is No. 1.) FamilySearch.com, a database maintained by the Church of Jesus Christ of Latter-Day Saints, had more than five billion hits in its first two years of existence. Many of the Web-based family-history sites combine rich genealogical resources with naked hucksterism. At www.familyheritageshop.com, for example, you can get a detailed history of your surname, but only if you buy it on a piece of parchment, such as the "Family Name History Masterpiece Scroll," for nineteen dollars and ninety-five cents. As the family Web site gradually takes the place of the family Bible as the standard repository of family history, the controlling structure for the family seems to be evolving from a tree into something more like a root system, hairy with adoptive parents, two-mommy families, sperm-bank daddies, and other kinds of family appendages that don't fit onto trunks and branches.

Genealogy serves two often incompatible human impulses: the

desire for self-knowledge and the desire for status. On the one hand, genealogists ask the most profound questions we can ask about ourselves—Where did we come from? and Where are we going? On the other hand, genealogy is the oldest form of social climbing in the world. Long before the ancient Hebrews put their genealogies in writing in order to prove they were the "chosen people," humans have claimed status and inherited privilege by establishing the superiority of their forebears. The longevity of the British aristocracy, in which a relative few enjoy the majority of the property and wealth, is due in part to the persistent belief that entitlement is inherited "in the blood."

Our Founding Fathers abolished the hereditary aristocracy, but in its place we have an extraordinary variety of hereditary societies. There are early-settler societies, Colonial societies (both Revolutionary and Tory), religious societies, and ethnic societies—everything from the National Society of Daughters of the Barons of Runnemede ("for women of lineal descent from one or more of the barons who served as sureties of the Magna Carta in 1215") to the Society of the Descendants of Washington's Army at Valley Forge. In New York, the headquarters of many of the city's hereditary societies are at the New York Genealogical and Biographical Society, a stately Italianate building on East Fifty-eighth Street, where the quaint practices of New Yorkers long dead are preserved. At meetings of the Holland Society of New York (for male descendants of residents of New Netherland before 1675), a stuffed-beaver mascot, symbol of the fur trade, is carried around the room by a color guard while one of the guardsmen proclaims, "Gentlemen, the Beaver!"

Recently, new ways of identifying ancestors have been developed using DNA analysis. In addition to containing a complete set of instructions for the creation and maintenance of life, DNA is a vast new archive of human history, one that can be used both for answering questions about one's own ancestors and for shedding light on the ancestry of the human species. In our DNA is a history of genetic heritage that includes not only our human ancestors but also our chimpanzee ancestors, our fish ancestors, and our protozoan ancestors, going all the way back to LUCA (an acronym for "last universal common ancestor")—a thermophilic bacterium that lived some four billion years ago, whose DNA all living things share.

But if DNA can help us discover who we are, it can also tell us who we aren't. If the only purpose of genealogy were biological ancestry, then the surname should follow the mother's line because, as any genealogist will tell you, the father is only ever the presumptive parent, whereas the mother is almost always the genetic one. The rate of false paternity in the United States is estimated to be between 2 and 5 percent—not large, but over ten generations the likelihood that a bloodline suffers what geneticists refer to as a "nonpaternity event" could approach 50 percent. This means that many of the fancy pedigrees cherished by great families may not, biologically speaking, be accurate. In the age of DNA, the Daughters of the Barons of Runnemede may end up belonging to the Daughters of the Paleozoic Invertebrates instead.

I have been a casual family historian for quite a while, but I was not a serious researcher into my own genealogy until I became a father, an ancestor in my own right—no longer a tender young shoot on the family tree but a stouter limb farther back. I don't exactly know why I am so interested in my ancestors. It's not as if I were particularly intimate with my parents, siblings, and cousins. We are close in an unspoken way, but there's a lot about them that I don't know, and that they don't know about me, and most of us seem to be reasonably content with this arrangement. But the lure of ancestors is not like the desire for intimacy with relatives. Ancestors are mostly dead, and while this is the main problem with them—they rarely left behind adequate records of their thinking at crucial junctures in their lives—it is also what makes obsessing about them acceptable. They are less likely to embarrass you, or to show up and stay with you.

Like many Americans, I first became interested in my "crossing ancestors"—the forebears who made the passage from the Old World to this one. Almost every family has a crossing story of some kind to tell: it's the story of the way we became Americans. In African-American family history, the crossing is a nightmare of oppression, and for many other families it is a story of hardship and persecution. But it is also a source of pride, because it's the start of a kind of spiritual pedigree.

Crossing stories are rarely written down. They usually exist in the oral legends that families tell about how they got here, in which truth often yields to a good story and an illustrious forebear.

My paternal crossing ancestor—the one who brought my branch of the Seabrooks to these shores—was easier to trace than my maternal ancestor (a Toomey), because recordkeeping favors the male line. He was my great-great-grandfather Samuel Seabrook. Samuel came with his family from England sometime between 1855 and 1860, far too late to qualify our family for any of the hereditary societies. My father seems to feel that our family didn't cross soon enough, and for many years he has hoped to prove a connection between our line and the storied South Carolina Seabrooks. Their crossing ancestor, Captain Robert Seabrook, came around 1675, and the family owned several large plantations on the sea islands of Edisto, Johns, and Seabrook, off the Carolina coast, before its fortunes were wrecked by the Civil War. According to the story my father heard from his father, a son of the Carolina Seabrooks could have been sent back to England, to be educated at Cambridge University, where he became an abolitionist. His slave-owning family disowned him, and so he settled in the nearby county of Suffolk, where Samuel's family came from.

Virtually everything I know about my Seabrook ancestors is from a genealogy that my grandfather commissioned from a professional genealogist in London, and which he paid the American Historical Company to include in a sixty-five-volume tome called *Colonial and Revolutionary Lineages of America,* published in 1954. My grandfather was a self-made man, and like many other Americans of undistinguished origin who achieve some eminence in the world, at a certain point in his life he found himself wanting the ancestors he deserved. Even though our Seabrook lineage is neither Colonial nor Revolutionary, the American Historical Company counted it among its elite, who are, according to the volumes' foreword, "those who sound their belief in the principles upon which our country was founded, and their adherence to the lofty aims and ideals that were written into the early documents of our government." We all believe that men are created equal, goes the logic here, but let's not forget that some of us believed it first.

Shortly after my son was born, in 1998, I began to try to sort out what about this family history was fact and what was fiction. The following details seemed accurate. Samuel was born in England in 1815. His father was the Reverend Thomas Seabrook, who was the curate of a church in Denston, a village in Suffolk about twenty miles east of Cambridge. Thomas's father, a farmer named John, was born in the same area in 1746, and died there in 1801; John's father, Richard, also came from there, although there was no record of his birth. Beyond Richard, nothing, although my grandfather had somehow convinced the editor that he should include a legend about an earlier ancestor who happened to share my grandfather's name:

> According to tradition, in the time of Charles II there resided in Wood Ditton, now a part of Newmarket in Suffolk, Charles Seabrook, a doctor. On an occasion when the king was traveling nearby his coach overturned, and the monarch suffered a broken arm and shoulder blade. Dr. Seabrook was summoned, and did his work so well that he was brought back to London where he was made Chief Surgeon to the King.

I do not know why Samuel came to America. All I know is that Samuel's first wife, Clara Peters, had died, and he and his second wife, Fanny Peaters, were married in 1855, in London, where, according to the marriage certificate, Samuel was working as a "warehouseman." Sometime in the next five years, they emigrated, with two of his children from the first marriage and one of their own. On arriving in New York, they found their way up the Hudson River and settled in Rhinebeck. Here, according to family legend, Samuel worked as a caretaker for Horace Greeley, the famous editor of *The New York Tribune*. This seems highly unlikely, since Greeley's farm was in Chappaqua, eighty-five miles downstate from Rhinebeck, but I have always liked the detail. On East Nineteenth Street in New York, which was the site of Greeley's residence when he was in town and where, 130 years later, I lived on first moving to the city, I used to walk along the street imagining different scenarios in which Greeley and my great-great-grandfather might have met.

At some point in the 1860s, Samuel went down to the far southwestern corner of New Jersey, to a part of the state so rural and untraveled that even today hardly anyone knows it's there, and he settled among the truck farmers and muskrat trappers near the Cohansey River. Why here, of all places, I have always wanted to know. Whatever the reason, it is where my family has lived ever since, and it's where I grew up. Samuel died not long after he arrived, in January of 1871, and was buried in what is known as a "stranger's grave," at the back of the Presbyterian church in the village of Upper Deerfield. A brook running behind the graveyard has overflowed many times since Samuel was placed in it, and whatever stone marked the grave has long since been washed away.

One hot summer afternoon, I went into the Irma and Paul Milstein Division of U.S. History, Local History, and Genealogy in the New York Public Library. The Milstein Division is in a narrow, high-ceilinged room that used to house the science-and-technology collection, and the terra-cotta tiles there felt cool on the stifling day. My purpose was to search the census records and see if I could find some mention of Samuel's existence. The index for the 1860 census is on the open shelves, and I found the listings for Dutchess County, where Rhinebeck is situated. I could find no Seabrook, but there was a Samuel "Seabrood." The index gave a number, 934, which corresponded to the page on which Seabrood's entry could be found.

The actual census records are on microfilm, stored in large metal filing cabinets in Room 119, next to the main genealogy room. The tables are filled with microfilm readers. The cowl-like, vaguely ecclesiastical shape of the machines, the users' supplicant posture, and the dim light make research in Room 119 feel a little like prayer. As I scanned the names of the dead, the spooled microfilm whirring, the realization that my life too will soon end washed over me. This was not the pleasant sensation of melancholy that comes from wandering around in cemeteries, where grass and old worn stones offer a kind of sensual comfort. This was a complete disaster: everyone was gone.

It was hard to read the faded numbers at the tops of the pages, but after some hunting around I found page 934, and there was Samuel Seabrook—it was definitely a *k* and not a *d*—along with a wife and a daughter and two male children, living in Dutchess County, New York, on April 21, 1860, the day the census-taker came to visit. The age was right, forty-five, and the country of origin,

England, and place of dwelling, Rhinebeck, all matched the information I already had. Under "Occupation" there was a word that
looked like *herdsman,* or maybe *handyman.* This discovery was un-
expectedly thrilling, and I made a sound, a sound I have since heard
others make in Room 119: a sort of exultant grunt that arises spon-
taneously when you "get" an ancestor. It was like finding something
that has been lost for a long time—a kind of redemption.

That was a promising beginning, but after a lot more searching in
libraries and archives I didn't learn anything new. The genealogist my grandfather had hired seemed to have found what could be
found in the records, and the more tantalizing but undocumented
material—the doctor from Wood Ditton, the employment with
Greeley—I could neither prove nor disprove. If only there were another way to trace ancestry, a method that didn't rely on the vagaries
of records and on the whims of forebears who invented or destroyed
documents in order to make themselves more impressive to their
descendants. In the hope of finding one, I began to surf the new
DNA-based genealogical sites on the Web.

I found a number of services offering DNA-fingerprint tests,
mostly for the purpose of proving paternity. In this procedure, lab
technicians examine a representative number of sites spread throughout the chromosomes in the human genome. Humans have twenty-
three pairs of chromosomes—tightly coiled double-helix ladders of
information inside the nucleus of almost all human cells—one set
each from the mother and the father. Chromosomes are sequences
of chemical compounds, or "bases"—adenine, cytosine, guanine,
and thymine, designated by the letters A, C, G, and T—and by re-
cording these sequences scientists can derive a unique genetic fin-
gerprint for every individual on earth.

For years, a suspicious father's only recourse was to make jokes
about the milkman; now he can log on to www.genetree.com and
send away for the GeneSwab Specimen Collection Kit, which includes DNA swabs in three pastel colors, and promises an answer in
seven to ten business days ($290 for the first test; $125 for each additional child). Gene Tree also offers a complete line of products to

test your brothers and sisters and your grandparents, as well as SecureGene DNA Banking, which archives your DNA. There's even ToothFairy DNAPassport for storing the kids' DNA.

However, while DNA fingerprinting can establish a pattern of genetic inheritance between people who are separated by one generation, it doesn't work if you're trying to locate a characteristic genetic signature in distant relatives, or among putative family members who lived hundreds, or even thousands, of years apart. This is because during the formation of sperm in men and eggs in women, the paired chromosomes in the nucleus exchange DNA randomly, a process known as recombination. Shuffling the deck like this contributes to a varied gene pool, but it also makes DNA fingerprints very difficult to trace over many generations.

There is one chromosome, the Y, carried only by men, that does not undergo recombination and remains essentially unchanged, except by rare mutations, as it is passed down through the male line. Since Y chromosomes and surnames are both handed down through the male line in Western culture, genealogists have the opportunity to match the record in our genes with the written records, and to use the former to bridge gaps and dead ends in the latter. In 1997, for example, an ingenious amateur genealogist named Dr. Eugene A. Foster realized that he could use a Y-chromosome test to help settle a genealogical controversy—whether Thomas Jefferson really did father a child with his slave Sally Hemings—that had kept a cottage industry of historians busy for more than a century. As Foster reported in *Nature* in 1998, tests comparing the Y chromosome of male descendants of Sally Hemings with the Y chromosome of proven descendants of Jefferson showed that there was a strong probability that Hemings's youngest son, Eston, was a Jefferson. (However, the Monticello Association, which oversees the graveyard for lineal descendants of Thomas Jefferson, still won't let any of the Hemings descendants be buried there, partly on the ground that the common ancestor could have been a different Jefferson.)

The Y has also been used to prove ancient tribal affiliations. According to the Old Testament, the descendants of Aaron, the older brother of Moses, are part of the priestly tribe of Jews known as the Cohanim (*cohan* means "priest" in Hebrew). The priesthood could pass only from father to son, and for the last three thousand years or so certain Jewish men have been telling their sons that they are Cohanim. Michael Hammer, a geneticist at the University of Arizona, sampled about three hundred Jewish men, and as he and his collaborators reported in a 1997 paper, "Y Chromosomes of the Jewish Priests," published in *Nature,* more than 50 percent of the men whose fathers had told them they were Cohanim shared a similar signature on their Y chromosomes, while only 10 percent of the non-Cohanim had that signature. Another study used the Y as a kind of molecular clock to approximate how far back the common ancestor of all these Cohanim lived, calculating that the man was alive between 2,100 and 3,250 years ago, which is consistent with the dates given for Moses and Aaron in the Old Testament. At www .FamilyTreeDNA.com, Hammer's Cohanim test is available to anyone who would like to find out if he has the priestly gene.

Perhaps the most dramatic example so far of the potential of Y-chromosome-based family history was demonstrated in 2000 by Bryan Sykes, who is a professor of human genetics at Oxford University, and a colleague, Catherine Irven. Sykes and Irven obtained DNA from forty-eight male Sykeses, who were not, as far as the respondents knew, related either to Dr. Sykes or to each other. By studying the men's Y chromosomes, Sykes discovered, to his astonishment, that there was a distinctive Sykes-family signature on the Y chromosomes of twenty-one of the forty-eight men tested. Four other Sykeses were only one mutation away from those twenty-one. In a paper on the study, published in *The American Journal of Human Genetics* in April 2000, Sykes reasoned that since the DNA of the remaining Sykeses was not at all similar, there was probably one original founder of the surviving Sykes line, and that the unrelated Sykeses must be the results of a steady accumulation of nonpaternity events or adoptions. Sykes was offering a commercial version of that test, called Y-Line, on a Web site, www.oxfordancestors.com, where the motto was "We put the gene in genealogy."

It occurred to me that the Y-chromosome test could answer my father's question of whether our Seabrooks are related to the South

Carolina Seabrooks. In order for it to work, I would need to find a patrilineal descendant of Captain Robert Seabrook, persuade him to give me his DNA, and compare his Y chromosome with mine. After logging a number of hours on the Web, I found, at one of the thousands of surname-based chat rooms—www.genforum.com/seabrook—the e-mail address of Jeffrey Scott Seabrook, a resident of Argyle, Texas, who has a well-documented paper trail leading to the South Carolina Seabrooks and all the way back to Captain Robert, Jeffrey's great-great-great-great-great-great-grandfather. I sent Jeffrey an e-mail, and he sent me his cell, work, and home phone numbers. I reached him in his car and explained that I needed a little more of his information—his DNA. Not a problem, Jeffrey said. "I used to work for a company that helped develop DNA-testing kits," he said. "So I know what this DNA stuff is about."

I looked for some other male Seabrooks to sample. According to a database of telephone directories on www.ancestry.com, there are 830 Seabrooks listed in the United States. Seabrook is not so rare a surname as Crapper (29 listings) or Lump (63), but it is not so common as Bundy (3,963) or Reed (91,414) or Adams (142,720). At any rate, it is uncommon enough that whenever I meet another Seabrook we are quick to exchange family histories to see if our respective branches might be connected by a common ancestor. The Internet has made these random encounters much more likely, and in recent years I have received e-mails from Seabrooks around the world, each trying to find his place in the larger family tree, if indeed one exists. The most active of these family e-storians are Australian Seabrooks, followed closely by Canadians, then by Americans, and finally by British Seabrooks. The general rule seems to be that the farther the bearers of a name get from its motherland the more interested in their roots they become.

It wasn't easy to find Seabrooks around New York who were willing to give me their DNA. First of all, many of the Seabrooks living in New York City are black. This is a cultural legacy of slavery, and specifically of the South Carolina Seabrooks, who at the height of their fortunes owned more than a thousand slaves, some of whom took the name Seabrook on being freed. Larry Seabrook is a former state senator whose district was in the Bronx and part of Westchester. Norman

Seabrook is the head of the city correction officers' union ("New York's Boldest"). It is remotely possible that these Seabrooks share some of my DNA, but it seemed insensitive to ask them to take the test in order to find out. (I did fax Senator Seabrook's office, asking for his DNA, and followed up with several calls that were not returned.)

If I hoped to discover a Seabrook signature from a relatively small sample, I would probably have more success if I sampled Seabrooks living near the place where our common ancestor—the original Mr. Seabrook—might have lived. This is how Sykes had conducted his study: he obtained DNA from Sykeses in Yorkshire, Lancashire, and Cheshire, where, historical records show, the name Sykes comes from (the word means "moorland stream" in Old English) and where the largest concentration of Sykeses in England still live. The results of Sykes's study appeared to confirm the research of George Redmonds, a British-surname historian and the author of *Surnames and Genealogy: A New Approach,* published in 1997. According to Redmonds, in many cases even relatively common surnames derive from a single ancestor, rather than from multiple progenitors, as is generally believed.

Redmonds came to the May 2000 annual conference of the National Genealogy Society, held in the Rhode Island Convention Center in Providence, to give a talk on DNA testing and its role in genealogy, and I took the train up from New York City to meet him. The conference is the big yearly event on the calendar of thousands of enthusiasts. I looked around the Exhibit Hall, where genealogical products were on display. There was a lot of software for sale, much of it produced by the Church of Jesus Christ of Latter-Day Saints, which has amassed by far the largest collection of genealogical records in the world. (Donny and Marie Osmond would be appearing later to promote a software package called One Great Family.) In the Mormon faith, it is believed that family members remain together for eternity, not just for their time on earth, and it is the duty of Mormons to help unite families by locating their ancestors and performing a "sealing ceremony," a ritual binding the family together forever. Thanks to the zeal with which they have pursued their mission, Mormons have collected more than two billion names. The bulk are contained on microfilm and include many of the parish registries from England—births, marriages, and deaths, town by town, going back to the fifteenth century. The main collection is stored in the Family History Library, a 142,000-square-foot facility in Salt Lake City, but some databases can be searched at any one of the nearly two thousand family-history centers around the country. These records are not complete, however, because some parishes refuse to turn their papers over to the Mormons, arguing that their departed parishioners would not have wanted to be baptized by the Mormon Church. Survivors of the Holocaust brought a successful suit against the LDS Church to prevent Holocaust victims from being included.

I met Professor Redmonds in a café upstairs, where he was assembling a batch of scribbled-over sheets of paper for his upcoming lecture. His wife, Ann-marie, was sitting next to him, eyeing with a certain apprehension the large-bodied Americans who were circling us, holding their NGS tote bags, hoping for a little free genealogical advice from the Master. (Whenever Redmonds speaks, he is asked by family historians to perform a kind of genealogical parlor trick: they tell him their surname, and he endeavors to tell them where it comes from.) Redmonds was a bearded, snaggle-toothed Englishman in his midsixties, who spoke with a thick Yorkshire accent. For a long time, his views on the single-place origin of surnames contradicted the mainstream academic view, which held that surnames appeared at multiple spots, adopted by different families. He has subsisted over the years, in part, by doing surname studies for families who request them and by leading groups on heritage tours—those peculiarly American pilgrimages in which you attempt to relive your ancestors' struggles by dragging the spouse and kids back to the Old Country. Redmonds takes the Fairbanks to the fair bank where their name comes from, and so forth. He generally offers the caveat that one can't be entirely sure that this is the exact fair bank, but his audience rarely seems to mind. It makes a good picture for the Fairbanks back home.

We talked about DNA testing and its impact on genealogy as it is currently practiced. "What DNA represents is a shift in the nature of authority—a shift away from the authority of the book to the authority of the test, away from the library to the lab," Redmonds said. "There has never been absolute proof in genealogy before. As scholars, we work with that understanding. Then DNA comes along and seems to answer the question once and for all in the lab. And whether or not the answer really is definitive, people believe it in a way that they don't necessarily believe what they read in books."

I asked Redmonds for some practical advice on how best to go about finding where the Seabrooks came from. He directed me to the English Place-Name Society's publications on the development of names in English counties, which had lots of details on the origin of words like *Seabrook*. Back in New York, I enjoyed another couple of days in the Milstein Division, where I discovered that a variant of Seabrook first appears in written records from the fourteenth century, in the county of Buckinghamshire, near the village of Ivinghoe, where a now vanished hamlet called Seabrook was once located. I checked this against a database of present-day phone listings on Yahoo, which showed that the greatest concentration of Seabrooks still lived in Buckinghamshire and the neighboring counties. So it appeared that a strip of territory roughly following the Chiltern Hills, running from the south-central part of the country east into the old Anglo-Saxon kingdom of East Anglia, was the Seabrook heartland. That was where I should go looking for Seabrooks to sample.

Y-chromosome analysis is available only to men, but there is another type of DNA test that traces ancestry in the maternal line. These tests use mitochondrial DNA, which is the DNA inside mitochondria, the cellular helpers memorably described in biological texts as "the powerhouses of the cell." Every human cell contains a thousand or more mitochondria, and each mitochondrion has its own DNA. There are mitochondria inside both human eggs and sperm (they help power the tail), but only the mitochondria in the mother's egg remain in the fertilized embryo, where they begin again to multiply and soon produce a body full of mtDNA that is exactly like the mother's mtDNA. Sons get the mother's mtDNA, but, lacking eggs, they can't pass it along to their children.

Because there are so many copies of mtDNA within each human cell, mtDNA is easier to obtain from degraded specimens than nuclear DNA. Perhaps the most famous genealogical use of mtDNA was in helping to identify nine skeletons, exhumed in a forest in Siberia in 1991, that were believed to be those of Tsar Nicholas and his family. The test relied on an mtDNA sample given by Queen Elizabeth's husband, Prince Philip, who was a grandson of the Tsarina's sister. The mtDNA matched, proving that the skeletons found in the grave were indeed Romanovs. Researchers then used the Romanov sequence to answer another long-running mystery, by comparing it with the mtDNA of Anna Anderson Manahan, a woman claiming to be the Princess Anastasia, who had escaped execution. Manahan had since died, but a sample of her intestine taken during a 1979 operation had been preserved. There was no match, and she was exposed, posthumously, as a fraud.

Mitochondrial-DNA analysis can also provide a record of ancestry where no paper trail exists. Dr. Michael Blakey, a biological anthropologist at Howard University, was the lead scientist with the African Burial Ground project, in New York City, which is documenting a large eighteenth-century graveyard that was discovered in lower Manhattan in 1991. As the skeletons are analyzed, Blakey had been assembling a database of early African-American mtDNA. That database may one day be used to match living African-Americans to their ancestors. In theory, it would also be possible to collect mtDNA signatures from different parts of West Africa with which African-Americans could compare their own mtDNA in the hope of identifying the village their ancestors came from. In May 2000, when Rick Kittles, also of Howard University, announced plans for a business venture to provide this kind of genealogical service, his office was overwhelmed with calls from African-Americans. (Kittles himself used DNA testing to trace his African ancestry, and discovered that he was part German on his father's side.) But his plan also drew criticism. "That's like charging Holocaust victims to confirm their relatives were in fact gassed," Fatimah Jackson, an anthropologist at the University of Maryland, said. Other geneticists pointed out that in order for Kittles's applicants to obtain any meaningful result about their ancestors he would need a much larger database of African DNA than is currently available.

Finally, and most weirdly, mtDNA data offer living people connections to female ancestors who lived tens of thousands of years ago. These ancestors are not based on archeological evidence; they are statistical constructs derived from comparing mtDNA samples taken from modern humans all around the world. In a 1987 paper published in *Nature,* Rebecca Cann and Mark Stoneking, together with the late Allan Wilson, of the University of California at Berkeley, claimed that similarities in worldwide mtDNA samples showed that there must have been a "mitochondrial Eve," a woman who lived in Africa some two hundred thousand years ago whose mtDNA all humans share. Studies carried out in the laboratory of Douglas C. Wallace, of the Emory School of Medicine in Atlanta, have identified twenty-eight major branches in the mitochondrial family tree. Wallace has given letter designations to these "Children of Eve," as the different lineages were dubbed in a *Nova* television documentary on DNA-based ancestry, and has shown that many of the branches are continent-specific.

The enterprising Dr. Bryan Sykes had gone a step further, establishing a sort of ancient-pedigree business that allowed people of European heritage to find out which of the Seven Daughters of Eve—as he calls these ancestors—they are descended from. In taking this step, Sykes may have crossed a line between good science and entrepreneurship—between telling people the truth about who they are and plying them with a fiction about who they may be. Sykes sold his service (MatriLine) through his Web site, charging $180 per test. Sykes's names for his Seven Daughters—Xenia, Ursula, Jasmine, Tara, Velda, Helena, and Katrine—correspond to Wallace's single-letter designations for seven of the mtDNA lineages in Europe (X, U, J, T, V, H, and K), and on his Web site Sykes had added slightly overheated summaries of each of the daughters' epic achievements in the Pleistocene. Tara lived in Tuscany seventeen thousand years ago, and her descendants walked across the land bridge that used to connect England and France, where they founded the Celts. Xenia managed to survive the last Ice Age, and some of her descendants crossed the Bering land bridge to get to North America—X is the only one of the mtDNA European lineages also found in Native Americans (mostly among members of the Ojibwa tribe, who live around the Great Lakes). In Sykes's book, entitled *The Seven Daughters of Eve,* he expands on the daughters' biographies.

When I logged on to Sykes's site and looked over the material on the Daughters of Eve, my immediate thoughts were, in quick succession: (1) What a scam! (2) How many people are actually paying for this? (3) It would be kind of interesting to know which of the Daughters I am descended from. The service was a little pricey, but I was on the verge of getting a new ancestor, and what more can a family historian ask?

About a month later, a package containing several DNA-testing kits arrived in the mail—slender plastic cytology brushes with tiny nylon bristles on the end, packed in sterile translucent envelopes. I carried the instruction sheet into the bathroom. "Holding the stem, brush your inner cheek about ten times on each side to remove cells." I rinsed out my mouth, and scraped ten times on each side, watching myself in the mirror. As I was feeling the coarse bristles cutting through the mucus inside my cheek, collecting my "buccal cells" (producing a bitter taste, which made me gag slightly), I tried to conjure up an image of this warrior-princess ancestor, my Daughter of Eve, whose mtDNA has been passed from woman to woman, down through twenty thousand or so years of mothers and daughters, in order to get here to this bathroom. It was something of a stretch.

Both mtDNA- and Y-chromosome-derived lineages represent a relatively small part of the total contribution of your ancestors to your genetic makeup. If I go back four generations, I have sixteen ancestors, but since my mitochondrial DNA comes only from my mother's mother's mother's mother, and my Y chromosome comes from my father's father's father's father, together these two ancestors represent only two-sixteenths of my actual ancestry. The farther back you go, the smaller that fraction becomes. But this is exactly what Sykes is selling through MatriLine—exclusivity.

I had e-mailed Dr. Wallace, in Atlanta, about Sykes's Daughters of Eve business. He wrote back that his own group had not tried to seek commercial gain from its mtDNA work, implying that he disapproved of Sykes's efforts to do so (a criticism I heard from other geneticists too). He also pointed out the potentially misleading aspects of DNA-derived ancestry: an individual who thinks of himself as, say, Anglo-Saxon could find out from an mtDNA test that his deep maternal ancestor is in fact Middle Eastern or African. "For example an individual might consider himself as belonging to a particular group 'A,'" Wallace wrote. "If the individual being tested was subsequently told that his mtDNA is from the 'B' group, he might mistakenly think that his personal identity is misplaced. This could be devastating. Tragically it would also be untrue since the vast majority of this individual's genes would in fact be 'A.'"

I finished collecting my DNA, slipped the brush back inside the envelope, sealed it with tape, and mailed it, along with a check, to the Institute of Molecular Medicine in Oxford, where Sykes had established his genealogical venture in partnership with Oxford University. I had a couple of DNA-testing kits left over, and I wondered what to do with them. It would be easy to sneak a sample from my son and send it off to Gene Tree. There was no reason to doubt he was "mine," and yet the comfort of certainty was hard to resist. But I resisted it, bearing in mind what may be the golden rule of the age of household genetics: Never ask for an answer you don't need to know.

When I got to England, I went to see Sykes at his lab in Oxford. He was already analyzing my mtDNA, and I had decided to use his Y-Line service to evaluate my male Seabrook samples too. We talked in the institute's common room. Sykes, then forty-nine years old, was dressed in a dark-green suit with a black T-shirt underneath. He was fair-haired and ruddy, and he spoke in the musical, aware-of-itself voice of the star geneticist, used to holding the rapt attention of classrooms and labs full of students. Sykes had a knack for using DNA testing in dramatic, media-friendly contexts that generate headlines. He was part of a team that extracted mtDNA from the five-thousand-year-old Ötzi Man, the body of a Neolithic hunter found frozen on an alp near the Ötztal Valley, on the Austrian-Italian border, in 1991. Sykes also recovered mtDNA from a nine-thousand-year-old skeleton of a man found in the Cheddar

Gorge, in the English county of Somerset, in 1997. After testing people living in and around Bath, a city near the gorge, Sykes announced that a local schoolteacher named Adrian Targett was a relative of the Cheddar Man.

Sykes's study of male Sykeses increased his fame. His conclusion—that there was an original Mr. Sykes, and that the nonrelated Sykeses were the result of nonpaternity events or adoptions—was questioned by some geneticists, who argued that the nonrelated Sykeses could derive from founders of other, less prolific Sykes lines. (Alan Savin, an amateur genealogist in Britain who has conducted a similar study of British Savins, did not find evidence of a single progenitor.) But the idea that people with the same name might belong to the same genetic family was eagerly lapped up by the press.

Sykes himself had the Sykes Y-chromosome signature, although he told me that it would not have mattered to him if he had discovered evidence of a nonpaternity event at some point in his male line. "There are two ways of doing genealogy, both equally valid," he said, putting down a mug of coffee. "There is your cultural family, and there is your genetic family, and the two are often not the same, though you may think they are. There have already been quarrels over this, and there are going to be others, so we have to make it absolutely clear as we go forward: the biological and the paper families are not the same thing, but they are both equally valid."

Sykes said that the joint venture with Oxford University is "genetics for fun." He planned to open genetics shops, where people can stop in to get all their DNA work done, Kinko's style—sequencing, banking, database searching, as well as Daughters of Eve T-shirts. "It's all in the marketing plan," he said.

I asked whether MatriLine, his Daughters of Eve test, had much business yet.

"Hundreds and hundreds of customers," Sykes said. "Most of the interest is in the States, of course. Sometimes it's sons getting their mother's mtDNA sequenced for Mother's Day, or friends giving MatriLine to newlyweds as a wedding gift. People really don't have a personal relationship with their DNA yet. It's been thought of as a chemical, basically. But what it actually is, it's a part of your history. Think of how far your genes have come to get to you. They survived the Ice Age, lived lives very different from the lives we live now. When you reflect that at any point in the last twenty thousand years or so, there was only one individual woman who carried the same mtDNA you carry, and that she had a daughter, and that daughter had a daughter, and so on, throughout history—it's quite powerful. It's not like nuclear DNA, where you keep multiplying your ancestors as you go back. It's one woman, or, in the case of a Y test, one man. That's what people relate to."

Sykes took me on a brief tour of the laboratory, where students and lab workers were involved in the labor-intensive practice of preparing and sequencing DNA samples. In his office, a harried-looking assistant was busy printing out customers' mtDNA sequences and Daughters of Eve genetic trees. Sykes disappeared, returning a little later with a page fresh from the color printer.

"Congratulations," he said. "You're a Xenia. The rarest one. Only six percent come from Xenia." He paused for a moment to let this sink in, then asked, "How do you feel?"

"Only six percent!" I said.

"And you are the mysterious X branch," Sykes went on. "Let me ask you, would you seek out other Xenias?"

I didn't think so. I might buy the T-shirt, though.

With a flourish, Sykes signed his name under my mtDNA sequence. A vellum copy, suitable for framing, would be sent to me in the mail.

After seeing Sykes, I rented a car in Oxford and headed north, toward the Seabrook heartland. In Sykes's lab, with its racks of test tubes and its pipette-wielding technicians, I had felt out of place; there were none of the bookish comforts of the Milstein Division. But now that I was once again navigating by written records, which I had found mostly in the English Place-Names books, I felt more sure of myself. I had my papers on the seat beside me, with the research I had done into the name Seabrook. Like DNA, the name has mutated over time, as mistakes, copying errors, and elisions have crept in, producing variations from Seybroke to Sebroc to Seabrooke. Seabrook is a compound word, which Anglo-Saxons were fond of. The first part of it, *sea*, modifies the second part, *brook*. A *sea* in Middle English meant "a dweller by a lake or pool of water," but in Old English *sea* may have come from the word *saege,* which means "slowly moving or trickling." Or it could be from Saega, an Anglo-Saxon personal name—Seaga's Brook. The Anglo-Saxons had many more words to describe landscape features than we do, and they seem to have been especially concerned with water. There were seabrooks, shirebrooks (clear), sambrooks (sandy), skidbrooks (muddy and dirty), and holbrooks (brooks running through hollows). *Brook* always seems to have meant a brook, though it was once spelled *brock,* which also meant "marsh." According to the Oxford Dictionary of English Surnames, a *brock* was also "a stinking or dirty fellow."

The Anglo-Saxons had only one name, and this was, in the manner of modern pop stars, distinctive enough to be unique: Cerdic, Lemma, Pymma, Ugga, Sprott. But in the centuries following the Norman Conquest in 1066, partly owing to the popularity of biblical and royal names—in fourteenth-century England, 34 percent of the men were named John—it became necessary to have two names. In England, most people chose surnames between 1250 and 1400. Surnames were not at first intended to be hereditary but were, as the word suggests, "bynames," more like first names today. Some people chose their bynames from places and topographical features (Hawthorne, Goodwood), some from relationships (Johnson), some from trades (Arrowsmith, Cartwright), and some were descriptive nicknames, both kind (Armstrong, Fairchild) and cruel (Vidler, meaning "wolf-face," and Greeley, "pockmarked").

The road to Ivinghoe was dotted with mutant remnants of Anglo-Saxon words. I passed the village of Tring, which in Old English meant "slope on which trees grow." Ivinghoe itself was in a valley below the ancient Pitstone Hills. Just outside the village, I found a farm called Little Seabrook. As I was walking alongside a hedgerow that marked the boundary of a cow pasture, I heard the farmer and his wife on the other side. I called out that I was a Seabrook, come looking for my roots, and they invited me into the field. We walked through the pasture to the spot where, according to the farmer, Bernard Keable, the hamlet of Seabrook had once stood. "Supposedly, if

THE TREE OF ME    131

you look at it from the air you can see discolored patches in the grass," Mrs. Keable said, pointing around at the patchy ground. A little farther along, they brought me to a brook that flowed through the field. Bernard said, "When it rains, you see, that brook floods, and this field becomes a shallow lake."

"A sea, like," his wife added.

I shot a glance at her to see if she was putting me on. An American on a heritage tour is in a pitifully credulous state, willing to believe almost anything the locals tell him. But the Keables appeared sincere. I began composing in my head the e-mail I would send my father about this; it would be a variation on the telegram the German archeologist Heinrich Schliemann dispatched when he found the tomb of Agamemnon, in Troy—"I have gazed on the brook from which we came."

There were no Seabrooks left in Ivinghoe, but there were Seabrooks in the towns around it, and the next day I returned to the area to see if I could collect DNA from a few. The first Seabrook I tried wasn't home when I turned up at his door unannounced, and after I told his wife what I needed she looked alarmed. "My husband's not here now, but I'm sure he wouldn't be interested in something like that." She closed the door.

After another rejection, I decided that the best method would be to call first, explain as best I could what I was after, and suggest popping by. The wives of the male Seabrooks often were the ones who answered the phone, and they seemed much more leery of the idea of DNA sampling than the men were, perhaps because women are more aware of the perils of loosely passed out DNA.

One Mrs. Seabrook who answered said, "Not another one of these shady Seabrooks coming out of the woodwork!"

Were there a lot of shady Seabrooks around? I asked.

"Oh, yes—loads of them!"

By the end of a long day, I had found three Y-bearing Seabrooks, all of them elderly, who didn't seem to have much else to do when I called, and allowed me to come over and sample them. The first was

Gerald, who lived alone in a cul-de-sac in the town of Hemel Hempstead; the second was Keith, whom I sampled on the High Street in Bedmond; and the last was Allen, whom I got in his parlor in Chesham, as his wife sat next to him drinking tea. My technique was to chat about our respective families until the moment seemed right to withdraw the sampler from my pocket.

I asked each of these Seabrooks what he knew of his own ancestors, and was surprised to discover that not one of them knew anything more about his family history than the name of his grandparents. On the other hand, all the Seabrooks knew a lot about their houses, and the history of the villages I found them in. Could it be that Americans' fascination with genealogy springs in part from our lack of interest in the history of the buildings and towns we live in? In the United States, everything gets thrown out or torn down too fast, until all we've got left is our genes.

On Saturday I drove up to Suffolk to see if I could find the grave of Thomas Seabrook, my crossing ancestor's father. According to my grandfather's genealogy, he is buried in the village of Stradishall. I left the motorway and entered the part of the country my ancestors came from. The land became hilly, and from the highest elevations I had glimpses of the ancient market towns in the distance—Newmarket, Saffron Walden—with the spires of the churches poking up over the old walls. My ancestors must have walked within sight of these views for at least 140 years. What struck me most about the land was that it looked a lot like the place where I grew up, in South Jersey. Maybe that's why Samuel finally settled there—because he had heard it looked like home.

When I reached Stradishall, at about three o'clock, the town was deserted and silent. Some crows were sitting high in the yew trees that grew around the churchyard. The church itself had been built in the fourteenth century and was not well preserved; the interior was dank and smelled strongly of mildew. The register was filled with entries from other ancestor-seeking Americans—"Found my g g g g grandfather in back!!!!" I went outside and began looking for the grave of Thomas. The grass was long and wet, and the ground

was uneven, especially behind the church, where some of the older
graves were.

As I was walking back there, the earth gave way under my foot. I
staggered backward and then cautiously peered down into the hole.
It seemed to go all the way down into a grave.

I looked everywhere, but could find no Seabrook. Then I noticed
a row of four stones that were so covered with ivy that I had mis-
taken them for part of the ground. I pulled the ivy away from the
first stone. The lettering was too worn to read by eye, but by tracing
with my fingertip along the declivity in the stone I could spell out
the letter S, then e, then a, until I got *Seabrook*. It was a moment
that DNA couldn't touch.

While searching online for Seabrooks to sample, I had sent an
e-mail to a Colin Seabrook, who lived just outside Ipswich, a
medium-sized city in southeast England. Shortly after returning to
New York, I received a reply from him. He declined to take the
DNA test, but by comparing genealogies we discovered we had a
common ancestor in Richard Seabrook, my great-times-five grandfather and Colin's times-six—which made us sixth cousins once removed. Colin added that he had a "shedful" of information about
the Reverend Thomas Seabrook. "With what I know about the Reverend, I could write a small book," Colin said. Apparently the grave
I had found in Stradishall was not Thomas's—he was in a different
village altogether. If I felt like coming back to England, Colin wrote,
"I'll take you to where the Reverend is buried."

So on a cold, black December day I drove up the A 12 from
London, heading northeast past Colchester, the oldest settled town
in Britain, and reached Ipswich about midday. The historic meeting between the two branches of the family tree that were separated by Samuel's crossing took place in a car park outside a Toys Я
Us. I had no idea what Colin looked like, and although we shared
the same Y chromosome, the only known physical traits the Y ex-
presses, apart from maleness, are hairy ears in Indian men and
shape of the tooth. As I walked around peering at the shoppers in
the rain, I spotted a nose that looked exactly like the one on my

brother's face, Norman in size but Anglo-Saxon in aquilinity—quite a honker. Sure enough, it was Colin.

Colin was fifty-one and had curly salt-and-pepper gray hair and a long neck (like mine). He was friendly—not the least bit brocklike. His father had been a butcher, his grandfather a farmer, and he was a mechanical engineer with British Telecom. Colin had made a large family tree of Seabrooks, which he printed out on a continuous-roll printer, the kind engineers use for making circuit diagrams. We sat in his car and unrolled it, and he traced our connections on the paper with his index finger. I kept stealing glances at his teeth.

I was eager to see the documents Colin had brought with him, but he suggested we have lunch first. He told me about his work for British Telecom, and his two children, a girl and a boy who are eighteen and twenty respectively, and his wife, Angela. He said his interest in genealogy started when his grandfather died. "I realized how much is lost when a person dies. All that oral history, all that knowledge of who did what to whom, disappears."

After lunch, we spread out the documents. The "shed," it appeared, was a figure of speech. Colin had some interesting odds and ends, including the e-mail address of a California branch of the family, who are now called the Fitzpatricks, but he had nothing to explain what Thomas was like, or why his son Samuel might have left this country. Like me, Colin had got no further back than Richard. He had never heard of the Dr. Seabrook who set the king's arm.

I did gain a better sense of what life as a clergyman had been like in this part of Suffolk. Colin showed me a document from the Barnardiston parish registry, which is stored in the records office at Bury St. Edmunds, making Thomas a curate. He was to receive a hundred pounds a year, plus surplus fees—weddings, burials, baptisms—to be paid by the Reverend John Maddy, who was the rector of Stansfield Church. Thomas was responsible for three churches, in three villages, although the contract specified that he was not required to travel more than fifteen miles on a Sunday. And "We do further assign and alot unto you the rectory house for your residence, with the offices, stables, gardens."

That night the winds were so strong that they blew the roofs

off houses in Cardiff. Nothing so organized as a nor'easter or a
hurricane, the gale was nevertheless a great blow. As I lay in my
hotel room listening to the wind roaring, I remembered the way
Colin's nose looked, when I first glimpsed it in the Toys Я Us
parking lot. I couldn't get that nose out of my mind. I knew that
the similarity to my brother's nose was probably a coincidence,
but I clung to this bit of physical kinship. Perhaps this was what I
was looking to my ancestors to find—some echo of myself.

The next morning, as I was coming out of the dining room after
breakfast, I saw Colin waiting for me in the lobby. He had arisen
early to see Angela and some of her friends off for a bit of shopping in
the outlet malls on the French side of the Chunnel. I got my things
and we set off in Colin's car, heading for Bury St. Edmunds, resting
place of the martyred king of East Anglia, Edmund, whose lungs
were ripped out by the Viking leader Ivar the Boneless in 869. Leaving the modern Britain behind, we entered the timeless English
countryside, with its perfectly worked fields, deep lanes, and ancient
hedgerows.

As we entered the cemetery at Rede, the northernmost of the
churches on Thomas's route, there was a rumbling sound, and several huge, extremely healthy-looking workhorses charged across the
neighboring pasture to have a look at us, water flying from their
steaming bodies, their vitality making a vivid contrast to the dank,
licheny silence of the churchyard. The sky had clouded over and
rain was threatening again. There were molehills everywhere.

"Moles like worms," Colin said.

We continued on to the village of Wickhambrook, where Thomas
had succeeded John Maddy as vicar, although he served for only a
year, until his death, at the age of fifty-eight.

The interior had the bone-chilling cold peculiar to old churches,
which perhaps contributed to Thomas's untimely death. Bits of the
original building had been preserved, and there was a north door,
typical of the way the Vikings built churches. The stained glass in
the windows had been smashed by Puritans in the seventeenth century, all except for a few panes high above the altar.

I walked around, peering at the inscriptions in the walls, until

Colin said, "You just walked over Thomas." I looked down, and there
was a cracked stone with his name and dates, saying he had been the
vicar here. The stone was broken in five or six places, and the words
were fractured, the letters beginning to tumble into one another. I
took a picture of Colin in front of it, and took another close up, so that
I could show Colin's nose to my brother.


Just before Christmas, I got back from Sykes's lab the results of my
first six Seabrook-DNA samples. Sykes had compared nine sites
on the Y chromosomes. The first two English Seabrooks I sampled,
Gerald and Keith, matched one another at all nine sites, and the DNA
of Allen, the third English Seabrook, was very close to that of Gerald
and Keith. A white American Seabrook, William, of Farmingdale,
Long Island, who had also volunteered for my experiment, turned out
to be an exact match for my Y at all nine sites. We are only one mutation from Allen, and two from Keith and Gerald. The sole Seabrook
who didn't match any of the rest is Jeffrey Scott, of Texas, the scion
of the South Carolina Seabrooks.

Sykes called me about my chart shortly after New Year's. He
told me what I wanted to hear: he believed the study showed a
characteristic Seabrook-family signature on my Y chromosome.
"It's a very interesting study, really. It shows all of you except Jeffrey Scott are connected by a common ancestor at some point,
though it's hard to say when. Between five hundred and a thousand years ago. Better say fifteen hundred years ago, to be safe.
Still, based on this, I'd say there was very clearly one original Mr.
Seabrook, from which all five of you come. And you and William
are identical. You could be brothers. Are you his brother?"

Not as far as I knew, I said, my mind racing over the possibilities.

I asked about the discrepancy in Jeffrey Scott Seabrook's sample. Did this mean we are conclusively not related to the South
Carolina Seabrooks? The prospect of telling my father this news
pained me—he would take it hard—but I was pleased that I
wouldn't have to feel any more white guilt than I already feel. However, Sykes did leave our family myth some wiggle room: "It would
appear from this small sample, especially since three samples come

from the homeland of the name, that Jeffrey Scott has a nonpaternity event somewhere in his line." Sykes added that the fact that
five of the six Seabrooks do have a similar signature is quite a testament to the integrity of the Mrs. Seabrooks. "Their descendants
have every reason to be proud of their mating behavior."

I called William Seabrook, to tell him that according to our
Y chromosomes we're related. I reached him at the insurance company where he works, on Pine Street in downtown Manhattan,
about a ten-minute walk from my home. If the point of this ancestor-
hunting was to get more connected, then shouldn't finding a living
relative matter more than finding a paper ancestor? But now that I
had found a new cousin and he was right across town, I felt more
wary than curious.

Bill turned out to be a genealogy buff too, and knew that his
crossing ancestor, Fred Seabrook, had come from Sussex in the 1880s
with his family, and settled in Queens. He hadn't traced his line any
further back than that, so it's possible that his people came from my
people in Suffolk, and then got to Sussex before emigrating.

"What I'd like to find out," Bill went on, "is if we're related to the
South Carolina Seabrooks." It seemed that those Seabrooks figured
even more prominently in his family's mythology than in mine. He
told me the story of how, in the 1950s, a couple of lawyers representing Seabrook Island, in South Carolina, had written to his grandfather, who was a carpenter in Queens, and offered him the island,
saying he was the rightful heir to it—"all the land, the old plantation, everything, for payment of back taxes"—but his grandfather
had turned the lawyers down.

"I mean, could you imagine what would have happened if my
grandfather had accepted that offer?" he said, his voice dead serious,
the way you get when you're telling the family's history. "We'd have
the whole island."

—2001

# FRAGMENTARY KNOWLEDGE

In October 2005 a truck pulled up outside the National Archeological Museum in Athens, and workers began unloading an eight-ton X-ray machine that its designer, X-Tek Systems of Great Britain, had dubbed the Bladerunner. Standing just inside the National Museum's basement was Tony Freeth, a sixty-year-old British mathematician and filmmaker, watching as workers in white T-shirts wrestled the Range Rover–size machine through the door and up the ramp into the museum. Freeth was a member of the Antikythera Mechanism Research Project—a multidisciplinary investigation into some fragments of an ancient mechanical device that were found at the turn of the twentieth century after two thousand years in the Aegean Sea, and have long been one of the great mysteries of science.

Freeth, a tall, taciturn man with a deep, rumbling voice, had been a mathematician at Bristol University, taking a Ph.D. in set theory, a branch of mathematical logic. He had drifted away from the academy, however, and spent most of his career making films, many of them with scientific themes. The Antikythera Mechanism, which he had first heard about some five years earlier, had rekindled his undergraduate love of math and logic and problem solving, and he had all but abandoned his film career in the course of investigating it. He was the latest in a long line of men who have made solving the mystery of the Mechanism their life's work. Another British researcher, Michael Wright, who has studied the Mechanism for more than twenty years, was coincidentally due to arrive in Athens before the Bladerunner had finished its work. But Wright wasn't part of the research project, and his arrival was anticipated with some trepidation.

It had been Freeth's idea to contact X-Tek in the hope of finding a high-resolution, three-dimensional X-ray technology to see inside the fragments of the Mechanism. As it happened, the company was working on a prototype of a CAT-scan machine that would use computer tomography to make 3-D X-rays of the blades inside airplane turbines for safety inspections. Roger Hadland, X-Tek's owner and chief engineer, was interested in Freeth's proposal, and he and his staff developed new technology for the project.

After the lead-lined machine was installed inside the museum, technicians spent another day attaching the peripheral equipment. At last, everything was ready. The first piece to be examined, Fragment D, was placed on the Bladerunner's turntable. It was only about an inch and a half around—much smaller than Fragment A, the largest piece, which measures about six and a half inches across—and it looked like just a small greenish rock, or possibly a lump of coral. It was heavily corroded and calcified—the parts of the Mechanism almost indistinguishable from the petrified sea slime that surrounded them. Conservationists couldn't clean off any more of the corroded material without damaging the artifact, and it was hoped that the latest in modern technology would reveal the ancient technology inside.

The Bladerunner began to whirr. As the turntable rotated, an electron gun fired at a tungsten target, which emitted an X-ray beam that passed through the fragment, so that an image was recorded every time the turntable moved a tenth of a degree. A complete 360-degree rotation, resulting in three thousand images or so, required about an hour. Then the computer required another hour to assemble all the images into a 3-D representation of what the fragment looked like on the inside.

As Freeth waited impatiently for the first images to appear on the Bladerunner's monitor, he was trying not to hope for too much, and to place his trust in the skills of the group of academics and technicians who were there with him.

Among them, waiting with equal anticipation, were John Sei-radakis, a professor of astronomy at the Aristotle University of Thessaloniki; Xenophon Moussas, the director of the Astrophysics Laboratory at the University of Athens; and Yanis Bitsakis, a Ph.D. student in physics. (Mike Edmunds, an astrophysicist at Cardiff University, who was the academic leader of the research project, remained in Wales.) "I was just focused on my relief that this was happening at all, with all the delays of the past four years," Freeth told me. "Honestly, there were times when I thought it would never happen."

One day in the spring of 1900, a party of Greek sponge divers returning from North Africa was forced by a storm to take shelter in the lee of the small island of Antikythera, which lies be-tween Crete and Kythera. After the storm passed, one of the divers, Elias Stadiatis, put on a weighted suit and an airtight helmet that was connected by an air hose to a compressor on the boat, and went looking for giant clams, with which to make a feast that evening.

The bottom of the sea dropped sharply, and the diver followed the underwater cliff to a shelf that was about 140 feet below the surface. On the other side of the shelf, an abyss fell away into total darkness. Looking around, Stadiatis saw the remains of an ancient shipwreck. Then he had a terrible shock. There were piles of bodies, all in pieces, covering the ledge. He grabbed one of the pieces before surfacing in order to have proof of what he had seen. It turned out to be a bronze arm.

The following autumn, the sponge divers, now working for the Greek government, returned to the site, and over the next ten months they brought up many more pieces of sculpture, both marble and bronze, from the wreck, all of which were taken to the National Museum to be cleaned and reassembled. It was the world's first large-scale underwater archeological excavation. Evidence derived from coins, amphorae, and other items of the cargo eventually al-lowed researchers to fix a date for the shipwreck: around the first half of the first century B.C., a time when the glorious civilization of ancient Greece was on the wane, following the Roman conquest of the Greek cities. Coins from Pergamum, a Hellenistic city in what is now Turkey, indicated that the ship had made port nearby. The style of the amphorae strongly suggested that the ship had called at the island of Rhodes, also on the eastern edge of the Hellenistic world, and known for its wealth and its industry. Given the reputed corruption of officials in the provinces of the Roman Empire, it is possible that the ship's cargo had been plundered from Greek temples and villas, and was on its way to adorn the houses of aristocrats in Rome. The sheer weight of the cargo probably contributed to the ship's destruction.

Most of the marble pieces were blackened and pitted from their long immersion in the salt water, but the bronze sculptures, though badly corroded, were salvageable. Although bronze sculptures were common in ancient Greece, only a tiny number have survived (the bronze was often sold as scrap, melted down, and recast, possibly as weaponry), and most of those have been recovered from shipwrecks. Among the works of art that emerged from the waters near Antikythera are the bronze portrait of a bearded philosopher, and the so-called Antikythera Youth, a larger-than-life-size naked young man: a rare specimen of a bronze masterwork, believed to be from the fourth century B.C.

Other artifacts included bronze fittings for wooden furniture, pottery, an oil lamp, and item 15087—a shoebox-size lump of bronze, which appeared to have a wooden exterior. Inside were what seemed to be fused metal pieces, but the bronze was so encrusted with barnacles and calcium that it was difficult to tell what it was. With so much early excitement focused on the sculptures, the artifact didn't receive much attention at first. But one day in May 1902, a Greek archeologist named Spyridon Staïs noticed that the wooden exterior had split open, probably as a result of exposure to the air, and that the artifact inside had fallen into several pieces. Looking closely, Staïs saw some inscriptions, in ancient Greek, about two millimeters high, engraved on what looked like a bronze dial. Researchers also noticed precisely cut triangular gear teeth of different sizes. The thing looked like some sort of mechanical clock. But this was impossible, because scientifically precise gearing wasn't believed to have been widely used until the fourteenth century—fourteen hundred years after the ship went down.

The first analyses of what became known as the Antikythera Mechanism followed two main approaches. The archeologists, led by J. N. Svoronos of the National Museum, thought that the artifact must have been "a kind of astrolabe." A Hellenistic invention, an astrolabe was an astronomical device that was widely known in the Islamic world by the eighth century and in Europe by the early twelfth century. Astrolabes were used to tell the time, and could also determine latitude with reference to the position of the stars; Muslim sailors often used them, in addition, to calculate prayer times and find the direction of Mecca.

However, other researchers, led by the German philologist Albert Rehm, thought that the Mechanism appeared much too complex to be an astrolabe. Rehm suggested that it might possibly be the legendary Sphere of Archimedes, which Cicero had described in the first century B.C. as a kind of mechanical planetarium, capable of reproducing the movement of the sun, the moon, and the five planets that could be seen from Earth without a telescope—Mercury, Venus, Mars, Jupiter, and Saturn. Still others, acknowledging the artifact's complexity, thought that it must have come from a much later shipwreck, which may have settled on top of the ancient ship (even though the Mechanism had plainly been crushed under the weight of the ship's other cargo). But in the absence of any overwhelming evidence one way or the other, until the 1950s the astrolabe theory held sway.

Looking back over the first fifty years of research on the Mechanism, one is struck by the reluctance of modern investigators to credit the ancients with technological skill. The Greeks are thought to have possessed crude wooden gears, which were used to lift heavy building materials, haul up water, and hoist anchors, but historians do not generally credit them with possessing scientifically precise gears—gears cut from metal and arranged into complex "gear trains" capable of carrying motion from one driveshaft to an-

other. Paul Keyser, a software developer at IBM and the author of
*Greek Science of the Hellenistic Era,* told me, "Those scholars who
study the history of science tend to focus on science beginning with
Copernicus and Galileo and Harvey, and often go so far as to assert
that no such thing existed before." It's almost as if we wished to reserve advanced technological accomplishment exclusively for ourselves. Our civilization, while too late to make the fundamental
discoveries that the Greeks made in the sciences—Euclidean geometry, trigonometry, and the law of the lever, to name a few—has excelled at using those discoveries to make machines. These are the
product and proof of our unique genius, and we're reluctant to share
our glory with previous civilizations.

In fact, there is evidence that earlier civilizations were much
more technically adept than we imagine they were. As Peter James
and Nick Thorpe point out in *Ancient Inventions,* published in 1994,
some ancient civilizations were aware of natural electric phenomena
and the invisible powers of magnetism (though neither concept was
understood). The Greeks had a tradition of great inventors, beginning with Archimedes of Syracuse (c. 287–212 B.C.), who, in addition to his famous planetarium, is believed to have invented a terrible
clawed device made up of large hooks, submerged in the sea and
attached by a cable to a terrestrial hoist; the device was capable of
lifting the bow of a fully loaded warship into the air and smashing it
down on the water—the Greeks reportedly used the weapon during
the Roman siege of Syracuse around 212 B.C. Philon of Byzantium
(who lived around 200 B.C.) made a spring-driven catapult. Heron of
Alexandria (who lived around the first century A.D.) was the most
ingenious inventor of all. He described the basic principles of steam
power, and is said to have invented a steam-powered device in which
escaping steam caused a sphere with two nozzles to rotate. He also
made a mechanical slot machine, a water-powered organ, and machinery for temples and theaters, including automatic swinging doors.
He is perhaps best remembered for his automatons—simulations of
animals and men, cleverly engineered to sing, blow trumpets, and
dance, among other lifelike actions.

Although a book by Heron, *Pneumatica,* detailing various of
these inventions, has survived, some scholars have dismissed his

descriptions as fantasy. They have pointed to the lack of evidence—no trace of any of these marvelous machines has been found. But as other scholars have pointed out, the lack of archeological evidence isn't really surprising. No doubt the machines eventually broke down, and as the know-how faded, there was no one around who could fix them, so they were sold as scrap and recycled. Very few technical drawings or writings remained because, as Paul Keyser observes, "the texts that survive tend to be the more popular texts—i.e., those that were more often copied—and textbooks, not the research works or the advanced technical ones." Eventually, following the dissolution of the Roman Empire, the technological knowledge possessed by the Greeks disappeared from the West completely.

But if the Greeks did have greater technological sophistication than we think they did, why didn't they apply it to making more useful things—time- and work-saving machines, for example—instead of elaborate singing automatons? Or is what we consider important about technology—which is, above all, that it is useful—different from what the Greeks considered worthwhile: amusement, enlightenment, delight for its own sake? According to one theory, the Greeks, because they owned slaves, had little incentive to invent labor-saving devices—indeed, they may have found the idea distasteful. Archimedes' claws notwithstanding, there was, as Keyser notes, cultural resistance to making high-tech war machines because "both the Greeks and the Romans valued individual bravery in war." In any case, in the absence of any obvious practical application for Greek technology, it is easy to believe that it never existed at all.

In 1958 Derek de Solla Price, a fellow at the Institute for Advanced Study in Princeton, went to Athens to examine the Mechanism. Price's interests fell between traditionally defined disciplines. Born in Britain, he trained as a physicist but later switched fields and became the Avalon Professor of the History of Science at Yale; he is credited with founding Scientometrics, a method of measuring and analyzing the pursuit of science. The study of the Mechanism, which incorporates elements of archeology, astronomy, mathematics, philology, classical history, and mechanical engineering, was ideally suited to a polymath like Price, and it consumed the rest of his life.

Price believed that the Mechanism was an ancient "computer," which could be used to calculate astronomical events in the near or distant future: the next full moon, for example. He realized that the inscriptions on the large dial were calendrical markings indicating months, days, and the signs of the zodiac, and postulated that there must have been pointers, now missing, that represented the sun and the moon and possibly the planets, and that these pointers moved around the dial, indicating the position of the heavenly bodies at different times.

Price set about proving these theories, basing his deductions on the fundamental properties of gearing. Gears work by transmitting power through rotational motion and by realizing mathematical relationships between toothed gearwheels. The Mechanism concentrates on the latter aspect. Price seems to have assumed that the largest gear in the artifact, which is clearly visible in Fragment A, was tied to the movement of the sun—one rotation equaled one solar year. If another gear, representing the moon, was driven by the solar gear, then the ratio of wheels in this gear train must have been designed to match the Greeks' idea of the moon's movements. By counting the number of teeth in each gear, you could calculate the gear ratios, and by comparing those ratios to astronomical cycles, you can figure out which gears represented which movements.

However, because only a few of the gears appear at the surface of the Mechanism, and because many of the gear teeth are missing, Price had to develop methods for estimating total numbers from partial tooth counts. Finally, in 1971, he and a Greek radiographer, Dr. C. Karakalos, were permitted to make the first X-rays of the Mechanism, and these two-dimensional images showed almost all the remaining gear teeth. Price developed a schematic drawing of a hypothetical reconstruction of the internal workings of the Mechanism. In 1974 Price published his research in the form of a seventy-page monograph titled "Gears from the Greeks." He had written, "Nothing like this instrument is preserved elsewhere. Nothing comparable to it is known from any ancient scientific text or literary allusion. On the contrary, from all that we know of science and technology in the Hellenistic Age we should have felt that such a device could not exist."

Price expected his work on the Mechanism to change the history of technology. The Mechanism "requires us to completely rethink our attitudes toward ancient Greek technology," he wrote, and later added, "It must surely rank as one of the greatest mechanical inventions of all time." Price also pointed out that the Mechanism cannot have been the only one of its kind; no technology this sophisticated could have appeared suddenly, fully realized. Not only did the Mechanism demonstrate that our concept of ancient technology was fundamentally incomplete; it also contradicted the neo-Darwinian concept of technical progress in general as a gradual evolution toward ever greater complexity (technological history being the last refuge of the nineteenth-century belief in progress)—an idea firmly embedded in A. P. Usher's classic 1929 study, *A History of Mechanical Inventions*. As Price writes, it is "a bit frightening to know that just before the fall of their great civilization the ancient Greeks had come so close to our age, not only in their thought, but also in their scientific technology."

But Price's work, though widely reviewed in scholarly journals, did not change the way the history of the ancient world is written. Otto Neugebauer's huge *A History of Ancient Mathematical Astronomy*, which came out the year after "Gears," relegates the Mechanism to a single footnote. Scholars and historians may have been reluctant to rewrite the history of technology to include research that had lingering doubts attached to it. Also, Price's book was published at the height of the popularity of *Chariots of the Gods*, a 1968 book by the Swiss writer Erich von Däniken, which argued that advanced aliens had seeded the earth with technology, and Price got associated with UFOs and crop circles and other kinds of fringe thinking. Finally, as Paul Keyser told me, "Classical scholarship is very literary, and focuses on texts—such as the writing of Homer, Sophocles, Virgil, or Horace, or it is old-fashioned and historical, and focuses on leaders and battles, through the texts of Herodotus and Thucydides, or it is anthropological-archeological, and focuses on population distributions and suchlike. So when an archeological discovery about ancient technology arrives, it does not fit, because it's new, it's scientific, and it's not a text. Plus, there is only one such device, and unique items tend to worry scholars and scientists, who quite reasonably prefer patterns and larger collections of data." Whatever the reason, as one scholar, Rob Rice, noted in a paper first presented in 1993, "It is neither facile nor uninstructive to remark that the Antikythera Mechanism dropped and sank—twice"—once in the sea and once in scholarship.

The National Museum in Athens took no special pains in displaying the lumps of bronze. Item 15087 wasn't much to look at. When the physicist Richard Feynman visited in 1980, there was little information explaining what the Mechanism was. In a letter to his family, later published in the book *What Do You Care What Other People Think?*, the physicist wrote that he found the museum "slightly boring because we have seen so much of that stuff before. Except for one thing: among all those art objects there was one thing so entirely different and strange that it is nearly impossible. It was recovered from the sea in 1900 and is some kind of machine with gear trains, very much like the inside of a modern wind-up alarm clock." When Feynman asked to know more about item 15087, the curators seemed a little disappointed. One said, "Of all the things in the museum, why does he pick out that particular item, what is so special about it?"

For the Greeks, as for other ancient civilizations, astronomy was a vital and practical form of knowledge. The sun and the moon were the basis for calendars by which people marked time. The solar cycle told farmers the best times for sowing and harvesting crops, while the lunar cycle was commonly used as the basis for civic obligations. And of course for mariners the stars provided some means of navigating at night.

Xenophon Moussas, one of the two Greek astronomers who are part of the research project, is a compact, soft-spoken man. He grew up in Athens, and as a boy, visiting the museum, he often pondered the Mechanism; now, as a professor of astrophysics, he uses it to

connect with his undergraduate students, for whom ancient technology is often more compelling than ancient theory.

One winter evening, Moussas led me on a memorable walk
around the archeological park in central Athens, which includes
both the Greek and the Roman agoras. As a quarter moon shone in
the clear night sky, illuminating the ruined temples and markets,
Moussas narrated the story of how the ancients slowly learned to
recognize patterns and serial events in the movements of the stars,
and to use them to tell time and to predict future astronomical
events. "It was a way of keeping track not of time as we think of it,"
he told me, "but of the movement of the stars—a deeper time."

For the Greeks, like the Babylonians before them, the year consisted of twelve "lunations," or new-moon-to-new-moon cycles, each
of which lasted an average of twenty-nine and a half days. The problem with a lunar calendar is that twelve lunar cycles takes about
eleven days less than one solar cycle. That means that if you don't
make regular adjustments to the calendar, the seasons soon slip out
of sync with the months, and after eighteen years or so the summer
solstice will occur in December. Finding a system that reconciled
the lunar year with the solar year was the great challenge of calendar-
making.

Most ancient societies readjusted their calendars by adding a
thirteenth, "intercalary" month every three years or so, although
methods of calculating the length of these months, and when they
should be added, were never precise. Babylonian astronomers hit
upon an improvement. They discovered that there are 235 lunar
months in nineteen years. In other words, if you observe a full moon
on April 4, there will be another full moon in that same place on
April 4 nineteen years later. This cycle, which eventually came to
be known as the Metonic cycle, after the Greek astronomer Meton
of Athens, was an extremely useful tool for keeping the lunar calendar and the solar calendar in sync. (The Metonic cycle is still used
by the Christian churches to calculate the correct day for celebrat-
ing Easter.) The Babylonians also established what would come to
be known as the saros cycle, which is a way of predicting the likely
occurrence of eclipses. Babylonian astronomers observed that eighteen years, eleven days, and eight hours after an eclipse, a nearly

identical eclipse will occur. Eclipses were believed by many ancient societies to be omens that, depending on how they were interpreted, could foretell the future of a monarch, for example, or the outcome of a military campaign.

The Greeks, in turn, discovered the Callippic cycle, which consisted of four Metonic cycles minus one day, and was an even more precise way to reconcile the cycles of the sun and the moon. But the Greeks' real genius was to work out theories to explain these cycles. In particular, they brought the concept of geometry to Babylonian astronomy. As Alexander Jones, a professor of classics at the University of Toronto, put it to me, "The Greeks saw the Babylonian formulas in terms of geometry—they saw all these circles all spinning around each other in the sky. And of course this fits in perfectly with the concept of gearworks—the gears are making little orbits." Some Greek inventor must have realized that it was possible to build a simulation of the movements in the heavens by reproducing the cycles with gears.

But who? Price called the inventor simply "some unknown ingenious mechanic." Others have speculated that the inventor was Hipparchus, the greatest of all ancient Greek astronomers. Hipparchus, who is also believed to have invented trigonometry, lived on the island of Rhodes from about 140 to 120 B.C. He detailed a theory to explain the anomalous movements of the moon, which appears to change speed during its orbit of the earth. Hipparchus is also thought to have founded a school on Rhodes that was maintained after his death by Posidonius, with whom Cicero studied in 79 B.C. In one of his letters, Cicero mentions a device "recently constructed by our friend Posidonius," which sounds very like the Mechanism, and "which at each revolution reproduces the same motions of the sun, the moon, and the five planets that take place in the heavens every day and night."

As Moussas and I headed uphill toward the Acropolis, he pointed out the spot where Meton's astronomy school and solar observatory had been. On our way back down, we stopped at the famous Tower of the Winds, the now gutted shell of what was the great central clock of ancient Athens. Designed by the renowned astronomer Andronicus of Cyrrhus, it is thought to have been an elaborate water clock on the inside and a sundial on the outside. "But in light of what we know about the Mechanism," Moussas said, "I am beginning to wonder whether this was a much more complicated clock than we think."

When Derek Price died, of a heart attack, in 1983, his work on the Mechanism was unfinished. Although his fundamental insights about the device were sound, he hadn't figured out all the details, nor had he succeeded in producing a working model that was correct in all aspects. That year, in London, a Lebanese man walked into the Science Museum on Exhibition Road with an ancient geared mechanism wrapped in a piece of paper in his pocket. Later, he showed it to Michael Wright, one of the curators of mechanical engineering. J. V. Field, another curator at the museum, was summoned to examine the artifact, which was in four main fragments. According to Wright, the man said that he'd bought the artifact in a street market in Beirut several weeks earlier. The Science Museum eventually bought it from him, and Wright and Field proved that it was a geared sundial calendar that displayed the positions of the sun and the moon in the zodiac. Wright also built a reconstruction of the sundial. The style of lettering on the dial dated the device to the sixth century A.D., making it the second-oldest geared device ever found, after the Antikythera Mechanism.

In addition to his job as a curator, Wright helped to maintain the old clocks exhibited in the museum. Among them was a replica of the oldest clock that we have a clear account of, constructed in the early fourteenth century by Richard of Wallingford, the Abbot of Saint Albans. It was a fantastic astronomical device called the Albion ("All-by-One"). Another reconstruction was of a famous planetarium and clock built by Giovanni de' Dondi of Padua in the mid-fourteenth century, known as the Astrarium. Like many students of mechanical history, Wright had noted this odd upwelling of clockwork in Europe, appearing in several places at around the same time. He was familiar with the theory that many of the elements of clockwork were known to the ancients. With the decline of the West, goes this theory, technical expertise passed to the Islamic world, just as many of the Greek texts were translated into Arabic and therefore preserved from loss or destruction. In the ninth century, the Banu Musa brothers, of Baghdad, published the *Book of Ingenious Devices,* which detailed many geared mechanical contrivances, and the tenth-century philosopher and astronomer al-Biruni (973–1048) describes a Box of the Moon—a mechanical lunisolar calendar that used eight gearwheels. The more Wright looked into these old Islamic texts, the more convinced he became that the ancient Greeks' knowledge of gearing had been kept alive in the Islamic world and reintroduced to the West, probably by Arabs in thirteenth-century Spain.

In the course of this research, Wright became intensely interested in the Antikythera Mechanism. Upon studying Price's account closely, he realized that Price had made several fundamental errors in the gearing. "I could see right away that Price's reconstruction doesn't explain what we can see," he told me. "The man who made the Mechanism made no mistakes. He went straight to what he wanted, in the simplest way possible." Wright resolved to complete Price's work, and to build a working model of the Mechanism.

Whereas Price worked mainly on an academic level, approaching the Mechanism from the perspective of mathematical and astronomical theory, Wright drew on his vast practical knowledge of arbors, crown wheels, and other mechanical techniques used in gear-train design. His experience in repairing old grandfather clocks, many of which also have astronomical displays that show the phases of the moon, led him to one of his key insights into the engineering of the Mechanism. He posited that there must have been a revolving ball built in the front dial that indicated the phases of the moon—one hemisphere was black, the other white, and the ball rotated as the moon waxed or waned. Wright also showed how a pin-and-slot construction could be used to model the movement of the moon.

Wright, who was fifty-eight, had a British public-school demeanor, which was generally courteous and hearty and seemingly rational. But he was prey to dark moods, wild, impolitic outbursts, and overcomplicated personal entanglements—"muddles," he called them. Although, he told me, "I really hate confrontation, and antagonism of any kind, even competition," he consistently found himself in disastrous confrontations with people who should be his allies. Whereas academic researchers are used to collaboration and to sharing resources and insights, Wright was temperamentally more like a lone inventor, working away in secrecy and solitude until he had found the solution.

He did have a collaborator once—Allan Bromley, a lecturer in computer science at the University of Sydney and an expert on Charles Babbage, the nineteenth-century British mathematician who was the first to conceive of the programmable computer. Bromley used to come to the Science Museum to study Babbage's papers and drawings, and Wright would often lunch with him. In 1990 the pair took new X-rays of the Mechanism, the first since Price's. But Bromley brought the data back to Sydney and would allow Wright to see only small portions of the material. (According to Wright, Bromley confessed "that he had it fixed in his mind that it would be his name, preferably alone, that would be attached to the 'solution.'")

Meanwhile, Wright got into a muddle with his boss at the Science Museum, an "out-and-out bully" who would allow Wright to work on the Mechanism only in his free time. ("We don't do the ancient world," Wright remembered another colleague saying.) This meant that while Wright's wife would go on holiday with their children, Wright would go to the museum in Athens. (Eventually, after years of this routine, he and his wife divorced.)

By the late 1990s, Bromley was dying of cancer. Wright went to see him in Sydney, and Bromley turned much of the data over to him. Just as Wright was finally able to work up their findings for publication, however, he learned of the research project and the effort to take a new set of X-rays of the Mechanism. Instead of viewing this new investigation as a potential boon, he saw it as an improper encroachment on his own turf. "There is a long-established unwritten law concerning the study of Greek antiquities, which is that when one researcher has access to the material, any other researcher is denied access until the first has finished," he wrote to me. "In my case, this understanding was swept aside through the machinations of the group." So, when he arrived at the National Museum while the Bladerunner's X-rays were in progress, he was not excited, like the others; he was "angry, tired, and depressed."

The first images of Fragment D to appear on the Bladerunner's monitor were stunning—"so much better than we dared to hope," Freeth told me. "They took your breath away." Inside the corroded rock was what looked like a geared embryo—the incipient bud of an industrial age that remained unborn for a millennium.

Then the team spotted an odd-looking inscription. Andrew Ramsey, X-Tek's computer-tomography specialist, who was operating the viewer, zoomed around inside the 3-D representation until he found the right slice. Written on the side of the gear were the letters *M* and *E*—ME. Was this the maker's mark? Or could ME mean "Part 45"? (ME is the symbol for forty-five in ancient Greek.) Freeth joked that Mike Edmunds had scratched his initials on the fragment. Others suggested that this particular piece of the Mechanism could have been recycled, and that the ME was left over from some earlier device.

Altogether, the team salvaged about a thousand new letters and inscriptions from the Mechanism—doubling the number available to Price. Together with earlier imaging, the new inscriptions support theories that both Price and Wright had advanced. On Fragment E, for example, the group read "235 divisions on the spiral." "I was amazed," Freeth said. "This completely vindicated Price's idea of the Metonic cycle of two hundred and thirty-five lunar months on the upper back dial." They also read words explaining that on the extremity of "the pointer stands a little golden sphere," which probably refers to a representation of the sun on the sun pointer that went around the zodiac dial at the front of the Mechanism. Wright had proposed that the rings of the back dials were made in the form of spirals; the word *eliki,* meaning "spiral," can be seen on Fragment E. On Fragment 22, the number 223 has been observed, pointing to the use of the saros dial as an eclipse indicator.

It was, as Xenophon Moussas put it to me, as if "we had discovered the user's manual, right inside the machine." What had been regarded mainly as an archeological artifact took on a different sort of artifactual status, as an important astronomical text. Very few copies of original astronomical texts remain from the period; most of our knowledge about ancient astronomy comes from other, later astronomers. Little of Hipparchus's writing survives; we rely largely on Ptolemy of Alexandria, who some believe took much of Hipparchus's work and called it his own.

Many of the inscriptions took months to read. Yanis Bitsakis, the Ph.D. student, collaborated with Freeth and the X-Tek team in rendering the X-ray data as computer images, while Agamemnon Tselikas, a leading Greek paleographer, did all the readings and most of the translations. As Bitsakis explained to me, "One of the difficulties in reading the texts was that in ancient Greek there were no spaces between the words, and there are many alternative readings. Also, in many cases the edges of the lines are missing, so we don't know what is continuous text." He and Tselikas would work on the readings through the night, frequently e-mailing and calling other members of the team about new discoveries. Moussas remembers this period, lasting until the spring of 2006, as "the most interesting time in my life." For example, finding the words *sphere* and *cosmos* was extremely moving, Moussas told me: "I felt as though I were communicating with an ancient colleague, through the Mechanism."

One day, I paid a visit to Michael Wright, in his book-and-clock-cluttered home in West London. Wright was reading Xenophon, the Greek historian, in ancient Greek. He put the book down and brought out his model of the Mechanism from a cabinet underneath the stairs. In size, it is startlingly similar to a laptop computer, though a bit thicker. On the front dial, in addition to the pointers for the sun and the moon that Price posited, Wright added pointers for the planets and a separate pointer for the day of the year. On the back dial were 223 divisions, marking months in the saros cycle; a similar dial above that showed months in the Metonic cycle. The gears were hidden inside a wooden casing, which had a large wooden knob on one side.

Wright was still a little upset about what he considered the sweeping claims that the research group had made when it published its findings, in the November 30, 2006, issue of *Nature*. He almost stayed home from the two-day conference on the Mechanism that the group put on in early December. In the end, he decided to go, taking his wife, Anne, whom he married in 1998, "to stop me from lifting my knee in some chap's groin."

We went upstairs to Wright's workshop. It was filled with tools and pieces of metal, and the air held the pleasantly acrid scent of machine oil. Scattered across the tables and the floor were clever devices that Wright had fashioned out of gears—clocks, astrolabes, engines of various kinds. I recalled Price's description of the maker of the Mechanism—"some unknown ingenious mechanic"—and wondered if this mysterious maker might have been a bit like Wright, with a workshop similarly cluttered with machines.

Wright took his model apart and showed me how all the gears fitted together. I noticed some writing on a rectangular metal plate in the middle of the mechanism, and Wright told me that it was made of recycled bits of brass left over from some previous incarnation.

"So you think that the letters ME—"

"Precisely," Wright interjected. "I think they must relate to whatever that bit of metal was used for before."

Then Wright put the machine back together and turned the hand knob that drives the solar gear. It engaged with the smaller gears through the various gear trains, and the pointers began to spin around the dials. The day-of-the-year pointer moved forward at a regular pace, but the lunar and planetary pointers traced eccentric orbits, sometimes reversing course and going backward, just as the planets occasionally appear to do in the night sky. Meanwhile, the pointers on the back dials crept through the months in the saros and Metonic cycles; eclipses came and went. I noticed that as long as he kept turning the knob, Wright himself seemed, for once, perfectly unmuddled.

Until this moment, I had, like many others, continued to puzzle over why, if the Greeks were capable of building such a technically sophisticated device, they used that capacity to construct what is essentially a toy—an intellectual amusement. But as I beheld this whirring, whirling symphony of metal, a perfect simulation of a mechanistic and logical universe, I realized that my notions of practicality were foolish and shortsighted. This machine was much more than a toy; it embodied a whole worldview, and it must have been, for the ancients, wonderfully reassuring to behold.

—2007

# INVISIBLE GOLD

Set near the midpoint of Interstate 80's long trip through Nevada, the town of Battle Mountain is for most travelers merely a pit stop, a place to get gas or to eat a hamburger in one of the twenty-four-hour cafés. In another time, it served passengers on the Southern Pacific Railroad in a similar way; now the trains carry freight only and rarely stop. The railroad neatly bisects the town, and there is a right side of the tracks and a wrong side. The houses on the right side are mostly one-story frame structures, with tidy, treeless yards, white picket fences, and concrete sidewalks, which the seasons—bitter winters and blazing-hot summers—have buckled eccentrically. The houses on the wrong side are in rattier condition, many of them shingled with faded asbestos and surrounded by junked cars—little more than shacks, really, with the exception of the town's two brothels, the Calico Club and the Desert Club, both prosperous-looking establishments. A gritty, salt-flavored wind gusts indiscriminately over right side and wrong, shrouding the town in a thin curtain of dust, and this, combined with the heat rippling up from the desert, makes Battle Mountain, viewed from a distance, difficult to distinguish from other desert mirages, at least by day. By night it is a small oasis of neon, a low saucer of light on the horizon.

During the 1980s, over forty million ounces of gold had been found all around Battle Mountain. Forty million ounces was more gold than came out of any of the bonanzas that feature so prominently in our national mythology, including the California bonanza of 1849. There was gold in the Battle Mountain Formation, the range that runs southeast of town; gold in the alluvium to the west; gold in the Black Rock Desert to the northwest; gold in the Sheep Creek Range and in the Tuscarora Mountains to the northeast. The Tuscaroras were especially rich. Along the Carlin Trend, a forty-mile stretch of this range, were twelve deposits. Some people believed that a much richer swath of ore, a deposit to rival South Africa's Gold Reef, ran unbroken under the Carlin Trend, perhaps three thousand feet down—more than three times as deep as the deepest mines there now go. Other people thought such talk was merely boomtown hysteria—but, because the last gold bonanza in this country, the rush for Goldfield and Bullfrog in 1904, was fading from living memory, a sober historical perspective was much more the exception than the rule.

The physical as well as the social center of town was the Owl Club, a café-restaurant-bar-casino that stayed open twenty-four hours a day, three hundred and sixty-five days a year. At all hours, there passed through the Owl the array of people that a contemporary gold rush attracts: drillers, miners, construction workers, surveyors, geologists, metallurgists, engineers, federal marshals, stock promoters, corporate executives. Everyone shouted over the clangor of the slot machines—levers ratcheting, counters clicking and whirring, payoff bells sounding, coins clanking into aluminum trays. Miners came into the bar with the latest gold prices from the metals markets, just as their ancestors supposedly rushed into the saloon with bags of glittering dust. Two engineers discussed the economics of extracting gold from seawater, which the Japanese had recently attempted. A metallurgist described a microbe that digests sulfur, and could be used to eat gold free from certain refractory hosts. A "black-box geologist," a sort of modern dowser, explained how his contraption works: "I have a magnet in there, and it's attached to a quartz spring. The idea's pretty simple. I just walk around out there, and whenever I get over some big metallic object—an ore body, in other words—my magnet gives a tiny tug on my spring, and my

spring sends a signal to my instrument." The drillers told driller stories. Stretch, six feet eight and two hundred and fifty pounds, told
Tiny, six feet ten and about three hundred, about a buddy: "There
was this old boy who was drilling down at Round Mountain when
the pit floor gave way on him. He sees the rig sliding toward him,
and he goes, 'Oh, man, it's going to crush me to death.' Then the dirt
starts falling in on him, and he figures he'll be buried alive. Then
the water—they got a lot of groundwater down there—starts jetting
up over him, and he thinks it's going to drown him. Then he realizes
it's hot water, and he thinks it's going to boil him. All in the space of
like two seconds. Said his life flashed before his eyes four times."

Though the gold had brought some three thousand people to
town, almost doubling the population, jamming the trailer parks and
tying up the motels, the transients were nearly all industry professionals. A gold rush in the romantic sense—a stampede of would-be
millionaires, a long trail of U-Hauls snaking along Interstate 80—
was not what I found here. There was in town only one amateur ar-
gonaut, a former maintenance worker from Syracuse who read about
the bonanza in *Treasure* and decided to come West and find a fortune. So far, fortune had eluded him. He was forced to take a job in
the Owl—maintenance again—but was fired not long ago for playing the slot machines on duty.

Still, housing was a serious problem. Potential developers considered the shortage an opportunity; the local government, however,
mindful of the ruinous consequences of a bust—a phenomenon
nicely illustrated by the ghost towns in the surrounding desert—
wanted to deal prudently with the situation. Fortunately, the principal developer in town, a portly, red-faced, easygoing man named Bill
Elquist, also happened to be the chairman of the County Commission, so some agreeable solutions to the housing problem were in the
works. "More trailer parks," Elquist said, pointing out what will be
the town's fifth, on a parcel of land he had recently sold to Echo Bay
Mines, which was one of the large companies operating in the area.
Next to the park was a colony of modular homes, also an Elquist
enterprise.

Elquist said he wouldn't mind seeing the town grow in an orderly
way to twice its present size but didn't think it would happen. People

in Battle Mountain tended to distrust mining booms, no matter how promising. They had lived through plenty of them: uranium in the 1950s, copper in the sixties, mercury and molybdenum in the seventies, barite in the late seventies and early eighties. All those booms brought with them the same infectious optimism that has now come with gold. "These mining boys, they all say this boom's going to last till the year 2000, and I hope it does," Elquist said. "But nobody's counting on it, see?" Nobody wanted to repeat the recent barite debacle. The price of barite, a mineral used in drilling oil wells, rose dramatically in 1978. Barite deposits were discovered all around Battle Mountain. The county put in a sewage system designed for a community of eight thousand, built a new high school, paved the main street. Some local miners decided, in a moment of hubris, to erect a sign on Interstate 80 that said "Battle Mountain—The Barite Capitol of the World." It was a bad sign, and not only because the word *capital* was misspelled. Shortly after it went up, the oil business collapsed, and the price of barite plummeted. By 1982, the boom was over, though the taxpayers were still paying for the civic improvements. One of the howling desert winds took care of the sign.

Now there was a new sign, erected by the Chamber of Commerce, which says "Battle Mountain—No Riddles, No Jokes."

"It's kind of catchy," Elquist said.

"But what does it mean?"

"Well, right there's what catches people. Nobody really knows."

About six miles outside town, in the middle of a lonely basin lightly sprinkled with sage, sat a Cadillac plated with gold. Hubcaps, grille, headlights, fenders, and even the locks on the doors, were plated with gold—a burnished, coppery gold that shone fiercely enough to be seen from the Interstate, about a mile away. Emeralds, diamonds, and rubies glittered in the Cadillac hood ornament and in the two Cadillac insignia, on either side of the canopy. The license plate said P Davis, and in the rear window was some red neon lettering, rigged to the brake pedal, that said Davis Gold Mining. A few steps away was a battered white trailer home with some Keep Out signs near the door.

Phillip A. Davis rarely came into Battle Mountain, and some of the town's inhabitants considered him reclusive and eccentric. He hardly ever came into the Owl, where gossiping about him is a popular pastime. The theory was that Phil changed when, seven years ago, he began receiving regular payments from his gold mine, which lately had averaged seventy-five thousand dollars a month. He became "a little weird" and "real suspicious," people said, some of them sympathetically. Then, elaborating, they told the story of how he was robbed by a girlfriend and several cowboys who worked on a nearby ranch. The girlfriend, whose name was Pinkie, or maybe Red—nobody could remember exactly—knew that Phil had hidden his first payment, which he'd insisted on getting in cash, under the floor of his trailer home. After Phil went to sleep one night, the girlfriend unlocked the trailer door; the cowboys came in and clubbed him unconscious, breaking his jaw and damaging an eye, then ripped up the floor and made off with the money. That happened in 1982, and Davis had been much less sociable with his old friends since (and he now kept his money in banks); some said he had turned mean, but more charitable people thought his orneriness was merely a pose, and that in reality he was a nice guy—take, for example, the fact that he carried candy in his pockets to give to children.

There were lots of people in town who believed that soon—next spring, maybe, or maybe next year—they too would get rich from their claims, but so far only Phil Davis had struck gold. His mine was the Dee, one of the twelve deposits in the Carlin Trend. Ten of the others belonged to the Newmont Gold Company, and the eleventh, the Goldstrike, belonged to American Barrick Resources. Compared with the ore reserves and the production capacities that its corporate neighbors possess, the Dee was a pint-sized operation. Newmont had some sixteen million ounces of gold in the ground, worth about six and a third billion dollars at the current price, and in 1988 produced 895,000 ounces, which made it the largest producer of gold in North America. American Barrick produced 341,000 ounces in 1988. The Dee produced some 50,000 ounces. Provided that nothing interfered with the production schedule, and no new ore was discovered, the Dee deposit would be exhausted in 1994. Phil Davis was expected to earn about nine million dollars from it, all told.

Phil liked to refer to himself as "the little guy," as in "I'm the little guy, the last of a breed," and "Mr. Big Company don't care for the little guy, I'll tell you that." Don Smith, a local resident who introduced me to Phil, also advertised himself as a little guy; a lot of the locals did. He, too, drove a Cadillac—a non-gold-plated 1976 Eldorado with almost three hundred thousand miles on it—and we were riding down Front Street in it when he spotted Phil, going into the new Econ-O-Mart, right next to the Chevron station. We parked and followed him in.

"I hear they got this mug here," Phil was saying. "I got to have one of those mugs." He was straightening shelves as he went, picking up cans—a can of peas, a can of Chef Boy-ar-dee spaghetti—muttering over them awhile, then putting them back. He bustled over to the manager, shook his hand enthusiastically, complimented him repeatedly on the store, and asked about the mug. "That's the one, that's the baby," he said when it was shown to him. It was an ordinary mug, the kind that coffee shops use. Phil bought it, and lingered a little to compliment the manager some more, turning the mug over and over in his hands as he talked.

When we were outside, I said I was interested in the story of how he had come by his gold mine.

"That's what they all want to know, that's the one they all ask," Phil said. He was jaunty, flexing up and down in his boots, and although it was twilight, he was squinting fiercely. The big neon Chevron sign over us made a cherry-red glow in his eyeglasses. He went on, interrogating himself. "Yep. 'How did you do it, Phil? What's the secret, Phil?'"

"And what do you tell them?"

"Depends on who's asking. The little guy's got to watch out for himself. He don't get much help." He rattled off a list of some of the little guy's enemies: large mining companies, banks, politicians, the Bureau of Land Management, the Forest Service, Wall Street.

Don said that just last spring he himself had put off taking his wife to Reno in order to talk to two financial reporters from the East. "And you know something? They didn't put anything about the little guy in the story they wrote. It was about how great your big companies are, your Newmonts, your American Barricks."

"That's bad," Phil said. "That's real bad."

"That's the way outsiders think, you see," Don said heatedly. "They think this gold is all about Wall Street. Who do they think owns the gold in the first place? Some investment analyst? Some smart-ass geologist? Nope. The little guy owns it. He has the claims, see?"

Phil shook his head and smiled, unmoved by Don's grievances. Lazily, he took a small leather case from his back pocket and opened it far enough to show a pistol inside. Then he winked theatrically and tucked the case back into his jeans. "There are those who have done what they shouldn't have done," he said. "I got to be careful." He lowered his voice confidentially. "I got people following me around whenever I'm out in those hills. Yes, sir. They sit up on top of that mountain over there and watch me with telescopes. There are a lot of people who want what I've got—know what I mean?" He laughed, and hollered, "Too many cans of pork and beans, know what I mean?" Still laughing, he climbed into a Toyota pickup, one of his everyday vehicles. Don and I watched him drive away.

"Guess he don't take the Cadillac out much," Don said soberly.

Don Smith was the president of Citizens for Mining, a local advocacy group that he helped organize in 1977 to protect, in his words, "the interests of the little guy." He was often to be found in one of the window booths at the Owl; he came in almost every morning for his breakfast, a maple bar, and sometimes for his lunch, another maple bar. He watched the parade of transients, a somewhat cynical expression on his face. He was a leathery man, sixty-two years old, with sloping eyes and prominent cheekbones, who was invariably dressed in a short-sleeved machinist's outfit; his forearms were festooned with tattoos. He had an incongruous high-pitched giggle. Like many longtime residents of Battle Mountain, Don was a miner more by avocation than by trade. He prospected when he had time, and mined placer gold when he had the inclination. Placer mining had the advantage of being relatively simple and cheap. Erosion has already done the hardest work: it has washed the gold out of the mountains and into the valleys, where, in the form of specks, flakes, and nuggets, it lies mingled with the alluvium. One has only to wash the sand and gravel, a task that the primitive miner performed with a pan. A more modern miner does it with a dredge—a large floating contraption equipped with scoops, whirling buckets, and a sloping riffled table. But placer mining is much less lucrative than hard-rock mining, also known as lode mining—the kind of mining that was going on along the Carlin Trend. Nature had scattered placer gold widely. Don cherished the hope of finding an exceptionally large nugget, but worried that one of his crew—he generally employed three helpers—might find it first, and pocket it. He tried to encourage honesty by handing out bonuses, but as a rule, he said, "hawk-eyed watchfulness is your best policy." He also had a cash-flow problem: he hated to sell the gold he found. He had six raisin-size nuggets soldered around the face of his Timex watch. Only the direst conditions could induce him to liquidate part of his hoard. When his wife had a heart ailment, Don sold his backhoe to pay the medical bills. He would grow silent, a rare state for Don, when he looked at his gold. He would tell the story that each nugget carries: where he was when he found it, who was with him, the weather, the angle of the sun.

But the big money is in lode, not placer. Don had 345 lode claims—down from an all-time high of 782 but nonetheless, at twenty acres a claim, an impressive amount of property. Each of these claims is supposed to represent a discovery: so stipulates the Mining Law of 1872, that quintessentially American law which entitles United States citizens to mine hard-rock minerals on public land. However, the Mining Law does not define the word *discovery*, and the legal definition, which a secretary of the interior wrote in 1894, is vague: "Minerals have been found and the evidence is of such a character that a person of ordinary prudence would be justified in the further expenditure of his labor and means, with a reasonable prospect of success, in developing a valuable mine." Don may or may not have displayed "ordinary prudence" in staking these claims, but it was highly unlikely that his prudence would be challenged in court. In practice, the courts rely on the doctrine of *pedis possessio*, which means roughly "first come, first served."

In Nevada, the cost of a lode claim was then fifteen dollars. The

Mining Law stipulates that the claimant must perform a hundred dollars' worth of work on his claim each year in order for it to remain valid. In 1872 a hundred and fifteen dollars was a steep enough price to discourage people from staking claims frivolously or from hoarding large blocks of claims, but the price has remained the same over the years, and a hundred and fifteen dollars is a bargain today. Still, $34,500, Don's annual bill for the work on his 345 claims, was rather steep, or it would be if Don had to pay it. Actually, he paid not a penny; his lessees paid him. A mining concern—it may be a large company or it may be a fly-by-night exploration outfit assembled by stock promoters—paid to explore a package of Don's claims over a fixed period. The price varied according to the size of the package and to how attractively situated the properties are. The Carlin Trend was considered prime real estate, and Don had a small parcel of claims at the northern end of it. In general, the nearer a claim is to a known deposit, the higher its rental value is. Any encouraging piece of evidence enhances the value of adjoining claims, and Don listened to miners' gossip, fanning the rumors when it was in his interest to, and checked the land-status maps in the courthouse for unclaimed patches in up-and-coming areas. All his leases contained a discovery clause, which obliged the lessee to pay Don a royalty, usually between 3 and 5 percent, on whatever was found. The clause had never been put into effect.

The Owl served as an office of sorts for him.

"Where you been lately, Don?" said a man wearing unmuddied boots and a freshly laundered plaid shirt—evidently a city person trying to look rustic.

"Oh," Don said. "Out. Enjoying the scenery."

"Heard you've been up by Mountain City."

"Some real nice scenery up that way." Don slipped a Pall Mall out of his breast pocket. "You might want to see it sometime."

"I'd like that, Don."

"I think you'd like it."

"That's a real nice watch you've got, Don," the man said, bending toward it, and then, "Hell, I'm late. I got to go. I'll be talking to you, Don."

"You know where to find me."

"Promoter," Don said when the man had gone. "These boys come down here from Vancouver looking to lease some of my claims. Oh, they act like they don't really want 'em. It's always, 'Oh, by the way,' or 'So as long as we're at it, here's a few bucks, give us some of your claims.' They're not interested in finding gold, really. They're just looking to set up some kind of exploration company that they can list on the Vancouver Exchange. Then they spread the rumor that they got a gold mine, and the stock goes up some—maybe from a quarter to two dollars a share—and the promoter and his buddies sell quick and make a bundle. Course, they don't always make a bundle." A burst of giggling. "Sometimes they can't sell at the right time and they lose a bundle. Anyway, those are the types of guys I do most of my business with, and it's fine by me, 'cause it's real straightforward. If they actually found gold on my property—oh, hell, then I'd have headaches. Contracts, lawyers—all kinds of headaches."

"But you'd be rich."

"Oh, I'm doing okay as it is."

"How much do you make from renting your claims?"

More giggling. "Enough to keep me in T-bones."

Don held the Mining Law to be "the best damn law ever written." It was "the only friend the little guy's got." He often heard people argue that the little guy was abusing the law—that in passing it Congress did not intend to make real-estate merchants of prospectors; rather, it hoped to encourage the prospector to develop the nation's mineral resources and, in doing so, to help colonize the West. In current practice, goes this argument, the Mining Law actually inhibits mining: it gives licenses to squatters, speculators, and extortionists, with the result that the miner who actually finds a mineral deposit can expect to face a nightmarish snarl of title suits and contractual negotiations, often involving three, five, maybe ten different claimants.

Don believed that Congress, in passing the Mining Law, meant to give the individual a means of competing with capital, and that the individual is within the spirit, if not the letter, of the law in doing what he can to safeguard that privilege. "In the old days, guys like me could go out and with some luck we could find a surface deposit. We'd get a couple of buddies together and mine it ourselves. Now the surface deposits are all gone. You got to drill to find an ore body, and these drill holes run you about twenty-five thousand bucks a pop. That's for one six-hundred-foot hole. You may have to drill ten, maybe twenty holes before you discover the ore body. Where's the little guy going to get that kind of money? Banks? Hell, no bank's going to loan him the money. They only loan to the big companies. People say, 'Well, if the little guy can't afford to make the discovery he should just butt out of the whole process.' But I say, 'Why should the gold go to the ones who have already got money?' If Congress had wanted it that way, it would never have passed the Mining Law in the first place."

In 1987 the House Subcommittee on Mining and Natural Resources held an oversight hearing on the Mining Law. Chief among the topics debated was whether or not the current policy of free access to hard-rock minerals on federal lands ought to be replaced by some kind of discretionary permitting system, such as exists for oil, natural gas, and geothermal deposits. Under this system, the prospector would have to apply to the federal government for the right to explore in the public domain. If the government approved his application, it would grant him a lease, the terms of which would resemble those of the leases that Don writes—a certain time for a certain price—and the government would get a share of whatever the prospector discovered. If more than one party was interested in the same piece of ground, the government would auction the lease. The advocates of this system, among the most outspoken of which is the Sierra Club, believe that it has several advantages over the policy of free access: it is consistent with the manifesto contained in the Federal Land Policy and Management Act of 1976; namely, "It is the policy of the United States that . . . the public lands be retained in Federal ownership." It would bring the federal government billions of dollars of extra revenue. And, by rationalizing the laws concerning mineral exploration, it would stimulate mining.

"It would be the death of the little guy"—that was Don's opinion of a leasing system, and he was probably right. People like Don could never hope to outbid a corporation for the right to explore public land. Perhaps, however, the little guy's time has come and gone;

perhaps he, like the nineteenth-century law that keeps him in business, is an anachronism. To this argument Don had two responses. The first is a sentimental one—"When you talk about wiping out the prospector, you're talking about wiping out just about the most American type there is"—but it played well with politicians. The second was that little guys are indispensable to the discovery process. They perform the tedious and, to many industry geologists, unacceptable task of primary exploration—tramping the deserts and the mountains searching for surface anomalies. They can then broker that information to companies well enough endowed to act upon it. Don felt that the mining industry would suffer dramatically if the prospectors were squeezed out, and as an example he cited what happened to uranium. The Atomic Energy Act of 1946 excluded uranium from the provisions of the Mining Law and set up a leasing system administered by the Atomic Energy Commission. A small army of geologists was dispatched to build up the government's reserves of this suddenly strategic mineral. Very little uranium was discovered. In 1954 the Atomic Energy Act was repealed, and within two years private prospectors had discovered so much uranium that there was a huge oversupply. "You can't put the job of finding minerals in the hands of geologists" was Don's conclusion. "I'd rather have a guy with a crooked stick walk my property than a geologist." He pronounced the word "ge-o-lo-gist," dismantling it piece by piece.

Don's opinions were often seconded by Andy Hampton, a fellow prospector and a regular patron of the Owl. Andy was eighty-six years old, and pudgy and cute, like an elderly cherub; he was a great favorite of the waitresses in the Owl, who were forever cooing and fussing over him, and giggling over his proposals of marriage. Andy took up prospecting in earnest twenty-one years ago, when he retired from his job as a tool designer and moved to Battle Mountain with his wife, Grace. Grace died in 1984, and Andy's best friend and prospecting partner died in 1987, at the age of ninety-one, but Andy said he didn't feel lonely or old. "In a way, my whole life is up ahead of me. I could end up a millionaire. How many guys my age can say that?" A lot of his time was spent studying his "microfish," he said, meaning the land-status transparencies that he pored over in search of unclaimed pieces of land. He had a parcel of seventy-two claims about fifteen miles west of town, near an old mine called the Marigold.

"Let's say it's a smallish sort of a deposit I got on my property, around two hundred and twenty-five thousand ounces," Andy said one morning in the Owl, pouring syrup over his pancakes. "So, with the price of gold what it is, four hundred and fifty-two dollars I believe it was this morning, that comes to—What's that come to, Don?"

"Around a hundred and two million dollars," Don said, with the air of a man for whom nine-figure discussions are routine.

"So if I lease my claims for a three-percent net smelter royalty . . ."

"Well, you figure one percent would earn you a million, so three percent gets you just over three."

"Say three and a half million." Andy had not yet mastered the sangfroid with which Don bandies great fortunes about: he made a game stab at it, though, squeezing his lips together and bobbing his pink, nearly hairless head rapidly.

"You could probably get four percent," Don said, taking out another Pall Mall. "Four's what Phil Davis gets. Or what he's supposed to get, anyway."

Andy pulled a face at the sound of Phil Davis's name. It bothered Andy, it offended his sense of justice, that Phil Davis, of all people in town, should be the one to strike it rich. "The truth is," Andy said, "me and Don were the ones who really found the Dee mine. Isn't that right, Don?"

"Well, no," Don said, with a worried glance at my pen and pad. "That isn't exactly right."

"But we were the ones responsible for Phil getting those claims, wouldn't you say?"

Don sighed, blew out a plume of smoke, and looked rather glumly out the window. Personally, it seemed, he was inclined to agree with Andy that Fortune, in making a darling of Phil Davis, had played a cruel little joke on the other prospectors in town. Ideologically, however, he felt a certain allegiance to Phil.

"Tell about how Davis came by those claims, Don," said Andy.

"Well," Don said, turning toward us again. "It was in 1975. Phil

Davis had that trailer of his pulled up on my property. I let him have
free use of the electric and all, and he just lived there in my yard. He
worked as a driller on and off, and before that he was a mechanic.
Supposedly, he went to Pakistan once."

"Yeah, Pakistan," Andy put in. "Or Thailand, maybe."

"Anyhow, he met a guy named Russell Perry over in Elko in
1975. Perry was an oilman, and he was messin' around over in Elko,
doing his six weeks for his divorce. I don't know how Phil met him.
Can't have been in a bar, 'cause old Phil don't hold with drinking
much. I remember once there was this guy standing outside drinking a beer, and old Phil just hauled off and hit him. Just hit him for
drinking a beer."

"He's some kind of health nut," Andy said.

"Oh, yeah. First thing he does in the morning is fifty pushups.
Right out of bed—I seen him. So. Anyway, he meets Perry, and
Perry says as long as he's got to stay in Nevada six weeks he might as
well stake some claims. Like I said, this is in 1975. In 1975 everybody around here was getting crazy for barite. Now it's gold. It's always something. Anyway, then it was barite, and Phil works out a
deal where Perry will pay him to go out and stake some barite claims
for him. So Phil comes back to me and says, 'Where am I going to
stake some barite claims?' And I say, 'Why don't you put 'em next to
my claims up by Rock Creek?'"

Andy harrumphed.

"That's where Andy come in," Don said, reaching for a cigarette.

Andy leaned forward and said, "Phil asked me if I'd help stake
some claims, and I didn't have a whole heck of a lot to do right then,
so I said sure, why not, okay, and I did. Me and this other fellow
went up there. And you know something? We just about did the
whole darn job ourselves. Phil hauled some stakes up from town in
the back of his pickup, but that was it." Andy and Don smirked for a
while.

"Course, we never saw any money," Don said. "Old Perry, he
went off to Europe and got married again, then went back to New
York or someplace—he sort of disappeared. Phil kept the claims
valid by doing the assessment work, and after a couple of years he
advertised Perry out. You know what advertising out is?"

"It's when you put an ad in the local paper," Andy said. "You say, 'If So-and-So wants these properties, he better come forward.'"

"Perry never answered, so the properties went over to Phil," Don said. "Then John Livermore's people, the Cordex group, went up there and found the gold."

"Didn't we hear Perry was involved in some kind of oil scandal down in Louisiana?" Andy asked.

"Yeah, but then we heard that he wasn't. Anyway, that's how Phil got hold of the claims. And you know something? When Phil started getting his money? He just hauled that trailer right off of my yard without saying good-bye or thank you, or anything. I just woke up one morning and it was gone. I ever tell you that, Andy?"

"Believe so," Andy said.

Don nodded, and looked out the window again. "Well, it don't matter. I don't want that kind of money anyway." He put out his cigarette carefully. "You?" he asked Andy.

Andy chewed on his upper lip.

"Two million would be fine," Don said.

"Oh, I'm with you there, Don," said Andy. "You don't need more than two."

To drive to the Carlin Trend from Battle Mountain, one goes eighteen miles east along the interstate to a little colony of mobile homes that is the hamlet of Dunphy, turns left at the cattle guard there, and heads north through the Boulder Valley. The road skirts Boulder Creek for a few miles, climbing, then forks at the top of the valley, where the Sheep Creek Range butts into the higher, craggier Tuscaroras. The right fork, known locally as the Yellow Brick Road, goes to the Bootstrap, Blue Star, Goldstrike, Post, Gold Quarry, and Carlin mines; the left fork leads to the Dee. Though the deposits vary widely in size and also differ in subtle geological ways, they all employ roughly similar production methods. All are open-pit mines. The miners do not tunnel underground for the gold, drifting as the vein drifts and blasting out stopes and adits, as different parts of the tunnel are called. They simply blast and haul out a huge, cone-shaped wedge of earth. To someone whose notion of a gold mine involves little ore carts pushed by men with lights on their hats, it is perhaps disenchanting to see these pits: the work is essentially an earth-moving operation, and the miners are really just truck drivers. But in their own way the pits are fantastic. Standing in them insults one's sense of scale. The axles of the hundred-ton haul trucks are ten feet from the ground, and the shovels on the Demag 285s are eleven yards wide. Everything is almost cartoonishly large. A typical pit descends in concentric circles, in a sequence of tiers: tier, twenty-foot drop, tier, to the bottom. Some pits are shaped like coliseums; others, cut into the sides of mountains, are more like ancient Greek theaters. Sometimes the job is simply to tear a mountain apart. Nearby there is always a new mountain, of waste rock, going up. The largest of the pits, the one that Newmont is digging to mine the Gold Quarry deposit, would be an oval more than a mile wide and twelve hundred feet deep when it was mined out, in 1994. From the air it would look like one of the craters of the moon. But from the Boulder Valley road the pits are hard to distinguish from the gouges and gashes of erosion. Only the occasional dull thud from a blast and, on a windless day, the hazy billows of dust rising tell you that something unnatural is happening in the mountains.

I made this drive early one morning with a geologist named Andy Wallace. Wallace worked for the Cordex Syndicate, the partnership that developed the Dee mine, and one of whose partners operated it. As we drove along, I mentioned my encounter with Phil Davis. Wallace said he had never met the man, but it looked as if he "might be having that pleasure soon." In court, he added, and he went on, "You know about this lawsuit between us? Oh, yeah. Well, it wouldn't be an honest-to-goodness gold mine if it didn't have a lawsuit attached to it." He said that the kernel of the dispute was the royalty that Cordex was supposed to pay Phil. It was to be 4 percent of the net value of the gold if the company mined more than a thousand tons of ore a day, and 6 percent of the net if it mined less than that or if the value of the ore mined was greater than fifty dollars a ton. The ambiguity lay in the word *mined*. To Phil's way of thinking, *mined* meant "milled," and since the mill was treating only about 850 tons a day Phil felt he should be getting 6 percent on some of the ore. But to Cordex *mined* meant "processed," and since the company was blasting and hauling about 1,800 tons of ore a day it was paying 4 percent on all the ore. "That's the main issue, I guess, but there's a whole shopful of other things that have been bothering Phil over the years. He thinks we ought to be exploring for barite. He thinks we're not looking hard enough for more gold on his property. He never thought we knew how to look for gold in the first place. You get that all the time out here—guys who just know they got gold on their claims, and they know right where it is, and they aren't going to take any contradiction from anybody, and especially not from some pointy-headed geologist. They think it's their land, so they know about it. Well, it is their land, sort of. I think the Mining Law is a great law in principle, but when you've got guys tying up big chunks of land, not letting you explore on it unless you do it their way, that's not doing anybody any good—not the country, not them." He shook his head. "You got to talk to John Livermore about Phil Davis. He's the only one who deals with Phil."

We came to the turnoff for the mine. The Dee pit, dug into the far side of the mountain, was hidden from us as we ascended toward it. Thick flurries of grasshoppers were ringing like hail on the sides of the Bronco. Flinders of chert and shale and ragged patches of cheatgrass covered the slope, and the ground was steaming slightly in the early-morning heat. At the top of the ridge was a mechanical gate in a wire-mesh fence, operated from within by a security guard. Wallace spoke to her over the intercom, the gate slid aside, and we drove up to a Quonset-style administration building.

In the reception area, where I waited while Wallace went to see about hard hats and protective glasses, was a computer-generated three-dimensional picture of the ore body, dry-mounted and framed. Mining people have a habit of stretching the metaphor when they talk about their ore bodies. They say how beautiful, how satisfying, how tantalizing their ore body is, they make hourglass shapes with their hands, knead with their fingers, smooth with their palms as they talk. The ore body before me looked something like a bowling pin laid on its side. The ore was depicted as undulating pink ribbons against an inky background. The higher-grade zones were pinker, the lower-grade more anemic-looking.

To someone untutored in the methods of modern mining it

seems marvellous that miners can X-ray their ore as a doctor can X-ray the human body, and many mining companies, conscious of how reassuring these pictures are to nervous investors, reproduce them lavishly in their annual reports. Before any mining began at the Dee, Cordex had announced that the deposit contained 2,670,000 tons of .115 ore (.115 ounces of gold per ton) and 3 million tons of .025 ore, for a total of 382,050 ounces of gold. Actually, there is a good deal of poetry in these figures. They are based on statistical models, a kind of three-dimensional game of connect the dots played by a computer. Each dot represents an assay taken from a drill hole. At the Dee, 247 holes were drilled on hundred-foot centers to an average depth of six hundred feet. An assay was taken every five feet, so there were nearly thirty thousand assays on which to base the reserve projections. The gold values within adjacent five-foot sections varied widely—.120 gold at the 245-foot level, .009 gold at 250—and the ratio of ore to waste within the minable part of the deposit was one to six. Nevertheless, by applying all the assay data to a logarithmic formula the computer was able to make a reasonably accurate estimate of the size, shape, and grade of the ore body. That was the picture I was looking at.

Wallace returned with the safety gear, and we climbed back into the jeep and drove to the lip of the pit. The chasm appeared before us suddenly: grassy tufts one moment, a sheer precipice the next. The pit was an oval about nine hundred feet long, four hundred feet wide, and three hundred feet deep—half as deep as it will be when the mining is finished. Swallows were living high up in the walls, and there were ravens floating on a hot breeze that blew up from the pit floor. The walls were scored as though by claws, from the teeth of the shovels, and streaked with purples, indigos, and orange-yellows, as if enormous globs of colored wax had melted and run down the sides. The colors were mineralized chert, shale, and siltstone, and their variegations indicated folds, faults, dikes, and sills.

The blast crew was working down in the pit, dribbling a gooey paste made of ammonium nitrate and diesel fuel into blast holes that had been drilled twelve feet apart and twenty feet deep. The rock from these holes had been samples, and the high-grade, low-grade, and waste rock had been marked with red, yellow, and white flags, so that the miners would know whether to haul it to the mill, the heap, or the waste pile. In another part of the pit, miners were working on rock that had been blasted the day before. The shovels loaded rock into the haul trucks. The trucks with high-grade rock drove up to the primary crusher, a huge set of steel jaws that chewed the rock into fragments three-quarters of an inch in diameter, then spat it onto a conveyor that ran to a silo just outside the mill. The trucks hauling waste rock drove to the eastern edge of the mountain and dumped their loads. The low-grade rock went to one of four outdoor heaps, the largest of which was thirty feet high and hundreds of feet long. Bulldozers were flattening the tops of the heaps. Irrigation sprinklers were spraying the rubble with a weak cyanide solution. Gold is a noble metal, which is to say that it resists combination with all but a few substances, and cyanide is one of the few. Over the next three weeks, the cyanide solution would gradually percolate through the pile, leaching the gold out of the rocks. The gold-bearing cyanide solution, which miners call the pregnant solution, would eventually reach a sloping rubber pad at the bottom of the heap and run into sluices at the edges. These sluices, as we drove past them, were agurgle with precious, poisonous streams of "preg" that had dripped through the rocks. They flowed downhill into a rubber-lined reservoir, the pregnant pond, and from there went into the mill.

Heap leaching, as this process is called, is an exceptionally inexpensive method of treating low-grade ore, and it is practiced at all the mines along the Trend. It cost Cordex five dollars to mine and leach a ton of ore; that meant that rock with a grade as low as .0125 can be leached profitably when the price of gold was at least four hundred dollars an ounce. However, the process is effective only when it is applied to a particular kind of gold, called invisible gold: tiny particles of gold that are more or less evenly disseminated through the rock. If a nugget turned up in a heap, the cyanide would leach only a fraction of it, but a speck of gold one three-thousandth the size of a grain of sand is easily dissolved; the recovery rate in a heap-leach operation is usually between 60 and 75 percent.

A metallurgist named Frank Hanagarne showed us around the mill. Entering the mill was just as dislocating to the senses as entering the pit had been, but the shock was more to the ears than to the eyes: the rhythmical gnashing of the grinders was amazingly loud. The place, a cavernous barn made of aluminum siding, was windowless and gloomily lit, and smelled vaguely of almonds from the cyanide. We walked to the spot where the high-grade ore, having been smashed by the primary crusher, was conveyed from its silo into the rod crusher, a spinning steel barrel filled with five-hundred-pound rods that smash whatever rock is caught between them. Cyanide and water were being pumped into the barrel, and lime was added to prevent cyanide gas from forming. The pulp from this crusher went up to a centrifuge, and from there the larger pieces went into another crusher, full of fifty-pound steel balls. When the rock was ground to four-hundred mesh (that is, it could pass through a mesh with four hundred openings per square inch, and was about the consistency of talcum powder), it flowed out of the mill into a large open vat. Once it had clarified sufficiently, the liquid on the surface of the vat flowed into a ladder of five columns. Each column contained ground and roasted coconut shells—activated carbon, which is even more attractive to gold than cyanide. The carbon stripped the gold from the cyanide; sterile again, the cyanide went back to the rod crusher at the beginning of the circuit.

The gold-loaded carbon went into four tanks filled with hot caustic soda and antifreeze, which washed the gold from the carbon, and this new pregnant solution flowed into electrolytic cells—hoppers filled with negatively charged bales of steel wool. The gold, which has a positive charge, was plated onto the steel. These metallic golden fleeces were carried to a retort and heated to eleven hundred degrees to purify the gold and to partly oxidize the steel. Then several fluxes were added, chiefly soda ash and borax, and the mixture was heated again—this time to two thousand degrees, in a convection furnace, to liquefy it. The slag—mainly residue from the steel wool—was removed and the remainder was poured into a rectangular mold about the size of a shoebox. Impurities formed a crust of leaded glass on the surface of the mold, which the refinery workers shattered with hammers. What remained was a bar of doré—pale yellow in color, containing roughly equal portions of gold and silver. Wells Fargo carried it to the Johnson, Matthey refinery in Salt Lake

City, where it was melted again and purified to .995 fine. The mill produces one thousand-ounce doré bar a week.

John Livermore, who was mainly responsible for exploring and developing the Dee, had found or helped to find four gold deposits. The Carlin deposit, from which the current bonanza evolved, was the first. His extraordinary success was venerated by both prospectors and geologists, and that was in itself an achievement, since prospectors and geologists rarely agree. Livermore had the credentials to call himself a geologist—a bachelor's degree from Stanford, two years in the United States Geological Survey—and he could speak the ten-dollar words if it pleased him to, but he preferred to think of himself as a prospector. I asked him to elaborate on the difference between the two. "A prospector is a guy who just goes out and tramps the hills. He just looks at the rocks, gets used to them. He doesn't have a definite exploration program in mind. He has ideas about where the gold is, sure, but he doesn't have that methodical, scientific approach that a geologist has—hypothesis, experiment, conclusion. The geological approach is useful when you've got the target sighted in—you're not on the bull's-eye yet, but you're close—whereas the prospector is better at grass-roots exploration."

Most of the prospectors I met viewed the lonesomeness and tedium of their lives as a regrettable but justifiable evil, a means to a magical, scarcely imaginable end: gold, millions, luxury. With Livermore it was just the reverse. Searching for gold was a way of escaping the comfortable life into which he, a member of a wealthy San Francisco family, was born. The Livermore name is a prominent one in San Francisco. Various monuments bear it: on Angel Island, there is a Mount Livermore, named in memory of Livermore's mother, Caroline, who helped preserve the island from further development; there are five stained-glass figures over the eastern portal of Grace Cathedral, and under each is a name of one of the Livermore brothers: John, George, Putnam, Robert, and Norman. John grew up in a big redwood house at the top of Russian Hill. The house still stands, and next to it is a smaller house, where his aunt Elizabeth used to live, and where his brother Putnam lives now. When John Livermore was growing up, in the twenties, Russian Hill was still considered a bohemian community, and the Livermores, though they were prosperous, were not out of their element there. Caroline Livermore was a conservationist before it was fashionable to be one. She was also a founder of the San Francisco branch of Planned Parenthood. Livermore's aunt was a close friend of Norman Thomas and Carl Sandburg. John's father, Norman, ran a machine-manufacturing business and, from his own father, who came to California in the 1850s, inherited Montesol, now a seven-thousand-acre ranch in the Coast Range, about twenty-five miles north of Napa, where John and his four brothers spent each summer. "Altogether, it was, I guess you'd say, a pretty perfect childhood," he told me. "But when I got older, you know, people were aware of what I was doing. If I took a girl out, people talked about it. I'd get invited to society things. I was a Livermore. My brothers stayed in the city, but I really didn't care for it. I wanted to do something that would get me out of all that."

The prospector's existence—days in desolate climates, nights in motel rooms, weeks of solitude, years of tantalizing clues and frustrating near-misses—was certainly a radical change. But a nomadic life suited Livermore. He was seventy-one years old and unmarried; though he numbered marriage high among his priorities, second only to finding another gold mine, there was little reason to suppose that these two pursuits, hitherto incompatible, would be reconciled soon. He owned a one-bedroom apartment in Reno and a vacation house on the Montesol ranch, but neither of these places was in any sense a home. He cannot remember the last time he stayed in one place for more than a week. His wardrobe, as far as I could tell, consisted of hiking boots, a pair of khaki frontier pants, and several shirts. His car, which he drove with alarming abandon, was a battered AMC Eagle. The money he had earned from his discoveries was an acute embarrassment to him. Though he was extremely reluctant to admit it, he had donated millions of dollars to charities.

He had an office on Second Street in Reno, a street that, though its western half was cheerful enough, gliding past a spanking glass-and-steel flank of Harrah's Hotel Casino, deteriorated rapidly as it ran east and crossed the Truckee River. Desert weeds cracked the sidewalk, ten-dollar-a-night rooms were everywhere, the wind was prickly with grit. There were three bail-bonding operations within two blocks of Livermore's office—Art's, Mac's, and Big Jim's—and right next door was Reno Plasma, a plasma bank in front of which, every morning at seven-thirty, about a dozen luckless people usually gathered, waiting to sell their blood for eight dollars a pint.

One day, shortly after Livermore returned from a prospecting trip to South America, I sat in his office with him and a prospector named Whit De La Mare. On the desktop was a small brass burro, about three inches tall. It was nearly buried under prospecting paraphernalia: geological reports, assay figures, maps, contracts, aerial photographs, electromagnetic surveys, gravitometer readings, lawsuits, letters from people who think they have gold on their property, letters from people who know people who have gold on their property. Cardboard boxes full of more of the same covered the floor. The office was low-ceilinged, adorned only with a yellowed and curling map of Colombia and some dusty glass shelves filled with rocks. It was raining—unusual weather for Reno—and water was dripping steadily through the roof.

Livermore began searching the drawers of his desk for a diary. He was a handsome man with a noble forehead, lined now in puzzlement. He couldn't find the diary. Despite his talent for finding ore deposits, he was forever forgetting and losing things—hats, gloves, car keys, wallets. He was, as an associate puts it, "one of the most absent-minded men I've ever met." Nevertheless, he had a phenomenal memory for rocks. "You're out exploring with John," said Larry McIntosh, one of the people who work with him, "and he comes to an outcrop he likes. So he gets all excited, hopping around going, 'Gee, golly, heck'—you never hear John swear—and, 'Boy, oh, boy, this reminds me of that jasperoid we sampled near Beatty in 1965. Our fifth sample ran .195 ounces of gold,' and on and on. It's amazing, really, the stuff that's inside his head. Then you leave that outcrop and cross over onto another ridge and John says, 'Whoops, I forgot my rock hammer,' and goes sprinting off to get it."

"Oh. Here, here it is," Livermore said now, holding up a small blue notebook with "1981" written on the cover. He opened it and quickly found what he was looking for: "'1/18/81: Contacted Phil Davis about Boulder Creek claims.'" He looked across the room at

De La Mare, a frail man in his seventies with porcelain-blue eyes. "So you must not have gotten up there till around Christmas, huh, Dee?"

"Was it as late as that?" De La Mare, universally known as Dee, said, in a high, reedy voice. "I guess it was an open winter that year."

"What-what? Oh. Hmm. Open winter, yes. Hmm."

Dee resumed a story he had been telling. In 1980, when he was working as a prospector for Cordex, he noticed peculiar lines in an aerial photograph of the northern end of Boulder Valley. Lineaments, he called them. It didn't matter that no one else who looked at the photograph could see the lineaments—dark stripes running north by northeast across the basin and range. To Dee they were plain, and using a blend of scientific and rustic knowledge he had acquired over the years, he reasoned that the stripes were the result of discolored sagebrush, that the sage had been altered by an increase in groundwater, that the increase in groundwater could have been caused by a fault, and that the fault might be a "feeder"—a conduit for mineral solutions. He decided to sample the area. This, as Livermore had just figured out, was in December of 1980.

Dee drove up to the top of the Boulder Valley and climbed the low, shaley ridge that fuses the Sheep Creek Range with the craggier and more impressive Tuscarora Mountains. "I came over the top of it, and down before me was a valley. I started down the slope. I came to this big ol' outcrop, and it had that winy, purplish color you like to see, so I whacked off a hunk of it. But I was thinking to myself, It's too obvious. If that's the ore body sticking its snout up, somebody would have found it by now. So I hunted around some more. About, oh, fifty feet away, I came to another outcrop, same type of rock—that altered limestone—but much smaller and less impressive. Kind of tucked away. So I took a sample of that, too. I took maybe eight samples in all—not that many—and then I hopped back in the truck and left. Later, when I got the assay results back from the lab, it was like I figured—that big, handsome-looking outcrop was just about dead, but that little outcrop kicked like a mule."

Livermore stood up. While listening to Dee's recollections, he had been fidgeting, trying to find a way to accommodate his body, which was six feet five inches long, to his desk, which was hope-lessly small for him. He tried leaning forward on his elbows, but no, that doubled him over like a jackknife; he tried leaning back, but his knees jammed, under the center drawer; he stuck his large feet up on his papers, and, just for a moment, looked comfortable; then, as though remembering himself—he had guests, he ought to act civilized—snatched them away again. Now he strolled over to the shelves where the rocks were displayed and picked up one of the samples.

There were some attractive specimens among the samples: na-tive silver, for example—soft, snaky stringers writhing about in the host rock—and porphyry copper, a delicate green wafer, like a lace cookie. The rock that Livermore picked up was not so fetching: a lusterless lump of gray with rust-colored blotches on it. "This is what Dee's sample looked like," he said. "Calcareous siltstone. Very fine grains of sand which were cemented together with limestone. The whole thing has been heavily silicified—cooked, you might say—in a mineralizing solution. The iron staining is obvious, and here you can see these pores left by pyritic crystals."

Dee smiled at the geological jargon, and went on with his story. "I had noticed some claim posts when I was up there, so John and I went down to the courthouse and had a look at the maps. The sam-ples came from the Russ claims, owned by a Phillip A. Davis. So John went to see him about getting an option to explore, but—isn't this right, John?—Davis didn't want to negotiate."

Livermore consulted the diary again. "'1/22/81: First spoke to P. Davis about Boulder Creek claims. 1/31: Met Davis. Davis not inter-ested,'" he read; and he went on, "Phil wanted to prospect the prop-erty himself. He had the idea there was barite up there. He didn't ask what we wanted to look for, and I didn't tell him about Dee's sample. That's standard procedure. Anyway, it was a hundred to one that the sample did not represent a minable ore body. But I just couldn't let it go. So I called him a couple of times more, and then I had the idea of sending him an invitation to the opening of our Pinson Mine." He hunted through the diary. "'4/10: Met Davis at opening of Pinson Mine. Davis impressed by operation. Entered negotiations.'"

"Those were some ticklish negotiations, weren't they?" Dee said.

"Oh, boy. Well, in the first place, I never dealt with Phil himself. He had a pal named Frank Solaegui who would come and go over the contract with me and then report back to Phil. Then Phil would call me up and get mad, and then he'd call me back and say, 'We're still pals, aren't we, John?'"

"Turned out he couldn't read, isn't that right?" Dee asked.

"Well, that's right, yes. I didn't find that out until a couple of months ago. I guess that's one reason he'd get so mad—he was frustrated. I think this lawsuit he's started grows out of that. When you can't read the contract—well, all sorts of worries can come into your mind."

On June 26, 1981, Davis and Livermore signed a lease-option agreement. Livermore agreed to pay Davis fifteen thousand dollars for three months of exploration, a hundred thousand dollars at the end of the first ninety days, and an additional hundred thousand dollars for every six-month period after that. Well before the ninety-day option expired, they knew they had something. Like all the other explorers I spoke with who had been involved in discoveries, Livermore could not recall any especially joyous or triumphant moment: he never cried "Eureka!" or danced a Walter Hustonesque jig. The modern discovery process is too attenuated to furnish much suspense. Since the modern explorer cannot see the gold, and has to wait for the assay results to come back from the lab, the drama is somewhat muted: if the celebratory moment occurs at all, it is often in front of a computer terminal. And the discovery is only a potential discovery until the metallurgists have finished testing the ore. The ore might be unoxidized, meaning the sulfides would have to be roasted out of it; it might be carbonaceous, meaning that much greater amounts of cyanide would be needed; the gold particles might be locked up inside the matrix of silica molecules, meaning the rock would have to be very finely ground. And even if the metallurgical tests yield a favorable cost-per-ounce estimate, the mine engineers still have to design an economically viable pit. They might discover that there was too much waste rock on top of or inside the deposit, so that the expense of stripping it would be greater than the value of the ore. Finally, assuming the deposit is found to be viable, the backers have to come up with the financing to put the ore body into production. Therefore, although the Dee was officially discovered in July 1981, it took the Cordex Syndicate until April 1983 to figure out whether or not it had a gold mine. The exploration and feasibility testing cost about two million dollars—a risk that, though it turned out to be well taken, stood a nine in ten chance of being for naught. Eighteen months more went by, during which the mill was constructed and the mine developed. Finally, on October 15, 1984, almost four years after Dee noticed his lineaments, the first bar of gold was poured.

"By that time, things had started to go pretty sour with Phil Davis," Livermore said. "He didn't like it too much that we'd named the mine after Dee, here, not after him. The big blowup came when Phil brought some friend of his up to the mine. He wanted to show him some carbonaceous ore. Phil must have got confused or something—we don't have any carbonaceous ore at the Dee, and I told him that. Phil got so mad. He called me a liar and went storming off. The thing that upset him so much, I guess, was that he'd been embarrassed in front of his friend. He's so darn sensitive. Anyhow, after that it was only a matter of time before he found a lawyer. I'll tell you, these mining lawyers—now there's a good business."

Mining people venerate Livermore not only for the deposits he had discovered. He was also known as the man who discovered invisible gold. His search for it began in 1949, when he took a job at the Standard Mine, a small, marginally profitable gold mine outside Lovelock, Nevada. Like nearly all the gold mines in the country, the Standard had closed during the Second World War, and Livermore and his colleagues were supposed to get it running again. To do so, they needed to find some additional ore. For a few months, they searched for the structure that controlled the Standard deposit—that is, for the vein. Their work was predicated on the universally accepted theory of how North American lode deposits formed. The theory held that hydrothermal, gold-bearing solutions rise through the earth's crust along faults. Once they encounter the cooler temperature near the earth's surface, the gold is precipitated out of solution and into the wall rocks of the fault. How far the gold is disseminated into the rock can vary: if the host rock is extensively fractured, or if, over time, the mineralizing solutions rise repeatedly, the gold can form a kind of halo of low-grade ore around the rich heart of the deposit. At the Standard, the low-grade zone was extensive—it covered about 360,000 cubic feet of rock—but the exploration staff could not locate any profitable ore. After a few months the owners ran out of money, and Livermore was out of a job.

He spent the next two years prospecting by himself in Nevada. He tried to get mining companies to hire him on a retainer basis (an arrangement he has instituted at Cordex) but had no luck. During his wanderings, he had a lot of time to think about gold. He went over and over in his mind the geology of the Standard deposit, and he became more and more convinced that his fellow geologists had been incorrect in assuming the ore body to be merely an inferior version of the typical lode deposit. For one thing, the gold was in sedimentary rocks—limestone, siltstone, chert, shale—though according to the prevailing theories about ore deposits it ought to have been in volcanic rocks, like granodiorite or basalt. For another thing, the particles of gold were extremely small—invisible to the eye and to all but the most powerful microscopes. The gold was broadly and more or less uniformly disseminated over a relatively large area, so the ore body was more typical of a deposit of porphyry copper than of a gold deposit. From these pieces of knowledge Livermore began to assemble his own theory of how the Standard deposit and others like it formed. He thought that it might be a genetically different type, a type not classified by the theorists of ore deposits. As was the case with vein-type occurrences, his theory went, the gold had come up from the earth's magma in a hydrothermal solution, channeled by faults. However, the gold did not precipitate in the walls of the fault, forming a vein. The gold-bearing solution, being acidic, reacted with the limestone in the host rocks, dissolving the calcium-carbonate molecules and creating, as it were, pores, through which the tiny particles of gold could pass. Its progress would be aided if the host rock was already extensively fractured, as it was inclined to be in north-central Nevada, an area of intense tectonic activity.

During the early fifties, Livermore visited two other small, fitfully operating gold mines in the north-central part of the state, the Getchell and the Gold Acres, and at both he saw ore similar to the ore at the Standard. In each case, the ore was low grade, but because the gold was broadly disseminated and close to the surface, it could be mined with an open pit, a much cheaper and simpler method than underground mining. If he could find a similar deposit with a slightly higher grade of ore, it could turn out to be very profitable.

"A lot of people said, 'Oh, come on, John, every creek and wash in north-central Nevada was gone over by the old-time prospectors,'" Livermore recalled. "Well, that was true. But the old-timers all used pans. What they'd do is they'd grind a sample up and pan it with water, and if they didn't see any colors in the bottom they'd move on. Of course, they'd never be able to see the gold I was talking about. They would have just rinsed it out without knowing it was there. But I could send all my samples back to the lab for assays. That was my advantage." His disadvantage was that he didn't know exactly, or even roughly, where he should look.

"A lot of days I'd go out and not take any samples at all," he said. "It's hard to explain exactly what I was doing—just getting to know the land. And I'd think about the research I'd done, and what I knew about gold anomalies, and after a while I'd see something that sort of fit in with what I was thinking about, and I'd pick that up and put it in my gunnysack. But for a long while I never got so much as a sniff. Still, I really and truly believed I would find gold. Of course, I could have been wrong—I have been wrong plenty of times when I had that feeling. But as a prospector you've got to have optimism. You have to believe you're going to find an ore body. A lot of geologists are so aware of how slender the chances are of ever finding gold that they sort of have a negative attitude. If you think you won't find gold, you can be darn sure you won't. Gold will always surprise you—more than any other mineral, I think. You can't predict it. You get some decent gold values in a sample and you sort of think to yourself, Aha, I'm on to you, I've got your secret this time. Then it turns out you don't—the gold was just playing with you.

"That's another thing you need as a prospector—an awful lot of patience. The gold will tease you and tease you, give you just enough hope to keep you going, but one way or another, it almost always breaks your heart. Maybe the gold you find isn't an economical deposit, maybe somebody else got to it first, maybe it's a Bureau of Land Management or a Forest Service restriction, maybe the financing falls through. There's so much stacked against you. I know sometimes I've felt so awfully disappointed that I've thought about quitting and doing something else. But I keep at it. Really, I love it. I love going out and walking the land. Then again, sometimes I've wondered if the world was just passing me by. I'll see my friends, a head geologist here, a vice president there, all rising up through the ranks. And what am I doing? Still the same old thing—walking around looking at rocks. I get lonely sometimes too, living in those motel rooms, spending all day by myself. I ask myself why I'm prospecting. It's not to be rich. It's nice to have the money, but honestly, that's not why I do this. I don't know. It's something about—about the finding. If I could just find that gold, then everything would be okay. It's this endless puzzle, and sometimes—I don't know—it seems more important than it really is. But it has become really important for me, finding it. Not for the money, not for . . . I don't know what for. I just want to find it."

In 1952 he joined Newmont Mining's exploration staff. The company sent him to South America, where he prospected for copper; to Morocco, where he assisted a French company in a zinc-mining venture; and to Turkey, where he contracted hepatitis. In 1958, when he had recovered sufficiently, he was given an administrative job at the company's headquarters, in New York. Fred Searls, who was then the chairman of Newmont, thought that Livermore would make an excellent executive, but Livermore wasn't happy behind a desk. He was convinced that if he could prospect in Nevada he stood a reasonable chance of finding a gold mine. He explained his ideas to the head of Newmont's exploration program, a man named Robert Fulton. In 1960 Fulton, who had assigned Livermore to a base-metals mine in Eureka, Nevada, reluctantly agreed to give him a year or two more there to look for gold.

Copper was the metal of the moment; gold was not an attractive prospect in 1960. The price, thirty-five dollars an ounce, had remained unchanged since Roosevelt pegged it there in 1934, while the cost of mining had risen sharply over that period. By 1959, the only sizable gold-mining operation in the United States was the Homestake Mine, in Lead, South Dakota. No large deposits of gold had been discovered since the first years of the twentieth century; it was the general opinion of the mining industry that all the spectacular deposits in the continental United States had been found. North-central Nevada—Lander, Eureka, Humboldt, and Elko Counties—was a particularly improbable place to look: in more than a century of relatively intense prospecting there, only a small amount of gold, about 120,000 ounces all told, had been found.

In the evenings, it was, and remained, Livermore's habit to read mining journals and geological bulletins. In their pages he occasionally discovered a useful clue: perhaps an unusual assay value, or a tantalizing rock formation—something that focussed his research. One evening early in 1961, having settled in with an issue of the United States Geological Survey's Professional Papers series, he came across a two-and-a-half-page paper entitled "Alinement of Mining Districts in north-central Nevada." Its author was a field geologist with the USGS named Ralph J. Roberts.

"I remember I got terribly excited when I finished reading that little paper. Here was a guy, this fellow Roberts, who, totally independent of me, had worked out a theory to explain where the gold I was looking for was. I found out he would be lecturing soon to the Eastern Nevada Geological Society, which was meeting in the Nevada Hotel in Ely. It was about a four-hour drive from Eureka. Altogether, about thirty other exploration geologists showed up, most of them just for the free dinner and a little conviviality—Nevada was considered Siberia in those days. Finally, when the coffee was being served, someone introduced Dr. Roberts. This very scholarly-looking gentleman stood up and began droning on in an academic way about why he thought north-central Nevada was a good place to look for mineral deposits. It was all very dry, and had I not encountered his ideas in that paper beforehand I might not have paid much attention. No one else in the room did. Anyway, the speech ended, people began drifting off to the bar; I walked up to Roberts and introduced myself. We shook hands. I guess that was the most important handshake of my life. Then we strolled into the bar together and started talking."

About twenty-seven years after that fateful meeting, I was eating at the counter in the Owl one evening when a tall man with professorially thick glasses and graying, tangled hair came through the door. Head bowed in thought, he moved at a stiff-legged gait, more like skating than walking, past the blackjack tables and into the Miner's Room, as the restaurant is called. The following evening, he came in again, and then on a third evening. Each time, he was trailed by three or four other men who, to judge from their conversation—"I'd say we're in Pumpernickel Formation," "Nope. It's Vinini," "But we're seeing graptolites," "*You're* seeing graptolites"—were geologists. Once they were all seated, the leader of this little party would contribute occasionally to the conversation, and he had a trick to his voice—a habit of giving a quizzical, ethereal lift to the end of his sentences—that made even the most commonplace remark sound thoughtful. But more often he was silent, rocking his head, a slight smile on his lips—the master indulging his disciples.

Other men in the dining room, and especially newcomers to town—corporate executives who had flown out from Denver or Houston on reconnaissance tours, or property men discussing deals with one of the local prospectors—glanced furtively toward the geologists' table, whispered together, stared again, more boldly. "So that's him," these looks seemed to say.

On the third evening, I asked the waitress who he was.

"Oh, that's Doc Roberts," she said. "He's a real big shot around here."

Eventually I introduced myself, and Roberts invited me over to his apartment for a chat. He occupied three rooms in a barracks-style cinder-block bungalow, which were littered with rock samples and maps. He pushed my way a bag that contained oatmeal cookies and wadded-up tissues, saying gravely, "It's my belief that food of this type stays fresher when moistened tissues are added to it. These cookies were drying out rather badly at first, but now we seem to have arrested the problem." I noticed his right thumb, an awful-looking thing, shriveled and nailless and splinted, with a pin poking out of the top of it and no bandage. He examined it curiously and dispassionately for several seconds, turning it this way and that, almost admiring it. He had fallen, he said finally, on an outcrop outside town. An outcrop of calcareous siltstone, he added. Havallah Formation. Deposited in Pennsylvanian and Permian time.

There was, I eventually perceived, a good deal of humor in Roberts's show of pedantry. It was an exceptionally dry humor, and whether you responded to it or not was, it seemed, all the same to him. He amused himself. He did not suffer mildly colleagues who challenged his contributions to geology, the greatest of which are his papers on the Paleozoic history of north-central Nevada. At the same time, he relished controversy. Though he was by no means ill at ease in the spotlight, to be universally lionized was not altogether satisfying to the contrarian in him. Mining people refer to Ralph Roberts as "the father of the Carlin Trend." Thirty years ago, when he was unsuccessfully trying to convince people that the Carlin Trend existed, he was thought to be a sort of quack. He admitted to a certain nostalgia for those days.

Ore deposits were only an occasional interest of Roberts's during his career with the USGS, which lasted forty-five years and ended in 1980, when he retired at the age of seventy. The paper that had so excited John Livermore was rather incidental to the work that Roberts had been engaged in for the better part of the previous decade: studying and mapping the structure and stratigraphy of the region, trying to unravel the mystery of its origin. "To me," he said, "ore deposits have always been just a part of the general geological picture, a small piece in the great puzzle, no more interesting than the other pieces." However, he did not believe, as some of the other geologists in the USGS did, that "one had to remain entirely free of any commercial considerations in order to be a good scientist." Floating around the Survey was the idea that geologists who labored in the name of science were superior to geologists who labored in the name of Anaconda, Kennecott, Texaco, or Mobil. "Some USGS members welcome the opportunity to work with the mining industry, and some don't," he told me. "I would say the majority don't, but

I'm not with the majority there. I just don't see anything wrong with it. I think you can do commercial things as well as scientific things—it's useful to do both. You need both to make advances in the sciences and to communicate that knowledge."

In the late fifties, Roberts said, he began attending geological meetings around Nevada, lecturing, talking privately, telling whoever would listen that in his opinion a mineral belt, a vast swath of ore, ran through the north-central part of the state. It was only a theory, but Roberts, being a conceptual geologist, felt the charm of theory more warmly than most of his listeners. North-central Nevada had been of acute interest to geologists since 1878, when Clarence King, the leader of the Fortieth Parallel Survey, pointed out that the Paleozoic rocks of eastern Nevada are lithologically distinct from the Paleozoic rocks of the western half. The eastern rocks are carbonates, mostly limestone and dolomite, and the western rocks are siliceous—chert, shale, sandstone, and quartzite. Carbonate rocks form in shallow water, where carbon (from decaying marine life) and oxygen are abundant; silicas form in deeper water. Geologists therefore deduced that the North American continent must once have ended in the middle of Nevada, that the carbonates came from the continental shelf, the silicas from the ocean floor. That explained the origin of the rocks but not their structural juxtaposition. Some tectonic event must have uplifted the deep-water rocks and pushed them eastward onto the shallow-water rocks. And if that is what happened, then a fracture zone between the rocks ought to exist. In 1939, the year Roberts began working in Nevada, two older geologists, C. W. Merriam and C. A. Anderson, discovered and mapped a low-angle thrust fault, which they named (coincidentally) the Roberts Mountains thrust. They traced it north by northwest for nineteen miles, and speculated in their paper, published in 1942, that it might run much farther. They also discovered windows in the upper plate of the thrust—eroded patches in which the lower-plate rocks, the carbonates, were exposed. The two plates overlapped by a margin of at least thirteen miles, they believed.

In his doctoral thesis, published in 1949, Ralph Roberts identified the tectonic event responsible for the Roberts Mountains thrust. He named it the Antler Orogeny, after Antler Peak, one of several peaks in the highlands southwest of Battle Mountain. He traced the thrust fault through the Tuscarora Mountains and the Independence Mountains and into southern Idaho, nearly as far as Sun Valley. He also showed that the western rocks had traveled farther than Merriam and Anderson had suggested—approximately a hundred miles over the eastern assemblage. Finally, he identified additional windows in the upper plate—the Lynn Window, the Pinyon Window, the Bootstrap Window, and the Carlin Window.

In studying the windows along the Roberts Mountains thrust, Roberts noticed a peculiar circumstance: most of the ore taken out of north-central Nevada had come from mines in or near the windows. Upon visiting the mines, most of which had closed down by the fifties, Roberts found stalks of much younger, intrusive rock near the ore bodies. He made several deductions. One was that the ore-bearing solutions rose along with the intrusives, about thirty-eight million years ago. A second was that the thrust zone, because of its structural weakness, provided less resistance to the intrusives than the more competent rock to the east and west did, and so they rose closer to the surface of the earth. And a third was that the windows were caused by doming; erosion had then scoured away the siliceous crust of these domes, leaving the underlying carbonate rocks exposed.

Two of the mines that Roberts visited were gold mines—the Bootstrap and the Gold Acres. In each case, the ore was in carbonate rocks. Like Livermore, Roberts knew that this was unusual, and like Livermore, he figured that the porosity and the high alkalinity of the limestones were responsible. Furthermore, Roberts believed that the overlying layer of siliceous rocks had acted as a sort of seal, concentrating the mineral solutions and protecting the mineralized carbonates from erosion and dispersal. Where the seal had worn thin—in the windows—miners had discovered ore. But these discoveries had been serendipitous. Roberts suspected that a good deal more ore could be found by systematically prospecting the windows. He also believed that other windows might be discovered along the thrust. And he thought it possible that between the windows, under the extant siliceous layer, lay a long, precious stripe of ore.

His audience, composed for the most part of economic geologists and mining engineers, did not respond as enthusiastically to his theories as Roberts would have liked. "They just didn't take me very seriously," he told me. "Nobody said to my face, 'Oh, this is just a lot of malarkey.' They simply yawned. I persuaded a few people to come on field trips with me. I brought the people from Kennecott up on the thrust—we stood right out there on Popovich Hill, right over the Carlin deposit. I brought a fellow from Homestake too. Homestake could have had the whole of the Carlin Trend if it had wanted to. But these company geologists weren't going to listen to an academic type like me. They were all quivering with fear about losing their jobs."

I asked Roberts whether he had ever considered leaving the Survey and trying to capitalize on his ideas.

"Yes, at one time I was tempted very strongly to leave, when the Copper Canyon mine went on the market," he said. "It was being sold for a hundred and forty thousand dollars, and I had a friend with millions of dollars who would have supplied the money. That was a terribly good price, I knew, even at the price of gold then. Battle Mountain Gold now has six hundred million dollars' worth of gold there. In other words, it would have been a good bet, and I knew it. Quite possibly, I could have had the whole Carlin belt. I knew what was there before anyone else, and that gold is now worth about fifty billion dollars." He stopped to do a few calculations. "About sixty billion dollars, actually. But I was in the middle of my career, and I was working on publications that were important to me—important, I thought, to geology as a whole. So I just went on speaking my little piece, hoping that sooner or later I would encounter someone with enough inquisitiveness to test my ideas." He paused and examined his broken thumb for a while. "One always wonders what would have happened if John hadn't driven over from Eureka that day. What if he'd been held up? How long would the Carlin have sat there?"

At any rate, Livermore did drive over, and as a result of his chat with Roberts he and another Newmont geologist, Alan Coope, began prospecting just outside Eureka, near the Gold Acres mine, slowly working their way north along the Roberts Mountains thrust. Eventually they came to the Lynn Window, up near the old Blue

Star Mine. In October 1961, three months after the Ely meeting, Roberts spent several days in the field with Livermore.

Roberts: "They were having some trouble differentiating the mineralized carbonates in the eastern assemblage from the silicified shales in the western assemblage. I helped set them straight."

Livermore: "Ralph was terribly concerned that we get the regional geology straight. Of course, it was very interesting, what he told us, but by then we were mainly concerned with the gold values we were getting in our surface samples."

Roberts: "There was a good deal of unnecessary busywork going on up there, in my opinion. Exploration geologists like that kind of thing—sampling this and sampling that. Once I've figured out the regional geology, I know where the ore body is. It's like shooting fish in a barrel, really."

Livermore: "Ralph wanted us to get a drill rig out there and take some core samples—deep ones, the deeper the better. Of course, he was desperately curious to know what the geology was like down there—one thousand, two thousand feet down."

Roberts: "After several days in the field, I said to myself, 'Well, at least I've put them on the right track. I'll let them do it their way.' And I left."

Livermore: "At a certain point, Ralph's advice became counterproductive to the discovery process. We didn't want him to go away mad, we just . . . Well, anyway, he left."

By this time, Livermore and Coope had collected a number of surface samples with low-grade gold values, around .03 ounces per ton. The most promising samples came from the area called Popovich Hill—named for Henry Popovich, an old prospector who lived up there in a shack. They chartered a bulldozer and cut three trenches. In one of the trenches they encountered eighty feet of rock averaging .20 ounces of gold per ton. "After that, we knew we had something very interesting," Livermore said. "We didn't know how big or how rich yet, but we knew that it was there. The drilling began the following summer. The third hole hit eighty-five feet of ore grading about one ounce to the ton. It was fantastic—even better than any of us had hoped for. Over the next two years, Newmont proved twelve million tons with an average grade of .32. It was that same submicroscopic gold I had first seen at the Standard, uniformly disseminated, no major metallurgical problems—it was just a beautiful ore body. My God, it was a beautiful ore body."

The Carlin, as the ore body came to be called, turned out to be a three-million-ounce deposit, at that time the second largest deposit ever discovered in the United States. The mine went into production in 1965.

Livermore's discovery brought many more explorers to north-central Nevada. Gold briefly came back into fashion. The fickleness of the mining industry was amusing to men like Don Smith. "I had been trying to peddle my claims as copper properties," he told me. "Copper had been the big thing around here since nineteen-sixty. Round about sixty-four, everyone starts going, 'Have you got any gold for me? Invisible gold, that's what we're looking for.' Suddenly everybody's crazy for invisible gold. So I said, 'Sure, I got gold properties. Sure it's invisible. That's all I got, invisible-gold properties.' You see, it don't make no difference so far as the Mining Law's concerned whether you're staking for copper or gold."

By the end of the decade, however, the enthusiasm for gold had waned. Only one other ore body, the Cortez, was discovered during the sixties. Livermore, who had been transferred to Canada immediately after the Carlin discovery, returned to Nevada in 1970 and, along with a geologist named Peter Galli, established Cordex. In 1971 they and their small staff found the Preble and the Pinson—two Carlin-type deposits, much smaller and less profitable ore bodies than the Carlin itself. In 1976 a prospector found the Alligator Ridge deposit, near Eureka. But none of the really extraordinary deposits that lie along the Carlin Trend—the Gold Quarry, the Post, the Goldstrike—were discovered until the first five years of the eighties.

In a sense, these ore bodies did not exist until 1979 or 1980—not in their present size, at least. Nature cannot create gold so quickly, but the marketplace can turn a mass of waste rock into an ore body virtually overnight. The definition of gold ore—of any kind of ore, for that matter—is rock that can be mined profitably. The average rock contains infinitesimal amounts of lead, zinc, copper, silver, gold, and many other minerals. The granite in the Empire State Building contains five parts of gold per billion. If the price of gold rose high enough, the Empire State Building would turn into a sky-scraper of gold ore. But if it then turned out that all the incidental costs of mining the building—buying it, paying lawyers to negotiate with the Landmarks Preservation Commission, complying with the city's environmental standards—exceeded the market value of the gold, the Empire State Building would revert to being a skyscraper of waste rock. What the alchemist once conjured for with a caldron and a mandala, the accountant, it seems, can figure on a calculator and a computer. All kinds of transmutations are possible. A hundred tons of rock sitting in the back of a haul truck can be a hundred tons of ore when it leaves the mine and a hundred tons of waste when it reaches the mill, because of the cost of the diesel fuel.

Calculations of this kind mattered enormously in the Carlin Trend ore bodies, for most of them were low-grade deposits. For ex-ample, the average ton of rock at the Dee deposit contained .07 ounces of gold—less than a big cavity's worth. If the price of gold was four hundred dollars an ounce, the gross value of that ton was twenty-eight dollars. Cordex could mine, treat, and transport that ton for about nineteen dollars. So the rock was gold ore, highly prof-itable ore: in 1988 the Dee netted over ten and a half million dollars. If the price of gold fell to a hundred and fifty dollars an ounce, though, the gross value of that ton would be ten dollars and fifty cents, less than the total cost of producing it, and so the rock would be considered waste. Then if the production costs fell to ten dollars, the rock would change back into ore. The reduction in costs could come from any part of the budget: maybe a new technology would make milling cheaper, maybe the state legislature would vote a tax decrease for gold mines, maybe a financial officer would figure out a way of borrowing money at a lower rate of interest. But the great-est variable in the economics of these deposits was the price of gold. Each time the price rose, a certain portion of the country rock around Battle Mountain turned into ore; each time the price fell, some portion of it changed back into waste. It was a peculiar sensa-tion to wander in a desolate scrap of rangeland outside town—a cow's skull here, a rusty wagon wheel there, a dust devil moving among the scuttling tumbleweeds—and to think that maybe tomorrow, because of a buying spree in, say, the Hong Kong market, the ground under your feet would be a viable gold mine.

The daily permutations in the price of gold were a phenomenon unique to this bonanza—a phenomenon that was unknown in the gold rushes of old. Until the mid-1970s, the price that an American miner could get for his gold was decided by the government, not the market. From 1792, when Alexander Hamilton defined the value of a U.S. dollar as twenty-four and three-quarters grains of pure gold, to 1971, when Richard Nixon formally abandoned the last vestige of the gold standard, gold was a monetary institution. Gold (and from time to time, silver) guaranteed the value of paper money, and in order to keep that value constant, the price of gold had to be controlled. Although the gold standard as most people understand it—a guarantee that the government will redeem anyone's dollars for their value in gold—was suspended in the Emergency Banking Relief Act of 1933, a related system, the foreign-exchange gold standard, was adopted eleven years later at the Bretton Woods Conference, and was used thereafter to regulate international trade. The currencies of the participating countries were valued in terms of the dollar, and the dollar was valued in terms of gold. In theory, the United States would redeem the dollars in foreign treasuries for gold bullion; in practice, since the dollar was generally considered to be as good as gold, such transactions were rare. During the sixties, however, as the United States sank into its now familiar slough of annual trading deficits, this system began to disintegrate. Foreign creditors, no longer so sure of the integrity of the dollar, began demanding payment in bullion. In 1971, hoping to correct the chronic trade imbalance, the Nixon administration raised the official price of gold from thirty-five dollars an ounce to thirty-eight dollars, in effect lowering the value of the dollar. Fourteen months later, the price was raised again, to $42.22 an ounce. But the run on the dollar continued, and so the Nixon administration abandoned its efforts to control the price of gold. Thereafter, the dollar would be valued in terms of other major currencies, not in terms of gold. Gold, relieved of its monetary authority, became a commodity. Like wheat, sugar, copper, and cattle, gold could now be traded on the open market, and the market, not government policy, would determine its value. Franklin Roosevelt's sanctions against private bullion transactions were repealed by President Ford in 1974. In 1975 a gold market opened on the New York commodities exchange.

It was widely supposed that with the freeing of restrictions on gold ownership, the demand for and thus the price of gold would rise, and this is indeed what happened. By the end of 1975, the Comex price was a hundred and forty dollars an ounce. Then, as the novelty of owning bullion wore off, the price began to sink, and by mid-1976 it was below a hundred and ten dollars. Over the next two years, it rose—at first very gradually, then more quickly: it broke two hundred dollars an ounce in August 1978. For the next six months, it rose and dipped fitfully, falling below two hundred again in November of that year, rising above two hundred and fifty the following February.

A lot of the exploration that went on in Nevada in the 1970s was "head frame" geology—prospecting around the glory holes and tunnels sunk by the old-timers—and some small-scale mining was done on the waste dumps, now become ore dumps, outside the old mines. But the mining industry did not plunge into the gold business. Miners, who are, whether by nature or by experience, generally cautious, skeptical people, distrusted the instability in the price of the metal. None of them wanted to commit millions of dollars to a project and discover five or ten years later, when the development work was complete, that a bear market had turned their gold ore back into waste.

Every mining endeavor must contend with variations in the price of the mineral it is producing, but the behavior of products used in industry—such as copper, barite, and molybdenum—is on the whole easier to predict than the behavior of gold. The demand for industrial minerals was relatively stable from year to year. The price of molybdenum, an alloy used in hardening steel, rises or falls with the fortunes of the automotive industry. The price of copper depends mainly on the performance of the housing industry. And the number of new cars and new houses built each year depends, in turn, on the state of the economy in general. Though no one can exactly predict the future of the national economy, one can at least make educated guesses.

The price of gold, however, doesn't conform so neatly to the fundamental laws of supply and demand. The supply is drastically limited. If you took all the gold mined in the last six thousand years, melted it, and poured it into a cube, the cube would measure fifty-four feet a side. It would weigh 137,500 tons. (The American steel industry produces the same amount of steel in four hours.) Yet the industrial demand for gold—dentistry, wiring, and jewelry are the main industrial markets—consumes only 67 percent of the annual production in non-Communist countries, which in 1986 was over sixty-three million ounces. (The Soviet Union, thought to be the second-largest gold producer in the world, doesn't release its production or sales figures, so the industry must rely on Central Intelligence Agency estimates.) The rest is bought by governments, banks, bullion dealers, and individuals, for reasons that a historian, or a psychologist, is perhaps best equipped to explain. Roy Jastram, an economist, demonstrated in a book called *The Golden Constant* that gold, over a period of centuries, has maintained its purchasing power in terms of basic goods and services—bread, tea, cloth, land. He proved that people who buy gold as a hedge against economic fluctuations—a motive that impels many investors—will, in the long run, benefit from their investment. But toward the end of his analysis he felt compelled to add, "It is not easy to be dispassionate where gold is concerned," and he went on, "However scientific one may try to be, there is a nagging feeling that something deeper than conscious thought, not an instinct but perhaps a race-memory, distorts perspective. For gold is inexorably entwined with two of man's primordial needs: the imperative to survive and the desire to possess and enjoy beauty."

One must also take into account what Jastram calls the Attila Effect. Many people use gold as an insurance against economic, political, or natural catastrophes—as an asset that will fit under the mattress or, if necessary, in one's pockets as one flees. This attitude is not prevalent in America; the American investor who feels uncertain about the future is more likely to put money into blue-chip stocks, treasury bills, or an account in a reliable bank (or into a handgun) than into gold. But in North Africa, the Middle East, the Persian Gulf states, and Southeast Asia, in countries whose financial institutions are less reliable, gold is the basic form of savings. Therefore, the demand for gold usually rises as the level of international tension rises. Earthquake, war, revolution, financial panics— almost any kind of truly miserable news is likely to be good news for the price of gold. People who are "in" gold, whether as investors or as producers, tend to acquire a kind of apocalyptic attitude toward world events. Almost everyone I met in Battle Mountain, from the lordliest chief executive to the lowliest prospector, was able to quote the latest price of gold, and if the New York price differed substantially from the London price, I was likely to get both. In the evenings, subjects like the Persian Gulf war, the West Bank rebellion, and the downing of the Iranian airliner were discussed at the bar in the Owl as enthusiastically as, say, the forthcoming stock-car race or the new girls in the Calico Club, across the tracks. A deterioration in the monthly U.S. trade figures, a jump in the Consumer Price Index—these were joyful tidings. The budget deficit was the subject of more than a few boozy fantasies. In a favorite scenario, foreign creditors finally realize that the United States can never repay its debts; the ensuing panic destroys the value of the dollar; to restore confidence in its currency, the federal government goes back to the gold standard; the price of an ounce of gold is pegged at a thousand dollars, maybe two thousand dollars (to bring the value of the government's bullion reserves in line with the money supply); and everyone sitting here in the bar this evening gets rich.

There comes a moment in the life of every bonanza when the explorers and the small miners are eclipsed by the speculators and the entrepreneurs, when the rush of humanity is replaced by a rush of capital. In Nevada, that moment came around January 21, 1980. The rapid sequence of crises in the late seventies—the revolution in Iran, the taking of the Embassy hostages, the Soviet invasion of Afghanistan, a recession in the United States—caused a vertiginous ascent in the price of gold. Between January 2, 1979, and January 21, 1980, the Comex price of gold rose from $222 an ounce to

$825 an ounce. Gold—not just gold coins and raw metal but all gold-based financial instruments (futures, options, securities)—became a seductive investment. Gold stocks were especially attractive, since the shareholder was, in theory, making two investments at once: both in the company's earnings and in the gold it had in the ground. To meet the demand for gold-mining equities, scores of new companies were formed. The combined value of North American gold-mining stocks rose from about two hundred million dollars in 1980 to twenty-seven billion dollars in 1987. During the same period, and partly for some of the same reasons (mainly recession in the United States), the price of most base metals dropped. Silver collapsed. Oversupply ended the oil boom. Mining companies like AMAX, which was mostly in molybdenum, and Duval, which had been in copper, and Echo Bay, which had been in silver, began mining gold. By 1985, ten of the twelve deposits along the Carlin Trend had been "discovered." By February of 1985, the price of gold had fallen below two hundred dollars an ounce, temporarily taking the edge off the financial world's enthusiasm, but it swiftly regained three hundred, and during the next two years it established itself in the three-hundred to four-hundred-dollar range. Since the average cost of mining a Carlin-type deposit was two hundred and fifty dollars an ounce, any price over three hundred dollars was comfortable, and as the market, after its youthful fickleness, settled in the neighborhood of four hundred dollars, the metals analysts began to say that gold had found its "true" value.

Among the financiers who recognized the potential of the North American gold-mining industry, none has been more successful than Peter Munk, the founder and chairman of American Barrick. Munk's company grew with spectacular speed: it was the fifth-best performer on the New York Stock Exchange in 1987 (the price of the stock rose almost 178 percent). Barrick was the third-largest producer of gold in North America. Its richest property is the Goldstrike deposit, just a few miles south along the Trend from the Dee.

Munk was a Hungarian-born, Swiss-educated Canadian citizen; he spoke with the kind of Slavic accent favored by villains in James Bond movies, and he articulated his words with a military precision.

He made his first fortune selling hi-fis in Canada in the 1960s. He went into the hotel business in the seventies, and by the end of the decade, he and a partner, David Gilmour, had built up the largest chain of hotels in the South Pacific. In 1980 he sold that business for $130 million and began looking for a new venture. In the spring of 1980, Munk told me, he watched on television the events leading up to Zimbabwe's independence: "I thought of Ian Smith, who had fought for ages to keep Rhodesia from becoming Zimbabwe, and yet he was just overwhelmed by events. And I said to myself, 'Aha!' I said. 'Peter, if Rhodesia can go, why not South Africa? And if South Africa goes, what will happen to gold?'"

Munk's office in Toronto, where our conversation took place, was a spacious room with silk-covered walls. A table with crystal glasses on it sat in one corner of the room, and Munk strolled over to it and poured himself a glass of water. "Those South African mining companies showed a profit by sending people twelve thousand feet below the ground, where they worked in inhuman conditions, on their hands and knees in hundred-and-ten-degree heat. In conditions beyond my comprehension and yours, my dear friend. And they did this for just over forty pounds a week—not a day, a week. I said to myself, 'How long will this last, Peter? How long?'" He took a drink of water, then answered himself: "'Not long.'" He snatched from the pocket of his suit an artfully arranged handkerchief, dabbed at the corners of his mouth, repocketed it with a poke, set the glass noiselessly down, and began pacing the carpet.

"Now, the large European institutional-fund managers traditionally invested around ten percent of their portfolios in South African gold stocks. Excellent growth, excellent discipline, huge market caps—above all, secure. This was their insurance, you see. If some monstrous calamity destroyed the value of the rest of their portfolio— well, that same calamity would presumably cause the price of gold to soar. That was the theory, at any rate. But I was thinking, What if the calamity occurs in South Africa? Do you see? Hmm? I didn't think it would be long before the investment-fund managers started realizing you don't build your insurance house on top of a volcano. I knew it wouldn't be long before they started looking for insurance houses in more stable countries. So I asked myself, Peter, what is the most secure country in the world for investment? Of course, the answer was obvious. The United States of America."

An assistant buzzed to announce a phone call that Munk had been waiting for. I was escorted next door, to a dining room. When I returned, some ten minutes later, I found Munk pacing again; he immediately resumed his speech.

"I looked at the New York Stock Exchange. I saw not a single major diversified gold company listed on it. There were hundreds of manufacturing companies, maybe a hundred and fifty utilities— Here you had the largest stock index in the world, and yet only four or five companies listed there mined gold. And none of them was at that time a gold-mining operation exclusively, which is what the Europeans require. Of course, there were hundreds of gold-mining companies listed on the Vancouver and Toronto exchanges, but they were much too small to attract the institutional investors.

"You see, the gold-mining business in 1980 was still in a remarkably primitive state. It was like the last dinosaur, financially speaking. Almost every other North American industry you look at, you find people have gone into them and modernized them, but the gold-mining business remained fossilized for over one hundred years. A lot of small companies loaded with debt going about things very conservatively, without the benefit of modern technology or modern finance." He shook his head sadly. "The typical company had an explorationist, and he would root around, find the perfect site, which was his baby, and he wouldn't tolerate anyone's looking anywhere else. He would sit on it for twenty-five years, as though to make it hatch from inertia. You had a situation where people couldn't see the forest for the trees. A miner becomes worried about such things as milling capacity and refractory ore, and he loses sight of the big picture—which is why a fellow like me, who knew nothing about mining, could come in and shake things up."

Munk walked over and sat down in one of the armchairs. He lowered his voice to a cozier pitch. "You see, the great locomotive of change is money, always money. Nothing changes without money. I have foreseen a period of dramatic consolidation and rationalization in the gold-mining business, all caused by this money—exactly what happened in the oil business, the automotive business, the computer business. Well, my God!" He stood up. "Look at what has happened just in the past five years! A whole new sector—gold producers—has been created on the major North American exchanges, and that sector was the best performing in most of 1986 and 1987. An industry has flowered. People talk about a gold rush. The Nevada gold rush. What we have here is a gold rush of capital. Money!" Out came the handkerchief again; this time, Munk pressed it to his forehead. "It's the money, you see. It always brings about mergers, acquisitions, takeovers, and that's the way an industry matures. The small companies come more and more into the shelter of the benevolent big companies, until there are only four or five enormous producers, much as is the case in South Africa now. That's the future of the mining industry in North America. Right now there are thirteen large North American producers." He ticked them off on his fingers. "Newmont, Homestake, Barrick, Echo Bay, Battle Mountain Gold, AMAX, Placer Dome, Pegasus, Freeport McMoRan, FMC, Hemlo, Lac, Corona. That is too many—thirteen. Half, at least, will have to be swallowed. And I realized this right from the beginning.

"So it was my objective to form a diversified company for European investors, to give them a viable alternative to South Africa. We announced that at the beginning. I was totally committed to that idea, for I believed that there would be a major shift of funds away from the South African market, be it for economic or political reasons. And I also felt that such an enterprise would generate enormous wealth for the people involved."

He began pacing rapidly. "Now, in contrast to the tradition of mining, I didn't go hunting for gold, I didn't hire anyone to look for it. I didn't want to wait for some prospector to find it, then have the geologists and the engineers come in and run feasibility studies—a process that could take ten years. We had to forget about exploration. I wanted to act immediately, to grow by acquisition, not exploration. So I thought I would go to the oil companies that had bought up the mining properties during the oil boom of the late 1970s. By this point, of course, the boom was over. So I went to them"—he pantomimed opening a door and walking into an office—"and I said, 'What are you doing in mining? Do you think your investors buy your stocks because you are in mining? No. They would buy your stock if they saw an improvement in your balance sheet. I'll give you cash. You don't want to be in mining anyway. Hell, you're not a miner.' And so you know something? They said, 'Peter, we agree with you.'

"So I bought the Renabie Mine in eighty-three. Then I bought Valdez Creek. You see, I would only buy mines with proven reserves—I didn't care to take on any more risk than I had to. And then I needed people to mine my properties. So I went to analysts, put my feet up, and said, 'What is the best mining company around in terms of personnel?' And they all said, 'Why, Peter, it's Camflo.' So I bought it. In nineteen-eighty-five, I bought the Mercur mine. And in nineteen-eighty-seven I bought the Goldstrike property, on the Carlin Trend. I paid sixty-eight million dollars for it. Everyone said, 'Oh, Peter, that's too much, sixty-eight million.' Now we have found six billion dollars in reserves at the Goldstrike, and everyone says 'You paid only sixty-eight million? What a deal!'

"Of course, now it's a different story as far as buying mines and mining companies goes. It's not so easy. I know. I sat in Hugh Liedtke's office—the chairman of Pennzoil—and tried to get him to sell me one of his companies. And as I came out the door the investment bankers were waiting to go in, and they went in and said, 'Don't sell this company to Munk. Let us take it public for you.'

"Still, this is a great business. This is the greatest business there ever was. The feeling I have, being in this business, it's like the feeling of Christmas. You have no selling cost, no advertising cost, no inventory cost, and you can borrow off your product and sell it forward at a premium. To me, this is Christmas. You can get gold out of the ground for two hundred and fifty dollars an ounce and sell it for four hundred and fifty. There's never been a business like this. It's a great business when the price of gold is three hundred and fifty dollars an ounce. I've got bullion dealers lined up outside my door, from J. Aron, from Citibank, just waiting to buy my gold." He gestured toward the door, as though they were waiting to get in. Then he shot his hands forward, so that his cuffs slid back. "Look at my hands. You see no gold rings on them. I'm not a gold bug. I would go into these companies I was thinking of buying, and they would have charts going up to the ceiling, figuring their profits with the price of gold at one, two, three thousand dollars an ounce. They all lived with this dream, you see. Well, I'm not interested in dreams. I get gold loans, I sell forward and option a certain percentage of my production, I have so much upside that I can trade off a portion of it to protect my downside. And I can still hand over to my shareholders a hundred-percent profit.

The intercom buzzed again: Munk's next visitor was waiting for him. Touching my elbow lightly, he escorted me to the door.

"A lot of people in this business, they walked around with gloomy faces after October nineteenth, when the market crashed. They thought the price of gold would skyrocket when the crash came. They were betting on it, and it didn't happen, so they got depressed. But I was happy. An October nineteenth makes it harder for the investment bankers to take mining companies public, you see. And it makes the mining companies cheaper, because their shares go down. That's how it works. In bad times, you buy other companies. In good times, you sell shares. That's how ITT, Phillips, and GM grew, and we're seeing that right now with gold. If the price of gold goes down again, I'm going to be in a very favorable position. I'm not saying the price of gold will go down. In some ways, the price of gold is tragically low right now. I'm saying I can run this company if the price drops. Anyone can make money when the price of gold goes up—it's running a company in a downturn that makes you worth your salary. After all, what are brains for?"

Toward the end of my stay in Battle Mountain, I ran into Phil Davis again. I spotted him coming out of a tanning parlor in the center of town. On his shoulder he was carrying a long, flat cardboard box; he carried it to his Toyota and carefully rested it in the bed. "Tanning machine," he said. "Got myself a tanning machine. Might as well have it all, that's what I say. Might as well have it all."

He was in a state of high excitement, positioning the box just so in the truck, stooping to rub a tarnished spot on the hubcap, patting his pockets for the receipt. "What you doin'? Say, I talked to my lawyers, and they told me, No way, man. No way can I talk to you. See, this thing is just too big. There are people, see, people who are going to get hurt. Some people have got just a little big for themselves, know what I mean? Kind of puffed themselves up too big. And now they're going to be brought down. People think that they can insult you. Well, let 'em. I don't hate anybody. But you talked to Don Smith, and I know you're talking to John Livermore"—he winked— "ain't ya? So I guess you know pretty much what goes on here."

From a truck going by on Front Street someone yelled out "Hey, Phil!" and Phil looked up, startled. Then, recognizing the man, he began signaling for him to come back, but the truck kept going.

Phil climbed into his Toyota. "You see, I'm not fooling around with no couple of claims. I got me fifty-eight square miles of property. Think about that. That's more than any of these big companies got. I got forty square miles of claims right in one place. Mines all around me. And when I find my mine I'm going to do it myself. I got the Rothschilds trying to loan me money. They want to give me a hundred million bucks. I told the Rothschilds, No way, man. See, I don't need to be fooling with any Rothschilds or anybody else. No-o-o way." He banged his hand angrily on the side of the truck.

I said I was disappointed because I hadn't been able to see the gold-plated Cadillac up close.

"Yep. It's the one they all dream about." He laughed for a couple of seconds. "Well, look, you follow me in that vehicle of yours and I'll show it to you."

We drove east into the desert, then turned down a little road that led to Phil's place. It was just a big seventeen-acre square out in the sagebrush, with some white gravel sprinkled around for a driveway. The white trailer was on one side of the graveled patch, and on the other side was a brand-new blue prefab. The place looked like a machine yard. There were machines everywhere—a Volkswagen with a Cadillac front end stuck onto it, a Ford pickup in which a Cadillac engine had been installed, a backhoe, a Caterpillar shovel, a tractor trailer, and—a surprising sight in so arid a climate—a boat, a thirty-foot cruiser. The boat looked new. "Never used it," Phil said. "It's there if I need it, though. Yep, it's there if I need it."

And, of course, there was the gold-plated Cadillac, a Biarritz model. Phil leaned over and stared at the hood ornament, lips pursed discerningly. "Got three diamonds, here, here, and here, and the

rest is genuine emeralds and rubies. Get down next to it so you see
the sun hit it. See that there? When you're driving and the sun hits
that son of a bitch, it just lights up like a fireball. Now, if you'll just
step over here"—his diction was rising with the solemnity of the
occasion—"here you see I got my emeralds, diamonds, and rubies
on this side, and over here emeralds, diamonds, and rubies too." He
said it like a chant: "emeralds, diamonds, and rubies." I remarked on
the color of the body—tan—and Phil said sure, that it was the right
color for this country. "This is some kind of country," he went on.
"There's more opportunity out here than a man can say grace over.
You're free, you know. You should move out here. See those mountains over there, and over there, all around? I can see all of them
from out of my windows." He pointed to the prefab. "See, I got my
new house over here. I could have had a house built, but that takes
time, and all, and I'm kind of in a hurry, so I just got one of these
things hauled in. We'll go over and take a look inside of her just to
see what we got."

At the door, he fumbled for a while with a fat ring of keys before
finding the right one. Then we went in. "See, I got me my living
room here, and this is where I'll do most of my living, when I get
around to it, so I got her fixed up pretty nice. This whole console
here"—he waved toward the TV, stereo, VCR, and CD player—"this
thing run me around six thousand. You should hear it when I get it
cranked up. It's about like to blow your ears off." There were no records, cassettes, CDs, or videos to do any testing with, so Phil
switched on the TV. "Sit down in that sofa there. Sits nice, don't it?
I had these curtains made custom, and I think they did a nice job.
Lot of custom stuff here, see, I wanted it just a certain way."

The tour continued. A display case built into the hallway wall
and covered with glass contained souvenirs and keepsakes: a Shrin-
er's fez with the words "El Farah" written on it in rhinestones; a
picture of Barry Goldwater; a certificate declaring Phil Davis to be
the legal uncle of a local bulldog (the meanest fighter in the whole
county, according to Phil), which the dog had authorized with its
paw ("It's her right paw, you see, she's right-handed"); and a picture
of Lucky, an Alsatian that had been Phil's dog for sixteen years.
"And I got me the kind of plants you don't have to water." He pointed

at a rubber plant. "I got my guest bedroom and my exercise room—that's where the tanning machine is going to go—and here's my master bedroom." Phil swung the door open ceremoniously, then shepherded me toward the closet. It was stuffed with suits and shirts, all new-looking and meticulously hung. There was a yachting outfit with yellow epaulets. On a shelf over the clothes rack were stacks of hats—about forty hats altogether. We looked at the big pink bath in the bathroom, and then went back toward the kitchen. "The main thing is I got enough food in here so I don't ever have to go into town if I don't want to." He opened a cupboard that contained neat rows of canned peas, canned beans, canned spaghetti, and yellow Gatorade—around fifteen items in each row—and nothing else.

Outside, the clean, fierce desert sunlight was particularly blinding, reflecting up from the white gravel. Phil walked me back to my car. I asked if he needed help with the tanning machine, and he said no, he would get to that later. "Right now I think I'll go over there and take a nap," he added. He waved toward his old white trailer, and I asked whether he was still living there. He said he was. "Yeah, I guess that old crate kind of grew on me in the days back before I got my gold mine. Became a living habit, you know. Now I can't seem to get out of it."

—1989

# SELLING THE
# WEATHER

Getting up early one winter morning, I thought the city seemed oddly quiet, but it wasn't until I looked out the window that I saw the snow. A "Surprise Storm" that hit the East Coast of the United States that morning was under way, dumping as much as twenty inches of snow in Raleigh, eight and a half in Philadelphia, and six in New York. For the previous three weeks, unseasonably balmy weather had been the topic of small talk everywhere: why was it so warm, wasn't it weird that there was no snow—was it another sign of global warming? Now the first big winter storm of the season comes along, and the National Weather Service, the federal government's weather agency, doesn't put out an advisory until ten o'clock the night before. (The NWS had been on the network news just a week earlier, announcing new weather supercomputers that were supposed to make forecasts even more accurate.) Forecasters had seen a low-pressure system moving toward the southeast on the National Weather Service's satellite pictures, but all the major computer models said the storm would head out to sea. As Elliot Abrams, the chief forecaster and senior vice president of the State College, Pennsylvania, forecasting company AccuWeather, told me later, "Who am I to say the numerical guidance is wrong?"

I turned on the Weather Channel, as I always do for big storms.

The forecast may have been inadequate, but the live coverage was superb. In New York City, the Weather Channel was out in force, filming cars driving through slushy puddles and reporters sticking rulers into the snow in Central Park. I settled in for a little "weatherporn"—the voyeuristic weather-watching experience that has become a condition of modern life.

Ever since widespread weather-data collection began, shortly after the invention of the telegraph, in the 1840s, accurate forecasting has been the goal of the weather report. But in recent years, TV weather had given increasing time and emphasis to live pictures of weather, usually in the viewing area but sometimes elsewhere if the weather is atrocious and the pictures dramatic—and this was transforming the weather report. In some respects, these broadcasts seemed more like news than like "weather" in the traditional sense. Weather "events" are hyped, covered, and analyzed, just like politics and sports. (The Weather Channel acknowledged this in a TV ad created by Chiat/Day which depicted weather enthusiasts in the guise of sports fanatics, their faces painted like weather maps, rooting for lows and highs in a fictional "weather bar" known as the Front.) At the same time, the news, which once stuck to human affairs, now includes an ever larger number of weather-related stories. From 1989 to 1995, according to the Center for Media and Public Affairs, weather coverage wasn't among the top-ten topics on the nightly network news. In 1996 it was eighth, and in 1998 it was fourth—more than eleven hundred weather-related stories ran altogether. (According to the American Red Cross, 1998 was the most expensive year ever for natural-disaster relief.) Wild weather is also a standard component of reality-based programming on Fox and the Discovery Channel. And in book publishing, bestsellers like *The Perfect Storm, Into Thin Air,* and *Isaac's Storm* had helped create a hot market for weather-related disaster stories. This was not so much a new market, though, as a revival of one of the oldest genres in publishing: Increase Mather's 1684 book *Remarkable Providences,* which includes several chapters on extreme weather around New England, was one of the early weather thrillers in the New World.

This newsier approach to weather, with its focus on weather

events to help boost ratings, means certain kinds of weather get overblown while less telegenic but no less significant weather is overlooked. Take heat, for example. Eight of the ten warmest years on record occurred in the 1990s, the two others in the 1980s. (If the planet continues to warm at the present rate, some climatologists predict an increase in global surface temperatures of between two and a half and six degrees by the year 2100.) But heat doesn't do particularly well on television. You can track a blizzard on Doppler radar as it moves up a map of the East Coast, but you can't watch heat. And drought, as Robert Henson, a writer at the University Corporation for Atmospheric Research and the author of a book about TV weathercasting, told me recently, "is the ultimate non-event. You usually hear about the drought only when some rain event comes along to end it."

This is an old complaint—that ratings-driven, storm-of-the-century-style coverage makes it harder to get accurate information about the weather—and it has been heard here in New York at least as far back as the overhyped Hurricane Gloria, in 1985. But it's not only the broadcasters' doing: the public's fascination with wild weather is apparently inexhaustible. Could our preoccupation with storms reflect a more profound shift in the way we think about the weather? Ever since that famous day, in June 1752, when Benjamin Franklin and his son flew a kite in a thunderstorm and proved that lightning was electricity, storm science has been the subject of reasoned deduction, free of the superstition that Puritan theologians brought to their doom-haunted accounts of terrible weather. Today's fears about global warming may represent the end of this age of enlightenment. With growing public awareness of changes in the climate, and a readiness to link those changes to any and all weather anomalies, we appear to be moving away from Franklin's school of meteorology and back toward an Increase Mather school, in which extreme weather is taken as a sign of cosmic displeasure for our failure as stewards of the earth.

Hurricane Floyd, the most damaging storm of 1999, was a good example of the collision of what might be called weather values and broadcast values—the need to give people an accurate forecast, on the one hand, and the desire to put on a good show, on the other. From a broadcasting point of view, Floyd was a perfect storm. Its frightful satellite image made its debut on the national screens on Friday morning, September 10, still fourteen hundred miles east of Florida, and then enjoyed several nights of analysis and commentary as it approached the United States, allowing the media time to deploy crews along the coast. By Tuesday, Floyd was the leading news story in the country. The Weather Channel set a new single-day ratings record, breaking the previous record it had set on January 7, 1996, during "the Great Blizzard of '96." Weather.com, the Weather Channel's Web site, also set a record, with twenty-three and a half million page views on Tuesday. Broadcasters in every field were trying to get those satellite pictures of Floyd on the air. (*Entertainment Tonight* led with the storm on Wednesday, under the rubric "Stars Evacuate.") President Clinton cut short his stay in New Zealand, where he was trying to mediate in the East Timor crisis, and came home. Both presidential candidates, Al Gore and George W. Bush, made statements about the storm; Gore, looking to solidify his appeal as the weather candidate, even did a phone-in interview on the Weather Channel.

But none of the news coverage of Floyd helped much to prepare for the actual storm, and in some ways it may have hindered preparation. The National Weather Service's Floyd forecast provoked the largest evacuation in American history, and it turned out that very few of the people who left their homes needed to go. Almost all the expensive beach houses that you saw on television were unharmed; it was the farmers inland who were wiped out by the flooding that followed the storm, and most people weren't prepared for that.

The NWS forecast—made by government forecasters working in the much photographed National Hurricane Center, in Miami—declared that an extremely severe storm would slam into Charleston, South Carolina, on Wednesday night. So advised, I flew to Charleston on Tuesday to join a Weather Channel crew waiting for Floyd. My flight was full of nervous property owners and media people. A man behind me said he lived in Boston and had a week-end house on Folly Beach; he was flying down to board it up. "I always wanted a place on the beach, so I figured why not," he said. "But this is scary."

As the plane descended toward Charleston, I looked down at Interstate 26 and saw the largest traffic jam I have ever witnessed; even from five hundred feet the cars stretched as far as I could see to the red horizon. (The local paper later reported that it took people fifteen hours to go sixty miles.) The old motto of Charleston, "Come hell or high water," seemed to have yielded to a new motto: "If the Weather Channel says go, go."

Heading toward Folly, I had the eastbound side of the Interstate pretty much to myself. A religious program was on the radio; a caller was explaining that God could not be in the storm, because in the Bible Jesus condemns the storm, and he wouldn't do that if his own Father was in it, would he? This was interrupted by a news conference in which Governor Jim Hodges was upgrading the voluntary evacuation order to a mandatory order for all residents along the Intracoastal Waterway. All the hotels and stores in Charleston were closing, and by the time I arrived at the Folly Holiday Inn, where the Weather Channel crew was filming, it had nearly shut down.

I stood on Folly Beach and looked down the beautiful curve of sand with those expensive homes built cheek by jowl along it—the stacked chips of twenty fat years in the American economy, combined with a quiet period in major Atlantic hurricanes that now seemed to be coming to an end. I wandered a couple of streets back from the beach, into a funky-looking convenience store called Bert's that hadn't yet closed, and I loaded up on supplies, buying items I hadn't bought since I was a kid—Pop-Tarts, Nilla wafers, Hawaiian Punch. Most of the customers were surfers, who had come out for the waves. The checkout girl was looking up at the TV as she absentmindedly bagged my purchases, and saying to no one in particular that she ought to get out to the beach to be interviewed by that dude from the Weather Channel.

Jeff Morrow, one of the channel's on-camera meteorologists, was

at Folly Pier getting ready to do a live shot. (At the Weather Channel, a forecaster is called an OCM, although Morrow refers to himself as "the talent.") A freelance cameraman—wearing black jeans,
no shoes, and a wild-man look you sometimes see in cameramen—was
framing the shot in a digital Betacam. A second cameraman was out
filming people getting ready for the hurricane: loading up on plywood, for instance, at Home Depot, a major Weather Channel ad-
vertiser.

Morrow had a winning lack of cynicism about his job in the media. Because OCMs cover bad weather, which is supposedly nobody's fault, they seem to be able to maintain a youthful enthusiasm.
(Every single OCM I met traced an interest in the weather back to
childhood.) They also get an enthusiastic reception out in the field.
"These Weather Channel guys are treated like frigging royalty," I
was told by Bruce Fauzer, a satellite-truck operator who was working
with Morrow on Floyd. "Usually, local people treat the media like
scum—vultures preying on a disaster. But local people love these
Weather Channel guys. When we were in North Carolina for
Dennis"—the hurricane that had threatened the East Coast a week
earlier—"people were coming to the truck with plates of ribs, cold
drinks, pie, you name it. It was amazing."

In between updates from Morrow, the Weather Channel was
broadcasting the National Weather Service's data. During storms,
the Weather Channel gave much play to its tropical-storm experts—
they included Dr. Steve Lyons and John Hope, the eighty-year-old
Cronkite-style coanchor of the Severe Weather Update desk. But as
far as severe-weather warnings go, the Weather Channel broadcasts
only the National Weather Service's bulletin. (In times of an emergency, such as a hurricane, the NWS's forecast is supposed to be
transmitted by all weather broadcasters.) Even if a staff meteorologist disagrees with that forecast, the channel will not break rank
with the NWS, a practice the Weather Channel's vice president,
Ray Ban, chalked up to the importance of "being on the same page,
weatherwise."

The National Weather Service's forecast was based in part on
a computer model running on a Cray T-90 supercomputer at the

Geophysical Fluid Dynamics Laboratory, in Princeton. Another computer model, which is used by the European Center for Medium-Range Weather Forecasts, in London, was beginning to spit out a different forecast for Floyd, showing the storm weakening and turning north, and eventually making landfall near Wilmington, North Carolina, between fifty and seventy-five miles farther east than the NWS's predicted track of the storm in the eighteen to twenty-four hours preceding its arrival. The European forecast would prove correct, and by Tuesday night AccuWeather—which for the past thirty-eight years has sold forecasts to newspapers and TV and radio stations—had started to use that forecast, which its clients passed along to local markets. Elliot Abrams said that the same computer model had worked well with Hurricane Dennis, and "when a model has a hot hand you stay with it." But Weather Channel viewers weren't aware of the other forecast. I had spent the whole day with the Weather Channel, and I heard the correct forecast only when I got back to the hotel that night and turned on the local news.

I grew up at the agricultural end of New Jersey, which is still remarkably open country—lots of farms, few trees, and houses spaced half a mile or so apart. My father had been a farmer for most of his life, as had his father and grandfather, and we were acutely attuned to the weather as a kind of adversary—at best benign, at worst terrible and awesome in the Old Testament sense. In the summers, I worked for a local farmer, hauling sections of metal irrigation pipe among the rows of vegetables. When you're a mile or so from cover, carrying around thirty-foot-long conductive tubes, you become used to watching the sky for signs of bad weather: getting caught by a thunderstorm under a single lonely tree out there in the midst of all that space, and facing the real possibility that lightning will strike, fills you with a kind of terror you never quite forget.

At breakfast, my father would read out the weather report from the newspaper, and we would discuss whether it was good or bad for the crops. It was usually either too dry or too wet, or both, as happened in 1972, when Hurricane Agnes came up the East Coast and hit South Jersey. I remember the lines in one farmer's face as he surveyed his peppers, covered in two feet of salt water. The road we lived on used to be connected to a causeway that was taken out in a 1938 hurricane (the NWS didn't start naming hurricanes until 1947), and I would ride my bike down there and look in wonder through the muddy water at the broken concrete slabs disappearing into the muck and ooze.

Back then, in the seventies, the weather on TV was somewhat comic, partly because the notion that anyone could reliably predict the weather was still funny, and also because TV weathermen were more likely to be monologuists than meteorologists. David Letterman began his career as a weatherman in Indiana, and his *Late Show* gags preserve the spirit of an era when weathermen would hit an approaching low with an uppercut that, with any luck, would send it back out to sea. Those days, when Willard Scott once read the forecast dressed as Carmen Miranda, are gone now, as, inspired by the Weather Channel's example, weathercasters have generally adopted the demeanor of a scientist rather than that of an entertainer.

I moved to New York City in the eighties. This common American experience, moving from farm to town, which in most families happened a generation or two ago, affects a person on many levels, but one of the most profound is the change in the weather. In my first New York apartment, which had a view of an alley and a fire escape, weather was no longer the Shakespearean epic of wind and sky it had been on the farm. Being weather-wise in the city means making weather inferences: seeing patches of sky between buildings and guessing what the rest might look like, or learning to measure wind speed by how violently the Stop sign you can see from your office is rattling on its pole, or knowing the weather patterns of particular streets, where the wind always seems to blow the same direction, regardless of meteorological change.

That's when I started watching TV weather. The satellite and Doppler-radar pictures that now illustrated the weather report were like really good views that I didn't have from my apartment. Images from the federal government's polar and geostationary weather satellites, maintained by the National Oceanic and Atmospheric Administration (NOAA), which hover twenty-two thousand miles above the earth, had begun to appear on television in the eighties, as had other pictures from the NWS's network of 161 radar observation stations around the country. (Many broadcasters and private weather companies have invested in their own equipment; WNBC's much publicized Doppler radar is a large white ball sitting on top of Rockefeller Center.) Doppler radar was a crucial innovation and allowed forecasters to show the weather moving—particles in clouds coming toward the radar compress sound waves, while particles in clouds moving away expand them—rather than merely diagramming fronts with a grease pencil on a clear plastic board.

I became what's known in the weather industry as a "tracker." To be slouched in an armchair on a hot night on Long Island, with the lights off, windows open, mosquitoes flitting around the colored lights of the satellite pictures, watching a hurricane that is still a thousand miles out in the Atlantic and bearing down on Florida is my idea of good TV. My best tracking experience was Hurricane Bob, which came up the East Coast in August of 1991. This was the same weekend that the coup took place in Russia, and I spent a good deal of Sunday night clicking back and forth between the Weather Channel, which showed Bob approaching Long Island, and CNN, where Boris Yeltsin could be seen confronting the tanks. The old world order was breaking down, and the new order would be less stable, more chaotic—more like weather. Weather was becoming a metaphor for a kind of uncertainty that exists inside any very large system. Politics, once like war, would be like weather ("HURRICANE GEORGE!" screamed the headline in the *Post* in February, when W. won the 2000 Republican primary in South Carolina). Media were becoming like weather too—the way a big story crashed through the culture, submerging all other discourse in its storm surge of repetition, then disappearing quickly, leaving behind a weird deadness, like the aftermath of a big storm.

I went to the Weather Channel's headquarters, in Atlanta, in July 1999, a visit that coincided with the beginning of a heat wave in New York. The day before I left, the *Times* reported that parts of the

Sunrise Highway, on Long Island, had "liquefied" in the heat. The cab I took to the airport overheated on the Brooklyn Bridge, and the cabdriver, a Haitian, peering under the hood, made the washing motions with his hands I had seen tut-tut drivers in Port-au-Prince use when their wretched machines broke down. I proceeded toward Tillary Street on foot, trying to stick to the curb on the inside of the roadway, but the hardy little bushes growing out of the concrete were sooty and began to begrime the khaki pants I was planning to wear the next day to the Weather Channel, so I moved off the curb and was now loping along on the roadway, inside the turn—a bad place to be. It occurred to me that this is how you get killed by the weather in New York City. I managed to reach the airport in time, only to find that the flight had been canceled. Explanation? "Weather."

When the Weather Channel went on the air, in 1982, it seemed like a bad idea. The morning shows like *Today* and *Good Morning America* did a national weather report, but generally gave it no more than a couple of minutes. People liked to watch weather on TV—the weather forecast had long been the most popular part of the local news—but who would be desperate or idle enough to watch a twenty-four-hour weather channel, mostly featuring weather in other parts of the country or the world? Today, the Weather Channel seems like a great idea. Tornadoes, floods, hurricanes, thunderstorms, blizzards—who doesn't like to watch that stuff? Fifteen million people tuned in to the Weather Channel at least once a day, and the service, which was in more than seventy-four million homes, reportedly generated about a hundred million dollars in operating profits in 1998.

The idea came from John Coleman, a weathercaster on *Good Morning America* in the 1970s. Coleman, tired of having his weather time taken away by celebrity coverage, was convinced that people would watch a lot more weather if they could. He advocated a no-frills approach, with none of the jokiness of network weather and a lot more science and analysis. (Coleman was himself a veteran of happy weather: residents of Chicago, where Coleman was a weatherman before going to *Good Morning America,* remember his threat to do the forecast standing on his head if it rained one more day.) He took his idea to Frank Batten, the chairman of Landmark Communications, a privately held company based in Norfolk, Virginia, which owns *The Roanoke Times,* among other media properties, and Landmark agreed to finance the channel.

Coleman had envisaged a purely national channel, but Landmark insisted on including regional broadcasts in order to sell the channel in local markets (which still account for a large part of the Weather Channel's advertising revenue), and developed a technology that allowed the channel to intersperse regional forecasts—tailored to more than three hundred areas—amid national programming. Known as the star system, this is the same technology that sends local emergency warning signals crawling across your TV screen.

In its first season, though, the Weather Channel lost more than ten million dollars and generated headlines like "WHEN IT RAINS IT BORES." The graphics were crude, Doppler radar hadn't been invented yet, and the programming was monotonous. Coleman, who was the president of the company, departed in 1983, after disagreements with Landmark about how the business should be run. (That year he filed a lawsuit against Landmark, but the matter was settled out of court.) After Coleman's departure, the Weather Channel began receiving significant subscriber fees from cable providers, and this helped make the business more viable.

It was its coverage of a hurricane—Elena, in 1985—that first brought the Weather Channel widespread public attention. Though the original aim was to cover weather in a sober, scientific manner, the Weather Channel noticed that there was a ratings spike whenever a big storm came along. By the time Hugo hit South Carolina in 1989, the Weather Channel had become the source to turn to during weather emergencies. Four years later, Hurricane Andrew extended that reputation. Now you can tune in to *Hurricane Season* (it lasts almost as long as hockey season, from June 1 to November 30), *Tornado Season, Nor'easter Season,* and *Winter Storm Season.*

Weather Channel meteorologists use National Weather Service satellite and radar pictures, which are made available by the NWS for a relatively modest access fee, to illustrate their national weather reports. These images are often further colorized to show the density of the cloud tops in different shades—red at the core, pulsing orange around that, and beyond that a malignant-looking purple, a new color in the Weather Channel's 1999 palette. (These colorized pictures—whether they're of hurricanes or mere "T-cell activity," as they say on the Weather Channel—may not always be accurate depictions of how severe a storm is on the ground. But the pictures look frightening. When they look really frightening, as was the case with Floyd, people leave their homes.)

Any hour of programming generally follows the same format. At the top of the hour is *Weather Center*, a seven-minute roundup of the nation's weather, followed by four minutes of *Travel Wise*, aimed at business travelers, and four minutes of the *Weekly Planner*, which offers forecasts of up to seven days. There's another *Weather Center* on the half-hour, and *Storm Watch* at fifty minutes past the hour. Much of the information is the same—it's only the context that changes. You know this, but you watch anyway, rendered impassive by the mind-numbing repetition of it all. A research study commissioned by Chiat/Day identified the channel's addictive potential. When regular viewers were denied access for more than a week, Jerry Gentile, Chiat/Day's creative director, told *The Washington Post*, "these people just sort of broke. They couldn't get their lives together without watching the weather. They had to know. They had to have control. They couldn't just look out the window."

The voices of the OCMs add to the channel's calming effect. They all strike the same tone—pleasant but not jokey, confident but never knowing. (Recently I said to a friend of mine, "Looks like snow," and instead of scratching his chin, squinting at the clouds, and saying, "Yep," he said, "Actually, this clipper is going to blow through here, moving this low out to sea, and tomorrow the picture looks pretty clear," and I could tell what he'd been watching that morning.) Lee Grenci, a meteorologist at Penn State who helped to write the weather page for the *Times*, told me that freshmen who come to meteorology school "already sound like little minions of the Weather Channel. Same language, same descriptions, same body movements. It's almost Orwellian. Though I have to say the

Weather Channel has increased enrollment in meteorological school."

Almost every meteorologist I spoke to, both inside and outside the Weather Channel, brought up the Internet and the way it was changing the weather business, by making information once available only to experts accessible to everyone. (According to the Pew Research Center for the People and the Press, in 1998 weather was the No. 1 form of news that people looked for online.) In spite of blunders like the Surprise Storm, forecasting has continued to improve—a modern three-day temperature forecast is as accurate as a one-day temperature forecast was thirty years ago, and the ability to pinpoint a hurricane's location has improved by more than a day, according to Ron McPherson, the executive director of the American Meteorological Society. Computer models, though not infallible or always consistent, have become steadily more reliable as the machines they run on grow in processing power, and as more data are fed into the system. And thanks to the Net, the average weather enthusiast can now take his pick from as many as eight computer models showing various scenarios for the same region in the United States.

There are more than a hundred private weather companies in the United States, and all have been confronted by this new world of ubiquitous weather information. One popular strategy is to offer weather forecasts tailored to the needs of a particular commercial enterprise. "Let's say you're a cement pourer," Elliot Abrams, of AccuWeather, told me, "and you want to do a big pour on a particular day. So you make a contract with us, and you call us and tell us where you're pouring the cement, and we tell you what the forecast will be."

Long-range weather forecasting is another growing business. An online venture, www.weatherplanner.com, offers a free service aimed at people who are planning weddings, vacations, or other outdoor events. Type in the date and the location and you can get a whole year's worth of predictions on your screen. Weatherplanner's parent company, Strategic Weather Services, also uses long-range weather forecasting, along with demographic and market analysis, to make predictions up to a year in advance for corporations that need to plan ahead. Many meteorologists scoff at the idea of predicting the weather that far in advance. Strategic Weather Services will not comment on its methods, but its approach derives from theories about recurring weather patterns developed by Dr. Irving P. Krick, a colorful midcentury physicist, that have long been in favor in the military (Eisenhower employed these theories in the Second World War, and meteorologists from Strategic Weather Services advised Norman Schwarzkopf in the Gulf War). The company's clients have included Sears (lawnmowers and house paint), Duraflame (logs), Arctic Cat (snowmobiles), and Kmart (garden hoses, barbecues, and patio furniture).

Another trend in the weather business is the trading of weather futures and derivatives—financial instruments offered to companies as a hedge against extreme weather (or "extreme mildness," if you happen to be in a bad-weather business). The weather officially began to be treated like a commodity when the Chicago Mercantile Exchange opened a market in weather futures on September 22, 1999, in which the investor can bet on how far the temperature in certain cities on a given day will fall below or rise above sixty- five degrees (known, respectively, as heating-degree days or cooling-degree days). A former commodities trader who ran a weather-derivatives business told me that many brokerage firms have established weather desks, providing a new and lucrative source of employment for the hundreds of meteorological BAs who graduate each year.

The Weather Channel seemed well positioned in this new information-drenched weatherscape, because it had never relied as much on forecasting as most weather businesses. The Weather Channel's real competition was less other weather companies than other cable channels, such as CNBC and CNN, with which it competed for a free-floating audience of people who spend the day with their television sets on, ready to click to the appropriate channel if some extraordinary event or disaster occurs, be it human or natural. And as weather coverage had increased on the networks and the cable news stations, the Weather Channel had adopted a more news-driven approach. It covered the war in Kosovo, when the bombing began, because the weather was a factor (cloudy skies inhibited the air strikes). It also covered the JFK, Jr., tragedy—weather again—and routinely covered airplane crashes. It did live reports from some major golf tournaments, and reported the weather on Fox's NFL pregame show. On Super Bowl Sunday 2000, the Weather Channel brought viewers constant updates on the weather in Atlanta, which was not exactly relevant to the game—it was played inside—but which did allow it to show plenty of pictures of an OCM in the parking lot of the Georgia Dome.

When I was in Atlanta, I spoke with the executive vice president of marketing for the Weather Channel, Steven Schiffman. We met in his office, which is filled with mementos that he brought along from his previous job, at Kraft. There was a miniature Kraft Singles tractor-trailer, some plastic cheese slices, and other cheese-related knickknacks. Schiffman made it clear that his approach to selling weather was pretty much the same as his approach to selling cheese. He told me that on taking over his job, in 1998, he'd commissioned a new "segmentation study" into the "need states" of the audience, and the study came up with three basic types of Weather Channel user. (At the Weather Channel, market research is cited at every opportunity.) The first group, the weather-engaged, who make up 41 percent of the audience, "know the weather statistics like sports fans know a star's batting average," Schiffman told me. The second group, the weather planners, who form 28 percent of the audience, "are scheduling flights, or golf games with clients on a Saturday, and want to plan ahead." The remaining 31 percent, the commodity users, "just want their forecast, as quickly as possible. They don't care if it's raining in California." Schiffman foresaw potential for growth among the commodity users, whom he compared to the "cheese rejecters" he had to contend with when he was at Kraft.

Down the hall from Schiffman's office, CNN and the Weather Channel were playing on separate TVs, but both were showing a picture of a burning apartment building, right there in Atlanta. It had been struck by lightning the previous night—part of the same line of unsettled weather I had flown through. The Weather Channel was keen to find ways in which to increase its use of news footage, in part to get away from showing nothing but meteorologists standing in front of maps. As Patrick Scott, an executive vice president, explained to me, "If there's a flood in Georgia and someone drowns, CNN will say, 'Man dies in flood,' while we'll say, 'There's been flooding and it's so bad one man has died.' But we can use the same picture CNN is using."

The Weather Channel had to be careful here, however, because, as it widened the context of weather to include more news, it risked compromising what made viewers loyal to the channel: the belief that they're getting just the facts, delivered not to help ratings but for the good of the community. "People trust us," Schiffman said, "because we're doing the weather, not the disaster." Weather in this case means something reassuringly straightforward, helpful, and civic-minded. It is not like news, which traffics in disaster and misery for its own sake. Traditionally, where the Weather Channel has drawn the line between weather and news is in covering the aftermath of a storm. "We haven't done much aftermath, because then it's news," Schiffman told me. He nodded toward the burning apartment building. "We're trying to figure out a way of doing more of it."

In January 2000, the channel introduced *Your Weather Today,* a two-hour morning show that was closer to the network breakfast shows than the Weather Channel's usual programming. (After ten weeks on the air, the show was the highest-rated cable news program on TV.) Instead of a rotating cast of on-camera meteorologists, there were the same two every day, with their coffee cups, doing the weather. The Weather Channel's founder, John Coleman, fled *Good Morning America* because ratings-grabbing fluff kept taking time away from the weather. With *Your Weather Today,* it was as if the idea has come full circle: a morning show in which the weather itself was the fluff.


There's a paradox at the heart of the weather report today: people watch weather on TV because it seems real, in a way that political scandals and stock-market gyrations sometimes do not. But the more weather we watch on TV, the less time we spend in it. One becomes attuned to the movement of energy around the globe—the jet stream, the flow of high pressure down from the North Pole, the path of the storm—while at the same time becoming detached from the weather outside.

I remember standing on the battery in Charleston, South Carolina, waiting for Floyd: Wednesday, September 15, 1999. The old town was eerily deserted, the windows of the great Georgian houses protected by plywood cut into neoclassical shapes. TV crews were lined up all along the stone promenade: weather paparazzi straining before the velvet rope of the ocean, waiting for the celebrity to arrive. A Weather Channel producer, Dwight Woods, tried the shot: Charleston Bay, with Fort Sumter in the background. He didn't like it, and decided to see whether a marina that Bruce Fauzer, the satellite-truck operator, had scouted out earlier offered better pictures. As Jeff Morrow, the meteorologist, was climbing into the truck, he pointed at the sky and said, "By the way, there's the hurricane."

I looked up, and there it was. You could see the cloud, a huge dark plume that went up at least fifty thousand feet into the atmosphere. It was astounding, almost biblical in size, especially in contrast to the televised satellite picture I had been seeing for so long. Television simply can't convey the immensity of weather—that feeling you get just from looking up at the sky.

The crew set up near the marina, under the covered courtyard of a deserted Hampton Inn, just outside Charleston. Fauzer had parked the truck between the hotel and a boat warehouse. At around 3 P.M., the skyline of downtown Charleston went dark: the power had gone out. Even though the hurricane's eye was going to miss us, gusts of wind from the squall band were already too strong to stand up straight in, and the rain stung like ice crystals. The light was very dim, and the air was beginning to fill with debris. Suddenly an especially strong blast blew the ceiling tiles out of the Hampton Inn canopy and knocked over a bank of lights, which knocked over the camera. On the Weather Channel, this looked splendid—very *Blair Witch*—but unfortunately, it broke the camera.

By nine that night, the storm in Charleston was at its peak. The boat warehouse next to the Hampton Inn was beginning to blow apart. The skyline was dark, but once in a while there was a bright-green flash—another transformer, the metal box toward the top of certain telephone poles, had exploded as the lines blew together and opposite charges arced between them. Everyone was packed into the truck, which was now thoroughly damp, and cold from the air-conditioning. Outside, the wind roared like a train.

"Let's make live TV!" Fauzer cried, firing up the troops. He flung on his foul-weather gear and bounded out into the storm.

Morrow and the cameraman followed him into the full force of the wind to do the shot. As they were shooting, there was a tremendous crash in the darkness nearby. A forty-foot gooseneck streetlight had blown over.

"What was that?" Morrow shouted, flinching from the deadly wind.

"Show it!" shouted Fauzer, who had returned to the truck. "Let's see it!"

"These things can become missiles," Morrow said to the viewers, glancing around. It was great live TV, but not great weather. The next day, Bryan Norcross, a Miami-based weatherman who made headlines for broadcasting in Hurricane Andrew, said in *USA Today* that he thought it was only a matter of time before the nation saw a weatherman decapitated on live TV. Would that be news or weather?

I was in Washington, D.C., on March 8, 2000, when the temperature hit a high of eighty-five degrees. As I watched the weathercaster on NewsChannel 8 crowing over the shattered records and telling us how lucky we were, I was struck by the extent to which coverage of the weather, in spite of all the newsier innovations, is still rooted in the happy weather of the sixties and seventies, when storms, heat waves, and blizzards were a cheerful alternative to the body count in Vietnam, racial unrest in the cities, and soaring crime rates.

Global warming—without doubt the biggest weather story of our time—is almost never discussed on the weather report. "They don't really want us to talk about the causes of global warming," Buzz Bernard, one of the Weather Channel's meteorologists, told me. The position of the Weather Channel is that if you look at the last thirty years, the evidence that the planet has grown warmer has nearly reached scientific consensus, and we may be at the warmest point in the last hundred years. But whether this warming is a result of environmental or human influences is still not known, nor is it clear how long the warming cycle we are now in will last. Stu Ostro, a senior meteorologist at the Weather Channel, told me, "Once you say global warming is caused by human means, you have to say whose fault is it, and what do you do about it, and then you're in a very difficult political situation."

Opinions concerning the causes of global warming remain highly contentious. But many climatologists now believe that rising temperatures produce more extreme weather—not only more frequent heat waves and droughts but also more storms and floods. Thomas Karl, the director of the National Climatic Data Center, a branch of NOAA, recently completed a study of extreme weather in the United States since 1910. Karl, who was for a long time the darling of global-warming skeptics, concluded in the study that there has been "a persistent increase in extreme events" since the 1970s—an anomaly he attributes to global warming.

On television, however, when it comes to the subject of global warming, Ben Franklin's cheerful optimism—the dominant tone of his *Poor Richard's Almanac*—still rules over the dour spirit of Increase Mather's *Remarkable Providences*. Perhaps that's good science—the time frame of climate change is far beyond that of a daily forecast—but it nonetheless works to intensify our superstitions concerning weird weather, because we get only spectacle without any scientific explanation whatsoever. And an ever-growing focus on short-term dramas further dulls our capacity to follow long-term changes.

The news about the weather—that it's hot and getting hotter, and that our species may be contributing to the problem—is not the kind of bad news people want to hear in a weather forecast, and so they don't hear it. And that is why, when the weatherman mentions the oddly balmy temperatures, he usually tells us to "get out there and enjoy it."

—2000

# THE SLOW LANE

Shannon Sohn, the blue-eyed, freckled young helicopter reporter for New York's Channel 7 *Eyewitness News,* was sitting in the office at the back of the hangar at Linden Airport, in northern New Jersey, fanning herself with a newspaper and waiting for the traffic to get bad. The office looked like a place where people keep odd hours. The couch had body-length indentations in its cushions, and soft-drink cans and coffee cups were spilling out of the wastebasket.

It was early in the afternoon on Friday, May 24, or "getaway day," as Channel 7 called it—the start of the Memorial Day weekend and the traditional beginning of the summer traffic season. On days like this, all the drivers who commute in and out of New York City on a typical weekday are joined by the drivers who live in the city and use their cars only on weekends, producing the kind of chaos that traffic reporters in Atlanta or Los Angeles take for granted but New York reporters don't experience every day. If there were truly appalling delays, Sohn had a shot at leading the six o'clock news. "As a helicopter reporter, that's what you want," she said. "To be first." Helicopter reporters in New York don't have the luxury of following high-speed car chases—there are too many bridges and tunnels in the way. Here a terrible traffic jam is as good as it gets. But would today's traffic be bad enough?

After September 11, as anyone who drove in New York knew, traffic patterns changed. Congestion cleared up when Mayor Giuliani used his special emergency powers to restrict bridge and tunnel crossings into Manhattan below Sixtieth Street. Not since the Second World War had traffic in the city flowed as freely. In April, restrictions were lifted on some crossings, but morning rush-hour restrictions on lone drivers entering Manhattan remained in effect below Fourteenth Street. Although the cleanup operation at Ground Zero had ended, Mayor Bloomberg—who, during his campaign, promised to improve the quality of life in New York by making the city less auto-reliant—decided to keep the restrictions in place while the reconstruction of lower Manhattan continued. Traffic had been getting steadily worse since April, but it was still less crowded in the city now than it was a year earlier.

The phone rang in the office. It was the Channel 7 news desk, in Manhattan. The police scanner was reporting an incident that had shut down all the northbound lanes on the New York State Thruway. Sohn and her pilot, Arthur Anderson, hurried outside and climbed aboard NewsCopter 7. Anderson gave me a quick review of the emergency procedures, explaining that if we had to ditch he preferred to do so on land, not in the water. As we took off, Sohn unwrapped a lollipop. She was fourteen weeks pregnant, and relied on cherry-flavored Charms to ward off motion sickness in the chopper. Grape worked better, but it turned her tongue purple.

Linden Airport is near Elizabeth, New Jersey, and just south of Newark airport. As we headed northwest across Newark's sprawling runways, Sohn gathered information from the traffic news desk. Around noon, a twelve-year-old boy called Scottie Van Dunk, of Mahwah, New Jersey, whose class had been let out of school early, had ridden his bike to a section of the Ramapo River known as "The Forty Foot," a well-known swimming hole just across the New York state line. At 2 P.M. the boy's body had been discovered at the spot where the river runs beside the Thruway. He had drowned, and police officers had shut down the highway for the recovery operation.

By the time we arrived above the scene, at 2:15 P.M., the traffic on the northbound Thruway was backed up for several miles beyond .

the I-287 interchange. Drivers who had been zipping along the highway minutes before were now trapped and unhappy, and their previously limitless sense of possibility had shrunk to a single option: whether to change lanes. The idea that the delay up ahead might be the result of a disaster far greater than anyone's personal inconvenience rarely occurs to the driver stuck in traffic.

NewsCopter 7's remote-controlled belly-mounted camera roved the river's edge, looking for a body or some other pitiless image of tragedy for the folks at home, but found only a couple of men from the Stony Point Fire Department, stowing rescue gear. Van Dunk's body had been taken away just before we arrived. Sohn directed Anderson to get some pictures of the traffic jam on I-87 and I-287, but said she doubted that this tie-up would be enough to make the six o'clock news: "For that to happen, we need some really, really bad traffic."

Since 1970, the population of the United States has grown by 40 percent, while the number of registered vehicles has increased by nearly 100 percent—in other words, cars have proliferated more than twice as fast as people have. During this same period, road capacity increased by 6 percent. If these trends continue through 2020, every day will resemble a getaway day, with its mixture of commuters, truckers, and recreational drivers, who take to the road without regard for traditional peak travel times, producing congestion all day long: trucks that can't make deliveries on time, people who can't get to or from work, air quality that continues to deteriorate as commerce suffers and our overall geopolitical position weakens because we are forced to become ever more dependent on foreign oil. This is the way the world ends: not with a bang but a traffic jam.

What can you do about the traffic? Take the train? The train may be out of commission; Amtrak, the nation's passenger rail service, may be out of business before too long. Fly? Airlines are cutting flights and raising prices to offset heavy losses. Manage traffic better? There are many schemes for managing traffic, but not very many practical ways to reduce the number of vehicles on the roads.

Even if people have an alternative to driving, as do many New Yorkers, over time an ever larger number of commuters choose to drive. In 2001, about 3.6 million people made their way into Manhattan's "hub" (the area below Sixtieth Street) each workday—about the same number who came on an average day fifty years ago. In 1948, 650,000 of the commuters drove; fifty years later, more than 1.3 million of them drove, and most of them drove alone.

It's not enough to build public transportation; you also have to get people to use it, either by making trains and buses more convenient or by prohibiting some people from driving during peak periods. But in the United States restricting people from using their automobiles whenever they like has always been politically difficult, and Mayor Bloomberg's efforts to do so are controversial. The new restrictions had brought joy to many of the city's residents—New York is the only city in the United States in which the majority of households don't own an automobile—but they had been a source of outrage for the parking-garage industry, restaurant and theater owners, retailers, labor groups, and some local politicians. Traffic is bad, but as some New Yorkers had discovered, a lack of traffic may be worse. "I think it's destroying the fabric of New York," Greg Susick, senior vice president of Central Parking, told the *Times* in November 2001. After a Christmas season in New York in which the traditional Five Days of Gridlock saw only light congestion, the Metropolitan Parking Association began investigating possible legal action against the city for maintaining the lone-driver restrictions.

If New York could do something permanent about its traffic, maybe other cities around the country could too. In Atlanta, the time that the average commuter spends annually in traffic rose from twenty-five hours in 1992 to seventy hours in 2000. Los Angeles has the worst traffic in the country, but San Francisco, Houston, and Seattle are challenging L.A. for this distinction. These cities may find it necessary to impose restrictions on driving when traffic becomes even worse—much worse—as it inevitably will. That is why what happens in New York's experiment in traffic control is so important. Will New York, which is building a state-of-the-art transit center in lower Manhattan, be the first city to implement a state-of-the-art traffic policy? Or will this period in the city's traffic history—a period in which the automobile is a privileged guest—pass, defeated by our insatiable desire to drive?

A t 12:15 P.M. on getaway Friday, Rudy Popolizio, the director of systems engineering for New York City's Department of Transportation, was in the DOT's Traffic Management Center watching the city's roads for signs of trouble. The word *jam* was first used to describe automotive congestion by the *Saturday Evening Post* in 1910, in a reference to New York City. (The British word *blockage,* a holdover from horse-and-carriage days, was too civil-sounding to convey the awful noise and smell of automobiles densely packed into a tight space.) Because of the limited space and the dimensions of its grid, the heart of midtown Manhattan can accommodate only nine thousand moving vehicles without succumbing to gridlock: the congested traffic on one of the cross streets blocks the traffic on an avenue, which in turn clogs the next cross street. A bad case of gridlock can tie up all the streets in midtown within minutes, which is why engineers like Popolizio keep close watch on the city's roads, especially on days like this.

Traffic seemed to be flowing well, Popolizio reported. He suspected that a lot of people hadn't gone to work. "We may see an early peak today—around two o'clock," he told me over the phone. "But so far traffic is okay, I'm looking at the Fifty-ninth Street Bridge camera, and traffic is moving well."

The Traffic Management Center is in a large windowless bunker in a nondescript white brick building just off Queens Plaza, in Long Island City. I had met Popolizio there when I visited several months earlier. He and the other engineers work in the glow of thirty-four large TV monitors, each displaying changing images transmitted from the 130 remote-controlled closed-circuit cameras that the city and state DOTs have installed at troublesome intersections within the city and at common choke points outside it. Traffic cams reduce the DOT's response time to accidents—the cause of 50 percent of all traffic jams. In theory, the cams, available online at www.metro-commute.com, are supposed to provide an advance-warning system for the public, but as a practical matter, most drivers aren't surfing the Web, you hope, while they're behind the wheel.

The most effective and equitable means of managing all the different users of the city's streets—bicyclists, in-line skaters, scooters, pushcarts, pedal cabs, and pedestrians, as well as drivers—is the traffic signal. "With the traffic signal, everyone's interests are reduced to red and green," Popolizio said. "It's 'You get yours, and I get mine.'" The electric traffic signal is an old technology, devised by an African-American inventor, Garrett Morgan, in 1914 (he also came up with an early version of the gas mask) and first deployed in the city in 1924, on Broadway; today, about 2,700 intersections in Manhattan are "signalized." Almost all signals in Manhattan run on ninety-second intervals, and over the decades the DOT has steadily improved and refined the way the signals work together. "In a grid this tight, you can't afford to have a signal thinking on its own," Popolizio said. (Two weeks earlier, a computer glitch had caused dozens of signals around the city to start thinking on their own, and the result was chaos.) The DOT times the sequence of the lights on most of the avenues progressively; and even if you don't know that the signals on, say, Ninth Avenue turn green at six-second intervals, you soon develop an instinct for just how much green you have left on the signal ahead of you before your progress is halted by red. E. B. White, writing in *The New Yorker* in the late 1920s, noted how quickly the citizenry had incorporated the newly invented timing progressions into its inner life. "These machinal rhythms are really very subtle," he wrote. "It is by such nice devices that man supplants the urge of hours and tides and the phases of a moon which he never sees."

More than half of the eleven and a half thousand signals in the five boroughs are connected to computers in the management center, and the city's traffic engineers can manipulate the timing of those signals throughout the day. During the morning and evening rush hours, for example, Sixth Avenue in midtown gets sixty seconds of the green time while the crosstown streets get thirty seconds, but during the middle of the day, when there's more crosstown traffic, the engineers change the signal timing so that both Sixth Avenue and the crosstown streets get forty-five seconds of green. Every one of Manhattan's signals is represented by a tiny light on a forty-foot-long tableau in the management center, and the lights are connected in real time to the signals on the streets. The model allows you to watch the sequences of lights sweeping along Broadway, or to study the subtlety of the signal pattern in Times Square. It represents the triumph of traffic engineering over traffic: a perfectly designed system, without drivers to mess it up. "We use very few left-turn signals in the city," Popolizio pointed out. "It's not like in the suburbs, where you have people going every which way in the intersections."

The day I had visited the management center, in March, there wasn't much traffic to manage. With all the rush-hour restrictions in effect, the roads in the city and outside it were quieter than usual; an engineer had tuned one of the monitors to daytime TV. Finally, at the end of the morning rush hour, a crew from the city's Department of Environmental Protection stopped its truck in the middle of the southbound FDR Drive, just south of Ninety-sixth Street, so that it blocked two lanes. The men got out, ambled over to the side of the road, and began peering into drains. Cars behind the truck immediately stopped, and, thanks to the DOT's cameras, we got to see the jam forming, traveling backward at eight miles an hour, a rolling wave of thwarted commuter desire that soon reached the Triborough Bridge. Meanwhile, a police car pulled up, its lights flashing, in the left lane of the northbound FDR, and the cops went over to see what the heck the DEP was up to. It was a pygmy traffic jam, in the general scheme of things, but it was the only thing happening that morning, and the DOT engineers got pretty excited. "What are those DEP guys doing?" one shouted. "Do they have a work permit?" Fifteen minutes later, the truck moved on, and the jam slowly cleared.

On getaway day, Popolizio told me, "We're going to be putting in our outbound timing progressions a little early this afternoon, maybe at one-thirty to two instead of three-thirty to four, to give more green time to the outbound lights. All to help get people out of the city as smoothly as possible."

Unfortunately, in getting people smoothly out of Manhattan, the city's DOT engineers weren't necessarily making their trips faster, and they may ultimately have been slowing down the drivers by flooding the highways outside the city with more cars than they were designed to accommodate. No major new highways have been built around New York since the 1970s, partly because there's no room left, and partly because many people believe that building highways makes congestion worse, because drivers who had previously used mass transit to avoid the traffic begin using the new roads. Even if no new drivers take to the new roads, scientists have shown that increased road capacity alone can increase congestion, a phenomenon sometimes referred to as "Braess's paradox," after a German mathematician named Dietrich Braess. In the twenty-three American cities that added the most new roads per person during the 1990s, traffic congestion rose by more than 70 percent.

But not building highways also causes traffic. The section of I-95 that runs from the New York state line to New Haven, for example, was designed to accommodate seventy thousand vehicles a day; it now carries more than a hundred and fifty thousand in places. Many parts of the nation's forty-seven-thousand-mile interstate-highway system, which was created in the 1950s, suffer similar overloads. Politically, it's almost impossible to build major new roads. David Schulz, the director of the Infrastructure Technology Institute at Northwestern University, said, "When you talk about building a new road, the number of people who benefit will be large, but their individual benefit will be quite small. The number of people who will be harmed will be small, but their disbenefit will be very large. And it's those people who will get involved in the public hearings and stop the road." NIMBY ("Not in my back yard") has given birth to BANANA ("Build almost nothing anywhere near anyone"), which has spawned NOPE ("Not on planet Earth").

The Federal Highway Administration spent hundreds of millions of dollars in the 1990s to make highways "intelligent," deploying a wide range of detection devices known collectively as ITS (intelligent transportation systems), which are supposed to track, predict, and possibly control traffic. Much of this technology was developed by the U.S. military and used during the Gulf War. (It is now part of our new homeland security measures.) It includes closed-circuit television cameras, vehicle sensors buried in the roads, overhead proximity radar, optical-image sensors, and the E-Z

Pass transponder—the small plastic box on your windshield that communicates with overhead "readers," and that may be the most significant advance in traffic management since the traffic signal. Mark Hallenbeck, the director of the Washington State Transportation Center at the University of Washington, said that the idea "is to add capacity with information, the way we used to add capacity with concrete. In highway agencies, we used to think of ourselves as being in the construction business. We build a road, go away, and then come back in twenty years and add a lane. Now all these agencies are having to learn how to increase capacity by adding intelligence to the system."

On Friday afternoon, after I had spoken to Popolizio, I called Transcom, a public interagency traffic-management organization based in Jersey City, to find out what was happening on the roads outside the city. Part of Transcom's mission is to coordinate information about I-95 that is supplied by the states the road runs through. Traffic, after all, doesn't respect city or county boundaries. Today, Transcom's managers told me, they were busy alerting travelers to problems on the highway that had started hours earlier, at Exit 34, near Milford, Connecticut. At 6:30 A.M., a tractor-trailer on I-95 northbound, carrying a load of car batteries, had hit a guardrail, overturned, and caught fire. The state police closed all lanes, in both directions, while they cut apart the truck and made sure no battery acid remained on the highway—a process that took eight hours. By noon, traffic was backed up for thirteen miles. Information about the delays was posted on electronic message signs mounted over the region's highways, and alerts were broadcast over highway-advisory radio. At the moment, Transcom does not provide drivers with alternate routes, but according to its executive director, Matthew Edelman, "Lots of these drivers know the roads, and if you tell them where the problem is they'll figure out how to get around it." This is assuming, of course, that drivers do what the system tells them to do. Dave Zavattero, the ITS program manager for the Illinois Department of Transportation, says that many drivers deliberately do the opposite. "We have variable signs on the Kennedy and Dan Ryan Expressways," in Chicago, he told me. "The signs tell you whether the local lanes or the express lanes are moving faster. But if

I put a message up there that says the express lanes are five minutes faster, a certain number of drivers will figure that the other drivers are taking the express lanes, so they're going to take the local lanes."

On this getaway day, any drivers heading out of New York early to avoid the afternoon rush hour who had checked the traffic cams and bulletins on the Web just before leaving would have known to take the Hutchinson River Parkway north to the Merritt Parkway, skirting the jam on I-95. But in fact the Hutch wasn't much better. Around noon, a truck driver had attempted an illegal dash along the parkway (which is off-limits to commercial traffic) to avoid the problems on I-95 and got stuck under one of the overpasses. This meant that by 1 P.M. all the New England–bound travelers that Popolizio and his colleagues were helping to leave the city were about to find two of the principal northbound routes blocked, and as we saw from the helicopter, by 2:15 P.M. a third—the northbound New York State Thruway—was a parking lot too.

Shortly after 4 P.M., the NYPD closed the Manhattan-bound side of the Brooklyn Bridge to investigate a suspicious package that had been found on the roadway. When those lanes reopened, at four-thirty, the police shut the Brooklyn-bound lanes for half an hour. The result was "terrorlock"—the latest gridlock neologism to enter New York's traffic vocabulary—on both sides of the bridge. Traffic on the neighboring Manhattan Bridge came to a standstill; the FDR Drive backed up with people waiting to get onto the bridges.

NewsCopter 7 was on the scene, hovering over the Brooklyn Bridge, taking pictures of the police activity below.

"Here comes the bomb squad," Anderson said, zooming in on the truck. I watched the streets of downtown Brooklyn filling with traffic. These drivers had been trying to avoid congestion by getting off the Gowanus Expressway before its merge with the Brooklyn-Queens Expressway, a trouble spot that causes seven and a half million hours of drivers' delays annually, and then taking Hicks Street through Cobble Hill and Brooklyn Heights. In using this time-tested solution to highway traffic—back streets—these drivers were creating a traffic problem for the people who live on those streets, some of whom had hoped to avoid the holiday traffic by staying home.

At 4:45 P.M., while the police were searching the Brooklyn Bridge (they found only a stray knapsack), a car caught fire inside the Lincoln Tunnel, closing the Manhattan-bound lanes and creating congestion on the eastern spur of the New Jersey Turnpike. NewsCopter 7 flew across the river to check out the fire, but there was nothing much to photograph. "Car fires make great pictures—if you can get to them in time," Sohn said. "The problem is that the Fire Department puts out car fires so fast."

Sohn and her pilot had a hunch that the George Washington Bridge was their best bet for the six o'clock news, so we headed up there shortly after 5 P.M., stopping once along the way to record a few "beauty shots" of the city skyline, which would be used to lead into the weather report. Sohn was careful to keep traffic out of the pictures. "Traffic is not what they're looking for in a beauty shot," she said.

As we came up to the bridge, we saw the jam: a solid line of traffic stretching from the New Jersey Turnpike to the bridge's toll plazas, then east all the way across the Cross-Bronx Expressway and north into Westchester County. The Major Deegan, the Grand Concourse, the Sheridan, and the Bruckner were also packed with cars and trucks. Only the traffic on the bridge was moving—the part you'd expect to be the most congested—offering travelers a brief respite between jams.

"Look at that," Sohn said admiringly. She directed Anderson to hover over Ridgefield Park, New Jersey, where I-95 joins I-80 and swings east for its approach to "the George"—and where she could get the best shots. She sent some of these pictures to Channel 7 and waited. It was almost six. Removing her lollipop, Sohn positioned the onboard "lipstick camera," mounted on the instrument console, so that it was pointed at her face, ready to go live at the top of the hour if she was called upon.

The jam at the George had begun hours earlier, at around 1:30 P.M., as a result of a minor accident on the bridge's lower level—a fender bender involving a truck and a car—that briefly blocked one lane. This tiny mishap was enough to turn a highway of free-flowing traffic into suet. It was a classic illustration of what is known among traffic engineers as "the Wile E. Coyote effect." Just as the curve of maximum "throughput"—moving as many cars between two points on a road as efficiently as possible—reaches its peak, it abruptly falls off the cliff and is squashed flat against the baseline of the graph.

Traffic engineering is the science of maximizing throughput. What makes traffic jams hard to understand, at least within traditional traffic-engineering practice, is that they tend to occur around the time that the road is performing according to the engineers' peak specification. One important development in understanding this "nonlinear" phenomenon came in 1992, when Kai Nagel and Michael Schreckenberg, two physicists at the University of Cologne, in Germany, began to apply a computational technique known as "cellular automata" (or CA) to traffic. In a CA model, highway capacity is represented as a two-dimensional grid. Each cell in the grid has one of two "states": empty or occupied by a particle, which in this case is a car. Unlike traditional mathematical models used by traffic engineers, where it is assumed that all drivers are the same, in a CA model the particles can be assigned values intended to represent different types of drivers: fast drivers, slow drivers, tailgaters, and lane changers can all be represented in the model. The result is virtual traffic.

Using a variety of computer techniques, engineers can build virtual roads on computers, add virtual cars to them, and sit back and watch what happens. KLD Associates, of Huntington Station, Long Island, sent me a simulation program for lower Manhattan, and I spent a morning watching virtual traffic flow up and down the West Side Highway. KLD was also using traffic modeling to plan evacuation scenarios for possible events like a terrorist attack on the Indian Point nuclear facility, in Buchanan, New York. "We work with ten different levels of driver aggressiveness," Mayer Horn, KLD's vice president, told me. "Also, we take into account that people who drive during the week drive more aggressively than those who drive only on the weekend—Sunday drivers."

Computer modeling has made it possible to study traffic not only as a physical system but as a social system, and several notable papers have appeared that explore the relationship between driver behavior and traffic jams. Two researchers, Donald Redelmeier, of the University of Toronto, and Robert Tibshirani, of Stanford, used computer modeling to demonstrate that changing lanes in traffic doesn't help, although it may seem to the lane changer that he is making progress. In a paper in *Nature,* the authors argued that this is because drivers mistakenly judge their progress relative to other drivers rather than to the overall time of the trip, and because drivers make decisions to change lanes based on short intervals, during which the other lane may move faster, rather than on longer intervals, in which the slower lane speeds up. The authors concluded that drivers change lanes for emotional reasons; namely, that they prefer overtaking to being overtaken. Their theory was recently contested by Nick Bostrom, a philosophy lecturer at Yale University, who argues in a short paper entitled "Cars in the Next Lane Really Do Go Faster" that certain lanes do move more slowly and the reason is that there are actually more cars in them, and that only by drivers' changing lanes can the highway as a whole reach equilibrium and maximum throughput.

After ten years of traffic analysis using CA models, Kai Nagel and his European colleagues have concluded that traffic jams can occur for almost any reason at all. A slight upgrade in the roadway, a light rain, or even a single road-rager getting cut off by a Sunday driver can provide the trigger for a traffic jam. Someone brakes, forcing the driver behind to brake harder, and the shock wave is sent backward through the traffic until eventually someone comes to a standstill. The Germans' gloomy position—that traffic jams will occur no matter how ingenious traffic managers are—is not popular with the engineers I have met around New York. "That stuff may work on the Autobahn," John Tipaldo, of the city's DOT, told me, "but not here. New York's traffic may be crazy, but it's not that crazy."

From time to time during the course of my traffic studies, when it seemed that traffic really was fundamentally chaotic, I'd go see Sam Schwartz. Also known as Gridlock Sam, Schwartz is the closest thing New York has to a traffic guru. He is unique in the polarized politics of automobiles in New York: he manages to be both procar and anticar, sometimes simultaneously. His support of rush-hour restrictions and East River bridge tolls, in a 1991 *News* op-ed piece, did not prevent him from conducting a study for the Metropolitan Parking Association which showed that the post–September 11 restrictions were hurting the city's economy. This apparent duplicity incensed the anticar contingent that had considered Schwartz an important ally. But Gridlock Sam has built his career at the crossroads of conflicting points of view.

In his "traffic forecast," which appears six times a week in the *News,* opposite the weather, Schwartz is the voice of every traffic-savvy driver who knows to avoid the Gowanus and the BQE by cutting through Brooklyn. His followers observe Sam's traffic calendar, which is an ecumenical mix of the Christian, Jewish, and Muslim holidays during which alternate-side-of-the-street parking is suspended. If Gridlock Sam's column was your only source of news, you'd have a pretty fair idea of what was going on around the city— the visiting dignitaries, celebrity-studded benefits, parades, political demonstrations, out-of-state lotto jackpots, block parties, and sports events in the area. Gridlock Sam has made traffic his worldview.

Schwartz was New York City's traffic commissioner for most of the 1980s, and during his storied career as a public servant he displayed a flair for the dramatic that is not the rule among traffic engineers. He was responsible for the "Don't Even Think of Parking Here" signs in midtown, and his antigridlock "Don't Block the Box" initiative created a lasting improvement in traffic flow. He waged war on "sitters," especially the limos waiting for fat cats to finish their power breakfasts in midtown hotels. The drivers didn't care about the thirty-five-dollar tickets they received for sitting (some of them even said thank you, which spooked the traffic agents), so Schwartz got the city to make sitting a moving violation, for which a driver incurs points on his license.

Schwartz ticketed Mayor Koch's car for illegal parking while they were having lunch together, revoked the parking spot of the archbishop of New York, which was next to Saint Patrick's Cathedral (it caused backups on Fifth Avenue and East Fiftieth Street), and had a TV-news van towed while the crew was interviewing him. But his finest hour was his assault on illegally parked cars with diplomatic plates. Not only did Schwartz ticket these cars; he began towing them, which caused an uproar in the diplomatic community. A special session of more than a hundred delegates to the UN was convened to meet with the traffic commissioner. The Russians cited the Geneva Convention, which they claimed guaranteed the right to free parking. The French said it was possible that the entire UN might move to Vienna if the diplomats didn't get their parking privileges back. But Schwartz was unmoved, and kept up his assault until, a week or so later, the U.S. State Department informed him that American diplomats in Norway and Togo had lost their parking privileges, and that to avert an international crisis Schwartz should consider refocusing his energies. "What I've learned from experience," he told me, "is that in New York people will go a long way to keep their parking privileges."

One fine afternoon in the spring, Schwartz took me for a drive around Manhattan. We drove in his car, a Volvo, which he keeps in a lot on Lafayette Street. We headed uptown, looking for some traffic. "I can't understand it," Schwartz said several times, shaking his head, as we sailed up Park Avenue South. "You never see it like this." We cut over to Madison Avenue; it was rush hour—surely we'd find some traffic there. Instead, we surfed along on the DOT's signal progression, and even made the light at Forty-second Street. Schwartz took no pleasure in these minor miracles. Without traffic, Gridlock Sam wasn't quite himself.

Finally, on Forty-seventh Street between Fifth and Sixth—the diamond district—Schwartz perked up. He began pointing out traffic violators. "Sitter. Sitter. Diplomat. Sitter—he's a Supreme Court judge, according to the plate." Up in front of us, traffic was squeezing into one lane to get around a "Mitzvah mobile," which is used by the Lubavitcher community in Brooklyn to transport people to the diamond district, and which had a large picture of their late spiritual leader Rabbi Menachem Mendel Schneerson painted on its side. Just as we were taking our place in the queue—bang!—the Volvo shuddered. The driver of the SUV behind us, locked in a battle with the driver of the Town Car beside him over who was going to get around the Mitzvah bus first, had struck Gridlock Sam's rear bumper. But the SUV driver didn't seem to notice. Or perhaps he didn't care. At any rate, the event delighted Gridlock Sam: "He doesn't even know he hit me!"

Since the spring, traffic in the city had grown steadily worse—or better, depending on your point of view. When I spoke to Gridlock Sam about this, he reported that the level of congestion was about where it had been in the midnineties. "It's not where it was at the height of the economic boom," he said. "But we're close." He was trying to sound dire about this, but I could detect a note of joy in his voice.

Most drivers see traffic jams as an impediment to their own progress; few think that their presence in the jam is an impediment to everyone else. But the true cost of a traffic jam is not only the time you are delayed; it's the accumulated time that your vehicle adds to everyone else's delay, because everyone else must travel the additional length of your vehicle to get to the barbecue. As Wolfgang Sachs, a German environmental scientist, points out in his book *For the Love of the Automobile,* "Once a certain traffic density is surpassed, every driver contributes involuntarily to the slowing of traffic. The time that the individual driver steals from all the others by slowing them down is greater many times over than the time he or she might have hoped to gain by taking the car."

The economic solution to traffic jams is to price roads the way we price other limited resources. Just as air travelers pay a premium to fly during peak periods, so car travelers should pay a premium to drive during times when everyone else wants to drive, such as the Friday before Labor Day. This form of traffic management, which is called "congestion pricing" (although its promoters like to call it "value pricing," because that sounds better), is a relatively easy system to implement; the technology necessary for it to work already exists, in the form of the E-Z Pass. Politically, the idea is a harder sell. (They're not called freeways for nothing.) But there are signs that congestion pricing is beginning to influence traffic management, and nowhere in North America is this more evident than in New York.

A year ago, the Port Authority began using congestion pricing in the Lincoln and Holland Tunnels, on the George Washington Bridge, and on the three New Jersey–Staten Island bridges; drivers crossing the Hudson eastbound at peak hours pay five dollars, while drivers at other times pay four. (Drivers without E-Z Pass always pay six.) The New Jersey Turnpike also uses congestion pricing. A form of congestion pricing is already in effect for parking, thanks to the new European-style Muni-Meters (the blue boxes that print tickets for display on your dashboard, which are replacing parking meters around the city).

Four East River crossings, however, remain free. This may be the single most irrational traffic-management practice in New York City: there is actually an economic incentive for a Long Island driver traveling to New Jersey to go through Manhattan, one of the most congested places on earth, rather than through Brooklyn and Staten Island, because the former trip costs nothing while the latter costs seven dollars—the price of the toll on the southbound Verrazano-Narrows Bridge. City planners have long argued for tolls, and Mayors Lindsay, Koch, and Dinkins all wanted them but could not build the coalition of city and state politicians necessary to implement them. Bloomberg floated the idea of East River tolls in his 2001 budget proposal, and he has been meeting privately with politicians and business leaders to gather support for the idea. Many observers think he will endorse the tolls publicly after the gubernatorial election this fall. Bloomberg also has the economic imperative of a budget deficit of five billion dollars. If New Yorkers are faced with the choice between losing city services (closing libraries, cutting back the number of police officers, adding more children to already over-crowded classrooms) and paying tolls on the East River bridges, many might choose the second option.

Instituting tolls on the East River and Harlem River bridges with E-Z Pass would, in effect, create what's known as a "cordon"—an electronic necklace of sensors surrounding the hub below Sixtieth Street. Singapore and Oslo have built cordons, and they are planned for other European cities. In London, thanks to the former mayor

Ken Livingstone, any nonresident entering central London between 7 A.M. and 6:30 P.M., Monday to Friday, has to pay a toll of five pounds per vehicle. Once a cordon is in place, it can be used to restrict or regulate entry to a city—or to any neighborhood, for that matter—in many ways. Vehicles could be charged according to how much time they spend inside the city; residents could be charged differently from out-of-towners; those driving a single-occupancy vehicle could be charged more than carpoolers; and if the SOV is an SUV the driver could be charged more than someone in a compact.

Sam Schwartz favors not only East River bridge tolls but also first-class high-speed lanes over the bridges, for which drivers would pay a premium that would guarantee them passage in a certain amount of time or their money back (all of which could be easily accomplished with E-Z Pass). In 1995 four new toll lanes opened alongside the Riverside Freeway in Southern California, which runs between Anaheim and Riverside County, allowing drivers who are willing to pay the toll ($4.75 during peak periods) a considerably speedier trip. Schwartz thinks that something similar should be done both on the East River bridges and on the Long Island Expressway. Critics of high-speed toll lanes say they would discriminate against lower-income drivers, creating "Lexus lanes" for the rich, but Schwartz disagrees. "First of all, the lowest-income workers aren't coming into Manhattan by car—they can't afford to park. Of the middle-class workers who drive, are you telling me that an electrician from Long Island who makes a hundred dollars an hour wouldn't pay ten dollars to save an hour in traffic?"


At 5:59 P.M., the crew of NewsCopter 7 heard from the studio: their report would be leading the six o'clock news.

"All right!" Sohn said.

"Okay, Shannon, to you in thirty seconds," a voice in the headphones said.

"I'm getting skid in the shot," Sohn said to Anderson, indicating the landing gear, and he angled the chopper downward so that the viewers at home would have an unobstructed view of the full horror of I-95.

Just before the news began, Channel 7 ran a car commercial. It showed a Jeep Grand Cherokee cruising along an empty road somewhere in the dreamscape of automotive fantasy. Then the clarions sounded, announcing the start of *Eyewitness News*.

"Shannon, what's it like out there?" one of the anchors asked.

Sohn reported that it was very bad indeed—"an unbelievable bumper-to-bumper jam leading from the George all the way up to the toll plaza at the New Jersey Turnpike—a solid hour-and-a-half delay," she said. She gave a rundown of the other traffic nightmares the city had suffered, and concluded, "This may be the worst holiday traffic I've ever seen."

"Thanks, Shannon," the anchor said when the spot ended. It was comforting to know that New York was getting back to normal.

At 6:15 P.M., NewsCopter 7 was whirring back to Linden Airport. The sun was sinking toward Kittatinny Mountain in northwestern New Jersey, and the hazy summer light was smudging the edges of Manhattan's skyline. It had been a terrible day for traffic, but a good day—"a five-lollipop day"—for Shannon Sohn.

"What's the next worst traffic you've seen?" I asked Sohn as we were once again flying over Newark.

"Yesterday," she said. "Yesterday was horrible."

How was she going to get away this weekend?

"I'm going to ride my horse," she said.

—2002

# THE TOWER BUILDER

Structural engineers make buildings stand up, but the public doesn't pay much attention to what they do until a building falls down. Although the safety of a building's occupants depends on its structure, most people notice only the aesthetics, the furnishings, and the view, and give the architects, not the engineers, all the credit (or blame) for the results. Very few inhabitants of modern high-rises know where the load-bearing columns are placed and how they are supported, or whether the building is a frame structure or a tube structure, and almost no one checks above the ceiling tiles to see how the floor overhead is attached to the vertical supports— all decisions that are worked out by the building's structural engineers. The anonymity of the high-rise structural engineer is the reward for his genius. Part of the awe that skyscrapers command lies in their apparent freedom from gravity: they're not just tall; they're effortlessly tall.

After the collapse of the World Trade Center towers, on September 11, structural engineers and their profession received a great deal of public attention. University engineering departments around the country staged public forums in which the "mechanics of failure" were debated; I attended one at Columbia University. The American Society of Civil Engineers and FEMA (the Federal Emergency Management Agency) were funding a team of twenty-four civil and fire-safety engineers to investigate what parts of the Twin Towers' structure failed first, and how much damage was caused by the impact and blast of the airplanes and how much by the ensuing fires. Dr. W. Gene Corley, a structural engineer with Construction Technology Laboratories in Skokie, Illinois, who led FEMA's investigation into the collapse of the nine-story Murrah Building in Oklahoma City in 1995, was the overall director of FEMA's inquiry into the World Trade towers. In addition to inspecting the site of the disaster, he told me, his team would review photographs and enhanced videos of the collapse, examine the debris, and use information from firemen, policemen, survivors, and other witnesses in an attempt to reconstruct the moment at which each structure failed.

Of course, you didn't need an engineer to tell you why the towers fell down: two Boeing 767s, traveling at hundreds of miles an hour and carrying more than ten thousand gallons of jet fuel each (if you converted the energy in the Oklahoma City bomb into jet fuel, it would amount to only fifty-one gallons), crashed into the north and south buildings at 8:45 A.M. and 9:06 A.M. respectively, causing them to fall—the south tower at 9:59 A.M. and the north tower at 10:28. Nor did we need a government panel to tell us that the best way to protect tall buildings is to keep airplanes out of them. Nevertheless, there was considerable debate among experts about precisely what order of events precipitated the collapse of each building, and whether the order was the same in both towers. Did the connections between the floors and the columns give way first, or did the vertical supports that remained after the impact lose strength in the fire, and if so, did the exterior columns or the core columns give way first? "That's the sixty-four-thousand-dollar question," said Ron Hamburger, a structural engineer with ABS Consulting in Oakland, California, who was also on FEMA's team, when I asked which of these scenarios he favored. Although there may never be another event like the attack on the towers, the disaster also highlighted several potential weaknesses in the way that many modern high-rises are constructed—weaknesses that the designers of the tall buildings of the future may want to consider.

Leslie E. Robertson was the engineer who, with his then partner, John Skilling, was mainly responsible for the structure of the

Twin Towers. Unlike most of his colleagues, who were widely quoted and interviewed, he remained largely out of the public eye since September 11. His only public appearance was at a previously scheduled meeting of the National Council of Structural Engineers Associations in New Hampshire, where, as *The Wall Street Journal* reported, on being asked by an engineer in the audience, "Is there anything you wish you had done differently in the design of the building?," Robertson broke down and wept at the lectern. Guy Nordenson, a structural engineer in New York and a professor at Princeton, who, like many of his colleagues, regards Robertson with great respect, showed me a recent e-mail he had received from him. It was a response to a letter Nordenson had written to the *Times*, praising the towers' structural design for keeping them standing as long as they did, and allowing some twenty-five thousand people to escape. "It's very Les," he said, referring to Robertson, and pointed at his computer screen. "Almost Shakespearean." Robertson had written:

> Your words do much to abate the fire that
> writhes inside
> It is hard
> But that I had done a bit more . . .
> Had the towers stood up for just one
> minute longer . . .
> It is hard.

On a brilliantly sunny fall morning in late October 2001, I visited Robertson's offices, on the top two floors of 30 Broad Street, a forty-eight-story building that stands a few blocks from Ground Zero. From the windows of the conference room where I waited for Robertson, there was a clear view down into the rubble where the south tower once stood. Fires were still burning inside the pit, and the smell, that sweet acrid odor of burning metal and decay, was noticeable in the room. Many of the firm's sixty employees, including Saw-Teen See, Robertson's wife, who is also a partner in the firm, stood by these windows and watched as the second

plane flew in over Hudson River Park, banked, and disappeared inside the south tower. See remembers closing her eyes at that moment, and didn't see the fireball come out the other side.

I turned away from the view and studied pictures of other buildings that Robertson's firm had worked on over the years, which were
displayed around the room, including the Bank of China Tower in
Hong Kong, a 1,209-foot structure engineered by Robertson for
I. M. Pei. Pei's characteristic triangular shapes had been seamlessly
translated into gigantic diagonal braces on the sides of the building.
Structural engineers commonly complain that architects don't understand how to construct high-rise buildings, from either a structural or an economic perspective, leaving it to the engineers to
wrestle with the problems posed by the architecture and to resolve
them in a way that allows the potential contractor to submit a bid for
the project that is within the developer's budget. Such a perfect
marriage of architecture and structure as the Bank of China Tower
is unusual in the creation of skyscrapers, but it is a distinguishing
feature of many of the buildings that Robertson has worked on over
the years, and especially the World Trade towers.

On entering the room, Robertson walked over and looked out
the window at the smoking pile where his structures had once been.
He seemed to do this casually, but as we stood there I noticed that
he was trembling slightly. He remained before the window for almost a minute, with the air of a man forcing himself to confront
something he didn't want to confront, nodding as though to say,
okay, this is reality, I know it—but looking bewildered at the same
time. When we sat down, he said, "The World Trade Center was a
team effort, but the collapse of the World Trade Center is my responsibility, and that's the way I feel about it."

Robertson, seventy-three, wore a gray silk shirt that was open at
the collar. His hair was mostly white, and longish, falling over his
ears, and with bangs in front, which gave him a slightly bohemian
look. His brown eyes were like very deep pools, and the flesh below
the eyes was swollen, either with fatigue or with grief. As we talked,
he frequently looked out the window. I felt the absence of the buildings in him. "That's how people introduced me," he said. "I was the
designer of the World Trade Center. Although that was wrong,

actually—I only assisted on the team that designed it. But that's who I was."

Robertson was in Hong Kong on September 11, having dinner with the developers of a skyscraper in Kowloon. "A woman's cell phone rang, and she said an airplane had hit the World Trade towers. I thought it was an accident, one of the helicopters that were always flying overhead. A short time later, my wife called me and said the second plane had hit, and I went upstairs and turned on the television. I knew both buildings were hit by planes, both on fire. I had no idea whether there were a thousand people or fifty thousand people at risk. I knew the fire was burning out of control, I knew people were jumping to get away from the heat . . ." His eyes searched the empty view again.

"Before the buildings collapsed," I asked, "did any part of your brain, calculating, say, There's probably this amount of jet fuel, this amount of fire protection—the building has this long to last?"

"I can't . . . I think there are times when logic just isn't the right way to think." Robertson's eyes were filling with tears. "This all took place in an hour and a half. The TV was on. I don't know if what I saw was the buildings falling down on rerun or whether it was live. I was just focused on getting back to New York City. I remember packing my bags. And when the building collapsed—it was totally devastating."

During the last hundred and twenty years, three major types of structures have been employed in tall buildings in New York City. The first type was used in the cast-iron buildings of the 1880s and 1890s, in which the "gravity load"—the weight of the building— was carried mostly by the exterior walls. This type of structure creates factory and warehouse spaces (and now, residential lofts) that are relatively free of internal supporting columns—more usable real estate for the tenants—but when combined with wooden floor beams and more lenient building codes, it also makes the buildings vulnerable to collapse. In a fire, the floors tend to collapse, and the iron frame loses strength and implodes.

The second generation of tall buildings, which includes the

Metropolitan Life Building (1909), the Woolworth Building (1913), and the Empire State Building (1931), are frame structures in which a skeleton of welded or riveted steel columns and beams, often encased in concrete, runs through the entire building. This type of construction makes for an extremely strong structure, but not such attractive floor space. The interiors are full of heavy, load-bearing columns and walls, and as you move toward the center of these buildings, the more cryptlike they feel. Charlie Thornton, of the Manhattan-based structural-engineering firm of Thornton Tomasetti Engineers, a leading designer of the structures of modern high-rises, said to me, "A building like the Empire State Building is way overdesigned and overbuilt. The building didn't need all that support. Those engineers didn't understand loads the way we understand them—they used slide rules to work them out, whereas we have computers—and so they erred on the side of caution."

Most high-rises erected since the 1960s use a third type of structure—a synthesis of the best aspects of the two previous kinds of structure. The perimeter structures of these buildings resemble tubes. Inside, a massive hollow core made of steel or concrete or both contains many of the services: elevators, stairwells, and bathrooms. Because the core and perimeter columns carry so much of the load, the designers could eliminate interior columns, with the result that there is more open floor space for the tenants. And because frame structures require ironworkers to weld or rivet the beams to the supporting columns on-site, which is both expensive and dangerous, reducing the extent of the frame means that more of the structure can be fabricated off-site, making the building safer and more cost-effective to erect. Finally, improvements in metallurgy increased the strength of the structural steel in these buildings, allowing engineers to reduce, or eliminate, the use of concrete in supporting the structure. Reinforced concrete, although it is more fire-resistant than steel, is messy and expensive to work with, especially in Manhattan, where traffic and space constraints at sites make it difficult to bring in the daily fleets of cement mixers necessary for a big job.

The floors in most of the high-rise buildings erected since the sixties are much lighter in weight than the floors in the older buildings. In a typical high-rise office floor, three or four inches of concrete covers a corrugated-steel deck, whose weight is supported by I-beams or, in the case of the Twin Towers, by long "trusses"— lightweight strips of steel that are braced by crosshatched webs of square or cylindrical bars, creating a hollow space below each floor surface. This space allows builders to install heating and cooling ducts within the floors, rather than in a drop ceiling below them—an innovation that means the developer can increase the number of floors in the entire building.

All of these improvements led to a high-rise building boom in New York City during the sixties and seventies; the World Trade towers, conceived in 1963 and opened in the early seventies, were the most famous products of that era. But as the new high-rises sprouted, some New York City firefighters began to point out that the same innovations that make these buildings more economical to erect and more pleasant to inhabit also make them more vulnerable to fire. In 1976 the New York City Fire Commissioner, John O'Hagan, published a book entitled *High Rise/Fire and Life Safety,* in which he called attention to the serious fire-safety issues in most high-rise buildings constructed since 1970, referring to such buildings as "semi-combustible."

Unlike the earlier generation of skyscrapers, which used concrete and masonry to protect the structural steel, many of the newer buildings employed Sheetrock and spray-on fire protection. The spray-on protection generally consisted of either a cementlike material that resembles plaster or a mineral-fiber spray, such as the one used to protect the floor joists in the World Trade Center. O'Hagan pointed out that, even when these spray-ons are properly mixed and applied to the steel (which must be clean), they are much less dense than concrete and can be easily knocked off. The swaying of the cables in the elevator shafts has been known to dislodge the fire protection from the columns in the cores of these buildings, and the coating used on floor supports is often removed by workers who install the ducts and wiring inside the hollow floor. The questionable performance of the fire protection used in these buildings, combined with the greater expanse of lightweight, unsupported floors, O'Hagan said, created the potential for collapse, of the individual floors and of the entire structure. He also pointed out that the open spaces favored by modern developers allowed fires to spread faster than the compartmentalized spaces of the

earlier buildings, and that the synthetic furnishings in modern buildings created more heat and smoke than materials made out of wood
and natural fibers.

O'Hagan's book did nothing to stop semicombustible buildings
from going up—a fireman's predictable lament about safety was not
what a city in love with its skyscrapers wanted to hear. It was not until
September 11 that the architects and builders of tall buildings began
to think seriously about whether the modern methods of constructing
high-rises needed to be revised. One indication that older high-rise
buildings may be more fire-resistant than the newer high-rise buildings is the performance of the twenty-three-story building at 90 West
Street—a Cass Gilbert–designed building, finished in 1907 (Gilbert
also designed the Woolworth Building), whose structure was protected by concrete and masonry—compared with the performance of
7 World Trade, an all-steel building from the 1980s, that had spray-on
fire protection. Both buildings were completely gutted by fires on September 11, but 90 West Street is still standing, and may eventually be
restored, while 7 World Trade, which had a gas main beneath it, collapsed after burning for seven hours.

Leslie Robertson was born in California in 1928. A poor student,
he dropped out of high school at the age of sixteen and spent
two years in the navy, where he became an electronics technician.
There, he said, "I learned that I actually knew how to do things, and
if I wanted to I could get them done." His father had been an inventor, "a brilliant guy, but he never stuck at anything." After leaving
the military, Robertson attended the University of California at
Berkeley, where he received a bachelor's degree in science. He began his career by designing electrical systems for factories, and from
there he moved into structural engineering. He worked for several
engineering firms around the country, including Raymond International, where he assisted in the engineering of offshore-drilling rigs
until he decided to go back to California. Driving from New York to
San Francisco in late 1958, he ran out of money in Seattle and took
the first job he could get—working at a firm of structural engineers
then called Worthington-Skilling.

In 1963 the firm entered a competition held by the Port Authority of New York and New Jersey to build in New York City what would be the tallest buildings ever constructed—the two towers of the World Trade Center. It was one of eight engineering firms—most of them large partnerships in New York—asked to submit proposals. Although the firm's tallest building up to that point was the twenty-story IBM Building in Seattle, the architect of that building was Minoru Yamasaki—the same architect the Port Authority had selected for the World Trade Center. At a meeting to present the firm's proposal to the architect and developers, John Skilling, one of the four partners, used only a drawing pad, an easel, and some markers to make his pitch.

The man the Port Authority had chosen as the architect of the tallest buildings in the world was afraid of heights. The glass curtain-wall skyscrapers, in which the only separation between you and the outside is a thinnish piece of glass, frightened Yamasaki. He thought tall buildings should have structural elements around the perimeter, so that the occupants would feel secure in them. In engineering the IBM Building for Yamasaki, Skilling's firm had come up with a structure in which the exterior walls were made of closely spaced steel pipes. Yamasaki liked the soothing effect that the pipes had on his acrophobia, and the building's vertical aspect—it appears to be dressed in a pin-striped suit—appealed to his aesthetic. Yamasaki had something similar in mind for the World Trade Center, but on a much larger scale: solid elements at the edges, which he could brace himself on before looking out. "And Yama was not a large man," Saw-Teen See told me, "so the columns couldn't be too far apart."

What Skilling proposed was a pure tube structure. His design was consistent with the general principles at work in the new generation of high-rises, but he carried the concept of the tube building farther than it had ever been taken before. (Or since: the Sears Tower, in Chicago, which replaced the World Trade towers as the world's tallest building in 1973, is also a tube building, but it is actually a cluster of nine smaller tubes.) The Twin Towers would be perforated steel boxes surrounding a hollow steel core. The outer box would be 208 feet on each side, and made of fourteen-inch-wide steel columns that were spaced on forty-inch centers—much closer than the fifteen- to thirty-foot spaces that separate most supporting columns in a building. Like the cast-iron buildings of the previous century, the exterior walls would be load-bearing; unlike most skyscrapers, which hide their supporting columns, the Twin Towers would proudly wear their structure on their sleeves. Because there were so many load-bearing columns around the perimeter of each building, the engineers could completely eliminate all columns within the office space. Joining the outside tube to the inner core were state-of-the-art lightweight floor trusses that spanned sixty feet from core to exterior walls on two sides, and thirty-five feet on the other two sides. Yamasaki liked the design because it reminded him of a bamboo tube, an important totem for him. The Port Authority liked the design because, among other things, the towers would offer the single largest expanse of column-free office space in Manhattan—a realtor's dream.

Skilling's firm got the commission, and Robertson, then thirty-five, moved to New York to open a new office, and to supervise the structural aspects of the building's construction. In 1983 the Seattle office and the New York office split, becoming two separate firms. Skilling (who died in 1998) and Robertson later argued about who was more responsible for the structure of the towers. "These are guys with big egos, and things got a little testy between them regarding who was ultimately responsible for the design," says Jon Magnusson, the chairman and CEO of the Seattle-based firm, which is now called Skilling Ward Magnusson Barkshire. "Skilling said, 'It was me,' Robertson said, 'It was me,' but I think the truth is that both of them made a significant contribution."

The trick to designing tall buildings in windy places (like New York City and Chicago) is to endow them with enough elasticity to move with the wind but enough stiffness so that the people working on the upper floors don't know the building is moving. The World Trade towers used the perimeter walls, rather than the core, to brace the buildings against the wind, a concept that recalled the first generation of high-rises. As Robertson described the models and experiments he had devised to test how the towers would stand up to external forces that might topple them, he looked almost happy for the first time that morning. He built models of the towers and placed them in a wind tunnel; he put people in motion simulators and observed their behavior; he invented a new kind of damper system to lessen the effect of the wind throughout the buildings. He rode on top of elevator cars in other skyscrapers to see whether the cables banged against the cores of the buildings.

He also designed the buildings so they would be able to absorb the impact of a jet airliner: "I'm sort of a methodical person, so I listed all the bad things that could happen to a building and tried to design for them. I thought of the B-25 bomber, lost in the fog, that hit the Empire State Building in nineteen forty-five. The 707 was the state-of-the-art airplane then, and the Port Authority was quite amenable to considering the effect of an airplane as a design criterion. We studied it, and designed for the impact of such an aircraft. The next step would have been to think about the fuel load, and I've been searching my brain, but I don't know what happened there, whether in all our testing we thought about it. Now we know what happens—it explodes. I don't know if we considered the fire damage that would cause. Anyway, the architect, not the engineer, is the one who specifies the fire system."

On September 11, each building took the impact of a 767 (which is nearly 20 percent heavier than a 707) and stood long enough to allow most of the people below the crash sites—the ninety-fourth floor to the ninety-ninth floor in the north tower, and the seventy-eighth floor to the eighty-fourth floor in the south tower—to escape. Had the buildings toppled immediately, nearly all those survivors would have died, and there would have been huge losses as well in the buildings and streets around the towers. The fact that the terrorists chose to hit the buildings on opposite faces suggests to some that they intended to knock the buildings over—which would have increased the destruction and loss of life. "Ninety-nine percent of all buildings would collapse immediately when hit by a 767," Jon Magnusson said.

But did the special structural characteristics of these buildings, qualities that made them so resistant to attack from without, also make them vulnerable to collapse from within, once the fires started? If one of the airplanes had hit an older skyscraper, like the Empire State Building, which has a frame structure instead of a tube structure, would the total disaster have been greater (the building falls over immediately) or lesser (the concrete in the building lasts longer in a fire, and the frame structure protects the building from complete collapse)? Of all the difficult questions that the FEMA investigators were asking about the disaster, this was one of the hardest.

In any fire, it is logical to assume that the weakest link in the structure will be the first to fail. In the towers, the weak link was the floors. "Floor beams or trusses will heat up faster than columns, because they're thinner pieces of steel," W. Gene Corley, the leader of the FEMA team, said. The floors were supported with sixty-foot-long right angles of steel (on the long sides), and these were bolted, not welded, to the inner and outer columns. "The whole floor system was a very lightweight construction," Eduardo Kausel, a structural engineer at MIT, told me. Another engineer described the floors to me as "flimsy." Jerome Connor, also of MIT, said, "The weakest link was definitely the connections of the floor trusses to the vertical members." Those connections were protected with the mineral-fiber spray, but most of it was probably knocked off by the impact of the airplanes. Ron Hamburger told me, "If you knock it, that spray-on protection will come off. When I visited the site, I went through the American Express and the Bankers Trust buildings, and I saw large chunks of the fireproofing in those buildings knocked off—and that was only by falling debris, not by an airplane hit. I think we can assume there was a lot of unprotected steel in the towers after the planes hit."

The columns in the core were massive, and were capable of bearing huge gravity loads, but they depended on the floors to provide lateral support. As the floors around the crash site began to give way in the intense fire, ever greater lengths of the core columns, which were already overloaded because of the destruction of exterior columns, became exposed. If you stand an inch-long drinking straw on end and press on it with your finger, you have to press pretty hard before it bends. But if you do the same thing with a seven-inch-long straw it buckles easily. The same principle was at work in the towers' core columns. Once the core columns buckled, the entire weight of the floors above the crash sites came down like a jackhammer on the remaining floors, starting a chain reaction of pancaking floors and buckling columns that demolished the entire structure within fifteen seconds—the same amount of time it took the people who jumped from the top of the towers to hit the pavement. "Once the collapse started, it was essentially a free fall," Eduardo Kausel said. Kausel, for one, thinks the terrorists knew exactly how to make the towers fall—not by knocking them over but by triggering a collapse from within. "You'd need a graduate degree in engineering to know exactly where to hit those buildings to make them fall. Hit them higher, and the weight above the crash sites might not be enough to bring the whole thing down. Hit them lower, and the core columns might have been strong enough to stand up."

Of course, it also could have been the case that the core columns were damaged by the airplanes, or weakened by the fires, and that it was the failure in the structural members themselves, rather than the lack of support caused by the collapsing floors, that led to the overall failure of the structure. The distinction here seems minor when set against the magnitude of the disaster, but it is important when you start thinking about how modern high-rise buildings are designed, and how safe they are. Although the Twin Towers were, in the words of Jon Magnusson, "of all the buildings in the world, the closest to being pure tube buildings," many other high-rises are based on the tube concept, and others have internal cores that are braced by the floors. How many floors would you have to remove in a tube-style building before it collapsed?

Robertson said he had thought a lot about the one-inch-thick cylindrical-steel webbing that was used in the support of the floors. He thought that the round steel rods might not hold spray-on fire protection as well as angled bars, but the contractor, Tishman Construction, could save money by using the cylindrical rods—they were a factory-produced item, and cheaper—and he approved them in the end. "On the other hand, there were other fires in the buildings over the years, and one quite serious one, and the fireproofing on those rods did okay." As the developer, the Port Authority had the ultimate say in making decisions about building materials, and although all developers are driven by economic considerations, the Port Authority was exceptionally profit-minded. "Remember, this wasn't a corporate headquarters—a monument building," Robertson said. "It was a moneymaking proposition."

W as there any way for the structural engineers and architects involved in building the towers to know that they were going to collapse, and how quickly? Yamasaki died, of cancer, in 1986. Robertson was in Hong Kong. A group of engineers from his office were on their way to the site after the first plane hit, but when the second plane hit they went back to the office or left the area. Most of the Port Authority engineers, including the chief engineer, Frank Lombardi, worked in the north tower, and they were in the stairwell when the second plane hit, unaware of what had happened. Only when they had regrouped in the Marriott Hotel, on the southwest side of the plaza, did they learn about the second plane, and not long after that the upper part of the south tower fell onto the hotel, partially collapsing it. "I thought a bomb had come through the windows," Lombardi told me. "We had no idea of the extent of the damage, and certainly none of us had the information to make a decision to keep the rescue workers who entered the buildings out of them." He added, "I do think it may be a good idea, in the event of something like this happening in the future, to have a structural engineer on the scene, who arrives with the firemen, and makes that cold, objective decision to send people in or not send them. But first of all, that person would have to have no emotional relationship to the people inside or to the building—I mean, for us, this was our second home—and secondly, that person would have to be absolutely liability free. Because that's one hell of a decision to make."

Among the dozens of people I spoke to who were experts in the construction of tall buildings (and many of whom witnessed the events of September 11 as they unfolded), only one said that he knew immediately, upon learning, from TV, of the planes' hitting the buildings, that the towers were going to fall. This was Mark Loizeaux, the president of Controlled Demolition Incorporated, a Maryland-based family business that specializes in reducing tall buildings to manageable pieces of rubble. "Within a nanosecond," he told me. "I said, 'It's coming down. And the second tower will fall first, because it was hit lower down.'"

Before September 11, the largest building ever to be imploded by accident or design was the J. L. Hudson department store in Detroit, with 2.2 million square feet of floor space, which CDI "dropped" on October 24, 1998. To do their work, Mark Loizeaux and his brother Doug need to understand the same forces and formulas that structural engineers study, but instead of using that knowledge to erect buildings, they use it to take them down. They are structural undertakers, which may explain why Mark, when confronted with the spectacle of the crippled buildings, lacked the sentiment that builders feel for their creations—that innate sympathy which helped blind the engineers of the World Trade towers to the reality of what was about to occur. "I thought, Somebody's got to tell the Fire Department to get out of there," Loizeaux told me. "I picked up the phone, dialed 411, got the number, and tried it—busy. So I called the Mayor's Office of Emergency Management"—which was in 7 World Trade. "All circuits were busy. I couldn't get through."

Loizeaux said he had an enhanced video of the collapses, and he talked about them in a way that indicated he had watched the video more than once. "First of all, you've got the obvious damage to the exterior frame from the airplane—if you count the number of external columns missing from the sides the planes hit, there are about two-thirds of the total. And the buildings are still standing, which is amazing—even with all those columns missing, the gravity loads have found alternate pathways. Okay, but you've got fires—jet-fuel fires, which the building is not designed for, and you've also got lots of paper in there. Now paper cooks. A paper fire is like a coal-mine fire: it keeps burning as long as oxygen gets to it. And you're high in the building, up in the wind, plenty of oxygen. So you've got a hot fire. And you've got these floor trusses, made of fairly thin metal, and fire protection has been knocked off most of them by the impact. And you have all this open space—clear span from perimeter to core—with no columns or partition walls, so the airplane is going to skid right through that space to the core, which doesn't have any reinforced concrete in it, just Sheetrock covering steel, and the fire is going to spread everywhere immediately, and no fire-protection systems are working—the sprinkler heads shorn off by the airplanes, the water pipes in the core are likely cut. So what's going to happen? Floor A is going to fall onto floor B, which falls onto floor C; the unsupported columns will buckle; and the weight of everything above the crash site falls onto what remains below—bringing loads of two thousand pounds per square foot, plus the force of the impact, onto floors designed to bear one hundred pounds per square foot. It has to fall."

Loizeaux said that when he demolishes buildings, he sometimes tries to make the top twist and fall sideways, which can generate enough "reverse thrust" to push the rest of the building the other way. "The top part of the south tower almost did fall off, which is what would happen in most buildings. Did you see how, when that top part started to fall, it began to rotate? If that piece had kept going out, it probably would have pushed the rest of the building the other way as it fell. But those long trusses saved the day—they gave way, guided that top downward just like a bullet through the barrel of a gun, and mitigated the damage." He added, "Let me tell you something. Far more people would have died if those buildings had been built differently. A conventional frame building would have fallen immediately—no question. Only a tube structure could have taken that hit and survived."

It is important to bear in mind, when discussing the towers' collapse, that most of the office workers who perished in the attack were trapped above the floors hit by the airplanes. Even if the buildings had stood for hours longer, the majority of them probably couldn't have been saved. Many of the people below the crash site who died in the collapses were the rescue workers, including 343 firemen, who entered the towers after the planes hit.

The firemen did what firemen do—they charged into the burning buildings and tried to save lives and put out the fire. There was little or no time to consider the potential for total collapse that was present in the tube structures. The chiefs and commanders were operating on standard FDNY procedure on how to fight a high-rise fire: stay below the burning floors, and attack from there. The city's Department of Buildings enforces the standards for how long the materials used in city buildings should stand up in fires. These standards are based on tests of individual building materials conducted at testing centers around the country. Each material is subjected to rapidly rising temperatures, to discover the point at which it fails. During construction, the appropriate amount of fire protection is applied to that material to bring its longevity in a fire up to the required amount of time. (Because the towers were owned by the Port Authority, a bistate agency, they were not subject to New York City fire regulations or inspections, but according to Alan Reiss, the former director of the World Trade Center, the Port Authority always had a policy of complying with New York City fire codes and inspection procedures.)

Unfortunately, the standard fire scenarios didn't match the conditions in the World Trade towers in several important ways. In the first place, the scenarios measure only the "fire load," or amount of combustible material, already in the building; the tests don't anticipate additional sources of energy that might be introduced into the building. Second, in calculating how long certain materials will last in a fire, most tests don't anticipate the sudden intensity of fires such as those in the World Trade Center; usually, a fire starts small and spreads, so that the curve of temperature over time is a gradual rise to the peak. Nor do the tests anticipate the added stress on structural elements caused by impact, such as that of an airplane—steel fails at lower temperatures when under extreme stress.

New York City firemen are very familiar with the crash of the B-25 into the seventy-eighth and seventy-ninth floors of the Empire State Building in 1945, which killed fourteen people; the department makes that event part of the standard training that every chief and commander receives. It is often true that those who don't remember history are doomed to repeat it, but it is also sometimes true that those who remember history can be misled by it. In the Empire State Building crash, the ensuing fire was a flash fire, fueled not by jet fuel but by gasoline (which has a slightly lower heat content); in addition, the B-25 carried only eight hundred gallons of fuel—much less than the ten thousand or more gallons that spilled into each of the towers. As a result, the fire was put out in thirty-five minutes and did limited damage to the building. The fires in the towers were far hotter—they may have burned at close to two thousand degrees—and because of the way the Empire State Building was "overbuilt," it was, in general, better able to resist fire.

Retired deputy chief Vincent Dunn, a forty-two-year veteran of the New York City Fire Department, who is the author of the book *Collapse of Burning Buildings: A Guide to Fireground Safety,* told me, "The technology of building high-rises has got way ahead of the ability to fire-protect them adequately." He added, "No one wants to be alarmist, but we in the fire service know that in any high-rise building built since 1970 the fire safety is questionable." Dunn speaks only for himself, but his opinion of the structure of the Twin Towers is shared by others who are closely affiliated with the New York City Fire Department. "Look, from a fire chief's perspective—and I'm not an engineer, but as a fire chief I know buildings—the World Trade Center buildings were not well constructed," Dunn said. "I'd call them fragile buildings. There were no internal columns supporting the floors, and those floor trusses were very lightweight. Essentially, it was a pinned construction, where the exterior walls are the bearing walls. That's the way the old cast-iron buildings in SoHo were built, and as every firefighter knows, in those buildings the floors collapse in fires. In my opinion, a skeleton steel building would have stood up better. Yes, you get sections falling off the building, maybe even the top part of the building falls off. But you don't get pancaking floors that bring the whole structure down." David Lucht, the director of the Center for Firesafety Studies at Worcester Polytechnic Institute, disagreed with Dunn's assessment of the safety of modern high-rises. "I can understand where the Fire Department is coming from—they don't build 'em like they used to," he said. "And that's true. But in many ways people are safer in high-rise buildings than they are at home." He pointed out that the newer buildings have the benefit of modern sprinkler and alarm systems, along with pressurized stairwells and floors that help keep smoke away from the fire areas. "High-rise buildings have performed amazingly well over the years in fires, although this event will cause both researchers and public officials to take another look at the performance of these buildings."

Dunn said that, had he been at the scene, he would have sent his men into the building too. "I don't care how strong they were—if you've got buildings collapsing on firefighters, there's something wrong with the way those buildings were built."

Leslie E. Robertson Associates was assisting the various teams that were investigating the towers' collapse, and Saw-Teen See was on the FEMA team. Robertson told me he was glad that the efforts were under way, but he doubted whether we would ever understand the mechanics of failure precisely. "If we could learn why the buildings collapsed, there would be value in that," he said. "But that other event, in Oklahoma City—that was more quantifiable. This is a huge task—it's probably an impossible task now to sort out all the proper evidence."

Because each steel column used in the exterior of the towers had a mark stamped on it, in theory it would be possible to reassemble the pieces from the damaged floors. But the time and manpower that such an effort would require were beyond FEMA's resources. Besides, the core columns, not the external columns, would yield the most information about the collapses, but the videos and still pictures of the injured buildings don't show the condition of the core columns, and those columns were marked only with paint, which in most cases has disappeared. Robertson said that he and his wife went out to one of the scrapyards in New Jersey where some of the steel is being held, to inspect a piece that one investigator thought had an airplane part attached to it. "But we figured out that that piece of steel was from the fortieth floor, well below either crash site," he said.

Behind Robertson were renderings of what would be two of the tallest buildings in the world, both from the architecture firm of Kohn Pedersen Fox—the Shanghai World Financial Center and an office building in Hong Kong. Robertson was assisting in the design of the structures for both buildings. He said he had met with the developers of the skyscrapers after September 11 and reassured them that the structures of both buildings were sound. "I said that it was not necessary to design buildings with the idea of planes running into them. It's prudent to see what we could do to make things better, but you can't design for every eventuality." He added, "I suspect tall buildings will always be with us. People need to be close to each other, in order to communicate effectively. But builders and architects are going to have to make the argument for why tall buildings should be built, and why people should move into them."

Charlie Thornton, of Thornton Tomasetti, told me, "One of the things you'll hear is 'Should we use more concrete?'" Thornton's firm did the structural engineering for the Petronas Towers in Kuala Lumpur, then the tallest buildings in the world; those buildings have a concrete core and concrete perimeter columns, but that decision was based in part on the fact that Malaysia had no steel industry, and imposes high tariffs on imported steel. "Should we at least require the cores of tall buildings to be reinforced in concrete, which would give them more fire protection and give people a better chance of getting out in a fire?" he went on. "Should we have refuge floors, spaced every ten floors or so, which would allow people some protection from smoke?" But Robertson says, "Thank God we didn't have refuge floors in the World Trade towers—people might have stopped there to regroup, rather than getting out of the buildings as fast as they could."

Every high-rise building represents a balance of power; incorporated into the final design are the various interests of developers, architects, engineers, and firemen. Will September 11 change this hierarchy? The public interest, which is safety, is protected by building codes and laws, but the way those codes are written is not a democratic process. Professional engineers, together with academics and the representatives of construction companies, articulate the "minimum" standard of safety as determined by each constituency. Guy Nordenson, who has expertise in seismic codes, said, "We have a predicament not only for engineering but for planning and design in general. Developers and many designers participate in the economy of wealth, image, and fame, and so they press against that minimum." Nordenson and his associates at Princeton were completing a seismic study for FEMA of the buildings in New York when, after September 11, they were called, along with the Structural Engineers Association of New York and

Charlie Thornton's firm, to help the city check the stability of the buildings around Ground Zero. His opinion was that the collapse of the World Trade towers would change building codes. "The building laws will change—more redundancy, stronger interconnection of parts, all attributes of good seismic design, by the way—as they have after every disaster."

Still, it doesn't make sense to design skyscrapers to withstand the crash of an airliner—the buildings would resemble nuclear silos, and as the chairman of the Nuclear Regulatory Commission suggested recently, even those structures might not withstand a fully fueled airplane. Engineers can't be asked to make every building safe from every possible event, yet that is just what people expect, and the engineers try to meet these impossible expectations. Sitting in Robertson's conference room, I said that his structures had saved a lot of people. He said, "A lot of things worked well—people got out. I suppose I'm proud of that." But he was looking toward that unavoidable view from the window. "It's a tremendous responsibility, being an engineer," he said, his voice breaking. "It's a very imperfect process. It's not so beautiful as science." He struggled to keep his composure. "I have a lot of tough nights. I'm still not sleeping. I go to sleep for a little bit, but I wake up thinking—I have so many thoughts."

He put his hands over his eyes, as though that would block out the thoughts. After a minute or so, he went on, "There are all kinds of terrible things that take place on this planet, that nature brings on us. But this event had . . . Not only was it man against man but it was live on television, and we watched it, and you could reach out and touch it"—he stretched out his hand toward the windows where the towers had once stood—"but there was nothing you could do."

—2001

# AMERICAN SCRAP

The Foot of Hawkins Street scrapyard sits on twenty-seven acres of industrial parkland, at the edge of Newark's old Ironbound District. The yard's metallic topography—large piles of scrap metal, mainly of steel, but also of copper, aluminum, and stainless steel—can be seen from the West Side high-rises in Manhattan. Sometimes, when the sun hits the piles, they glitter like honey-coated breakfast cereal. The yard also contains a range of machines used in the deconstruction business, including a shear, a baler, and two overhead cranes, which work through the piles of metal with the stately rhythm of large browsing ruminants. The air holds a tangy but not unpleasant metallic essence, and is periodically rent with the shriek of shattering steel, heard over a thudding backbeat of mangled appliances that the cranes drop into piles—food for a nearby shredder. If you listen closely, you can hear the tinkling of the "shred"—the fist-size hunks of metal that emerge from the shredder—raining down on the shred pile. That's a comforting sound to people in scrap, because it sounds like money.

It was a warm day in late September 2007, and I had arranged to meet Daniel Dienst, the CEO of Metal Management, which owns the yard. Dienst, forty-two, was a youthful and charismatic former investment banker from Gravesend, Brooklyn, who had recently become the head of America's first nationwide scrapyard. Only days earlier, Metal Management had announced that its already extensive network of yards was merging with the interests of the Sims Group, of Australia. Sims had an operating presence at more than a hundred locations on four continents, and traded annually in nine million tons of metal. The new combination would gather metal from all over the globe, process it, and ship it from the consortium's own ports to mills in the United States and abroad. It would be the largest metal-recycling company in the world.

There are two ways to make steel: one is to create virgin steel from iron ore and coke, and the other is to melt down used steel and recycle it. Recycled steel is just as strong as virgin steel. Unlike paper and plastic, steel can be melted down and recast indefinitely; it has no structural memory. Making recycled steel, in electric-arc furnaces, or EAFs, requires less capital investment than making virgin steel, which is manufactured in huge integrated mills; it also saves energy, and is easier on the environment, because not as much ore has to be mined. The only disadvantage of recycling is that it can be hard to know exactly what's in your raw material—the steelmaker must rely on the scrap dealer's ability to separate out other metals, particularly copper, which can weaken the steel. In 2006 two of every three tons of steel made in the U.S. came from recycled steel.

The U.S. steel industry is not the world leader it was once, but no one produces more junk than we do—scrap metal was among our most valuable exports last year. Yet the scrap industry remained a hodgepodge of mom-and-pop junkyards. The aim of the Metal Management–Sims merger was to create a scrap company with enough corporate heft to negotiate with steelmakers. As Jeremy Sutcliffe, the CEO of Sims, explained it to me, "The worldwide steel industry has consolidated, so it makes sense for the scrap business to consolidate. It gives us a seat at the table."

So far, Dienst's timing had been very good. The demand for metals had been soaring, largely as a result of the rapid growth of China, India, and other developing nations in Asia, driving up the prices not only of scrap but also of aluminum and copper. In 2001 the price of steel scrap was around seventy-five dollars a ton; in 2007, it reached almost three hundred dollars a ton. Copper had risen even more dramatically: in 2006 it briefly hit the unheard-of price of four dollars a pound. The stock of Metal Management had climbed from below four dollars in 2003, when Dienst assumed full control, to a high of fifty-seven in October 2007.

Dienst was wearing his customary jeans, button-down white shirt, and brown suede cowboy boots. An Allman Brothers fan, he owned a 1958 gold-top Gibson Les Paul—an exact replica of the guitar that Dickey Betts played in the band, right down to the cracks and nicks in the varnish—which was given to him by his business colleagues, and which he kept next to his desk at his office, on East Sixty-ninth Street. He looked nothing like Big Pussy, from *The Sopranos*—my idea of what a Scrap King was like. Or, for that matter, like Carmine Agnello, John Gotti's former son-in-law, a heavyset mobster who made millions from his scrap-metal business in Queens before he began serving a nine-year sentence for racketeering and conspiring to defraud the IRS, in 2001. (Metal Management now owns Agnello's yard.)

In the yard's office building, a map of the world hung on a wall. Dienst, gesturing with a half-outstretched hand, as though he were explaining his strategy in a Risk game, showed the company's control of American scrap. He wriggled his fingers over the New York waterfront, saying, "We've got New York and"—the fingers drifted west—"we've also got Chicago, and the yards on the rivers in the Midwest, and"—a cupping gesture over California—"we've got the ports in L.A. We've got the tracks, and the freeways; we can ship by rail, by barge, or by break-bulk ship." The way you win the game, I gathered, was to ensure that anyone who wants to ship scrap out of New York or Los Angeles would have to sell it to your company.

Dienst explained that he is not, like so many of the leaders of the scrap industry, from an old-time scrap family. In 2001 he was working for what's known on Wall Street as a "vulture capital" firm—a group of bankers and lawyers who take over troubled or bankrupt companies and try to salvage value from them, while helping themselves to a generous percentage of the remaining assets. Usually the situation is an unhappy one; Dienst knew that a restructuring job was complete when "everyone felt equally miserable." Dienst had become a specialist in steel-industry bankruptcies; there were a lot in the late nineties. "I had done maybe fifty steel-company restruc-turings, and I never wanted to be in the steel business," he said. Steel, once the premier American industry, is saddled with crushing legacy costs, and is subject to strict environmental regulations. The scrap business, on the other hand, requires relatively little invest-ment, has lower labor costs, and has generally remained below the radar of both regulators and, until recently, investors. Dienst had never thought much about it before he was given the job of restruc-turing Metal Management, a scrap company that went bankrupt in 2000. "And I had the classic epiphany. I said to myself, 'Wow, this is a great business—and no one knows about it!' You are the major raw material for steelmaking, and you are sitting on top of the richest scrap resource in the world, right here in the U.S.A.—that's a great place to be. You have these characters; it's gritty. But it's also green—you're taking a wastelike product and making something utilitarian out of it. There's something noble about it." Most people think of scrap dealers as part of the overall waste industry, but in fact the scrap and garbage trades are more like opposites. The garbageman has a financial incentive to throw things away because he is paid in pickup fees. The scrap man, on the other hand, is paid only for what he doesn't throw away. "Every last squeal of the pig," as they say in the trade.

Michael Henderson, a vice president of operations, joined us in the office, and we put on hard hats and went for a tour of Metal Management's three yards and nearby port. At Hawkins Street, we drove around the piles of metal, some five thousand tons in total—all of which, Henderson said, would be at the docks in the next twenty-four hours. Some of the scrap was still recognizable as for-mer products—so-called white goods, like refrigerators and stoves and air conditioners. Cars, which are processed at the nearby Doremus Avenue yard, are turned into shred—clean, high-quality steel that is loose enough to "charge" the steel mill's furnace easily, so scrap dealers can demand a premium for it. In a typical charge, the steel mill mixes shred with HMS, or heavy melting scrap—large structural pieces, sheared into four-foot lengths, piles of which could also be seen in the yard—layering the heavy melt and shred like sliced potatoes and diced onions in an au gratin casserole.

The nonferrous, or non-iron-bearing, metals had also been separated, and the copper had been further subdivided into grades. In the scrap trade, "barley" is the lariat-thick copper wire that is used for high-voltage electrical transmission in railroad signals, for example—the best kind of copper scrap; "honey" is copper with brass in it; and "candy" is No. 1 copper tubing, which is used for household plumbing. The bushy copper coiling that makes up the heart of an electric motor is called a "meatball." The terms were coined by scrap dealers in the early twentieth century in order to conduct business by telegrams—short words were cheaper. The Institute of Scrap and Recycling Industries has codified the language into its technical specs, although the precise meaning of certain terms may vary from yard to yard.

We drove to Doremus Avenue and watched the shredder work for a while. This type of machine, which was invented by the Proler brothers—Hymie, Sammy, Jackie, and Izzy—in Houston in the late 1950s (they called it a Prolerizer), is standard equipment these days in any medium- to large-sized yard. Cars were being loaded by crane onto a conveyor belt and brought up to a staging area. The shredder operator then tipped a car into two hydraulically driven feed rolls that revolve in opposite directions and suck the car into the shredder box. Inside, a rotor, which is powered by an electric motor, spins a dozen free-swinging steel hammers that smash down on the car, pulverizing it in less than a minute. The combination of torque and speed, Henderson explained, makes it possible to generate many pounds of force per square inch on the vehicle. After the car has been shredded, the shred passes through a number of "downstream" operations aimed at separating the metal from the "fluff"—chopped-up upholstery and dashboards. These include huge magnets, which pull the steel away from the rest of the shredded material; electromagnetism, which propels the big pieces of copper and aluminum away from the fluff; and water, which collects smaller pieces, like wires, at the bottom. Finally, at the "sorting line," a couple of workers watch for any remaining nuggets.

Dienst told me, with considerable excitement, that the shredder we were looking at, a twenty-year-old model, was about to be superseded by a much more powerful "megashredder." When operational, it would have the capacity to reduce a car to shred in seconds. The yards looked busy. Scrap was pouring in from many different sources: floating down the Hudson on barges; rolling in on rails, which were behind the yards; and entering in trucks, both large ones, owned by demolition companies, and small pickups, driven by "peddlers," as the individual scrap collectors are called. Some of their trucks looked not far from being scrap themselves. A steady stream of auto wreckers brought in flattened cars. At Doremus Avenue, all the metal comes in through one entrance, where it passes through a radiation scan. If the machine detects something, a siren and flashing lights go off, Henderson said. He added that it happens from time to time, though never intentionally; it might be tungsten from a scrapped X-ray machine that got mixed in with the rest of the scrap metal.

After the scan, the trucks are weighed, and the weighmaster radios to an inspector, who directs the drivers to one or another pile, depending on what kind of metal they're hauling. When the truck is empty, it's weighed again, and the driver is paid for the difference. Yards set prices about once a month, in general. The peddlers, who work for cash, can call around to smaller yards and try to get better prices than those offered at Foot of Hawkins Street, although at smaller yards the waiting can be longer. At Hawkins Street, peddlers are in and out in a hurry.

We came to a pile of "Zorba," which is the industry name for the heterogeneous mixture of aluminum and copper that remains after the shredded car has passed through the entire downstream operation— about 4 percent of the total car. It is made of small twisted pieces of aluminum from transmission casings, mixed in with chopped-up copper wires. In order to be recycled, the aluminum needs to be further sorted into different grades, and small pieces of copper wire have to be picked out. Advanced flotation systems exist that can accomplish this, but it requires a lot of water, and it costs far more to operate the machine than it does to send the Zorba to China. "We can't afford do the hand sorting," Dienst said, "but we have our guy we sell to in Shanghai, Tony Huang. He does it. You've got to see Tony's operation. They have these women who go over it, picking out all the pieces of wire by hand."

Leaving the yard, we drove to the twenty-five-acre deep-water port a few minutes away. In addition to shipping its own scrap from the port, Metal Management charges stevedore fees for handling other cargoes; currently, it was off-loading road salt that was being brought in for the winter. A large pile of Ukrainian rails was waiting to be shipped to a rerolling mill in the South, where the rails would be melted down and transformed into steel bed frames. We drove up to a high point, which was a mountain made of road salt. From here, we could survey the entire operation. In the distance, one of the company's giant cranes was loading scrap directly into the hold of a ship bound for Turkey.

At the third yard, on Roanoke Avenue, we came at last to the megashredder. As we approached it, Dienst and Henderson began hopping around in their seats like ten-year-old Giants fans who were about to meet Michael Strahan. In eight hours, the megashredder can process twenty-four hundred ferrous tons with a density in excess of eighty pounds per cubic foot—or about three hundred Cadillacs an hour. And that, Dienst said, "is a lot of grunt." The operator's cabin was four stories high, and the downstream operations were so extensive that they filled up a vast building. A nine-thousand-horsepower electric motor drove the hammers; it would be one of the single largest draws on the Newark power grid when it came online. The final wiring was taking a lot of time. "We don't want Cory Booker's office to go dark," Dienst said, referring to Newark's mayor. He said that he expected the megashredder to be up and running in a couple of weeks, and invited me to come back and watch it feed. "I myself can't wait," he said.

Scrap metal is as old as metalcraft itself. Copper smelting is thought to have begun about seven thousand years ago, in the Middle East. Taking elements from the earth and refining them into metals is so basic to civilization that we refer to eras in human history as the Bronze Age and the Iron Age. Through its highs and lows, civilization has always included a scrap trade, and unlike the arts and sciences, the scrap business has thrived in times of both darkness and enlightenment. The profession is founded on an inviolable truth: almost all the metal that has ever existed in the world still exists, and always will exist. Iron may rust, but the rust is still metal. (Scrap dealers collect rust from sandblasted trains, and sell it to steel mills to use in the furnace charge.) Metal takes a form—an I-beam, an airplane's hull, a paper clip, a bedspring—and it has a lifespan. In the U.S., the average car lasts a dozen years, while a lawnmower's life expectancy is seven years—four years longer than a leaf blower's. River barges last twenty-five years, on average; steel-truss bridges last fifty. But no matter how ingenious the fabricator has been in using the metal, sooner or later it will belong to the scrap man. "It's all inventory," Bill Heenan, the president of the Steel Recycling Institute, a trade association, said to me. "You might drive by the Golden Gate Bridge and say, 'Wow, what a beautiful bridge,' but I go by that bridge and I say, 'Wow, look at all that inventory.'"

The scrap dealer has a vested interest in a uniquely unsentimental outlook on human endeavor. The destruction of the World Trade Center freed up more than a hundred thousand tons of high-grade inventory, much of it handled by Metal Management. Hurricane Katrina was a similar bonanza for some southern scrap dealers. The collapse of Saddam Hussein's army and infrastructure in Iraq produced a great deal of scrap, and thanks to a scrap-export ban imposed by the Iraqi government in 2004, most of the metal remains in the country; it is the raw material for Iraq's future steel industry. Unfortunately, looters tore up most of Iraq's existing steel mills and sold them for scrap, so they'll have to be rebuilt first.

Many of the larger independent scrap-metal businesses around the U.S. trace their roots back to immigrants who came to America in the late nineteenth century or the early twentieth and scrounged the countryside looking for discarded farm equipment, which they sometimes carried on their backs to a metal recycler. These itinerant ragmen and peddlers were familiar figures in turn-of-the-century America: in addition to scrap metal, they took in rags, which were used in papermaking, and bones, which were ground to make gelatin, often bartering with needles, utensils, and tin-plated pans and pots. In *Waste and Want,* a history of trash in America, Susan Strasser writes, "Peddlers—traveling with huge backpacks, hand-pulled carts, beasts of burden, and horse-drawn wagons—became a major institution of nineteenth-century distribution and took their place at the center of the recycling system."

Over the next two generations, the businesses founded by these peddlers grew into the scrap fortunes of America. Because of the weight of the product and the cost of shipping, which cut into slim margins, the business was necessarily regional. Every big port city had a scrap family or two. In New York, it was Hugo Neu and his son John Neu, a cosmopolitan man who walks with a cane and cuts a Sydney Greenstreet–like figure. In Chicago, there were the Cozzi brothers, who in the late nineteen-nineties merged with Metal Management. In Portland, there were the Schnitzers, whose patriarch, a Russian immigrant named Sam, founded a one-man scrap business called the Alaska Junk Company in 1906; in 2007, the firm traded in more than four million tons of metal. In the scrap man survived some type of original American entrepreneur—Jefferson's yeoman farmer, tending not his land but his junk pile, doing just as he pleased.

Nathan Frankel was a thirty-four-year-old scrap dealer in Fontana, California, fifty miles east of Los Angeles. There was scrap in his family going back three generations. He was thin and artistic-looking, and had none of Dan Dienst's brashness; he was shy but somehow bold in his shyness. His grandfather, who was also named Nathan, emigrated from Russia in 1917, and became a ragpicker and peddler outside Buffalo, New York. In the late 1940s, "the old man" brought his family west, following Route 66 from Chicago, with the idea of founding a scrap business in the agricultural land east of Los Angeles. He forged relationships with farmers in the high and low desert, buying their old farming equipment and hay-baling wire (metal was used in place of twine in those days) and household junk, and bringing it first to a yard in Riverside, and later to a yard outside San Bernardino. His son, Leo, who was born in 1930, joined his father in the business in the midfifties, and they opened FIMCO (Frankel Iron and Metal Company) on a five-acre yard in Fontana, in 1961. They had a baler and a "snippy," a device for cutting up cars, and in 1971 they built a shredder at a second five-acre yard a few miles away. The old man, who had had a serious heart attack in 1959, died in 1968, of pulmonary edema, and Leo took over the business. His daughter, Nadia, was born in 1970, followed by his son, Nathan, in 1973.

During the war, Fontana had been transformed from Fontana Farms—a *Grapes of Wrath*–type oasis of little orchards, which drew settlers from the East—into a thriving mill town, as a result of the mighty Kaiser Steel company, which was opened by the industrialist Henry Kaiser in 1942 on thirteen hundred acres. Kaiser, the first integrated mill west of the Rockies, provided steel plate for the West Coast shipbuilding industry. Manufacturers of everything from steel file cabinets to steel buckets to chain-link fences grew up around Fontana, and so did large machine shops that serviced steelmaking equipment. There were dozens of auto-wrecking yards for vehicles from as far away as Nevada and Utah. With all this scrap around, the Frankels prospered. In the 1950s, a rebar-making company called Etiwanda (which is now called Tamco) built an electric-arc furnace in Fontana, and it became a reliable buyer of FIMCO's metal.

The sixties and seventies were a glorious time to be in scrap. Americans were throwing things away at a historically unprecedented volume. With government-mandated recycling programs still a decade away, tons of metal were simply discarded, and what the scrap dealers couldn't take went into landfills. The consumer society put the earlier, preconsumer system of rag-saving and recycling to rout. As a development boom hit Fontana—the first of several—the number of consumers tripled. The Santa Ana winds swept down over the new developments, filling the air with dust. For Joan Didion, and later for Mike Davis, the place was a model of a California warped by greed and development. "This is the California where it is easy to Dial-A-Devotion, but hard to buy a book," Didion wrote of the region in the 1960s.

In the midseventies, cheap steel flowed into California from Japan, and Kaiser quickly declined. It went bankrupt in 1983, laying off the last of its nine thousand workers. (U.S. Steel and Bethlehem Steel, which, like Kaiser, ran integrated mills, suffered similar economic problems: the former shut most of its mills in the 1980s;

the latter closed its vast Bethlehem, Pennsylvania, operation in 1995.) The decline of Kaiser didn't hurt the Frankel scrap business— it profited from the dismantling of the steel mill—but according to FIMCO's former manager, Victor Vollhardt, it did hurt the town of Fontana. "This was a close-knit community, when people worked around here," he told me. "But the politicians drove local businesses out, because people don't like to be around industry, and replaced them with all these malls and fast-food places and what have you, and forced people to drive into L.A. to work, and when people have spent three hours in the car they don't go to PTA meetings and community-oriented things—and so the community falls apart." Leo Frankel moved the family to Orange County in 1984, and Nathan went to high school in Newport Beach.

As a kid, Nathan loved hanging around the scrapyard. His father's small workforce was like a family, and Leo was known throughout the area for his fairness. Nathan learned from him that the scrap business should be about standing by your agreements, fulfilling promises, and delivering what you contracted to deliver, even if it means losing money. "I would drive there with my father in the morning and spend the day taking apart old machines," Nathan recalled. Using pieces of a scrapped motorized food-packing machine, he built a contraption that opened and closed his bedroom door automatically. He took special interest in the old mainframe computers that began to turn up in the yard as smaller computers gained popularity. He could spend the whole day tinkering, but his father made certain that he also practiced the violin in the office, which embarrassed Nathan. Leo was a self-trained violinist who played in the San Bernardino Symphony Orchestra, and his greatest ambition for his son was for him to be a distinguished violinist. Nathan was talented, though Leo thought he never practiced enough.

Frankel went to Brandeis University, where he majored in economics and was the orchestra's concertmaster. But after graduating, in 1995, he went to work in his father's yard. "I was eager to modernize everything about the scrap business—bring it into the digital age," he said. "But my dad thought what I should do was work in the yard, doing menial jobs, because that's the only way you can appreciate the foundation of the business.

"One day, about two months after I started, I was working on the sorting line on the shredder when I noticed there was this big piece of copper stuck between the belt and one of the rollers, and it was starting to push the belt off the roller. I thought if I stuck my hand in I could grab it and pull it out. I got hold of it, but my sleeve got caught in the roller, and before I really knew what was happening it had pulled my arm into the machine, and my face and shoulder were pressed up against the guard—and then I realized that it was going to pull my arm off. I could feel the skin under my armpit beginning to be pulled apart and this terrible stretching and it felt like things were snapping in there." He screamed and the next guy down the line hit the emergency stop. Some of the scrap workers carried him into the office and called his father, who was at a conference in Los Angeles, and told him there had been an accident, then took Nathan to the hospital. "I was throwing up and I was in shock—my arm was just dangling at my side and I couldn't feel it," Frankel said. "At the hospital, they got out all the metal that had been ground into my skin. But the next day I had no feeling at all in my arm."

The radial nerve had been crushed, and there was a good chance that the feeling in his arm would never return. To test if the nerve was regenerating, doctors regularly inserted a needle into Frankel's shoulder and sent an electrical impulse through the damaged nerve, attaching another electrical clip to his fingers that would receive a signal if the nerves were regrowing. For months, his fingers were dead to the signal. The situation seemed hopeless. Leo was devastated by the possibility that he had ended his son's violin career by forcing him to work in the yard. Finally, six months after the accident, the doctors picked up a signal in Frankel's fingers. About a year after the accident, he was able to play the violin again, and now he plays as much as he can (but never at the office). I heard Frankel play the violin part of Brahms's Piano Quartet in G Minor, at his place in Hancock Park, leading a group of three students from the Colburn School in L.A. They sounded terrific.

In the early 1990s, a wave of consolidation swept through the garbage business. Small garbage carters were acquired by several big companies, the largest of which was Waste Management. These companies had the resources to do long-distance garbage transportation, which became important for cities like New York, where the last local landfill, at Fresh Kills on Staten Island, closed in 2001.

By the end of the decade, the garbage business had been successfully consolidated, and the industry was looking for new ways to grow. To some investors, the obvious next move was the scrap-metal business. In the middle to late nineties, Metal Management was put together by some executives from the waste industry, who were backed by private-equity firms. By leveraging the value of the scrap in its yards, Metal Management borrowed money and expanded, but its timing was terrible: beginning in the summer of 1997, a financial crisis gripped a large part of Asia, and the value of metals plummeted. Metal Management couldn't meet its debt payments, and the company went bankrupt. As Dan Dienst explained the company's problems to me, "The garbage guys said, 'They have scrap, we have waste. They use trucks, we use trucks. They have scrapyards, we have transfer stations. They take it to a steel mill, we take it to a landfill—it's the same thing.' But it was a flawed analogy. The big difference was that their business was based on fees from people whose garbage they were picking up. It was a dependable cash flow that you can borrow money against reliably. But in the scrap business the capital is your metal in the yard, and that's a commodity, which means the value can change." Indeed, the scrap business is a commodity founded on other commodities—the price of steel, the cost of shipping, and the relative values of currencies—which makes scrap especially sensitive to changes in the national and global economy. Alan Greenspan, the former chairman of the Federal Reserve, once said that he didn't need to study a lot of economic indicators to sense where the economy was headed; he needed only to look at scrap-metal prices.

As part of that first wave of incorporation, Sims, the Australian company, bought Leo Frankel's two Fontana yards in 1998. Frankel recalled, "My father came to me and said, 'Do you want to run this business?' And I honestly could say that I didn't." An ardent foodie and an oenophile, Frankel was planning to open a restaurant. But soon after the company was sold, Frankel and his father began to hear complaints from their former employees and coworkers and clients. Victor Vollhardt told me, "The manager Sims appointed was in over his head trying to run two yards at the same time." He added that corporate decision making doesn't work in the scrapyard. "Nathan's dad did everything based on trust, a handshake, and that was it. But at Sims trust had been replaced by the new way of doing things, which was based on corporate bureaucracy."

When Frankel heard how unhappy his father's former employees and customers were, and how badly Sims was apparently managing the yards, he was roused from a Hamlet-like indecision about what to do with his life and decided to start his own scrap business. Borrowing money from some acquaintances, Frankel, then twenty-five, started on a rented three-acre lot in north Fontana in 1999. He rebuilt his father's old metal baler and began gathering scrap from local small industries. Later he added a guillotine shear, for chopping large structural pieces, and started courting some of his father's former clients. In 2001 his business, Advanced Steel Recovery, moved to its present location in south Fontana, not far from his father's old yards. He hired Vollhardt to be his manager, as well as a number of his father's other employees. Leo, however, was legally barred from assisting his son because of a noncompete clause he had signed when he sold to Sims. Leo Frankel died of colon cancer in 2002, at the age of seventy-one.

The south side of Fontana looks like a massive truck stop. Trucks bring containers from the L.A. docks full of Chinese goods, and unload them in gigantic warehouses on the outskirts of town. Most of the containers were going back to China empty, and Frankel wondered if there was a way of sending them back packed with scrap. Container shipping would allow independent, inland operators like Frankel to sell scrap directly to steel mills overseas without having to sell it through the big companies like Sims and Metal Management, which owned the ports. And because it costs only a few hundred dollars to send a container back to China (it costs much more to bring it here because the demand is much higher), it is cheaper to send the scrap to China than to ship it by rail to domestic steel mills, most of which are east of the Rockies. But loading containers took a lot longer than loading the hold of a ship, Also, the scrap tended to damage the sides of the containers.

One day, Frankel had an idea for a more efficient and less destructive container loader. He drew a sketch on a napkin. It looked like a big metal sleeve. A container-size hopper, open at the top, is filled by a crane, and wheels on the bottom allow it to slide all the way into the container. Then, while pressure from the detachable back wall of the loader keeps the scrap in place, the sides and floor of the loader retract, leaving the metal inside. In 2004—eight months and a million dollars after that sketch—the first FASTek (for Frankel Advanced Shipping Technology) was operating in his yard. Frankel owns five machines, and leases three of them—one to a scrap dealer in Bakersfield, another to a yard in L.A., and the third to a dealer in Phoenix. With the machine, one man can load a container in fifteen minutes. Frankel's business had switched from being exclusively domestic to 95 percent international—he sent his scrap all over Asia. Thanks to the FASTek, the little guy didn't have to sell to the big guy; he could participate directly in the global recycling economy.

Dienst told me that he didn't see Frankel's idea as a threat to his business model, but he quickly added that his company could focus on containers too, even if they didn't have a FASTek to do it with. "Just because something looks sexy doesn't make it cost-effective," he said, with his confident smile. "Look at my wife."

Frankel, for his part, would like to find partners from outside the scrap business, perhaps in another commodity business, to help him expand. "Opportunities are still enormous—we're just scratching the surface globally," he said. However, he also seemed ambivalent about his future in the scrap business. The second time I visited his yard, Frankel had recently come back from meeting with Asian steel-mill owners in Singapore, Korea, Taiwan, Malaysia, and Thailand, and the trip didn't sound like it had been much fun. "I'm still not really sure how it happened," he said. "People like my grandfather got into scrap because it required no investment, no education—just hard work. For me, it's not the same. I could do other things. I don't think my genetic destiny is to do scrap for the rest of my life. But it's what I'm doing now, so I am putting everything I can into it."

Most of the scrap metal that goes to China is turned into materials for the Chinese construction industry—rebar, beams, and floor decking. That steel flows into the skyscrapers sprouting all around Chinese cities and into new factory towns; the copper is used to wire the millions of houses being built for China's new middle class. (In this sense, China's industrial might is literally being constructed out of the ruins of our own.) But much of the aluminum returns to the U.S., in the engine casings of new cars, as well as in irons, coffeepots, grills, and frying pans, among millions of other consumer products, which are loaded into containers and shipped back to the ports in Newark and L.A.—to be bought, used, and thrown away all over again.

To trace the circle traveled by metal as it makes its way through the global recycling economy, I arranged to follow some of Metal Management's Zorba to its Chinese recycler. From Newark, the Zorba—the unsorted pile of aluminum and copper that comes out of the shredder—was loaded into a tilted container using a crane (far less elegantly than with a FASTek) and from there onto a Panamax vessel, which passed through the Panama Canal. Two weeks later, the container arrived at the port in Shanghai. It was loaded onto a truck and taken to an industrial area in north Shanghai, which is the corporate campus of Sigma, the largest recycler of aluminum in China.

Sigma's founder and chairman, Yaw Bin (Tony) Huang, was born in Taiwan. He went to Cornell for graduate work in food science, and when he received his degree, in the late seventies, he started two businesses: one exporting mullet roe to Taiwan, and the other a nonferrous-scrap business in New Jersey, which he later moved to Florida. He didn't own a yard—he bought from scrap dealers and sold the aluminum and copper in Taiwan. Over the years, the scrap business grew much bigger than the roe business. After fifteen years in America, he moved back to Taiwan. He was married to a Taiwanese woman and had two sons; one worked in scrap in L.A., and the other was finishing an MBA at Columbia University. In 1993 Huang expanded his business to mainland China, because the cost of labor was much lower than in Taiwan. The company flourished, and in 2005 he opened a ninety-acre plant in north Shanghai, which was where the Metal Management Zorba was trucked and then dumped into large bins.

I met Huang when he took me out for a night on the town in Shanghai. "CEO stands for 'chief entertainment officer,'" he said, and his laugh was followed by an explosive, throat-clearing cough. He explained that, like all private businessmen in China, he had to devote considerable time and attention to entertaining government officials, so that he could continue to operate more or less as he pleases. In a restaurant on the fifty-fifth floor of the Jin Mao Tower, in Pudong, with the city's sparkling Whoville of skyscrapers spread before us, we dined on Peking duck and Shanghai's famous hairy crabs, which are in season in October. Dinner was followed by a trip to the Paradise Club, a karaoke "hostess bar." We were given a private room in what appeared to be a large building with many such rooms, and we each selected a woman—Shirley for me and Mimi for Huang—from a lineup of a dozen. Then, settling into soft couches, we took up the mikes. Tony performed a solo version of "My Way," and he sang it as if he meant it. Then Shirley and I did a duet to the Carpenters' 1973 hit, "Yesterday Once More." *Every shing a ling a ling.* . . . In an informal survey conducted by a Chinese radio station in 2006, nearly a third of the listeners said that the first English song they learned was "Yesterday Once More." Shirley didn't need to look at the words on the screen:

> But they're back again, just like a long-lost friend
> All the songs I loved so well!

The next morning, that Carpenters tune was back again, just like a long-lost friend in my head, as I was driven from my hotel in the center of the city into the morning rush hour that clogs the overhead highways; the great commercial engine that is Shanghai was waking up to another day of moneymaking. Arriving at the Sigma plant, the driver crossed a moat that surrounded the property, and a uniformed guard at the gate saluted me. I saw a large parking lot, which had only a few cars, belonging to management, and a small covered shed that was jammed with the bicycles of the two thousand workers. It was a gray day, but the wind was blowing and the air was clear.

Huang took me to his office, which was airy and spotless and featured several large pieces of abstract art that he had picked out himself. "Cheap artist," he said, shrugging, when I mentioned them. Huang spoke English in gruff, somewhat percussive bursts of words, dispensing with most articles. He handed me a company brochure, and under the heading "Working in Paradise," I read about the plant's amenities: a soccer field, a basketball court, a marina, waterfalls, and exotic plants. There was even a karaoke bar, but "no girls," Huang said. The canals and the moat were filled with purified rainwater. There were tilapia in the water, he said, and the workers and Huang himself catch and eat them. It was a way of inspiring everyone to do a good job of keeping things clean, Huang explained, because "otherwise we get hurt first!"

We toured the facilities in a stylish golf cart. The grass and leaves around the huge sorting shed, where the Zorba had been taken, were covered with a thin layer of aluminum dust. Inside the open-walled shed, four hundred women, working in groups of twenty, surrounded fifteen-foot piles of metal. The women wore gloves and masks and white uniforms. They picked through the pieces by hand, sorting the aluminum into different grades (these also have colorful industry names—"tense," "twitch," "taint/tabor"), and each grade had its own bucket. They also separated out small pieces of copper wire and whatever else they might find in the Zorba—American coins, left in gummy car ashtrays, were not uncommon. I asked how much the women were paid. A thousand yuan a month, which is about $140, Huang said. He doesn't want men to do the job: "Men don't have the concentration for this type of work."

Men, wearing blue uniforms, worked on the smelting side of the operation. They loaded the sorted grades of metal into the furnace, and on the other side bright, thin streams of liquid metal ran out of pipes and into ingot molds, with a slightly metallic liquid sound—a silvery *shing a ling a ling*.

As we left the smelting shed, I noticed two life-size metal heads, which had clearly been severed from their bodies, sitting on posts beside the road, and asked who they were. "Those heads of Lenin and Stalin," Huang replied. He didn't seem concerned about the ideological influence that the heads might have over his workers; he was more sheepish about having given up inventory for sentimental reasons. "My workers found the heads in a load of Russian scrap and I guess it's okay they keep it," he said.

In 2006, when copper briefly hit a record price of four dollars a pound, it was driven both by demand from Asia and supply concerns in some of the world's large copper-producing areas—Indonesia and Central and South America. At that price, the U.S. penny became worth more as scrap metal than as coinage. The U.S. Mint received several queries about whether it is legal to melt down pennies and nickels on a large scale. In December 2006, foreseeing a potential run on the penny, the U.S. Mint issued new rules against melting the coins down.

The threat to the penny was only one of the unlikely social consequences of an era of higher metal prices. In 2007, police broke up a scrap ring in Albany: five men were stealing wire out of electrical substations and suburban railyards, and selling the copper. In May 2006, a huge fire at the Greenpoint Terminal Market on the Brooklyn waterfront was caused by homeless men who were burning the plastic coating off copper wires; the plastic-free wires earn more in the scrapyard. In graveyards around the country, the metal plaques marking graves of Revolutionary War soldiers are disappearing because a pound of bronze goes for a dollar and eighty cents. (In a scrapyard in Vancouver, an undercover officer was given five dollars for a bronze marker for a four-year-old child.) A metal street sign might bring a dollar; a manhole cover fetches about five. Beer kegs, swiped from behind an Applebee's, bring upward of forty dollars each. A phone booth will net fifty dollars or more. A condenser unit from a central-air-conditioning system is worth about a hundred dollars. Aluminum bleachers, guardrails, streetlight poles, storm-drain grates, copper flashing, and the nozzles of firehoses are also popular among metal thieves.

In the UK, lead theft from church roofs was rampant. Bronze statues had been sawn off at the ankles and carted out of public parks. The former Olympic running champion Steve Ovett suffered this indignity in September, when a life-size bronze replica of him, in full stride, disappeared from Preston Park in Brighton. (Police recovered a leg from a nearby bonfire.) In the U.S., a seven-foot bronze statue of the Buddha was stolen from an outdoor temple shrine at the Thai Buddhist Center in Elk River, Minnesota. The problem was even worse in Eastern Europe, where, in Ukraine, scrap thieves stole a thirty-six-foot metal bridge from the Svalyavka River in 2004.

Who was buying all this hot metal? The Institute of Scrap and Recycling Industries blamed fast-buck artists who weren't legitimate scrap dealers. However, anyone with a phone and an acetylene torch can get into the scrap business. Metal Management would not buy obviously hot scrap, but by the time the scrap has been processed by another dealer, the yard bosses might not recognize it. Also, container shipping makes it possible to move scrap in and out of the yard quickly, and get it on its way to Asia fast, before authorities can come looking for it. The ISRI suggests that dealers ask to see an ID, note license plates, and pay with a check, but it opposes measures, already enacted in several states, that require dealers to keep scrap for a period of time before reselling it. These "tag and hold" statutes were unpopular among scrap dealers because they subject the scrap in the yard to changes in commodity prices between the time the dealers buy the scrap and the time they can sell it, and that's the way scrap guys go under.

Metal theft seems like hard work—it's often heavy, and it's dangerous. "We had one in Kentucky up on the pole recently," Mike Dunn, the manager of security services at American Electric Power, told CSO, a trade magazine for security executives, in 2007. "He cut the wrong wire, got wrapped up in the lines and just hung there upside down, dead, until someone passed by and noticed." So why do so many people steal metal? The CSO reporter, Scott Berinato, noted that "hot spots of crystal meth abuse—Hawaii, the Southwest, San Diego, Oregon, and increasingly the rural Midwest and South— map to hot spots of metal theft." One of the conditions of a meth high is extreme focus, which is just what you need to unravel lengths of copper wire from a tightly corded braid of other metals. Not only does meth give you the patience to do the job but the reward—money for more meth—is right there in the metal.

The global metal-theft epidemic conjures a Mad Max world of desperate people mining civilization's infrastructure—a postcard from a future era of commodity scarcity. Economists have written about the concept of Peak Oil—the point, thought to be a distant possibility, at which oil becomes so expensive that its production begins to decline, triggering a wave of new energy technologies and a fundamental restructuring of industrial society. But perhaps that transformation will be brought about by Peak Metal, and it will happen sooner than we think.

Preparations for the megashredder took longer than Dienst had expected. His men worked on the wiring and final adjustments for months. Eventually, at 12:26 A.M. on November 16, 2007, the plant staff fed a Mitsubishi into the mouth of the machine and it passed through all the complex downstream digestive organs: the drum- shaped magnet, which plucks the steel pieces from the rest of the material; the magnetic field, known as an "eddy current," which flings larger pieces of aluminum and copper away from valueless debris; and the flotation system, which uses water to float bits of rubber and foam away from the Zorba.

James Mosebach, the overall supervisor for the megashredder assembly, reported to Dienst in an e-mail, written at 3:04 A.M. that night, that the shred "looks really good and squeaky clean." He added, "We have a big, beautiful baby."

The following Monday was a damp, freezing day at Foot of Hawkins Street; a light rain made the metallic scent of the yard smell more chemical. Dienst was outside pacing when I arrived. "It's been that kind of day," he said, with a nervous peppiness. Carmine Agnello was due to be released soon, and I wondered if Dienst was worried about hearing from him—but that wasn't the problem. The price of metal was dropping, and now the larger economy seemed to be following it—just as Greenspan said it would. But it wasn't that either, Dienst said. I gathered it was just the general stomach-churning pressure of trying to impose a corporate structure on a business that has never been incorporated before.

In the office, Mike Henderson brought in one of the pieces of shred from the Mitsubishi, and he presented it to Dienst. The shred felt cold and wet, and its torn edges were brutally sharp.

"That's one of the very first pieces," Henderson said.

"It's an honor," Dienst said, putting the steel down on the table.

"It's beautiful shred, Dan," Henderson said, with emotion. "Clean. Dense."

When I was in China, I had visited a Chinese scrapyard, operated by a private company called Fengli. It is situated at a big bend in the Yangtze River, about 150 miles upriver from Shanghai, in Zhangjiagang, a giant factory city built so recently that there's been no time to name all the streets. It is far larger than any scrapyard in the U.S., and it has two thousand workers. The day I visited, two hundred thousand tons of ferrous scrap were in the yard. With the Shagang steel mill, the largest private mill in China, thirty minutes away, the scrap did not have far to go. Fengli had no megashredder at the yard—it didn't need one. Instead, there were hundreds of men working at tables with alligator shears, cutting every piece of scrap by hand. The result looked like metal pasta. The megashredder, for all its grunt, couldn't do that.

Still, I was as excited as the rest of the Metal Management men; some kind of male pheromone was bouncing around the operator's cabin, which was directly above the mighty jaws of the machine. It was ready to take in a maroon Impala. But there were several delays. Looking out through the windows of the cabin, I could see the rail lines that defined the old Ironbound District. The turnpike and Routes 1 and 9 were ahead. Trucks were carrying new goods from the ports to the big-box stores, and other trucks were bringing old goods—scrap—to the yard. The global recycling economy was flowing all around us, and the beating heart of it—the megashredder—was about to be switched on.

There were more delays. At first it was one of the belts, then it was downstream, with one of the magnets. While waiting, Dienst went out on the balcony. We discussed what would happen if the price of scrap suddenly dropped, as it had ten years ago. "Bring it on," Dienst said, in his confident way. "I don't want to sound cocky, but we welcome the chance to prove that we can compete in any market."

We went back into the cabin, where the atmosphere was tense. I recalled hearing that one of the biggest problems in maintaining megashredders is to keep them from shredding themselves.

"Okay, they're jogging it"—trying to get a belt started—a worker in the cabin said, listening to his radio.

"It's just a teething problem," one of the engineers, who was on loan from the company that sold Metal Management the shredder, said soothingly.

"Well, why the heck didn't it have this problem Friday night?" Mosebach demanded.

"Maybe it's the rain," the engineer said, shrugging.

Finally, a voice on the radio said, "Ready to start!"

"We have liftoff!"

"Let's start shredding!"

The machine began to rumble, and the maroon Impala lurched halfway into the shredder box. The whole cabin shook. A cloud of smoke shot out, so thick that it obscured the jaws for a moment. When the smoke cleared, the Impala was gone.

—2008

# IT CAME FROM
# HOLLYWOOD

The DVD of *Jurassic Park III* comes with an F/X voice-over, in which the special-effects creators talk about their work. If you listen during the first gory sequence in the film, when the Spinosaurus jumps out of the jungle and, shockingly, devours a man in one bite, you will hear Stan Winston's voice—a gentle, sweet-sounding voice—exclaiming with delight, "I love it when dinos eat people!" He sounds almost moved. Dinosaurs provide Winston with an opportunity to evoke the ancient, hardwired horror of being eaten alive, as well as with a chance to display the disgusting remains of humans after the beasts have finished with them. For a creature-maker, it doesn't get much better than that.

At fifty-seven, Winston had, during thirty-five years in the movie business, almost single-handedly elevated the craft of creature-making from the somewhat comical man-in-a-rubber-suit monsters of the 1950s and 1960s to animatronics—electronically animated, part-robot, part-puppet creatures that have terrified millions of moviegoers. He won his first Oscar for James Cameron's 1986 film *Aliens,* of which the most spectacular creature was the Alien Queen—a fourteen-foot-high, crustacean-necked monster with a shiny cockroach carapace, yellow acid for blood, and two jaws full of mucus-smeared, razor-sharp teeth. (Before becoming a creature- maker, Winston studied to be a dentist.) He won his second and third

Oscars for Cameron's second *Terminator* movie (1991), for makeup and visual effects, and his fourth for Steven Spielberg's *Jurassic Park* (1993), for which Winston created, among other effects, robotic velociraptors and a forty-foot-long *Tyrannosaurus rex*, with hydraulically driven limbs and radio-controlled dilating eyes. His dinosaurs got better with each sequel, even if the movies didn't.

Winston's success had coincided with the rise of computer graphics, or CG—a technology that allows F/X artists to make monsters entirely out of pixels, greatly expanding the range of possibilities. Yet CG monsters rarely seem as scary as Winston's mechanical monsters, in large part because they aren't filmed in live-action sequences with the actors but are added to the film during postproduction. "When you come to the set," Steven Spielberg told me, "and there's a thirty-six-foot-high creature there, waiting to perform with the actors, it's inspiring—to all of us. If you make creatures only on the computer, it takes the fun out of it."

Nothing about Stan Winston seems monstrous. White-haired and bearded, he is slight of build, and has a soothing way of talking about creating pain and fear that probably would have served him well as a dentist. Directors like to work with him, Cameron said, because "Stan has never lost the love of putting on a show; he'll get all excited, saying, 'This is going to scare the crap out of people,' and he infects you with his enthusiasm." When I asked Winston about this one day—how can a guy who has scared so many people be so likable?—he said, "I hope I'm likable as a human being, but I do love to scare people. People like being scared. I'll tell you something, it's the people who don't go to scary movies who have nightmares. What I do is I allow them to get their fears out in the movie theater so they don't have to be scared at home."

Stan Winston Studio—a full-service special-effects shop, of which Winston was both the owner and the head artist—was a thirty-five-thousand-square-foot industrial space in the San Fernando Valley. In addition to making creatures for movies and television (these include appealing characters, like the duck in the Aflac insurance commercial, with its Chaplinesque walk, and the grumpy old frogs created for a series of Budweiser commercials), Winston produced a line of monster toys, and was in the process of creating a new Horror Channel, featuring twenty-four-hour horror on cable. Winston and his wife of thirty-four years, Karen, lived in Malibu, and he had his choice of a Hummer, two Harleys, a Ferrari, or a turbo-charged Porsche to make the drive to work.

The large workspace on the ground floor was full of the smells of creature-making—silicon, urethane, latex, glue. Scattered on worktables were arms and legs, some human, some animal. People were drawing, painting, sculpting, engineering, and wiring. Winston mostly managed his artists, several of whom have been with him for twenty years, though he occasionally sketched and sculpted. Some of his artists used computers to design the creatures, but Winston was proudly computer-illiterate.

Also downstairs was a diorama of the great Stan Winston monsters, displayed in a big, dimly lit conference room, with spotlights on the creatures. Here were Winston's takes on the mythic horrors—fire-breathing dragons, ogres, the Minotaur, the Harpies—that have been interpreted in art and literature for the past ten thousand years and reinterpreted, for the past century, in film. Winston's Predator, from the 1987 film by John McTiernan, refers to movie monsters such as the She-Creature, from 1956, which in turn harks back to Grendel, the monster in *Beowulf*. But the Predator's Rastafarian-looking quills and his fearsome mandibles made the horror fresh. Frankenstein, imagined by Mary Shelley in 1818, was a myth of modern hubris going back to Adam and Eve. It was made a modern classic in the 1931 Universal film starring Boris Karloff. That Frankenstein image was unsurpassed until James Cameron came to Winston with his idea for the Terminator.

Upstairs, some of Winston's serious artwork was on display, including a life-size, hyperrealist bronze sculpture of Arnold Schwarzenegger's head, each bone and muscle precisely rendered. Winston gave the original sculpture to his good friend the governor for his fiftieth birthday. (The idea to do these kinds of sculptures, Winston told me, came from another pal, the actor Rod Steiger, almost twenty years ago. "Steiger said, 'Do something serious.' As if making monsters wasn't serious. So I did a classic sculpture so that people could see that the monster-maker is also an artist.")

Winston cast himself alternately as a businessman and as an artist, swinging between pride and humility. He said, of his F/X atelier, "I have the greatest artists in the world working for me. The people here are the equals of the Renaissance artists of five hundred years ago. Michelangelo—what did he do? He created fantasies— gargoyles, images of Hell, demons, angels. Just like us. Or look at a great painting like *The Raft of the Medusa*—it's horrific! That parallels what we do." And, he went on, although making monsters does not rank high in the art world's hierarchy, "I guarantee you that long after the painting the snobs say is art—the painting and sculpture in the galleries—is forgotten, the face of the Terminator will be remembered." But soon Winston retreated from those remarks and assured me that he was just a monster-maker after all.

As an adolescent in Arlington, Virginia, Winston wrote and directed his own scary movies, which he shot on an 8-millimeter movie camera. His parents, who were in the garment business (Stan's family changed the name from Weinstein), wanted their son to be a lawyer or a doctor, but after two years of "predent," at the University of Virginia, Stan became an art major. "My parents' jaws dropped, but I had to let the artist inside me out," he said. "But I always had the businessman saying, 'Okay, Stan, indulge your passion for art, but how are you going to make a living at it?'"

Winston came to Hollywood in 1968, planning to be an actor. "Actually, I wanted to be a star, which is why I failed as an actor," he told me. While he was in Southern California, waiting for the acting jobs that never arrived, Winston decided to learn the trade of theatrical makeup at Walt Disney Studios. After graduating, he quickly began to get work in television. He did the makeup for *Roots,* and he aged Cicely Tyson some ninety years for her role in *The Autobiography of Miss Jane Pittman,* for which he won an Emmy. In 1977 he went to New York, where Sidney Lumet was filming *The Wiz.* (When Winston joined the cast and crew and "they saw that the black-makeup guy was this little Jewish white kid, they were stunned," he said.) Winston did the metallic makeup for the Tin Man and the mechanically articulated faces of the flying monkeys. He was then asked to work on *Heartbeeps*, which featured Bernadette Peters and Andy Kaufman as robots. "After that, I was no longer the black-makeup guy, I was the robot guy."

In the early 1980s, Winston met a young director named James Cameron, who had a script for a film called *The Terminator*. Cameron had a backer, a star in Schwarzenegger, and a character who was about to become one of the all-time great monsters in movies. Cameron had made several paintings of the monster he imagined—a face that was a nightmarish melding of man and machine, with part of the flesh stripped away, showing the gleaming metal underneath. In Cameron's vision, the face would deteriorate throughout the movie, until finally all the flesh was burned away to reveal an entire steel endoskeleton. Computer graphics—the technology that was used to create the morphing T-1000 in Cameron's *Terminator 2*—did not yet exist. To create a monstrous robot, Cameron had either to put a man in a suit or to use stop-motion animation—scale-model figures that are shot one frame at a time—which F/X artists had been using since the great Ray Harryhausen films of the fifties and sixties, like *Jason and the Argonauts*. But movie audiences had grown used to stop-motion animation in the intervening years, and the effects no longer looked as convincing.

"Technically, I didn't want the robot to look like a man in a suit, because the Terminator was a robot inside a man—a robot with flesh," Cameron told me. "We could not accomplish that visual by putting the robot outside a human form, then trying to imagine that it was also inside. It just wouldn't work. But nobody had ever created a robot that wasn't a suit." Cameron asked other directors if they knew of a makeup artist who could achieve the kind of effect he had in mind, and he soon heard about the robot guy. Cameron said, "I went to Stan with my drawings, and said, 'This is what I want the Terminator to look like. I don't know how to build it, but it's got to look like this.'" Winston altered the traditional man-in-a-suit formula— he made a mask out of Arnold Schwarzenegger's face, and cut part of it away to reveal mechanized-looking makeup underneath, which was applied to the actor's face. When Winston heard that Cameron was planning to shoot the endoskeleton scenes in stop-motion animation, he said, "Why don't you let us build you a full-size animatronic puppet—a robot, essentially, that would play the robot—and you can then shoot that sequence in live action?"

Cameron let him, and for *Terminator 2* Winston built an even more sophisticated robotic endoskeleton, which you see early in the movie, crunching a human skull under its steel foot. Winston's shop also designed scores of other effects, including the unforgettable image of the villain, Robert Patrick, his torso cleaved in two by a metal bar.

When Steven Spielberg collaborates with Winston, he sends the screenplay to Winston and then goes to see him. "Stan listens very intensely, until he gets the director's vision," Spielberg told me. "I swear, he must be the first Method monster man. He'll assume the creature's body position, make roars, do the facial expressions—trying to figure out how the creature is going to project the emotion you're going for."

Winston said, "We are all extremely attuned to certain expressions, and I think we understand character by a certain look—that sidelong glance that shows you the way we really feel." When designing a creature's face, he explained, "I sit in front of a mirror making faces." He imagines the emotion that the creature is feeling in a particular situation, watching for the distinctive twist of the eyebrow or the cruel curl of the lip in his own face, and then draws it.

After the creature's face and body have been designed in two dimensions, a three-dimensional model is created. At this stage, all the creature's cosmetic elements—color, hair, skin tone—are selected. Sometimes, if puppetry is part of the plan, Winston's staff of puppeteers begin practicing with the creature, at times wearing "gypsy suits"—full-body controls that allow the puppeteers to manipulate the creature's features. In many cases, a single creature is performed by multiple puppeteers—one for the ears, one for the eyebrows, one for the hands, one for the legs—who must all learn to work together so that the creature's movements are fluid and lifelike.

(When an animatronic doesn't move smoothly, the F/X artists in Winston's shop say it has the "wagga waggas.")

As Winston saw it, his job, after making sure that his creatures perform correctly, is to get the strongest possible performances out of the actors, and that often means terrifying them. "CG can't do that. How can you possibly get the best performance out of an actor when the thing he's acting with isn't there? Can't be done." The Spinosaurus in *Jurassic Park III*, for example, was a twenty-five-thousand-pound robot driven by a thousand-horsepower engine. "That robot could easily have killed someone," Winston told me excitedly.

The one aspect of making lifelike creatures that no F/X artist has yet mastered is "eye line"—a creature's ability to maintain eye contact with an actor and to track movements. "You've got multiple puppet operators moving the eyes, head, and neck," Winston said, explaining why eye line is impossible. "So if any one of them moves the head in a way that's slightly out of sync with the others, the eyes don't stay on the actor." If you could design eye line into robots, puppets, and animatronics, Winston believed, it would be a breakthrough in creature-making.

During his career, Winston had become a master creator of a certain kind of artificial life. It was not a scientific endeavor, like the pursuit of artificial intelligence launched at MIT in the 1950s by a group of researchers, including Marvin Minsky and Seymour Papert, with the lofty ambition of creating machines that think like people. Winston belonged to the older tradition of "automatons," which, as described by Gaby Wood in her book *Edison's Eve,* went back more than two centuries, to a famous mechanical duck built by the French engineer Jacques de Vaucanson in the 1730s. The duck could flap its wings, eat, and, most remarkably, defecate. (Voltaire observed, as Wood relates, that without the shitting duck there would be nothing to remind us of the glory of France.) The purpose of the duck, and other similar automatons, was spectacle and illusion, not science and technology.

These two notions of artificial life, the modern and the classical, came together in Spielberg's 2001 film, *A.I.* In order to create the illusion that robots really could look and talk like people, Winston built nearly a dozen animatronic puppets. Teddy, the talking and walking "super toy," was just a superior mechanical duck—a puppet who needed five, sometimes six, puppeteers to bring him to life—but within the movie he appeared incredibly real, and gave one of the most compelling performances in the film.

In the summer of 2001, just before the release of *A.I.,* a young computer scientist at the MIT Media Lab, Cynthia Breazeal, visited Winston. For her doctorate, Breazeal had built a "sociable robot," Kismet, which had a cartoonish, humanoid face that could imitate human facial expressions. When you praised the robot, it smiled back; if you looked angry, it looked sad. Kismet and Breazeal were widely covered in the science press, and often pictured together—an attractive young woman with dark hair and eyebrows and high cheekbones, and a robot with glued-on false eyelashes from a beauty-supply store, fur for eyebrows, and surgical tubing colored in with a red pen for lips. Kathleen Kennedy, the producer of *A.I.,* had seen a story about Breazeal in *Time,* and flown her to Los Angeles to brief Spielberg on robots and artificial-intelligence research, in preparation for doing press about the film.

Breazeal had a proposal for Winston. "She said, 'How would you like to build a real Teddy, a Teddy with a brain?'" he recalled. "Would I consider collaborating and sharing technology with MIT and creating the real thing?" Stan Winston Studio would fund and produce the design and construction of the robot, and MIT would supply the "brain": software that would allow the robot to see, hear, speak, and feel. Unlike Winston's creatures, this robot would be autonomous, its movements controlled not by puppeteers wearing suits or by operators working radio controls but by an internal mechanical system driven by its own software, and the software would give it the ability to maintain eye line. Breazeal would get a robot with a face capable of expressing the subtle cognitive processes embedded in its software; Winston would get a puppet without strings. Intellectually, their creature would, on its father's side, be descended from the classical world of automatons, and on its mother's side, from the modern world of artificial intelligence. It would, in short, be the most lifelike mechanical creature ever built, a state-of-the-art emotional machine.

"I had to think about her offer for two seconds," Winston recalled, "and then I said, 'Of course I'm going to do this.'"

Early in their collaboration, in the spring of 2002, Winston and Breazeal selected a name: Leonardo, "because this creature represents the ideal collaboration of art and science—an artist and a scientist working together to create something real," Winston said. Then, in Los Angeles, Winston went to work on Leo's body and face. One of the few guidelines from Breazeal was that Leo not look too human, lest he fall into the "uncanny valley," a concept formulated by Masahiro Mori, a Japanese roboticist. Mori tested people's emotional responses to a wide variety of robots, from nonhumanoid to completely humanoid. He found that the human tendency to empathize with machines increases as the robot becomes more human. But at a certain point, when the robot becomes too human, the emotional sympathy abruptly ceases, and revulsion takes its place. People began to notice not the charmingly human characteristics of the robot but the creepy zombielike differences.

Leonardo was built alongside Winston's other projects, including the robots he did for *Terminator* 3 and the animals he was making for Tim Burton's movie *Big Fish*. Winston wanted to design a creature that was almost compulsively lovable, but the principles that informed Leonardo's design were the same as those used to make monsters. "There are certain universal facial characteristics that are known to trigger a particular kind of response in people," Winston explained to me. (Many of these principles were codified at the Disney Studios in the 1930s and 1940s by the animators who created films like *Pinocchio* and *Dumbo* and *Fantasia*.) "Big eyes, a head that is bigger than a body, a cute mouth, and a pug nose are considered lovable everywhere."

Lindsay Macgowan, a "rendering artist" on Winston's staff who had helped design Teddy, drew the first sketches. Leo looked a little like a Gremlin, from the 1981 Spielberg movie, and also something like one of George Lucas's Ewoks. He had collie ears, a cougarlike snout, four-fingered hands, a round, cartoonish belly, and, most uncannily, a human tongue and teeth. He stood two and a half feet tall, with three-toed feet, and was entirely covered with thick, soft fur made mostly of mohair and the tail hair of yaks and hand-stitched into the skin, one strand at a time. His eyes and brows were youthful in appearance, but he had an old creature's hands, with lots of wrinkles around the knuckles.

Some of the aesthetic decisions about the creature's design were made with Leonardo's mechanical requirements in mind. The large head and the potbelly would allow more room for the motors, gears, cables, pulleys, and gimbals that constituted Leonardo's muscles. Big eyes, in addition to being adorable, would let more light in for the cameras, and the pettable ears would channel sound down to the microphones in the head.

As Winston and his staff worked on Leonardo's body, Breazeal and her students at MIT were working on his brain—assembling the software that would make the robot capable of speech recognition and synthesis, visualization, and basic cognitive skills. The work entailed adapting software written at MIT over a period of many years, and writing new bits of code tailored to Leo's requirements.

Breazeal grew up in California, where her parents were computer scientists. She majored in electrical and computer engineering at the University of California at Santa Barbara. (She also surfs.) After graduating, she went to MIT to study under Rodney Brooks, the head of the Artificial Intelligence Laboratory and one of the world's experts on autonomous robots. Brooks was trying to steer AI away from the absolutist goals of its founders and toward the more modest but reasonable aims of applied robotics. Breazeal built a rover with Brooks, and also worked on a primitive humanoid robot named Cog.

Some of Breazeal's ideas correspond with those of Donald Norman, a professor of computer science and psychology at Northwestern University and an influential writer on technological design. In his book *Emotional Design,* Norman argues that emotions play as important a part in intelligence as does cognition. Emotions do the work of judging, he says, while cognition does the work of understanding, but both kinds of thinking are necessary. "Our emotions protect us, guide us, make us inquisitive," he told me. "Robots will need the same kind of equipment so that they can learn about their environment, and how to get along in it." And robots need to display their emotions, Norman added, so that humans will be able to tell at a glance what's going on inside them.

I asked Breazeal whether she viewed her association with Hollywood as a kind of devil's bargain—in getting Leo's body and face from Hollywood, she was trading the world of science for the world of illusion. Breazeal pointed out that Hollywood has created many famous screen robots, from the Deco metal woman in Fritz Lang's *Metropolis* to Robby the Robot in *Forbidden Planet,* and from Hal in *2001,* on which Marvin Minsky was a consultant (Hal was totally disembodied, the opposite of Breazeal's robots), to the Terminator. Breazeal herself first became interested in robots in 1977, when she was eight, and her parents took her to see *Star Wars,* which featured the droids R2-D2 and C-3P0.

But while Hollywood robots may have sparked the general public's interest in thinking machines, and in some cases influenced scientists themselves, you're still watching a man in a suit, or a hunk of painted fiberglass masquerading as a complicated piece of electronic equipment, created not by scientists but by a "robot guy." Breazeal, however, saw her collaboration with Winston in less rigid terms: "Our approach to doing design is what I call bootstrapping— create robots for real-world applications, and then improve them based on how they perform."

Working with Winston to build a lovable robot, Breazeal believed, would help her to design robots that could eventually become human companions. "If you look at the statistics here, and even more so in Japan, in twenty years there are going to be too many elderly people who need care, and there won't be enough nurses or family members to take care of them," she said. "The solution could be a sociable robot, something that lives with you and that you can have a meaningful emotional interaction with."

In the summer of 2003, the creature came East, to Breazeal's lab on the MIT campus in Cambridge. Work on his brain continued, and Breazeal and her graduate students began training Leo to track objects with his eyes. In late August, Winston arrived for a demonstration, and I arranged to join him while he was in Boston.

On the morning of the demonstration, Leo sat on his metal base, with his eyes open, staring dully at a Tickle Me Elmo doll. When one of the students moved Elmo, the robot's eyes moved too, tracking it. There was a computer-generated Leonardo playing on a laptop in the lab, showing what the creature would look like one day, but that day did not appear to be imminent. Leo's expression was listless, and his appearance was somewhat disheveled—his ears had fur on them, but the rest of his fiberglass body was bare. (His yak coat was still in L. A.) The robot's facial expressions and body movements weren't being operated yet, although one of the students was moving his arms, using a gypsy suit. But the suit was a cheap one, and the student wasn't very skillful. Leo had a bad case of the wagga waggas.

Afterward, I brought up something that Marvin Minsky had said to me the day before, when I asked him for his thoughts about Leonardo. Minsky had said, "My objection to Leonardo is, it's just a trick. It doesn't really have emotions. It just knows how to fool you into thinking it does. Cynthia's an excellent engineer, but her work doesn't explain how emotions work. Leonardo is just an improved version of that software wizard, F1, that Microsoft tried to get people to buy a few years ago. People went, 'Oh, gee, that's neat,' for a couple of days, and then they got tired of it." In Minsky's view, Leonardo was more Hollywood than MIT.

"Shame on Marvin Minsky!" Winston declared dramatically when he had heard Minsky's views.

Breazeal, however, looked a bit taken aback. She said, "Well, I don't see Leonardo's emotions as being a trick. They serve a useful function for the robot. We're not trying to capture the human-feeling side of emotions, but we are trying to capture the pragmatic side—communicating with others and behaving more intelligently. If robots are going to have emotions, they're going to have robot emotions."

"And what is trick and what is real?" Winston added. "If you go to a film, a love story, and what you see on the screen makes you cry—isn't that a real emotion?" He leaned back in his chair and folded his arms confidently. "Let's say you tell me a joke and I laugh at it. Am I laughing because I think in my soul your joke is funny, or because I'm programmed to do it—I want to make you feel good because that then validates me? The point is, you can't know; I can't know. But the robot will be more honest—he won't laugh at my joke unless it's funny."

Building Leonardo had cost Winston almost a million dollars so far. (The creature's coat alone was tens of thousands of dollars.) "At first, it wasn't about the bottom line, it was about let's do something no one has ever done before," Winston told me. "But then my practical side started saying, 'Okay, Stan, this is cool, but what can I derive from this that's good for my business?'"

The most obvious application was a new generation of animatronic puppets, produced exclusively by Stan Winston Studio, that could lock eyes with actors. But more important, Stan Winston Studio would own the character of Leonardo. Directors generally have creative control of a creature while a film is in production, and the character rights are the property of the studio backing the film. The creature-maker, who, of all the artists involved in creating a film, comes closest to the primal act of creation, doesn't own his own creature. But Stan Winston was the auteur of Leo.

Winston hoped to make his creature a star. "I can envision a story written with Leonardo in it, and a movie with him as the main character—a wonderful, folksy, Disneyesque PG story that is all about him," Winston said.

Judging by the latest reports from Breazeal's lab, the creature was making progress toward that goal: he could nod, cock his head quizzically when he's confused, and blink almost flirtatiously.

I asked Winston whether Leo could be a monster.

"I don't think so," he said. "But anything's possible. I'll say this. He could be scary. You'll have an animatronic puppet actor that will never take his eyes off you. How scary is that?"

—2003

# TREMORS IN THE HOTHOUSE

In most parts of the world, people do not eat fresh tomatoes out of season. The supermarket tomato is a peculiarly American idea. Americans expect to have fresh vegetables in the supermarket all year long, regardless of season, and plant breeders have done what they can to accommodate them. Corn and peas have been bred to convert sugar into starch more slowly, lettuce to retain water longer, and potatoes to resist rot. The pepper, a cousin of the tomato, has been very satisfactorily adapted to supermarket culture—tricked out in a palette of designer colors and endowed with a shelf life of more than a month. But the tomato has stubbornly refused to go along with the program. Plant breeders have created attractive tomatolike objects that are durable enough to be transported long distances without turning into paste, but while these inventions are useful to tomato producers (they reduce "the shrink," which is the number of tomatoes lost in transit), they don't taste like tomatoes, a significant disadvantage to the consumer. The fresh tomato, endowed with every advantage on the vine, spectacularly fails to achieve its potential in the supermarket. The flesh is cottony and insipid, and the gel—the gluey liquid in which the seeds are suspended, and which is the source of most of the tomato's flavor—sometimes falls out when you slice the tomato, leaving a cavity surrounded by a tough tomato hide.

In spite of widespread unhappiness with the supermarket tomato—in one Department of Agriculture study, consumers rated the tomato thirty-first out of thirty-one produce items in order of satisfaction—the average American buys eighteen pounds of tomatoes a year, more than any other item of produce except lettuce and potatoes. The fresh-tomato market in the United States is four billion dollars, which is about the size of the whole biotechnology industry. How much more consumers might spend on a tomato that actually tastes like a tomato is a question that has long tantalized people in the business world. Charles Bluhdorn, the chairman of Gulf & Western, invested in the tomato business in the 1960s, and in the late seventies Jack Dorrance, the majority owner of Campbell Soup, made the development of a good supermarket tomato a personal crusade. The tomato got the better of these men. In recent years, Holland tomatoes, Israeli tomatoes, Sicilian cherry tomatoes, French hothouse tomatoes, vine-ripened tomatoes, and hydroponic tomatoes have turned up in produce aisles around the country, and while many of these varieties taste better than run-of-the-mill supermarket tomatoes, none have what people in the tomato business call "that backyard flavor." Cherry tomatoes occasionally do have the backyard flavor, but there isn't much of a market for cherries in the United States. According to market research, Americans like their tomatoes big and fat.

In the fall of 1993, around the time frost kills the last tomato plants growing in backyards around Chicago, and the taste of summer begins to fade from the palates of tomato-lovers everywhere, a new, genetically engineered tomato was scheduled to appear in Midwestern supermarkets. The name of the tomato was the Flavr Savr. It would be the first food created by the use of recombinant DNA ever to go on sale. Executives at Calgene, a small California biotechnology company that invented the Flavr Savr, were confident that theirs was the tomato others have sought for so long. "Our technology has allowed us to integrate the backyard flavor back into the tomato," said Stephen Benoit, a vice president of Calgene Fresh, a subsidiary of Calgene. Roger Salquist, the chief executive officer of Calgene, said, in a characteristic burst of optimism, "We're going to sell a hell of a lot of tomatoes, and the growers, the sellers, our shareholders—everybody is going to get rich."

That Calgene had been able to raise $210 million over the previous decade, a period in which the company had only once made a profit (last year, Calgene lost twenty million dollars), was a fair measure of how good Salquist was at inspiring investors. On Wall Street, anticipation of the tomato's arrival was keen. "The tomato is very important because it's the first genetically altered food to hit the market," said George Dahlman, a financial analyst with the investment firm Piper Jaffray. "If the tomato succeeds, it's going to be a big lift to all the other genetically altered foods coming along in the pipeline." A rumor that the Flavr Savr might not be the tomato Calgene had been saying it was—"I heard yesterday that Calgene's tomato doesn't work," one investor said to me at an investment conference in March—caused alarm throughout the biotech industry. Around the same time, Tom Churchwell, the president of Calgene Fresh, seemed to back away from some of Roger Salquist's promotional claims. "We don't have all the backyard flavor—yet," he told me. "We will. Eventually, we're going to design acidic tomatoes for the New Jersey palate and sweet tomatoes for the Chicago palate." Salquist, however, continued to claim, "We have the backyard flavor."

The Flavr Savr was not without competitors. DNA Plant Technology, of Cinnaminson, New Jersey, was experimenting with a gene it had manufactured that was based on an antifreeze gene from an Arctic flounder, in the hope of producing a tomato that can be chilled without being damaged. Other genetically engineered foods in the pipeline included a potato with a chicken gene, a potato with a wax-moth gene, and tobacco with a firefly gene (the plants glow in the dark), which had all been cleared by the Department of Agriculture for field-testing. Two of the country's largest breeders of chickens had done research to develop birds that will grow faster with less feed, and Auburn University in Alabama, with a similar aim, had spliced a trout gene into a carp. In the early 1990s, in an effort to produce leaner pork, researchers at the Department of Agriculture's main research center in Beltsville, Maryland, spliced a human gene into a pig embryo. The pig was born cross-eyed and with a strange, wrinkled face, and with arthritis so severe that it could hardly stand, but the meat was indeed much leaner.

Most people I knew said they would try Calgene's tomato, provided it was safe, and extensive testing indicates that it was. However, to Calgene's surprise and bewilderment, some people were actively campaigning against its tomato. The antibiotechnology activist Jeremy Rifkin was organizing a boycott of the Flavr Savr. "I'm here to tell you this tomato will be dead on arrival," he said. "This tomato will go under. This tomato will find no market." Rifkin's boycott had found support among people in different areas of environmental politics—organic-food people, biodiversity people, genetic-privacy people—who had their own reasons for not liking recombinant DNA, and all of whom were comfortable with the notion that instead of genetically altering a tomato to suit human habits we should alter our habits to suit the tomato. More than twenty-five hundred restaurants nationwide, including "21," Chez Panisse, and Spago, had said they would not serve Calgene's tomato, and in some restaurant windows one was beginning to see the boycott symbol—a coil of DNA with a red slash through it.

Roger Salquist, whose company had spent twenty-five million dollars to develop the Flavr Savr, believed that his tomato would prevail. "The nice thing about this situation is that all these issues—science, business, people's religion, what have you—come down to a tomato," he told me. "If people like our tomato, the rest of this stuff goes away."

George Ball's family had been in the genetics business for three generations. His grandfather bred asters, sweet peas, snapdragons, and calendulas, and eventually turned those interests into Geo. J. Ball, Inc., which has diversified holdings in horticultural research and seed production. George, who was forty-one years old, spent part of his youth on a petunia-breeding farm in Costa Rica and now ran the company. He was also the president of the American Horticultural Society and the chief executive officer of W. Atlee Burpee & Company, the country's largest supplier of seeds for home gardening. George's enthusiasm for what recombinant DNA offered the plant breeder was unclouded by any haunting feeling that man was going to have to pay for overstepping his place in the world. It puzzled George that people doubt or criticize rDNA, as it is known, and he sometimes thought that they must be motivated by some sort of "religious thing," although George's faith in rDNA more nearly resembled a religious conviction than anything I encountered on the other side. "I personally believe that this is another green revolution," George said. "It's quantum-leap technology. It's going to be bigger than frozen food."

Edward Madigan, who was secretary of agriculture under George H. W. Bush, was one of many informed and responsible people who agreed with George. "The coming of age of biotechnology in agriculture promises to make rapid and far-reaching progress that will dwarf the advances of the previous age of agricultural mechanization and the harnessing of chemistry," Madigan said. One of the brightest promises held out by rDNA is that it will allow farmers to stop using chemicals. In 1993, American farmers dumped some twenty-five million pounds of chemicals on corn alone, to kill rootworm. The Mycogen Corporation, of San Diego, was developing a corn plant that produces the toxin in a bacterium called *Bacillus thuringiensis* (Bt), which killed rootworm. "It's quite possible that in five years cornfields will be pesticide-free," said Michael Sund, the director of corporate communications at Mycogen.

Many other promises were also made for rDNA: It will increase productivity. It will create crops capable of growing in the deserts of Somalia and in the mountains of Peru. It will give us vegetables higher in nutrients, and cooking oils lower in saturated fat. It will feed the huge increase in population expected in underdeveloped countries over the next twenty-five years. Biotechnology is the one major industry in which the United States is the undisputed world leader; the profits from these products will flow into our country and make us rich again.

As a time- and labor-saving innovation, rDNA is to classical plant breeding as the computer is to the typewriter. Classical breeding is confining, because the breeder has to breed the selected plant with a close relative, and it is messy, because along with the desired trait the plant inherits a lot of unwanted traits. With recombinant DNA, the breeder can use genes from virtually any species, plant or animal—even human—and can target each gene precisely, cut it out, clone it, and splice it into the DNA of the selected plant. The basic techniques of recombinant DNA are not difficult. College biology students are using the technology now, and before long it will be possible to synthesize DNA with a home chemistry set.

"It's incredible!" George Ball said as we were eating lunch one day in Manhattan. "What used to take ten years now takes one or two. And the possibilities for new plant varieties are mind-boggling. You know, true blue is a very difficult color to achieve in nature. I believe we'll see a blue rose in three years."

I said, "But isn't there something unnatural about all this?"

George said, "I don't see why. Recombinant DNA is just a way of speeding up what takes place in nature—and maybe of taking nature in a direction it wouldn't go ordinarily, because nature isn't organized that way."

"But isn't recombinant DNA in fact a way of replacing natural selection with human selection?"

"I don't see how man, in using recombinant DNA, is doing something unnatural, when man is part of nature too."

"Well, what if a genetically engineered organism mutates out of control and attacks Cleveland?"

"Actually, recombinant DNA is safer than classical breeding in that regard, because it reduces the chance of escape mutations. Not that escapes ever happen outside of science-fiction fantasies."

"But don't you worry that we might be upsetting nature's delicate balance?"

"Nature isn't a delicate balance. What's so balanced about it?"

There was no shaking George's faith. Changing the subject, I asked, "So when will Burpee's first recombinant-DNA product appear?"

George looked aghast. "Oh, Burpee doesn't use recombinant DNA. Look at the trouble it's caused Calgene. I can't afford that kind of backlash."


The headquarters of Calgene was a plain concrete building surrounded by tomato fields, on the edge of Davis, California. Eighty percent of all the processing tomatoes grown in the United States were grown within fifty miles of the building, including the "square" tomato, which is bred for machine harvesting and represents the pinnacle of a certain kind of tomato technology. In the reception area at Calgene was an illustrated encyclopedia of fruits and vegetables, and I leafed through it while waiting for my tour to begin. The tomato was classified with the vegetables—it was, in fact, declared a vegetable by an act of Congress. Botanically, it is a fruit, because it forms an ovary. I turned to the illustration of the banana and wondered if one day it will look like an antique. Stephen Benoit, the Calgene Fresh vice president, appeared and led me into the employees' lunch area to talk. On the way in, he spotted a newspaper article about the Flavr Savr pinned up on a bulletin board: it was illustrated with a drawing of a tomato strapped to an operating table with electrodes attached to it and a mad scientist about to throw the switch. Benoit looked pained. "I just wish they would stop using these dumb drawings," he said.

Benoit explained what the Flavr Savr was designed to do. "Our tomato will stay firm for seven to ten days longer than the average tomato. The way we've done that is we've isolated the gene that tells the tomato to get soft, made a copy of it, and inserted it backwards, using our proprietary Antisense technology. So instead of telling the tomato to get soft when it's ripe, the Antisense gene tells it not to get soft. That will allow us to leave our tomato on the vine longer, and get more of the backyard flavor into it, but still have a tomato that is firm enough to ship."

I was confused about whether Calgene was going to keep the tomato on the vine an extra seven to ten days, which would make it taste better, and therefore would benefit the consumer, or whether the seven to ten days would be added to the tomato's shelf life, which would benefit the seller. Benoit said that the tomato would spend about half the extra time on the vine. It would be picked at the "breaker stage," when it is just beginning to show color. "As you know, the great majority of tomatoes you buy in the supermarket are picked green, before all the sugars get into them," he said. "Then they're reddened, using ethylene gas. The industry has come up with the concept of the mature green tomato, which means a green tomato picked just before it shows color. The trouble is that the pickers, who work on a per-basket basis, don't have the time to tell the difference between a mature green and an immature green, and they pick a lot of tomatoes long before they're ripe. We won't pick any tomatoes before they show color—that way we'll know how ripe they are."

I asked how the Flavr Savr would be different from vine-ripened tomatoes, which are also picked at the breaker stage.

"The vine-ripes have only four to seven days of shelf life," Benoit said. "So the distributors have to refrigerate them, and that destroys the flavor. Never refrigerate a tomato. We won't have to refrigerate our tomato, because of the extended shelf life. And we will control our tomatoes from the grower to the supermarket to ensure that they are never chilled."

I asked a few questions about Antisense, Calgene's patented method of manipulating the tomato's DNA, and Benoit suggested that we go find a plant scientist in the lab for a more detailed explanation. The lab was down the hall from the lunch area. Men and women in white lab coats were working at benches strewn with test-tube racks, dishes of agar, and microscopes. Steve Vanderpan, a young man wearing a lab coat and a ponytail, explained some of the details of Antisense. "The gene we're working with is the PG gene—for 'polygalacturonase.' PG is an enzyme that degrades pectin, a polymer in the walls of tomato cells. PG is there so that the tomato can get its seeds into the ground quickly. It would be extremely difficult, using sexual reproduction, to select for a non-PG-gene-bearing tomato. Our guys just cut the PG gene out, using restriction enzymes. Then we make up an Antisense gene. We attach a kanamycin-resistant gene to the Antisense gene as a marker, and we install this construct in the DNA of a disarmed agribacterium—the sort of thing that produces a crown gall on a tree. We expose tomato cells to the agribacterium, and it injects its DNA, which contains the Antisense gene, into the tomato DNA."

Vanderpan led the way out the other end of the lab into a corridor with a series of tightly sealed doors, and opened a door marked Tissue Culture Room Seven. We were bathed in pure-white grow lights. In metal racks below the lights were hundreds of petri dishes, each containing tomato cells, some already generated into plant tissue, resting in agar. Vanderpan said, "Now remember the kanamycin gene we installed in our Antisense PG? Well, kanamycin is an antibiotic. If the Antisense-kanamycin construct is successfully implanted in the tomato plant's DNA, the antibiotic will fight off the bacteria in the petri dish, and the tomato cells will live. If not, they'll die."

I asked, "So all these buds will grow into tomato plants?"

"Yes, but some of them we won't want," Vanderpan says. "We have no control over where the Antisense gene lines up on the genome."

I had not realized this. "Really?"

"Recombinant DNA doesn't give you that control—yet. Sometimes the gene is going to end up in the wrong place on the genome, which means that the tomato will probably develop into an undesirable mutant and we'll have to kill it. We may not know till we grow them out in the greenhouse."

The greenhouses were a quarter mile from the main building. Driving there, Benoit and I passed several tract-home developments, with no houses built yet—just big, forlorn, ugly stone walls standing in the middle of some tomato fields. Calgene's greenhouse manager, Karen McGuire, took us into the thick hothouse heat. We strolled among great expanses of genetically engineered tomatoes of all sizes and varieties. One plant was ten feet tall. McGuire fingered through some leaves and found a small ripe tomato, picked it, and handed it to me. The color was beautiful, almost ruby. McGuire said, "See how ripe that is? But feel the firmness."

I squeezed the tomato. I tossed it a few feet up in the air and caught it. I said, "So are you going to let me taste this thing?"

Benoit hesitated.

"Just one bite," I say.

McGuire said, "You might want to wash it first," carried it over to a faucet, ran water on it, and handed it to me.

In the eighteenth century, the tomato was widely believed to be poisonous, because it is a relative of nightshade, and to be diabolical, on account of its lurid color and the resemblance of its skin to human skin. A turning point in human-tomato relations came in 1820, when a man named Robert Gibbon Johnson sat on the steps of the courthouse in Salem, New Jersey, and, watched by a large crowd, ate two tomatoes. By a strange coincidence, I also come from

Salem, New Jersey. In my hometown, on a local holiday each August, a man in Colonial garb stands on the courthouse steps and raises a fresh South Jersey tomato to his mouth while spectators cry, "No! Don't do it!" I felt that the tomato I am holding was a transmitter connecting me to the real Robert Gibbon Johnson. I realized I was a little afraid of this tomato. I asked myself, "Do I want to do this?" Then I raised the tomato to my mouth.

If you live in a city but come from somewhere else, chances are that you have a perfect tomato somewhere in your past, which you picked from the vine when it was warm from the sun, and bit into like an apple, and will never forget, which actually tasted like a fruit, like a big grape, exploding juice into all parts of your mouth. But then you moved away from home and lost touch with the people you knew, and you left the backyard tomatoes behind. Your desire for a better tomato is in part the desire for the backyard you no longer have. There are people who say that through science the backyard can be restored to you, and there are other people who believe that placing your faith in science only carries you farther away from the backyard.

I took a bite of the tomato. Keeping in mind that it was a hothouse tomato, and that hothouse tomatoes are generally not as good as outdoor tomatoes, and that it was grown from a variety that might not be the variety I buy in the store, and that the circumstances of the tasting were unscientific, I have to say that the Flavr Savr was not the tomato of my dreams.

I walked around Manhattan wearing a pin with the symbol of the Pure Food Campaign, Jeremy Rifkin's organization—the double helix with a red slash through it. Under the symbol are the words "I DO NOT Buy Genetically Engineered Food." On the subway, people furtively glanced at the pin, squint uncomprehendingly, glanced away. No one expressed solidarity with me. I wore the pin to a cocktail party on the Upper West Side. People seemed angry with me. Sarah, a lawyer at a big Manhattan firm, says she was perfectly happy eating genetically engineered food and wasn't going to stop just because it's suddenly fashionable not to. "I mean, what isn't

genetically engineered? When you get right down to it?" she said. I
wore the pin while I was picking up an airline ticket in Rockefeller
Center. A woman behind the ticket counter said, "You could drive
yourself crazy thinking about this stuff. In church? On Sunday? When
the guy next to me offers the sign of peace? I'm thinking, Now,
where's his hand been? Because you don't know. Especially with the
men. But I take it anyway, because what else are you going to do?"

I called people who are on record as having a problem with recombinant DNA in agriculture. Many of them recalled similarly
optimistic predictions being made by manufacturers of agricultural
chemicals in the 1940s, and thought it was worth proceeding cautiously with recombinant DNA to avoid the biotechnological equivalent of DDT. Shepherd Ogden, a Vermont seedsman and the
publisher of The Cook's Garden seed catalogue, wondered why we
needed to prove that we can increase the production of corn when
we already have an oversupply and are paying farmers not to produce corn. "A lot of us think that high tech is just not in the long run
the way agriculture is going to go," he said. "When the petroleum
runs out, and when water in California gets too expensive, the economic basis of a large part of our current agricultural system, where
we grow something in California and truck it three thousand miles,
will be marginalized. We've been high-tech-farming for fifty years,
which is not a terrifically long time in human history. We've been
farming organically for ten thousand years."

When I told Margaret Mellon, a biotechnology expert at the National Wildlife Federation, about the guy from Mycogen who said
that engineering a corn plant to produce Bt will do away with pesticides in corn farming in five years, she made a derisive snorting
sound into the phone. "That corn plant is going to express Bt in every one of its cells, so that not just rootworm but anything that
chews on it gets the Bt. Bt is a safe, biodegradable pesticide. In anywhere from five to ten years, pests will evolve that are resistant to
Bt, and that will be the end of a perfectly good pesticide, and we
may have to start using even more chemicals on rootworm. And
what happens when Bt spreads into trees and grass and the butter-
flies and moths start chewing on it?"

I went to see Rebecca Goldburg, a scientist at the Environmental Defense Fund, on Park Avenue. Some of the work she did concerns herbicide-tolerant plants. She told me that the French chemical company Rhône-Poulenc funded Calgene's development of a cotton plant that tolerates bromoxynil, a herbicide manufactured by Rhône-Poulenc. Although farmers could use only limited amounts of bromoxynil without killing their cotton, Rhône-Poulenc hoped that Calgene's cotton plants would allow the farmer to use much more bromoxynil, which would be good for the farmer because it would increase yield, and good for Calgene, which would be selling the technology, and good for Rhône-Poulenc, which is already selling the bromoxynil. The public would also benefit, according to the industry, because supposedly bromoxynil was less toxic than some other herbicides, although, Goldburg pointed out, it was toxic enough to cause cancer in rats and to make the Environmental Protection Agency require that workers who apply it wear protective suits.

I said, "That doesn't sound like the road to chemical-free agriculture."

Goldburg studied me for a while. "No, it doesn't," she said.

Goldburg said there were two big questions that consumers should ask: "Will the use of antibiotics like kanamycin induce antibiotic tolerance, especially in children?" and "Will DNA taken from an allergenic food, like a peanut, make the host food allergenic too?" She said that the chance that either event will happen is low. Then she said, "I think a lot of people just don't feel right in their gut about recombinant DNA in agriculture—they feel on some level it's not right to mix plant and animal genes. But unfortunately, health concerns are the only mechanism available to them to express their doubts. We have to talk about whether these products are safe, not whether they are necessary or desirable."

I had lunch with an old college friend, Wilson Kidde, who was the president of International Agritech Resources, an agricultural technology information service, and who was the nearest thing I could find to an objective source. I pointed out to him that Kraft, General Foods, Kellogg, Beatrice, and Nabisco, which were among the largest food companies in the United States, had relatively small investments in recombinant DNA, and that the leaders in the field were DuPont, Upjohn, Bayer, Dow, Monsanto, Ciba-Geigy, and Rhône-Poulenc—companies with the research budgets, staff, and facilities to do advanced rDNA work. I said it seemed to me that the drug and chemical companies, whose own market in pesticides was being threatened by companies like Mycogen, were using recombinant DNA as a wedge to get into the food business, and that if they were successful, the companies that supply us with aspirin and weed killer might one day supply our produce, meat, and dairy.

Wilson said, "Well, it's a value-added revolution. Adding value to food, whether you do it by preserving it or cooking it or packaging it, or all three at once, as in the case of Swanson TV dinners, is the usual way a company gets into the food business. Kellogg adds value to corn by turning it into cornflakes. Recombinant DNA is just a new way of adding value to food, but doing it earlier in the production chain, as it were—at the level of DNA, before the food companies can get their hands on it."

Campbell Soup was one of the few traditional food companies that invested early in rDNA. Campbell had put millions of dollars into Calgene, and it owned the patent on the PG gene. In trying to exploit its investment, however, Campbell had been handicapped in a way that DuPont, say, had not. Campbell received a letter from Jeremy Rifkin threatening to boycott the company unless Campbell dissociated itself from genetically engineered products. In a letter to the *Times*, James Moran, the director of public relations at Campbell, said, "Campbell does not market any bioengineered products and has no plans to do so. . . . Before any such use would even be contemplated, we would have to be assured that such use has full governmental approval and strong consumer acceptance." The impression many observers got from this sequence of letters was that Campbell was so worried for fear the stigma of rDNA would damage its reputation for wholesomeness that it immediately gave in to Rifkin's demands.

I asked Wilson, "Do you really think Campbell's reputation could be hurt by using recombinant DNA?"

Wilson said, "Well, the very fact that Campbell even has to worry about it puts the company at a disadvantage. I mean, a manu-

facturer of pesticides doesn't have to worry so much about its reputation for wholesomeness."

When Roger Salquist took his tomato to the Food and Drug
Administration in 1991, the agency did not have a policy on
genetically engineered foods. The decision that the FDA had to
make came down to this: Is foreign DNA a food additive, in which
case a genetically engineered tomato is a processed food and requires a label, like a can of tomato soup, or is recombinant DNA
simply an extension of classical plant breeding, in which case the
genetically engineered tomato is a whole food, like a tangerine or
seedless grapes, and requires no label? Salquist argued that his tomato should be regulated and sold like any other tomato, without a
label. Many people in the industry felt that to label a genetically
engineered vegetable "Genetically Engineered" would hurt sales,
and that submitting a food-additive petition, which is a long and
expensive undertaking, would be a difficult burden for small companies like Calgene to bear.

The FDA's decision, announced in May 1992, was that DNA
from another organism is not a food additive, and that the use of
recombinant DNA is in no regulatory sense different from classical plant breeding. If the donor organism is a known allergen, the
FDA will require the manufacturer to do additional testing, but
the mere fact that the donor is a peanut, a pig, or a human being
will not require a label. It was the policy that Salquist and the
industry had asked for. Unfortunately, it was announced by Vice
President Dan Quayle. Quayle's Council on Competitiveness had
taken a special interest in the matter, and in his speech Quayle
welcomed the policy, saying that it would provide regulatory relief
for the biotech industry. "That was the dumbest thing Quayle
could have done, because it allowed the environmental groups to
raise the food-safety issue," Salquist told me. In an effort to restore his tomato's reputation, Salquist decided to go back to the
FDA and request that the marker gene be considered a food
additive—in effect, to ask for the very regulation he had argued
against. Now Al Gore was working with the FDA to determine

whether the 1992 policy on genetically engineered foods needs to be revised.

From Calgene's point of view, the worst thing about the FDA's policy was the inspiration it gave to Jeremy Rifkin. When you read one of Rifkin's jeremiads, or see Rikfin on a consumer-affairs segment of the evening news, you get the impression that he is a zealot. In person, however, Rifkin is pleasant and charmingly self-deprecating. With his shirtsleeves rolled up, his tie loosened, and a smile that makes his eyes crinkle at the corners, Rifkin seems more like a lobbyist than an activist. This is the Rifkin of "Life in the Third Millennium," a one-day interdisciplinary seminar he offers to colleges and other organizations around the country for five thousand dollars a pop plus expenses.

In his Washington office, on Seventeenth Street NW, Rifkin had two walls of books—one with all his intellectual influences, who include Mumford, Roszak, Marcuse, Rank, Jung, and Reich, and the other with various editions of Rifkin's own books, which include *Algeny, Beyond Beef, Biosphere Politics,* and *Declaration of a Heretic.* The books form a right angle; you enter through a doorway at the point of the angle. I passed through the doorway and took a seat. Rifkin came around from behind his desk and sat near me, looking into my eyes. I said that in my reporting I had been impressed by the speed and urgency with which intellectual property was being acquired by biotech companies. If a company comes up with a plausible use for a particular gene, it can obtain a patent that covers not only that use but also the gene itself. For example, Calgene's tomato is covered by two trademarks and two patents, including a patent on the Antisense method and, most important, a patent on the gene that causes pectin breakdown in the cell walls of the tomato. Therefore, even if the Flavr Savr doesn't work, Calgene (or Campbell) can demand a royalty from anyone else who uses the PG gene. The situation bore the marks of a landgrab, I said.

Rifkin leaned toward me and rested his forearms on his knees, and said, "What we're seeing here is the conversion of DNA into a commodity, and it is in some ways the ideal corporate commodity—it's small, it's ownable, it's easily transportable, and it lasts forever." A swift, allusive elaboration of that point followed. Then came a metaphor: "Genetic engineering is the final enclosure movement. It is the culmination of the enclosure of the village commons that began five hundred years ago. As we have developed as a society and we have moved from an agricultural to a pyrochemical to a biotechnical culture"—three sorting movements with his hands mark these cultures—"we have seen that whoever controls the land or the fossil fuels or, now, the DNA controls society. Control the gene pool and you control life!"

Rifkin's argument against genetically engineered food is composed of four different arguments—the safety argument, the ethical argument, the anticorporate argument, and the sustainable-agriculture argument—loaded into alternating chambers and fired so rapidly that the rounds are hard to distinguish from one another. His unique talent is to locate the metaphor that draws the disparate parts of his argument together and gives conjecture the force and solidity of fact. The thing about Rifkin that drives people in the biotechnology industry crazy is that they cannot understand why he is against them—he seems to be motivated neither by high principle nor greed. The obvious great pleasure he gets from encapsulating four hundred years of thought in five minutes, bundling it all up attractively, and delivering it to an audience must be, as far as I can figure, its own reward.

Rifkin floats more or less by himself in the galaxy of green politics, having had no long-term alliances with major environmental organizations. The environmentalists I know regard Rifkin as somewhat outlandish but savor him as a kind of guilty pleasure, since few people are better than Rifkin at getting under a corporation's skin. And the idea of Rifkin has many defenders. Even people in the biotech industry will concede that Rifkin provokes debate and that in the long run debate is good because it is the only way the public's apprehension about recombinant DNA will go away.

I asked Rifkin whether he thought that Calgene's tomato was safe. He leaned forward again, lowered his voice confidingly, and said that Calgene's tomato probably is safe. Then he gave me an argument. "The tomato is the classic example of the old way of thinking: whatever increases productivity is good and will find a market," he said. "I call it World's Fair thinking. But now we have a new way of thinking. What we will see in food today is going to be a battle between the World's Fair view of the world and the new, ecologically based stewardship of the world. Food is an intimate issue. I'm telling you food is going to be the focus of all green-oriented politics. And this is only going to gather momentum—in a year, this movement is going to be so strong that no genetically engineered product will make it to the supermarket. I think Calgene has miscalculated in the most profound way. It spent an enormous amount of money and it never asked the simplest question: Do people want this tomato? And I say people don't want this tomato. The bottom line is, who needs it?"

Jay Taylor, a Florida tomato grower who would be growing the Flavr Savr, told me a story to illustrate how the tomato business works. "A few years back, I sold a guy six loads of tomatoes in Virginia on August twelfth," he said. A load is a full semitrailer. "On September seventeenth, I was up in Detroit and I ran into the guy I sold those tomatoes to. I said, 'Hey, did you sell those tomatoes?' He said, 'Nope. I still got 'em.' He had those six loads of tomatoes in his coolers—he was waiting for the price to go up, so he could make a profit. You know who he ended up selling 'em to? McDonald's."

This is the main reason that supermarket tomatoes taste bad. Tomato distributors, in essence, run a futures market. The longer the shelf life of a tomato, the greater the probability that all the people who speculate on tomatoes—salesmen, repackers, warehousers, and retailers—can sell them for more than they bought them for. The wholesale market is very large, and a lot of money is involved; the price of a twenty-five-pound box of tomatoes can move from six dollars to eighteen dollars in ten days. Interests are entrenched. When I asked Calgene Fresh's Tom Churchwell how he was going to cope with this problem, he said, "We've changed the way the tomatoes are picked and the way the pickers are paid, we've changed the packing materials, we've invented our own packing machine, which will treat the tomatoes much more gently, and we're going to ship our tomatoes in good air-ride trailers, using truckers who are paid for the quality of what they deliver, not just the bulk, and we'll repack the tomatoes ourselves in our new service center outside Chicago."

"And how are you going to pay for that?"

"Well, if you can consistently deliver a quality tomato, you can put a brand name on it. And if you can brand your tomatoes you can charge a premium for them, and that allows you to pay for the other stuff." (Calgene plans to charge around three dollars a pound for its tomatoes.)

In Florida, most of the people I talked to felt that compared with reforming the tomato business, genetic engineering is easy. In Homestead, which is in one of the state's major tomato-growing regions, I talked about this with a tomato salesman named Ed Angrisani. Tomato salesmen enjoy a mythic status within the tomato business. They control dozens of truckloads of tomatoes a day, and they can earn more than a million dollars a year. Angrisani is a powerful-looking man, and he wears a gold necklace, a big gold ring, and a fabulous gold Rolex watch. I had previously met three tomato growers, and all of them wore gold Rolex watches, but Angrisani's was the biggest.

Angrisani's office had been wrecked six months earlier by Hurricane Andrew, and it had new doors, which made the air fragrant with oak. He was on the phone selling tomatoes when I came in. On his desk were invoices for loads to Vancouver, Los Angeles, Louisville, Hunts Point Market in the Bronx, and other destinations—his morning's work. When he got off the phone, I said that it seemed to me that when people at Calgene talked about reforming the tomato business they were talking about reforming people like Angrisani himself, and did Angrisani feel threatened by that?

Angrisani didn't look threatened. He smiled and put his hands behind his head and leaned back in his chair. "I personally would like to see Calgene succeed," he said. "Maybe Calgene's tomatoes will sell themselves, and I hope they do. Or it might be that they'll need a guy like me to sell their tomatoes for them. I mean, if it were just a matter of sitting here waiting for the phone to ring, growers wouldn't need guys like me. What separates the men from the boys in this business is whether you can sell your tomatoes when nobody wants them, when you've got a whole field that's just going to rot out there"—he waved toward the window—"unless you can move 'em out."

Angrisani scratched the side of his face for a while. Then he said, "I've got customers who know that when the supply is tight they can call me and I'll sell 'em a load. So when I get oversupplied I can call them and say, 'Hey, I know you don't need it, but how about buying a load?' And they'll say, 'We'll send the truck.' It took me sixteen years to get to where I had the relationships to do that. Now maybe the folks at Calgene think they can come in and do it overnight—and like I say, I wish 'em the best—but it's not a simple deal."

The phone rang. Angrisani said into it, "Make sure we get eight dollars a box. He owes us one dollar."

As I was leaving, I asked Angrisani for a card. He said, "I don't have any cards. They were all washed away in the hurricane." I drove through Homestead on the way back to Miami. Roads were lined with chainsawed sections of avocado and lime trees, and there were rotting piles of furniture and appliances on almost every street corner. All the street signs were uprooted and had concrete clinging to the bottom of the poles like hunks of sod. Tomatoes were just about the only living thing I saw. Tomatoes were everywhere, thriving.

A century ago, in June 1893, Luther Burbank began publishing his catalogue "New Creations in Fruit and Flowers." Burbank was already celebrated for creating the Burbank potato, whose resistance to disease was far superior to that of existing potatoes. But with "New Creations," which introduced to the world his hybrid plums and prunes, Burbank's celebrity climbed almost to the level of Edison's. In newspapers he was portrayed as a saint. Edward Wickson, a professor of horticulture at the University of California, wrote at the turn of the century, when Burbank was at the height of his fame, "He could hear the 'still small voice' without preparatory earthquake or whirlwind. Like David of old he could do his work with smooth pebbles from the brook; and he cast aside the elaborate armament of his scientific brethren lest it should impede his movements."

That kind of plant breeder, who was as much an artist as a scientist, and who, working within prescribed limits of nature, performed miracles, will probably disappear with the coming of recombinant DNA. While I was in Davis for my tour of Calgene, I went to see one of the last of the heroic master breeders, Dr. Charles M. Rick. That the tomatoes you are growing this year don't die of blight or yield unevenly or grow too leafy is ultimately attributable to Dr. Rick's efforts. Since the 1940s, Dr. Rick has been prospecting along the slopes of the Andes, the cradle of *Lycopersicon,* for novel tomato plants. He discovered a new species of tomato, *Solanum rickii,* bringing the total of known related wild tomato species to eleven. The specimens he has collected form the bulk of the C. M. Rick Tomato Genetics Resource Center, the largest collection of wild tomato species and genetic stock in the world. The center is on the Davis campus, across town from Calgene. It is the New York Public Library of tomato seeds. On the walls of the center are pictures of amazing tomato plants from around the world—a tomato plant growing on a sandy beach in the Galápagos, a tomato growing at thirty-six-hundred meters in Chile, a tomato growing in the Chilean desert, a tomato tree in northern Ecuador standing twenty-five feet high.

Dr. Rick was seventy-eight years old. He had a somewhat scraggly white beard, and long white wisps of hair curled out from under the faded khaki hat he often wears. In his shirt pocket he carried tweezers for emasculating tomato anthers and a probe for pollinating tomato stigmas. His dealings with tomatoes went back to a quasi-mystical experience he had in a tomato field in the early forties. "I was working in genetics at UC Davis, and a professor said, 'Charlie, why don't you go out to that field and see what causes those tomato plants to be unfruitful.' The guy was a cantankerous old fellow, and I thought, Oh, man, he would think of something like that. A month later, I woke up in the middle of the night in a cold sweat and said to myself, 'Rick! You damn fool! You'd better get out there and see those tomatoes!' So I spent the day in that tomato field, and by the time I came back I was hooked on tomatoes, absolutely hooked."

I was interested in knowing what Rick thought of Calgene's tomato. He laughed, and said, "I'll wait till I taste it."

I asked, "Well, do you think it's possible to produce a backyard supermarket tomato?"

Rick thought for a while, then said, "Well, it is important to keep in mind that, while we have become quite skilled at recombinant DNA, we still don't really know how genes work, and the more we find out about genes, the less simple their behavior appears to be." He laughed again and scratched his head through his old hat. "I mean, even something like the tomato, which has only a thousand or so genes, and a genome that has been extensively mapped—well, tomatoes are damn tricky things. There are so many things that can go wrong when you breed a tomato—yield, maturation time, quality, uniformity, coloration, size. One little cat face or growth crack and people won't buy the damn thing. Now color is relatively easy. It's not hard to breed a tomato that looks great and tastes like hell." He laughed. "I'm not entirely convinced that recombinant DNA will do any more for supermarket tomatoes than classical breeding has done. A few years back, the Israelis made a lot of noise saying that they had suppressed the same gene Calgene had, using conventional methods—only they called theirs the RIN gene. Said they suppressed it with a gene they got out of a wild cherry."

I spotted what appeared to be some ancient rolls of toilet paper high on a row of cluttered shelves. "What's that?" I asked, pointing.

"South American tp. The aboriginal stuff," Rick said. He told me to reach up and get a roll. It was yellow with age and looked as if it would do fine for finishing carpentry work. "Recombinant DNA can't hold a candle to this invention," Dr. Rick said. "Feel the consistency of that stuff?" He rubbed a sheet between his fingers. "Much better than American toilet paper for wrapping tomato specimens in."

—1993

# THE SPINACH KING

The town of Seabrook is in a part of South Jersey that almost no one visits, because there's no obvious reason to go there and it's not on the way to anywhere else. Even people who grew up in New Jersey have no clue what I'm talking about when I try to describe where Seabrook is—thirty miles south of Cherry Hill, across the state from Atlantic City, in the cul-de-sac that dead-ends into the Delaware Bay. Although Seabrook is only an hour's drive from Philadelphia, and two and a half hours from Washington and New York, it is surrounded by vegetable fields, and you can drive east for forty miles without seeing a mall or a Levittown. Road signs are perforated with bullet holes, and there are long snakes of tire rubber burned onto the road. The earth is chestnut-colored and looks comfortably worn. The fields drain into tidal creeks—pronounced "cricks" by the locals—which flow into salt marshes and on into the bay.

In 1995, the Japanese American Citizens League (JACL) held a fiftieth-anniversary celebration in Seabrook. About six hundred Japanese Americans attended the weekend—most of them former residents of Seabrook, about half of whom still live nearby. Between 1944 and 1947, twenty-five-hundred people of Japanese ancestry came to Seabrook from the internment camps around the

country where they had been corralled by the U.S. government after Pearl Harbor. They were recruited by my grandfather Charles
Franklin Seabrook—known as CF—who was the head of Seabrook
Farms, which by the 1950s was one of the largest producers of frozen vegetables in the country. My grandfather's basic idea, which
was to apply factory methods to agriculture, required a lot of labor.
In the early twenties, he published a message in a local paper,
which read:

## WANTED!

Some people who are mad enough to desire a quiet, comfortable home with modern conveniences, in the country, and a chance
to save money, rather than high wages with dirt, noise and uncertain employment. The place has nothing to recommend it except
good treatment, healthful living, steady position, and an opportunity for everybody to work their way up in a new and growing
business.

No sulkers or people with touchy feelings need apply. Anyone who says that he can get a job from "So and So" any time
he wants had better take it. It is better than this one. Our regular
work day is a ten-hour day. However, the work consists in doing
whatever the employer feels like asking at any minute of the day
or night.

Many of the workers at Seabrook Farms were refugees of
twentieth-century upheavals and hardships: Italians avoiding their
war with Turkey in the 1910s; former soldiers of the White Russian
Army in the late teens and early twenties; Americans who lost their
jobs during the Depression; Jamaicans and Barbadians and German
prisoners of war in the forties; Poles, Hungarians, and Czechs flee-
ing the advance of the Soviet Army in 1945; Japanese Americans
from '44 to '47; and Estonians and Latvians running from Stalin's
rule in the late forties and early fifties. My grandfather built "ethnic
villages" for the different groups, and this collection of villages became Seabrook. In the 1940s and 1950s, there were thirty different

languages spoken in Seabrook, a town of about five thousand people.

I drove down to Seabrook for the anniversary too. I went partly out of curiosity about my family history, and partly out of a dim sense of obligation. My wife, Lisa, and I took the Turnpike to my parents' house on Friday evening, and the next morning we drove over to Seabrook in two cars: Lisa and I with my sister Carol and her family; my mom and dad in Dad's car. It was a perfect Indian-summer day, too warm for the suit I had worn for the occasion.

When I was little, going to Seabrook gave me a stomachache. In Seabrook, something bad had happened between my grandfather and my father, and it resulted in a kind of family apocalypse that destroyed Seabrook Farms. The mystery of what went wrong in my family has become part of the landscape around Seabrook; it seems to linger in the orange lanes leading back into the stunted pines, and in the sun glittering on the spinach fields beside the road. The whole place feels haunted to me. As we got closer to town, conversation in our car slowed down, and the wind and the sound of the engine filled up the silences. We turned onto Route 77, a sturdy concrete road that CF built in 1921, on which he transported vegetables to Camden. We passed the Seabrook Buddhist Temple and went through an alley of plane trees, planted by my grandfather, which are big now and give the road a stately appearance, like a country road in Provence. The trees were the only obvious sign that something momentous had once happened here.

These days, Seabrook has the forlorn look of a company town without the company. The local grocery store no longer carries a large selection of Japanese food, although it's probably the only place along NJ 77 where you can buy roasted wasabi nuts. In the center of Seabrook is a huge empty space: the former site of the power plant, a four-story brick building with a tremendous 225-foot phallus of a smokestack, which was torn down in 1979. It's as if the empty land that my grandfather filled with energy, machines, buildings, and people had been distilled into an essence, and the essence had been poured right here.

The entrance to the Seabrook School auditorium was crowded with people registering for the weekend. Most of the crowd was nisei and sansei—second- and third-generation Japanese-American people, now mostly middle-aged, who were children at Seabrook, went away to college, and never really came back. There was a smaller number of issei, or first-generation Japanese, including ninety-six-year-old Fuju Hironaki Sasaki, who had been "mayor" of the Japanese community in Seabrook, and a few yonsei— fourth-generation—as well. We picked up our Seabrook Fiftieth Year Celebration tote bags and were shown to our seats, in a row near the front that was set off by a yellow ribbon. I nodded down the row to my father's brother Courtney, who is eighty-six, and to various cousins. The aisles were filled with people embracing each other. In front of me was a woman's face, squeezed over another woman's shoulder, tears overflowing her tightly shut eyes.

The anniversary began with a percussive blast from the Seabrook Hoh Daiko Drummers, who perform each summer in Seabrook for the Buddhist festival of Obon, a festival honoring the dead. (Legend has it that a disciple of Buddha had visions of his mother in Hell; by doing charitable deeds, he was able to attain forgiveness for her. The drumming announces her redemption.) Then the master of ceremonies, Ed Nakawatase, said, "I'm a former resident of Dormitory 8, Apartment 10, 819 Barnard Street, and I'd like to say to all of you, Welcome home." The local Boy Scout troop led the crowd in the Pledge of Allegiance to one nation under God indivisible with liberty and justice for all. The Reverend William Borror, pastor of the Deerfield Presbyterian Church, which was my grandfather's church (his employees called it "Saint Charles's Cathedral"), stepped forward and said a blessing: "We thank you that you are a God of mercy and that you are a God of justice, and that your purposes are worked out in time and in the lives of those who seek to do your good."

Children of Japanese internees often speak of the difficulty of getting their parents to talk about their wartime experience.

The younger generation want to know what happened in the camps, so they can pass along this almost biblical event in the family history to their children; the older generation don't want to talk about it, because the pain of the experience is still too alive. When members of the younger generation ask their parents about the camps, they often hear the phrase *shikataganai,* a Japanese bit of stoicism that translates as "It couldn't be helped." Richard Ikeda, who was at Seabrook as a boy and is now a physical chemist at DuPont, across the river, told me that *shikataganai* is a way of saying, "Okay, life is unfair. Now get back to work." Josie Ikeda, Richard's mother and a longtime Seabrook resident, says that parents downplayed the terrible experience of the camps, partly in order to protect the children. "When we were in camp," she told me, "I was very bitter, fighting everything, but then I became concerned that my bitterness would pass to my children, and so I tried to change my attitude. I did not want them to grow up feeling bitter toward their country. I wanted them to love their country." Theodora Yoshikami, the coordinator of multicultural programs at the American Museum of Natural History in New York, who was born in camp and spent most of the first twelve years of her life in Seabrook, told me, "You could never talk about the camps with my parents. I never knew what went on. Until I was nine, I thought when people said 'camp' they meant summer camp."

Events like the anniversary and the camp reunions are often arranged by the younger generation to help the older people talk about their wartime experience. Many of the kids go to the reunions with their parents in the hope of seeing through a rarely opened window onto the family past. The younger nisei and sansei tend to be more militant in their attitude toward the camp experience than the older people. The camp exhibit at the Los Angeles Japanese American National Museum, for example, which included a reconstructed barracks, would have been unthinkable thirty-five years ago. The sansei were the force behind the Redress Movement, which led to the creation of a federal commission to study the internment policy, and which concluded, in 1983, that "the broad historical causes which shaped these decisions were race prejudice, war hysteria, and a failure of political leadership." In

1990 the federal government began awarding every surviving internee twenty thousand dollars.

After the prayer, the mayor of Upper Deerfield Township, C. Kenneth Hill, talked about being the son of migrant laborers who came from Tennessee to work at Seabrook in 1947. Donna Pearson, forty-one, head of the Bridgeton City Council, also spoke. Her father, Samah Pearson, came from Jamaica in 1943 and went to work in the Seabrook bean fields. "We grew up in a multicultural household," Pearson said. "We learned to speak patois. Some of my first gifts were from Japanese Americans and German Americans. . . . We have to remember the reasons for coming here weren't always the best. There was a lot of pain, there was a lot of suffering, there was a lot of loss, but I think the biggest lesson is that people survive. We come together, and we learn how to live together." Pearson paused to collect her emotions, then continued, "There's no obstacle you can't get over. There's no excuse for 'can't.' There is always more in life to do and to achieve. Because if my parents could do it, so can I."

## BUILDING A DREAM

A hundred and thirty years ago, my great-great-grandfather Samuel Seabrook, who had been the caretaker of Horace Greeley's estate in Chappaqua, New York, brought his family down to New Jersey to live, ignoring his boss's advice to go west. His son Arthur became a sharecropper and sold vegetables door-to-door from the back of a huckster wagon. In those days, the word *truck* still meant "commercial produce," and New Jersey supplied most of the truck for Philadelphia and New York. In 1893 Arthur bought a fifty-seven-acre farm, partly covering the site now occupied by Seabrook. He worked it with his son—my grandfather. CF was small and thin and very serious. His pale-blue eyes, behind steel-rimmed spectacles, could appear icy. In almost all the photographs I have of him, he is glowering—his jaw pushed out, his mouth set stubbornly. He was proud of his body, especially of his feet, and was always showing off his high arches and tapered ankles as evidence that he was descended from good stock.

As a farmer, CF was distinguished by a strong dislike of dirt. Although his education ended at the age of twelve, when he went to work full time for his father, he had an intuitive understanding of the principles of engineering, and he applied this to the automation of the work on the farm. I was raised on his story: CF down on his knees as a boy, weeding onions in the heat, looking up to see a man towering over him on horseback, and resolving someday to ascend to that height; CF as a young man, hearing someone in Philadelphia talk about overhead irrigation one day, trying this new invention on his celery bed, and, banking on the value of his succulent irrigated celery, going up to New York and persuading some men to lend him the money to expand his business; CF as a budding industrialist, buying his father out and going on a building spree around Seabrook. Over an eight-year period, he put in thirty-five miles of roads, two railroads, a power plant, six enormous greenhouses, an ice plant, a sawmill (to make boxes for the truck), a canning plant, a cold-storage facility, and a school, and he laid out villages for his employees and their families: the "Italian village" for his Italian workers, and so on. In 1924 he went bust and lost the business, but he had got it back by 1930, and soon began freezing vegetables for General Foods, which had acquired the patents for Clarence Birdseye's quick-freezing process. In 1943 Seabrook Farms began selling its own brand of frozen vegetables. CF was often referred to in the press as "the Henry Ford of agriculture." In a dazzling picture story that appeared in 1955, *Life* called Seabrook Farms "the biggest vegetable factory on earth."

CF didn't own very much of Seabrook Farms outright. The plant, along with the rest of the infrastructure, was built with borrowed money, and all of it was periodically on the verge of being taken over by creditors. A lot of the land was owned by small farmers who had contracts to grow truck for CF. What my grandfather supplied was vision. He saw fifty thousand acres of small farms functioning as a single enterprise, and he put a lot of his energy into creating a community to bind the farmers and the workers together. The geographical isolation of the place made his creation seem like a separate world. It was a world of hard work and opportunity, the rewards of which were personified by CF himself, whom everyone called "the Old Man," even before he was forty.

In 1905 CF married Norma Dale Ivins, whom we grandchildren knew as Nana. She was the daughter of a successful farming family that had been in the area since Colonial times. She was taller and better educated than CF was, and she helped him finish his education through correspondence courses, and taught him grammar. My father, named John but called Jack, was born in 1917, the youngest of four children. When he was seven, the family moved into a large farmhouse on a dirt road called Polk Lane; everyone in town referred to it as the Big House. Around this time, CF made several transatlantic crossings, and he observed what rich people wore and what they ate and drank; he wanted his house to seem luxurious. He put in a tiled swimming pool—the first pool many people in the area had ever seen—and in the bean fields around the Big House he planted a grand formal garden, like the ones he had seen at great houses in England. High hedges separated the garden into elaborate sections. Wisteria vines trained as standards marched down the center of one section, banked on both sides by beds of hyacinths, tulips, snapdragons, rhododendrons, and chrysanthemums.

In my father's first memories of family dinners, everyone is discussing the business. For him and his two older brothers, Belford and Courtney, the family and the business were the same thing. Money was mixed up in everything. By the time he was nine, my father was working sixty-hour weeks during his school vacation. When he was thirteen, his father made him the quality grader. "It's unbelievable that CF would put this much trust in a thirteen-year-old boy," my father says. "His whole life depended on what he got for those crops." This, Dad says, is one of the most puzzling things about his father: a part of him wanted to trust his family members completely, but he also treated them badly, constantly playing one against another in order to get his own way.

CF educated his three sons to be engineers, sending Belford and then Dad to Princeton, and Courtney to Lehigh. Their sister, Thelma, was not included in the family business. (I often wonder what it must have been like to be the only daughter in that family— ignored by her competitive brothers as they carved out their fiefdoms.) My father married immediately after graduating from Princeton, in

1939, and returned to Seabrook to work. He and his wife, Ann, lived in one of CF's nicest houses; in fact, it had been previously owned by the man whose shadow fell across CF in the onion patch. As a young squire of twenty-five, my father had a Japanese cook and a Jamaican butler. His older brothers were already executives, each with his own area of expertise: Belford was the chief engineer, who designed and ran the freezing plant; Courtney was head of sales. My father took charge of labor recruitment and union negotiation and began building relationships with bankers in Philadelphia and New York.

The image of the Seabrook family was intrinsic to the value of the Seabrook brand. Pictures of father and sons working together frequently appeared in newspaper and magazine stories about the business. "The fact that there was a real family named Seabrook," my father says, "lent itself to a form of publicity that was far more effective than paid advertising." Seabrook Farms' frozen creamed spinach was better than Birdseye frozen creamed spinach because we Seabrooks grew it ourselves. "We grow our own—so we know it's good—and we freeze it right on the spot!" was the company motto. During the fifties, my father was dubbed the Spinach King by the company, and pictures of his handsome face were widely distributed in Seabrook Farms publicity.

But although father and sons worked side by side, they were not close. "CF was never close or intimate in any way with any of his family," my father has written in a memoir of Seabrook Farms that he has been working on. He goes on:

> None of us thought this was odd, it was just the way life was. In fact, it was not until 1953, when the three of us were grown men, and a psychiatrist pointed it out, that we realized how odd that was. We also realized that CF had had no close friends in his lifetime. Seen up close, he was cold and calculating, but in public he was highly successful at projecting a warm, caring, friendly image to a large group. At most family parties there was tension, because CF would be sarcastically critical of some family member, a daughter-in-law who was hard of hearing or a pre-teen grandson who happened to be overweight.

Nana did her best to shield "the boys," as everyone called her sons, from his fierce passive aggression, but she was no match for CF. My mother, Elizabeth Toomey Seabrook, once asked Nana how she could have allowed CF to be cruel to her sons, and Nana responded, "There was nothing I could do." She could hardly protect herself. On another occasion, she told my mother, "No one will ever know the person I was meant to be."

In the 1940s CF's health began to fail, and it became even harder for his sons to deal with him. It often fell to their wives to mediate. CF sent for a nurse who had once saved his life by curing him of dysentery in the Crimea—a large Australian woman named Miss Leila Small. From then on, anyone who wanted to talk to him had to go through her. Ann Seabrook remembers trying to plead her husband's case to her father-in-law during one of their disputes. CF was shut into a steam cabinet that Miss Small often put him in, with just his skinny old head poking out of the top of it, snarling, "Jack's got me by the balls!" When you ask my father about his stormy relationship with his father, he often says, "Well, it goes to show that you can't keep the old bulls and the young bulls in the same pasture," and that, usually, is the end of the conversation.

In the midfifties, CF began to show signs of what was then called "hardening of the arteries." He had a series of "spells" during which he would, say, show up in a Bridgeton clothing store wearing several layers of bathrobes. But he was capable of being rational when he had to be. My father was then between marriages—this was during his Spinach King phase—and he was often seen with actresses and models in New York hot spots like "21" and the Stork Club. His name appeared frequently in the gossip columns. Charles Ventura: "Frozen-food tycoon Jack Seabrook is planning an early merger with actress Eva Gabor." Dorothy Kilgallen: "The once-flourishing romance between Jack Seabrook . . . and Eva Gabor . . . has grown colder than his products." Earl Wilson: "Ann Miller and Jack Seabrook, the frozen foods fella, are a new duo." Dad's getting all this attention seems to have made his father envious and vindictive. One night, CF appeared at the New York apartment of one of Dad's girlfriends, wanting to take her out. He apparently wasn't ready to quit being the Spinach King himself.

Among the people sitting in the audience at the Seabrook anniversary was Ray Ono. On the day I interviewed him, in his house near Seabrook, his wife, Mariko, who is the grandmaster of ikebana, or Japanese flower arranging, for South Jersey, was holding a class downstairs for two women. It was cold that morning—the wind, which had been roaring in the trees the night before, had blown the cold in—and the spinach fields were glistening with frost. Six weeks after our discussion, Ray, who was in his early sixties, died suddenly, and when I heard the news the sound of the roaring wind came back to me. In Ray's study, where he and I talked that day, he kept his engineering degrees, five patents, and a picture of his father's fishing boat, which dates from his family's pre-Seabrook life on the West Coast. After Ray and I were finished, we had lunch with Mariko and her students and discussed flower arranging. Mariko said, "In ikebana, you can make the arrangements out of anything—grass, branches, rocks, even things you find in the road. You don't have to use only flowers."

Ray Ono's Seabrook story, like that of many other Japanese Americans, starts on December 7, 1941. Right after Pearl Harbor, the FBI picked up most fishermen of Japanese ancestry living in California, on the theory that they were in the best position to be spies. Ray's father, a tuna fisherman who owned a boat with his brother, was arrested one day as he was returning to the dock at Terminal Island, in San Pedro, where the Onos lived. For months, the family did not know what had become of him. They never saw the boat again. Ray told me, "We heard it was used by the navy as a minesweeper, and might have been sunk off the Philippines. But we're not sure."

There were immediate calls for the rounding up of all the 110,000 Japanese residents of the West Coast. Representative John Rankin of Mississippi said on the floor of the House, on December 15, 1941, "I'm for catching every Japanese in America . . . and putting them in concentration camps. . . . Damn them! Let's get rid of them now!" Henry McLemore, in a column published in *The San Francisco Examiner,* a Hearst newspaper (the Hearst papers were constantly warning their readers of "the yellow peril"), wrote, "Herd 'em up, pack 'em off and give 'em the inside room in the badlands. . . . Personally, I hate the Japanese. And that goes for all of them." Earl Warren, then the attorney general of California, said that placing the Japanese in camps was a good idea because "when we are dealing with the Caucasian race we have methods that will test the loyalty of them. . . . But when we deal with the Japanese we are in an entirely different field and we cannot form any opinion that we believe to be sound."

The men who contributed to making the final decision to send the Japanese to the camps—Franklin D. Roosevelt; Henry Stimson, who was secretary of war; John McCloy, assistant secretary of war, and Francis Biddle, the attorney general—were the kind of preppie Eastern-establishment types my father had vaguely in mind when he raised me. Biddle expressed reservations two days before the president signed Executive Order 9066, which gave the military the authority to carry out the operation. "A great many West Coast people distrust the Japanese [and] various special interests would welcome their removal from good farm land and the elimination of their competition," Biddle wrote to FDR. He added, "My last advice from the War Department is that there is no evidence of imminent attack and from the FBI that there is no evidence of planned sabotage." But FDR signed the order anyway, on February 19, 1942. No civil rights organizations, including the ACLU, actively protested the order. The Japanese American leadership did little to resist the camps either. The JACL stated that it opposed internment if the policy was motivated by West Coast anti-Japanese racism (which, in hindsight, it clearly was) but would go along with internment if, as FDR had claimed, it was to protect the Japanese *from* racism, and to help the United States win the war. The Japanese leaders suggested to their community that going quietly to the camps was the best way they could prove their loyalty to the United States.

In May of 1942, signs went up in Japanese neighborhoods like the Onos' that all people of Japanese ancestry had seventy-two hours to report to an assembly center, taking with them only as much as they could carry. The Los Angeles assembly center was the racetrack at Santa Anita. People lived in the horse stalls for five months, until the internment camps were finished. Josie Ikeda remembers showering in the big open area where they washed down the lathered-up racehorses in peacetime. "There was one elderly Japanese woman who was so embarrassed, she wore her clothes in the shower," she told me. "We laughed, but it must have been terribly humiliating for her." In October, the internees were moved to the camps, of which there were ten altogether, most of them in remote areas of Arizona, Idaho, and Arkansas.

Ray Ono's family went to Manzanar, one of two camps in California. They remained there for fifteen months. By December of 1944, Roosevelt had begun to have second thoughts about the internment policy, and the government announced that it was closing the camps down. Everyone had to get out. But many of the internees stayed until the government forcibly removed them, because they were afraid to return to their homes. Alfred Elliott, a congressman from Tulare, California, had said on the floor of the House in 1943, "The only good Jap is a dead Jap," implying that this statement would apply to "every one of them that is sent back" to California.

To permit nisei of draft age to serve in the military, the government devised a "loyalty test." Question 27 was "Are you willing to serve in the armed forces of the United States on combat duty, wherever ordered?" and Question 28 was "Will you swear unqualified allegiance to the United States?" The young men who answered no to both of these questions—about one in ten—were called "no-no boys," and the government made an attempt to segregate them at the camp at Tule Lake. The yes-yes boys were allowed to be drafted (many enlisted), and a large number of them served in the 442nd Regimental Combat Team, which became one of the most decorated units in United States military history.

## LEAVING CALIFORNIA

The war was good for Seabrook Farms. In one year, the company sold sixty million pounds of processed vegetables to the military, which was amazing business. But the war also made CF's labor problem, always the weak link in his operation, even worse. On this count, CF disliked the war. When Belford told CF, shortly after Pearl Harbor, that he was going to seek a commission, CF was furious, and never forgave him; that was the end of Belford's executive position with Seabrook Farms. It was as though Belford had committed an act of treason.

At the end of 1943, my father, who had stayed home from the war and had taken over some of Belford's responsibilities, heard from the American Friends Society, in Philadelphia, that the internees could be recruited as workers. Like many Americans, especially in the East, my father had been only dimly aware of the internment situation, but it sounded to him like one possible solution to the company's labor problem. Seabrook Farms sent scouts to the camps to offer them my grandfather's Fair Deal, and a small group of internees from a camp in Arkansas came to inspect Seabrook. CF promised every man and woman a job at the going wage, a house with heat and utilities, and decent schools for their children. In return, they had to agree to work for Seabrook for six months.

Many people who came to work for my grandfather had nowhere else to go. Seabrook became their refuge. Richard Ikeda told me, "Seabrook was a real community—there was kinship to the community, obligation to the community. Work was hard, but everybody was in the same boat and suffering together. If there was a funeral, people shared in the expense. If someone needed medicine, people contributed what they could." And there was far less overt racism in Seabrook than elsewhere. My uncle Courtney spoke to the men at the local clubs—the Elks, the Moose, and the Rotarians—and told them he didn't want any trouble for the Japanese.

Barry Semple, a former history teacher at Bridgeton High School, who spoke at the Seabrook anniversary, told me afterward, "I think South Jersey is more a part of the Deep South than it is a part of New Jersey. This is not recognized in Trenton. You say that South Jersey is more like Mississippi or Alabama than it is like Trenton, and those people in Trenton—it's impossible for them to comprehend that." Semple was an active participant in New Jersey's efforts to integrate the local public schools in the sixties, and he was threatened by the Klan. He went on, "So, with all the hatred of the war, for the Japanese to come in here, and for something this positive to happen—it's an amazing thing. And it says a lot about what your family must have done."

But Michi Weglyn, the author of *Years of Infamy: The Untold Story of America's Concentration Camps,* who also spoke at the anniversary, told me that life for her parents in Seabrook was hard. She remembers that her mother's hands cracked from sorting beans all day, and wouldn't heal. When she was planning her remarks, Weglyn told me, one elderly man said of working conditions in the plant, "It was awful. I hope you're going to give them hell." Weglyn thought, Oh my God, what have I got myself into? She also reread Seiichi Higashide's book, *Adios to Tears: The Memoirs of a Japanese-Peruvian Internee in U.S. Concentration Camps,* which contains a section about working life at Seabrook:

> We were required to work 12 hours a day. Initially, men were paid 50 cents an hour and women 35 cents an hour, with no overtime pay or differential for night work. If one arrived at work late, or if one went home sick, that portion would be subtracted from his hours in five-minute units. We had only one free day every two weeks, when we moved from one shift to the other. There were no paid holidays, no sick leave. Even for that time, these working conditions were considered to be severe.

In the end, Weglyn gave a mostly nostalgic speech, her voice vibrating with the emotion of what she could not say. She recalled working as a deejay on the night shift in the plant when she was in high school, playing Perry Como records to keep the workers awake, and especially remembered playing "Prisoner of Love," which was the hit song of the summer of '46.

Ray Ono and his family lived at 969 Roosevelt Street, in a concrete-block building that was not much of an improvement over the camp barracks, and in some respects was worse. In camp, they had had no refrigerator and a wood-burning stove; in Seabrook, they had an icebox and a coal-burning stove. Manzanar was temperate in the wintertime; Seabrook was freezing. In camp, internees did not have to work, and their food was prepared for them by the military; in Seabrook, people had to work very hard and provide for themselves. But Ray told me, "Psychologically, Seabrook was a lot better. There wasn't barbed wire around us. We were free."

For Ray, as for many of the boys and girls, camp had been fun, and Seabrook was more fun. "As a kid, you don't worry about hardship. You're going to school, and you have all these activities," he said. In the summertime, Ray picked beans, like all the boys, working beside Estonians, Latvians, Jamaicans, and Puerto Ricans. The Japanese kids organized their own gangs, with names like the Rainbows and the Blue Devils, but instead of fighting, the kids competed in baseball, football, and basketball. Ray was a good athlete, and went on to glory as a running back at Bridgeton High School. Barry Semple told me about watching him play in 1950: "Ray was behind a guy named Tex Robinson, who was a great football player. . . . But then Tex's jaw got broken, and everyone said, Oh, well, that's it, we've only got this little Japanese kid to fill in for Tex—we're done for." Ray, in his first game replacing Robinson, scored three touchdowns—two of them on long, spectacular runs. "That was the first time I really began to realize that the Japanese were really something special," Semple said.

After the war, Seabrook Farms grew rapidly. Under its own label, it produced a vast amount of frozen spinach, frozen baby peas, and frozen lima beans. The technology of frozen food was exploding, and Seabrook was at the forefront. Science was applied to every aspect of agriculture. Temperature, sunlight, water, and seed were all taken into account and factored together as "growth units," in a system that allowed Seabrook to react to changing weather and to determine the day when the crops would be ripest. Harvest was a highly organized military assault on vegetables—the agricultural equivalent of D-Day. The harvest of lima beans went like this: First, tractors dragged mowers through the lima-bean fields, laying the vines into windrows. A loader followed, gathering the windrows onto flatbed dump trucks. (This went on day and night, under floodlights.) The trucks carried the windrows to a viner, a very loud machine that separated the beans from the stems and leaves, which were fed to the company's beef cattle. (My father had to keep the cattle's existence a secret from CF, who hated all animals.) The beans were rushed to the plant to be washed in flumes, blanched in steam tunnels, and funneled downstairs into a circular container filled with brine. The heavier beans would sink in the brine, and the smaller ones—which would be packaged as "Extra Fancy Grade"—would float on the surface. After being sorted, the beans passed along a conveyor belt lined with women, who removed any refuse and stray smaller beans, and they went on to automatic packagers and then to giant "freezing trays," which were set at thirty-seven degrees below zero. If the beans came from nearby fields, less than an hour had passed since they were harvested.

Ray's father was one of about forty men who removed packages of frozen beans from the freezing trays and put them on racks, which were then moved by other men to a cold-storage warehouse or to waiting refrigerated trucks or railcars. "My father was a part of the precision machinery that Seabrook was famous for," Ray told me, "a worker in an assembly line of food." Ray's mother also worked in the plant, separating lima beans. The parents alternated their twelve-hour shifts, so that one of them would always be home with the children. Although a lot of Japanese-American families saw Seabrook only as a place to regroup, and returned to the West Coast in the late forties, Ray's father insisted that the Onos remain. "The boat was gone, and all we had were the clothes on our backs," Ray told me. "So we stayed. Dad's job was terribly monotonous. He knew about working on diesel engines, from his fishing days, and we tried to get him to work in the shop, where the work was more interesting, but he wouldn't do it." He unloaded freezer trays until he retired in 1958; he died in 1960. "He'd come home, eat supper, have his glass of wine, and go to bed," Ray said. "He didn't tell us much about it. We knew it was hard work. It was hard to determine what his feelings were. He had the Japanese attitude of *shikataganai*—'it can't be helped.'" Ray added, "The thing is, we were poor, but we didn't know we were poor. Our parents never let us feel like we were poor. This is something that came out very strongly at the Seabrook reunion—the incredible effort our parents made to keep the family strong and together, and the respect we owe them for that. You hear a lot about why the Japanese Americans have done all right, while other minorities can't seem to get going. I think the real difference is the strong family structure."

The point at which my grandfather began to hate his sons is hard to place. My mother, whom my father married in 1956, remembers my grandmother telling her it began when CF realized that he was old and his sons were young. Nana also thought that CF felt guilty over the way he had dealt with his own father. In 1911, without telling his father, CF went to meet with some financiers in New York, hoping to borrow money to expand the farm. He took the train to Jersey City and crossed the Hudson in a ferry, which landed not far from where I live now. After he had secured the money, he went home and offered to buy his father out for far less than half of what his New York creditors had proposed the farm was worth. Basically, he cheated his father. As CF grew older, Nana believed, the guilt he felt over how he had treated his father turned into paranoia that his sons would do the same thing to him.

The fall of Seabrook Farms was set in motion by Hurricane Hazel, which struck South Jersey in October of 1954 and wiped out all of Seabrook's spinach crop. An association of Philadelphia bankers, led by a man named Ben Sawin, told CF that they felt he wasn't up to the task of rebuilding the company, and that they wanted my father to take over. A three-man voting trust, composed of my father, Sawin, and CF, was established to manage the business. "CF seemed to accept this," my dad says. "He held a big family meeting in 1954, and announced that he was retiring and that I would be running the business from now on. Mother was overjoyed. Belford started clapping, which was rather indelicate."

In 1958 Seabrook had its best year ever. "Now in board meetings people didn't talk about 'truck' anymore," my father says. "We talked about expanding and diversifying sources of production. We were moving into frozen orange juice and gourmet frozen entrées. The Seabrook brand was a national brand now, and to keep it constantly supplied we needed growers in Florida and California. But your grandfather couldn't understand that." The truck-farming economy on which my grandfather's vision was based was giving way to a supermarket economy in which fresh produce would be available all year round and consumers wouldn't care where it came from.

In 1959 CF refused to renew the voting trust. The banks informed him that they would not continue to lend money to Seabrook Farms unless he renewed it. Like any farming enterprise, Seabrook could not survive without the banks. But CF was stubborn; he wouldn't budge. The head of Gerard Trust then told my father that, in order to save the business, the family should have CF declared incompetent to manage his affairs so that, if necessary, he could be forcibly removed.

Here my father faced an almost impossible choice. Did he stick with the bankers, who were offering him his livelihood, the salvation of everything he had worked for, and the chance to run the business on his own, even though this would mean condemning his father? Or did he stick with his father, even though it meant ruin for both of them? Dad chose the bankers: he was his father's son. For my grandmother, the choice was between CF and my father, and she chose her beloved Jack. My father's sister, Thelma, and her husband thought that what the boys were trying to do to CF was unfair—that whatever the old man's weaknesses were, he didn't deserve this humiliation. They sided with CF. A hearing was scheduled to determine whether CF was competent or not. Nana and her sons hired Richard Hughes, who later became the governor of New Jersey, to represent their side.

While the hearing was pending, CF had another "spell," and the family had him taken to a psychiatric hospital. CF soon got out on a writ of habeas corpus, and went to the Philadelphia newspapers with his story, accusing his family in print of having "shanghaied" him into a mental institution so that his sons, whom he called "Boy Scouts," could "take control of the business." He also said, "This is a conspiracy on Jack's part." These clippings have been carefully preserved by my father's former secretary, Elizabeth Gauntt, and are stowed in the barn at my parents' place, along with the glowing publicity from that time (things like a copy of Alice Hughes's column "A Woman's New York": "Not everyone is as fortunate as myself and 19 other . . . editors and writers invited to be the guests of a happy family of 'gentleman farmers' in New Jersey").

Shortly before the day of the hearing, CF played his trump card. On a Saturday night in May 1959, he sold Seabrook Farms to a wholesale grocery company for three million dollars. He had created Seabrook Farms, and to keep his sons from taking over, he destroyed it. On the day of the sale, CF appeared in a local barbershop wearing three neckties, and when someone asked him why, he said, "Three million, three neckties." CF also changed his will, to make sure that his wife and sons wouldn't get any of this money—effectively disowning them. He and Nana continued to live together in the Big House, but they took their meals separately, and rarely spoke. When CF died, in 1964, and the family saw that he had left virtually no money to Nana in his will, and hadn't even provided a place for her to live, they sued the estate, so that she was able to stay on in the Big House and receive enough money to sustain her.

A few months after Seabrook Farms was sold, my mother answered the door one morning to find a man, sent by CF, holding an eviction notice. CF had refused to let my parents buy their house, although they had offered to repeatedly, and now he was kicking them out. Exiled from Seabrook, Mom and Dad moved to a house outside Salem, about twenty miles away. My father was forty-two, was out of a job, and owed money. I was born in 1959, right in the middle of all this—my father's first son, his namesake, who in better times might have given my grandfather joy. But as things stood between them, my grandfather refused to recognize my birth.

All my life—in grade school, in college, at the different places I've worked—my reputation as a Seabrook Farms frozen-food heir has accompanied me. It's like a birthmark. I used to try to conceal it. At times, while shopping in supermarkets, I avoided the frozen-food section, not wanting to catch sight of that creamed spinach. (The Seabrook label lived on, even though my family didn't own it at first.) Even in cyberspace, a place where I had imagined, naïvely, that frozen-food heirs don't matter, someone in a discussion group I had contributed to posted:

He's the Seabrook Frozen Foods heir, I heard today . . . authoritatively.

To which I responded,

> As to my being the frozen-food heir, my grandfather started that business but he and my father had a terrible fight and he fired and disowned my father and sold the business to spite him . . . so in fact my only inheritance is bitterness.

The person replied,

> Never again will I buy that frozen creamed spinach.

And I replied,

> I know very well what that statement will cost you, and I appreciate it. Because in spite of all the pain that creamed spinach cost my family, it is still the best creamed spinach you can buy.

My grandfather did see me a few times before he died, at age eighty-three. Although my father and his father were never actually reconciled (and he and his sister, Thelma, were estranged for the rest of her life), our family sometimes went over to the Big House for Sunday lunch with Nana. I have only one memory of my grandfather. I am taken upstairs to see him by my father and mother. My grandfather is sitting on the floor, fully dressed, building something with an Erector set. My mother says, "CF, this is Johnny, your grandson. This is Johnny," and my grandfather just looks at me in a childishly mean way, his mouth curled down at the corners. I start to worry that his hands are going to snake out and grab my ankles, and I brace myself, putting my hands on my knees, ready for him. He never did say my name.

## A MAN OF HIS TIME

Because CF gave six hundred families a home after the camps, he is remembered by many people of Japanese ancestry as a kind of redeemer—a very different role from the destroyer he plays in my family mythology. One of my early memories is of going to the

Sunday service at the Deerfield church, and of Japanese faces outside the church looking extremely happy to see me, for reasons I couldn't understand but knew had something to do with my grandfather.

At the Seabrook anniversary, we watched a film called *Seabrook: A New Beginning*, made by William Brown. In the film, people spoke of my grandfather as a savior. "He was one of the finest persons you could ever meet," Samah Pearson said. "A wonderful person. And I'll never forget him." Esther Ono (no relation to Ray), who now owns a beauty parlor in Seabrook, said, "I always feel grateful that Mr. Seabrook did undertake to do this for us." I felt a familiar twist of sansei cynicism. Yes, CF helped these people, but it was always good business to help them. With the Japanese Americans, Seabrook Farms got a group of amazingly loyal, uncomplaining, hardworking people, who had a lot to do with the company's great success after the war. Later in the film, someone said of CF, "He was a little man, but he had a lot of noodles." That sounded more like the CF I know.

I have never met anyone who worked for Seabrook Farms—outside of my family, that is—who doesn't speak well of my grandfather. When I was doing interviews for this story, people would often open their conversations with me by saying, "I want to thank you for what your family did for my family," or "I just want to say what an honor this is"—not my usual experience as a reporter. Something about CF inspired people. He was the American Dream come true: the poor farmer's son who by wits alone becomes a captain of industry. He gave the Japanese-American workers something to believe in about America at a time when their faith was being tested.

Gene Nakata, who was ten when he arrived in Seabrook, told me that his father did not want to return to California, because of the loyalty he felt toward my grandfather. "'We're going to stay here and help Mr. Seabrook,'" Nakata remembers his father telling him. "'All our clothes, our furniture—all of this stuff—is from Mr. Seabrook. Without him, we wouldn't have this stuff.'" Richard Ikeda said, "I think your grandfather was a man of his time. Seabrook was a family-owned business, and he felt the obligations of the owner to the people. He felt that the workers were part of him. In a way, it was a very Japanese system. This feeling of belonging is what the modern corporation is trying to get back to."

But this benevolent, paternalistic C. F. Seabrook, the CF of the Seabrook anniversary, is not the CF that has been bequeathed to me. My CF is a racist and an ugly Red-baiter. It is said that CF enjoyed holding forth at the dinner table about the different races that worked for him, citing qualities of one that made it superior to another. He was enraged when one of his granddaughters became engaged to a Mexican, and sent a lawyer down to Mexico to threaten the suitor's family. He certainly did not hold the Latvians' and the Estonians' anti-Semitism against them. Many of the Japanese were anti-Communist, and CF approved of that: he liked to portray unions as a bunch of Commies. Throughout the thirties and into the forties, CF waged an epic battle with local labor unions, which repeatedly tried to organize Seabrook. (They eventually succeeded.) From a union perspective, what my grandfather had going in Seabrook was a precapitalist, feudalistic state, in which the workers were little more than serfs. My grandfather argued that the workers were happy as they were, and he was not above hiring thugs to beat up workers who didn't agree with him. In August of 1934, *The Nation* published an account of a strike at Seabrook:

> Our committee watched the peaceful picketing which was in progress. . . . When he [CF] thought that observers had disappeared from the scene, an attack of tear and nausea gas was launched on the strikers. . . . Belford Seabrook, son of the proprietor, himself threw a bomb into a house then occupied only by an Italian mother and two very small children. He had previously shouted to his men: "Get this woman; she talks too much." The bomb, hurled through the window, landed on a bed and set the sheets ablaze. The rooms were so filled with smoke and gas fumes that the place was uninhabitable for more than two days.

Needless to say, this version of village life at Seabrook was not mentioned at the Seabrook Fiftieth Year Celebration.

As I sat in the audience, I was a little bit nervous for my father, who was going to have to get up and speak. His topic, which the organizers of the anniversary had set for him, was his father. What were the qualities of C. F. Seabrook that had enabled him to create this unusual community in South Jersey? My father had had a lot of trouble writing this speech. He got lost in details about the engineering marvels of Seabrook Farms; and the more trouble he had in reckoning with CF, the more technical details about the farming operation he would accumulate. I sent Dad an e-mail saying:

> Perhaps some of the difficulty you are feeling in writing this is that you want to please these people by giving them someone to worship, but unfortunately the CF you knew doesn't fit the bill. If that is the case, well, I'm not sure what you should do. My inclination would be to tell it like it is but I am sometimes rash.

We talked on the phone. Dad said, "Well, I guess it's not a lie if it isn't the whole truth." His voice sounded kind of listless. I wondered if his weariness came from wrestling with the knowledge that if his father had been in the place of the California farmers who wanted the Japanese immigrants' land, he might have been just as happy as they were to put the Japanese away in the camps. Or maybe he was still angry over what his father had done to him. It didn't seem appropriate to ask Dad these questions: my sansei curiosity about the family past was butting up against his nisei reserve. Did he feel guilty over how he had dealt with his father? I could see how some of my cousins—Thelma's children in particular—might think that he should. I tiptoed around that subject with him, but he would say only, "Well, maybe CF's mistake was that he didn't raise one of his sons to be a psychiatrist." That made me think of something that Ron Uba, the president of the New York chapter of the Japanese American Citizens League, had told me, speaking of the older Japanese people's experience in the camps: "They sometimes have trouble separating the hurt of the experience out of their lives enough to talk about it."

I asked Dad whether he regretted not having a family business to pass along to his children. No, he said, he thought maybe it was a good thing that Seabrook Farms was no more. "To this day, I can't say that for me personally this was a tragedy," he said. "I was broke and out on my ass at forty-two, and I've made a lot of money since." Ben Sawin had helped him get a job with Howard Butcher, a Philadelphia stockbroker who owned several utility companies. (Today, Sawin's picture hangs next to CF's picture in Dad's office. Dad sometimes wonders whether in some way he was a surrogate for Sawin's own son, who committed suicide when he was fifteen years old.) In ten years, Dad built the utility companies into a billion-dollar business, International Utilities. Like his own father, he came back from midlife disaster to achieve even greater success.

"Of course, it's conceivable we could have done great things with the business," Dad went on. "Seabrook might today be one of the greatest companies in the food business. But when you inherit something, you always have that doubt: Could I have done it on my own? I think I have more confidence now than I ever would have if I had stayed at Seabrook. Also, it might not have been good for you, or for your brother, if Seabrook had lasted."

"I would probably be running the Seabrook PR department," I said. Actually, maybe I am.

"American family businesses just don't last long," Dad said. "I heard there was a get-together in Europe recently of families who have been in business together for four hundred years. That's unthinkable in America."

I asked Dad if he had anything at all that his father had written in his own hand, and he said he had one letter. "I'll give it to you someday," he said. With a shock, I realized that my father did not have much more information about his father at his disposal than I did. An inspirational article about CF that was published in a 1921 edition of *The American Magazine* (Ring Lardner's essay on being thirty-five is the cover story) provided my father with a lot of the material for his speech. Surely, I thought, there must be memories of CF that my father carried with him—moments of happiness or uncertainty that Dad and his father had shared? Where were they? They seemed to be unavailable, blown away. Of this extraordinary man and his immense creation there was so little left!

One quality of CF's that comes through clearly in people's memories of him is that he didn't like to tell you what he was thinking.

He hated it when you wrote down anything he said. Sometimes my father would try to take notes at business meetings, and CF would rail about it: "What're you doing? Stop doing that!"

Ten years earlier, I had interviewed Jonas McGallaird, who was one of my grandfather's most faithful retainers, and he told me the story of meeting CF for the first time, in the spring of 1924. His story is the most vivid snapshot of my grandfather's methods that I have.

JONAS: I went to CF's office on a Saturday afternoon, a lazy day, and there set CF, reading a magazine. "Lookin' for somebody?" he said. I said I'm lookin' for a job. "Hmm," he said. "Where you been workin'?" I said I'd been workin' on the railroad. "Live around here?" I said I was living in Bridgeton. "Have a phone?" I said yeah. "What's the number?" He wrote the number down. And when CF wrote a number down you knew it was down, because he made numbers like they made 'em in Bible times. He just made big numbers. He wrote big.

"Well," CF said, "I gotta get on. I gotta go," he said. "You lock the door when you go out." And I said, "Well I'm goin' out too, you lock your own damn door," I said. And that's just the way I said it too.

The next day the phone rang and it was Seabrook. He said, "You want to go to Atlantic City?" I said yes. He said, "Well you come out to my place and we'll go to Atlantic City." So I went over to his place and there set this big Packard outside the house, a Club See-dan. CF came out and said, "You want to drive or you want me to drive?" I said it doesn't make any difference to me. "Well," he said, "you drive. You know how to drive?" "Sure," I said. "You know how to get to Atlantic City?" I said yeah. So we went.

In Atlantic City, CF spent an hour in the President Hotel, probably making arrangements for some Atlantic City bootleggers to pick up the applejack he had been making from his apple crop that year. In those days, the long grass that grew in the marshes was harvested by local farmers and sold as salt hay to local glass factories, where it was used as packing material, so farmers like CF knew all the little cricks and meadows through which booze could be run to the bay.

JONAS: I bought the Sunday paper and set there in the sun and after a while CF came out and said let's go home. . . . We got home and CF said, "You got a place to keep this car?" "Yeah," I said. "Off the street?" "Yeah." He said, "Now I want to go to New York tomorrow morning, and I want to catch the seven o'clock train. Can you take me?" So I drove that Packard home and my mother said, "What in the heck are you doing with that car?" And I said, "I do not know."

In this roundabout way, Jonas became CF's chauffeur. When CF died, Jonas asked my father if he could drive the hearse that took CF to his grave, saying, "The old son of a bitch rode behind me for forty years, and this is the first time he won't be able to talk back."

## FATHERS AND SONS

My father rose to speak to long applause from the crowd. He wore a yellow bow tie, and although he is white-haired and over seventy, he looked boyishly slim in his gentleman farmer's suit. He said he was going to speak about "a man of incredible accomplishments and incredible contradictions." Japanese faces around me looked thrilled at the sight of him—the same expression I remember seeing on the faces outside the church as a boy.

Dad began to reminisce. He recalled the house about half a mile away, now gone, where he was born. He recalled his father's father, Arthur, "a genial man" with "great flowing white mustaches." He recalled the terrible fights that CF used to have with his father. He recalled the stable across the street from that house, where a blacksmith named A. B. Skilowitzsky worked. "He was always stripped to the waist and sweating, even in the wintertime, and he pounded red-hot iron, and there was the smell of soft-coal smoke and burning hooves." He described how, after agricultural prices had dropped sharply, CF lost the business. "He was out, and he didn't look back," my father said. "This was another of CF's great contradictions. He never cared about money."

My father is good at telling stories. His greatest talent may be his ability to make you believe his version of events. Over the years, I have occasionally sat listening to him explain something to me, thinking, You bastard, you expect me to swallow that, and then trying to give him my version and failing miserably, and later on, in my head, succeeding brilliantly in putting his version to rout. But on this day, sitting in the audience, I was pulling for him. I knew his view of the past wasn't the only view, but in his struggle to deal with his father's legacy I was completely on his side.

As his story got closer to its sad conclusion, I found myself hoping it would turn out differently. My father and his father would realize the madness of what they were doing. Angels would whisper in their ears. Then my father said something I had never heard before: "On October 3, 1941, CF had a very serious stroke, and he was incapacitated for a couple of years after that." Not even my sister Carol, who is seventeen years older than I am, had heard about this before.

"Prior to the stroke, he had exuded the confidence that he could do anything," my father went on. "His great heroes in life were the builders. Steve Bechtel and Henry Kaiser—the people who said, 'Show me the job, I'll do it. I'll get it done.' Well, that's the way CF was. But after that he never really had confidence that he could do things on his own. And although he eventually learned to project a public image of confidence, when he was with people who were his peers—his directors, his bankers—he simply lacked the old confidence."

My father was saying that physical weakness had cost CF his confidence, and that the effort to make up for lost confidence had caused all the trouble that followed. This was Dad's version of *shikataganai.*

A FTER the ceremony, many people visited the new museum in Seabrook—the Seabrook Educational and Cultural Center, which is in the basement of the municipal building. The collection there was assembled by Ellen Nakamura and John Fuyuume, who invited the collaboration of many other former residents of Seabrook, and there are hundreds of good pictures of life at Seabrook from 1900 to 1959. (CF apparently didn't mind having photographers around.) The rooms of the museum are also filled with John Fuyuume's friendly manner. John got a master's degree in music literature when he was young. But he returned to Seabrook to work, and did not leave to get a Ph.D. and teach, as he had planned, because, he says, my grandfather told him, "It doesn't matter how many Ph.D.s you have, it's how many Ph.D.s you have working for you that counts."

I said, "He sold you that old line."

"No, it's true," John said.

While I was reading in the museum, I saw some of the older people who had worked at Seabrook all their lives come in and go slowly from photograph to photograph. John would often join them. One elderly man paused at a picture of the Seabrook power plant, and asked John, "Were you there when they dynamited her? It was unbelievable. The dynamite took the first story clear out from under her, so that you could see clear through to the other side. But she just hung there in the air for about five seconds. It was like she didn't want to come down."

Other Seabrook-anniversary activities included a tour of my grand-parents' house, which is now Seabrook House, a drug-and-alcohol-rehabilitation center. Paul Noguchi, a professor of anthropology at Bucknell, told me, "That was something I really wanted to see. The image I had of your grandfather's house, as a boy growing up in Seabrook, was that it was an impenetrable place, surrounded by shrubbery—something I never thought I'd be in." Richard Lamke, the communication coordinator for Seabrook House, walked groups through the place quickly, pointing out odd patches of grandeur that remain from my grandfather's day, like the tiles in the bathrooms and on the floor of the porch. People also toured my grandfather's formal English gardens, which had seemed wonderful to me as a boy, and I was glad to see that they had kept some of their former glory. Time has not erased them as easily as it has some of CF's other works.

I hadn't been in the Big House since I was eight. With Lamke, I went down to the basement, where what Jonas called "a can-house band" used to play during CF's New Year's Eve parties. Some Seabrook House patients were sitting on beat-up furniture, watching daytime TV.

"And this was the bar," Lamke said, showing me an elaborate built-in wet bar.

"Guess you don't need that anymore."

"No."

Upstairs, we looked up the stairwell that leads to the room where I remember seeing my grandfather. The staircase is narrow, but it's not, as I remember it, winding, like the staircase in a chiller-theater feature that scared me when I was a kid. I put my foot on the first step, but then changed my mind.

"There's nothing to see up there but offices anyway," Lamke said.

FOR lots of families, including mine, the Seabrook anniversary was a chance to see relatives you rarely get to see. My family's reunion took place in the backyard of my parents' house on Saturday afternoon. My cousin Ivin Seabrook—actually C. F. Seabrook III, and the only one of us who looks much like CF—told me he had run into an old Estonian man right after the ceremony. "I said to the guy, 'Hey, Seabrook sounds like it was a pretty great place back then.' The guy goes, 'Oh, that was all a bunch of crap. They were just as prejudiced here as anywhere else.' I went, 'Whoa!'"

Everyone was talking about my father's speech. To Carol I said that the story of the stroke was a good compromise—a way of respecting CF while at the same time acknowledging that something had gone wrong—because it meant you could blame a physical infirmity for the trouble that came later in the family, and not blame CF. She said, "Of course, it's also nice to believe we didn't inherit the genes that caused this kind of behavior."

My mother had hoped that the younger generation would play a softball game, but nobody really wanted to. She turned to my cousin Wessie, a plant engineer, who is my age, and said, "Hasn't the weather this fall been incredible?"

"Good for the spinach," Wessie said.

Dad chatted with Lisa, my wife. "What actually happened," he told her, "was that CF was in Florida when the Japanese arrived, and when he got home and found all these Japanese people here he hit the roof." Lisa tried to follow up on this bombshell, but Dad, who was known as the Silver Fox among his Philadelphia business cronies, withdrew into his den, saying only, "Well, victory has many fathers." (The next morning at the Deerfield church, as he and my mother were walking out, the Reverend Borror complimented my father on his talk, saying what a good speaker he was. "It was on the tip of my tongue to say, 'Well, Reverend, my advantage is I don't have to believe in the gospel I preach,'" my father told me.)

At lunch, I sat next to my cousin Jim, who is Belford's son and Wessie's father. We spoke about our grandfather in our own way—a reserved way that could be described as "Japanese." With Seabrooks it is often hard to tell what people are thinking, and as we talked I felt that CF was the source of a strange diffidence between us, lingering from the days when family members were on opposite sides.

Jim, sixty-one, was the sansei who had the most to lose from the issei-nisei conflict that destroyed the business. He continued to work for the new owners, but quit in 1977; eight days later, he rented an office in town and, working with his brother Charlie (C. F. Seabrook II), established Seabrook Brothers & Sons, a frozen-food company that is situated three miles from the old plant. Jim's three sons work there, and so do Charlie's sons Ivin and Peter; and lots of other Seabrooks, including my brother, Bruce, have done seasonal work in the bean fields. Seabrook Brothers is very successful, and once again functions as a local buyer for the farmers in the area. At first, Jim packed vegetables only for other labels because he was not permitted to sell his vegetables under the Seabrook name. In 1994, thirty-five years after CF sold the name, Jim bought it back.

"It's a good feeling," he said.

After lunch, I threw a football with Carol's sixteen-year-old son, Rodolphe. My mind wandered back over the day, remembering the quiet indignation in Michi Weglyn's voice, which caused it almost to warble; and the triumph in Donna Pearson's voice when she declared, "There's no excuse for 'can't'. . . . If my parents could do it, so can I"; and the resignation in my father's voice when he said of CF,

"He simply lacked the old confidence." I remembered what the minister had said—that God is just and merciful, and that his purpose is worked out in time and in the lives of those who seek to do his good—and I wondered whether that was true. It did indeed seem to me that I had caught a glimpse of a purpose that morning. The Japanese-American families' experience at Seabrook was like the white light behind an X-ray, which was my family's experience, and in the X-ray I could see a hairline pattern I hadn't seen before. But was this God's pattern, or was it the lingering force of my grandfather's energy? Or was it nothing?

I thought about all the Japanese-American family reunions going on right then around South Jersey, and wondered whether any of those people had found any answers. Standing there in my parents' yard, I had the sense that the purpose I had glimpsed that morning was already fading, as all of us returned to our own lives, each to the effort to make sense of his or her story—Ray Ono and Josie and Richard Ikeda and Gene Nakata and John Fuyuume of their stories, my father of his, I of mine. CF was a father to all of us. But his legacy is harsh and difficult to understand. It says that you cannot expect fairness—although you may get it anyway—and you cannot expect forgiveness either. My grandfather's law is a strain of the Calvinism that abides in the Deerfield church, where, in the graveyard outside, he and his father lie beneath an eighteen-foot gray stone slab (Arthur's head at CF's feet), and where there are two plots set aside for my father and mother, and more space, if I want it, for me.

—1995

# WHERE DO GREAT IDEAS COME FROM?

In *Flash of Genius*, John Seabrook explores the moment when inspiration strikes in an otherwise average life, and what happens when that idea moves out into the larger culture and takes on a life—and commercial possibilities—of its own. The title piece in this collection is the David v. Goliath story of Bob Kearns, a professor and inventor who came up with something we all take for granted: the intermittent windshield wiper. When Kearns's patents were infringed, he fought General Motors, Ford, and Chrysler and eventually prevailed in a classic American story of never giving up, never backing down.

Seabrook has been fascinated by stories of invention and entrepreneurship since childhood, when he grew up with an uncle who invented something as ubiquitous as Bob Kearns's wipers: boil-in-bag vegetables. In *Flash of Genius*, Seabrook also writes about thirteen other iconoclastic visions that turned into the stuff of every day.

JOHN SEABROOK began his magazine career at *Manhattan Inc.* and *Vanity Fair* and has been a staff writer for *The New Yorker* since 1993. He is the author of *Deeper: My Two-Year Odyssey in Cyberspace* and *Nobrow: The Culture of Marketing, the Marketing of Culture.* He lives in New York City.

UNIVERSAL PICTURES and SPYGLASS ENTERTAINMENT PRESENT A BARBER/BIRNBAUM PRODUCTION A STRIKE ENTERTAINMENT PRODUCTION "FLASH OF GENIUS" GREG KINNEAR LAUREN GRAHAM DERMOT MULRONEY MUSIC BY AARON ZIGMAN MUSIC SUPERVISORS G. MARQ ROSWELL ADAM SWART
www.flashofgenius.net CASTING BY DENISE CHAMIAN COSTUME DESIGNER LUIS SEQUEIRA EDITED BY JILL SAVITT ACE PRODUCTION DESIGNER HUGO LUCZYC-WYHOWSKI DIRECTOR OF PHOTOGRAPHY DANTE SPINOTTI ASC,AIC EXECUTIVE PRODUCERS JONATHAN GLICKMAN J. MILES DALE THOMAS A. BLISS ERIC NEWMAN
PRODUCED BY GARY BARBER ROGER BIRNBAUM MICHAEL LIEBER WRITTEN BY PHILIP RAILSBACK DIRECTED BY MARC ABRAHAM A UNIVERSAL RELEASE

$14.95 / $16.95 Can.

ISBN-13: 978-0-312-53572-8
ISBN-10: 0-312-53572-4

51495

www.stmartins.com

# ST. MARTIN'S GRIFFIN
175 FIFTH AVENUE, NEW YORK, N.Y. 10010
DISTRIBUTED IN CANADA BY H. B. FENN AND COMPANY, LTD.
PRINTED IN THE UNITED STATES OF AMERICA

9 780312 535728